max bill global

Zentrum Paul Klee
Bern

max
bill
global

An Artist
Building Bridges

scheidegger & spiess

foreword and acknowl edg ments

Max Bill was at once painter, sculptor, architect, designer, graphic artist, and typographer; but he was also a theoretician, collector, curator, publicist, teacher, politician, and activist. He was an influential figure for mid-twentieth-century art and design, and well known far beyond Switzerland's borders. As a designer he was receptive to stimuli from diverse disciplines and the artistic currents of his time, producing work that was commensurably multifaceted. He also built up a worldwide network of contacts with whom he engaged in dialogue his whole life long. Holding firm to his convictions, he became one of the world's most prominent advocates, champions, and theoreticians of Concrete Art. He also set new standards for design principles in graphic art, product design, and architecture.

Bill was a passionate proponent of renewal in design, which he believed to be inextricably linked to the renewal of society at large. As a mediator between the generations, he carried the avant-garde's concepts over into the postwar period, updated them, and took them a stage further. In his own work as a designer he strove for solutions that were economical, sustainable, and aesthetically pleasing. While Bill believed applied art had the potential to bring about a material improvement in people's lives, he saw fine art as serving humanity's spiritual needs. His aim was not individual expression, but logical, intrinsically intelligible, and harmonious design.

Bill often had his finger firmly on the pulse and was an eager participant in social and artistic discourse.

Our exhibition is the first to turn the spotlight on Bill's international network. Through his contacts to artists at the Bauhaus in Dessau and those he met later in Paris and Zurich, to say nothing of the avant-garde circles he influenced in Buenos Aires and São Paulo and his exhibiting activities in the United States, he was engaged in an ongoing exchange of ideas with like-minded people all over the globe. As his ideas seeped into the most diverse contexts and there were reinterpreted and developed, so he himself, thanks to his global network, won acclaim in both Switzerland and Germany.

Acknowledgments

Our first debt of thanks is to the max bill georges vantongerloo foundation, first and foremost to Dr. Angela Thomas Schmid and Erich Schmid, who right from the start supported our undertaking with both expertise and numerous works on loan. Over a period of several months, Dr. Thomas Schmid repeatedly took the time to answer our questions and those of the catalog authors. Assisted by Emily Fayet of Hauser & Wirth, she granted us access to the collection from which most of the works loaned to this show were drawn. We would also like to thank James Koch for the productive cooperation with Hauser & Wirth.

These we were able to supplement with works kindly loaned to us by a number of Swiss and German museums such as the Aargauer Kunsthaus, Kunstmuseum Basel, Kunstmuseum Bern, Museum für Konkrete Kunst Ingolstadt, Kunst Museum Winterthur, Museum für Gestaltung Zürich, Haus Konstruktiv, and the Kunsthaus Zürich, as well as the Daros Latinamerica Collection, the Grażyna Kulczyk Collection, Galerie von Bartha, Galerie Bruno Bischofsberger, and various private collectors. Thanks to the generous support of the New York-based Institute for Studies on Latin American Art (ISLAA) we have also been able to present high-caliber works of Argentinian Concrete Art from its collection here in Bern.

We would also like to thank the catalog authors Heloísa Espada, María Amalia García, Guitemie Maldonado, Angela Thomas Schmid, and Lynn Zelevansky for their valuable contributions to our understanding of Max Bill's international network. This international aspect is also reflected in the original languages of the text contributions for this book, which range from Portuguese, Spanish, and French to German and English. We would like to thank ProHelvetia for their financial support of the translation work. We were fortunate in finding in the publisher Scheidegger & Spiess an experienced partner that has already published a number of books about Max Bill and his circle.

Sincere thanks are also due to Sabine Hahn for her elegant design of the catalog and to Studio ZMIK and the Büro Berrel Gschwind for their excellent exhibition scenography.

Closer to home, we would also like to thank those of our own staff who have played such an important part in this project. Myriam Dössegger, in particular, assisted curator Fabienne Eggelhöfer with her research work right from the start as well as taking care of the project coordination.

An exhibition project as ambitious as this one would not have been possible without the support of third parties. We would therefore like to thank the Canton of Bern, the Burgergemeinde Bern, and the Ernst Göhner Stiftung for their much-appreciated support.

Nina Zimmer
Director Zentrum Paul Klee /
Kunstmuseum Bern

Fabienne Eggelhöfer
Chief curator Zentrum Paul Klee

Preparations for a group photo at the Hochschule für Gestaltung in Ulm 1956, Max Bill seated on the right.
Copyright: René Spitz, photo: Hans G. Conrad

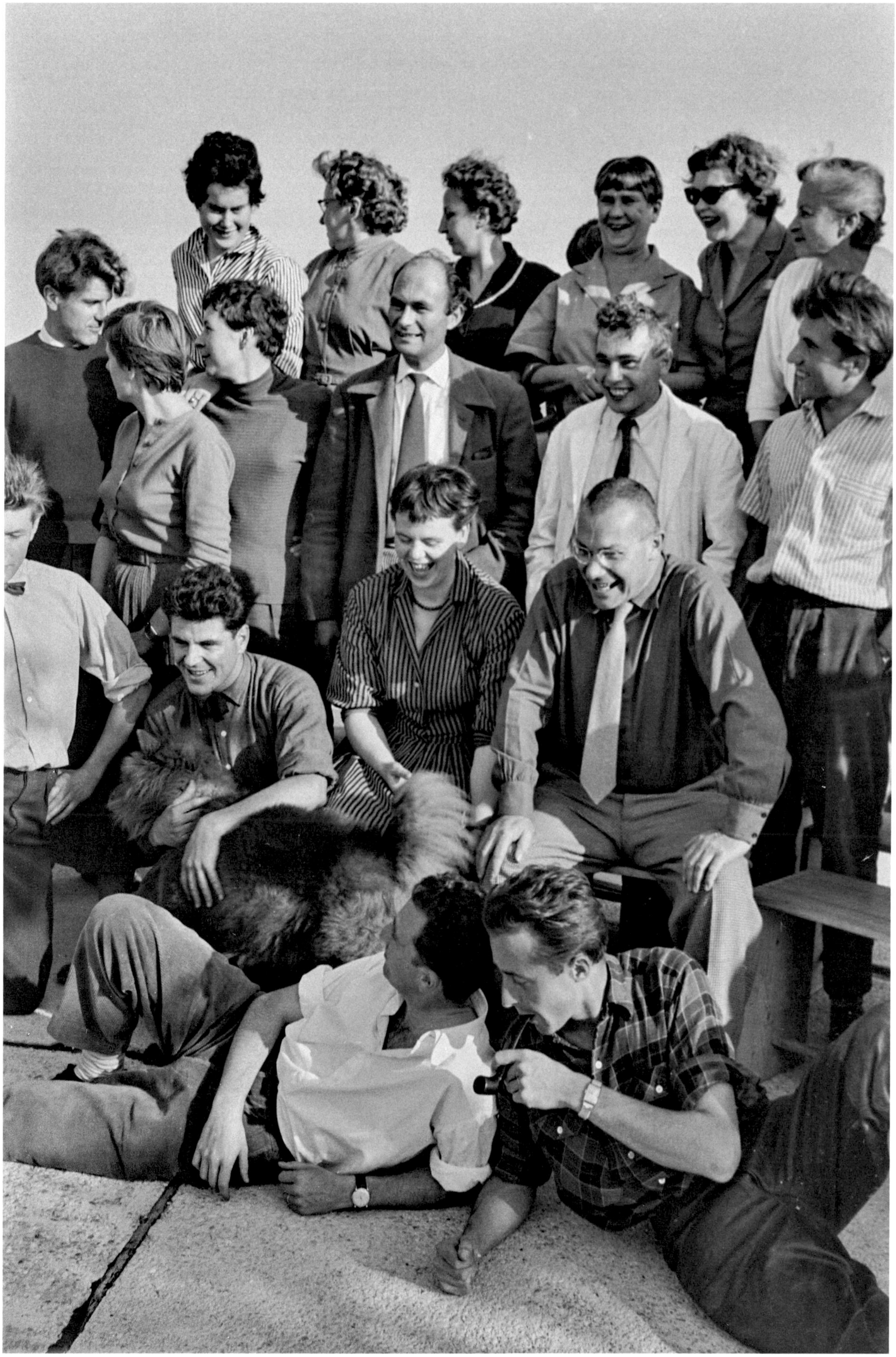

max bill

Fabienne
Eggelhöfer

An Artist Building Bridges

To cut to the chase: Max Bill was a networker par excellence. Even as a young man he cultivated contacts assiduously, whether by founding new artist groups like gruppe z and die augen, or by joining established ones such as Abstraction Création in Paris. He wrote his first theoretical text on Concrete Art at the age of twenty-eight and from the 1940s onward devoted more and more of his time to organizing exhibitions and publishing essays about his artist friends. Not only did he quickly establish himself as Switzerland's leading Concretist, but he also spread his convictions abroad, arousing considerable interest in his ideas in Latin America, especially Brazil and Argentina. His ties to players all over the world in turn helped him to elevate Concrete Art in Switzerland to a movement of global significance. As closer scrutiny of his career reveals, Bill was a consummate master at harnessing his sprawling network to his own personal goals. He was a bridge-builder between generations and across national boundaries and as such fostered dialogue on design issues in all sorts of disciplines, presenting these to a wide audience in both exhibitions and publications. He brought together people from all over the world, most notably at the famous Hochschule für Gestaltung (HfG) in Ulm. Bill's ambitious and forthright manner repeatedly met with rejection, more than once leading to acrimony and a parting of the ways; but as a closer look at his career reveals, his web of relationships with the most diverse players was pivotal to his success.

Dessau

Bill's career began in the spring of 1927 when he enrolled as a student at the Bauhaus in Dessau. He quit prematurely after only two years, just as he had previously aborted his apprenticeship as a silversmith at Kunstgewerbeschule Zurich. While the Bauhaus did not yet bring him his breakthrough as an artist, his time there did enable him to build up a network of associates from which he would continue to reap the benefits for years to come. His relationships of long standing with fellow students and even teachers, especially with Paul Klee, Josef Albers, Wassily Kandinsky, Gunta Stölzl, and Helene Nonné-Schmidt, thus began when he himself was just twenty. In addition to the obligatory preliminary courses, Bill also attended first László Moholy-Nagy's metal workshop and later the theater workshop led by Oskar Schlemmer. He also took care not to miss Klee's and Kandinsky's free painting classes. Bill's artistic work of the period bears the clear imprint of the avant-garde artists who at the time were teaching at the Bauhaus. Also striking is the fierce determination he brought to bear on the organization and promotion of his own works. Thus he teamed up with some other students to found the artist group gruppe z. "He wanted to bring together several young Bauhaus painters in a group and to organize touring exhibitions in Europe that would make us famous and our paintings coveted," Hans Fischli recalled later. "When we drew up our list of members, we started with Klee and Kandinsky and then added our own names, and because the list was in alphabetical order and there were no names that began with A, Bill came right at the top. gruppe z! The dernier cri! Beat that!"[1] Bill's practice of tying his own name to those of acclaimed artists, in this case his teachers Klee and Kandinsky, is one he would repeat in the coming years. The group drew up its own statutes and Bill took over as chairman and secretary, even printing letterhead and calling cards that he himself had designed. He also tried to persuade museums such as Kunsthaus Zurich to host gruppe z exhibitions, though not a single group show was ever held.[2]

Zurich to Paris

Back in Zurich, Bill initiated another artist group, a society called die augen that he co-founded with Swiss artist Hanns Robert Welti in 1929. The two men were actually making a statement, their works having been passed over for the show *Abstrakte und surrealistische Malerei und Plastik* being planned at Kunsthaus Zurich.[3] Although "artistically not yet anywhere near as great"[4] as the avant-garde artists from all over Europe on show at the Kunsthaus, the twenty-one-year-old Bill was audacious enough to stage a protest in the form of a rival exhibition at his home in Zurich, even if it featured only his own works and took no account of the other artists in die augen. He designed an invitation, which he sent to friends, acquaintances, and former Bauhaus students, and he even managed to solicit a review of his exhibition in the magazine *Das Werk*. That, however, was all that this latest group of his ever achieved. In December of the same year he again sought "permission for an exhibition at Kunsthaus Zurich," expressing his wish, "in the month of march or april, to exhibit around 25 paintings [. . .] [in the] glass-roofed gallery to the right of the central galleries."[5] This inquiry likewise failed to yield the desired response.

Interestingly, Bill tended to describe his own art as "surreal" during this phase. Angela Thomas Schmid speculates that one reason for this might have been the Paris Surrealists' enthusiastic response to Klee. For Bill, as one who was "hoping for success as an artist in his own right, but was still following in Klee's wake, as it were," perhaps that was motivation enough to attach himself to the Surrealist circle.[6] Bill did in fact travel to Paris in 1930—accompanied by the architect Ernst F. Burckhardt—and his stay in the world's art capital proved crucial to his development. When he tried to place his art in Jeanne Bucher's gallery, she turned him down on the grounds that as much as she loved everything by Paul Klee, Bill would have to work independently of Klee before she could consider exhibiting him.[7] This rejection must have disappointed the young artist, even if his visit to the gallery did at least yield some new contacts: the artists Serge Brignoni, Joan Miró, and Jacques Lipchitz, all of whom Bill met there in person. Acting on the advice of his friend Hanns Welti, Bill also took advantage of his time in Paris to visit the Uruguayan artist Joaquín Torres-García, founder of Cercle et Carré, an artist group that was swimming against the Surrealist tide and promoting Concrete Art. Torres-García's studio had already become a meeting place for the "anti-Surrealist" art scene, to which Georges Vantongerloo, Sophie

Taeuber-Arp, Hans Arp, Antoine Pevsner, and Piet Mondrian belonged. Alongside Cercle et Carré's magazine, Bill also discovered the Paris-based journal *ac* (art concret), edited by Theo van Doesburg, and would implement the theories of Concrete Art published there in his works.

The early 1930s saw Taeuber-Arp, who had taught at Kunstgewerbeschule Zurich, and her husband Hans Arp recruit Bill to Abstraction Création. This new, cosmopolitan group was based in Paris and numbered Vantongerloo and Pevsner among its members—along with Auguste Herbin, Marlow Moss, Jean Hélion, and many others both male and female. Even as a young man, therefore, Bill was welcomed into an avant-garde context in which the focus was firmly on non-figurative art. His first abstract works were even exhibited alongside those of well-known avant-garde artists at the Abstraction Création gallery as early as December 1933 and then again in March 1934. His involvement in Abstraction Création was thus significantly more productive than that in the two groups that he himself had founded.

Buoyed by the proximity of artists of international renown, Bill was able to strengthen his own position within Switzerland and with it that of his peers. Stimulated by the theoretical discussions of non-figurative art and anxious to win recognition as the movement's leading theoretician, he wrote an essay of his own inspired by the writings of van Doesburg. Called "konkrete gestaltung," it was published in 1936 in the catalog of *Zeitprobleme der Schweizer Malerei und Plastik*, an exhibition initiated by Leo Leuppi and Welti at Kunsthaus Zurich that ran from June 13 to July 22, 1936. That show also marked Bill's debut at the Kunsthaus, where seven works of his were presented alongside a further 152 by forty Swiss artists, some of whom he had nominated. The list of artists included not only names of international renown such as Arp, Klee, Le Corbusier, Alberto Giacometti, and Taeuber-Arp, but also artists of Bill's own generation such as Fischli, Fritz Glarner, Leuppi, Verena Loewensberg, and Richard Paul Lohse, with whom Bill would before long form a new artist group. The essay he wrote for the catalog, which was printed alongside an introduction by the curator Sigfried Giedion and a statement by Le Corbusier, explained Concrete Art as an approach to creative work that dispensed entirely with the mimesis of natural phenomena and instead grew out of its own materials and rules. *Zeitprobleme* was the first of many exhibition projects in Switzerland in which Bill was involved either as curator, artist, or poster and catalog designer. He also endeavored to strengthen the network of artist friends from all over the world that he had built up in Paris, whether by organizing exhibitions for them (and for himself, too) or by writing about them. The numerous articles that he wrote for *Das Werk* in the 1940s, for example, included appraisals of Klee, Taeuber-Arp, Kandinsky, František Kupka, Pevsner, Mondrian, and Albers.[8]

A year after the *Zeitprobleme* exhibition, Bill's friend Leuppi founded Allianz: Vereinigung moderner Schweizer Künstler, an association of Swiss artists with its own publishing arm.[9] Then, in 1942, Hansegger opened the Eaux Vives gallery in Zurich, which likewise published its own magazine, *abstrakt/konkret*. It was primarily through these media outlets that Concrete

Art came to the attention of a wide audience. Bill himself explained the development of modern art in a series of theoretical articles, while some of his fellow Allianz artists regularly contributed texts of their own. Excerpts from the writings of Mondrian, Klee, Adolf Hölzel, and Kandinsky were also reprinted. Many Allianz members had already taken part in the *Zeitprobleme* exhibition and through the Bauhaus or Abstraction Création were in touch with kindred spirits all over the world. Bill, flanked by Lohse and Anton Stankowski, soon became the driving force on the Zurich art scene, where the Concretists established themselves as the hard core of Allianz. The group's objective was to organize regular exhibitions in Switzerland. Their first success came in 1938, when Kunsthalle Basel, a year after its show *Konstruktivisten*, in which many former Bauhaus masters and members of Abstraction Création had taken part, staged an exhibition called *Neue Kunst in der Schweiz*. Four more major exhibitions would follow before Allianz was finally disbanded in 1954.[10] The non-figurative art on display at these shows provoked controversial responses from press and public alike. A review by Peter Meyer, who dismissed Concrete Art as "cultivated nihilism" and hence of no value—or rather valueless—, sparked an exceptionally heated debate, in which Bill, too, had a say in the form of his essay "Ueber konkrete kunst" published in *Das Werk*.[11] To lend his piece the necessary weight, he asked artist friends such as Friedrich Vordemberge-Gildewart, Mondrian, Vantongerloo, Naum Gabo, Pevsner, and Kandinsky to supply the visuals to illustrate it, adding to their works a photograph of his sculpture *unendliche schleife* (1936) taken by his wife Binia Bill. His aim was twofold: to anchor his own art in the context of international Concrete Art, and to lend contemporary Swiss art the necessary legitimacy. Thus he was able to cast the concept of Concrete Art as something of enduring value and to present it as a major global development of the twentieth century. Concrete Art, Bill argued, was neither a self-contained category nor even a definite style; it was more an attitude. Hence his description of his own art and that of his fellow artists as the logical outcome of the abstracting momentum that had begun with Cubism, as Jörg Stürzebecher so appositely puts it.[12] With his experience at the Bauhaus and his contacts to Abstraction Création, Bill was the ideal candidate to spread the word of abstract art across national boundaries and across the generational divide.[13] In the course of the 1940s, for example, he was involved in the conception and implementation of a series of exhibitions of contemporary art. Among these was the show *konkrete kunst* at Kunsthalle Basel that he curated in 1944 and that featured not only single works by international artists, but also whole groups of works by fellow artists from Paris and Zurich. He also designed the *konkrete kunst* poster and catalog, to which he contributed an essay called "ein standpunkt" in which he sought to define Concrete Art.[14] Bill was good at positioning his own paintings and sculptures to maximum effect—and at giving them a theoretical underpinning. The geopolitical turbulence prior to and during World War II had turned Switzerland into a refuge for artists from all over war-torn Europe and some of them—Max Ernst, Vordemberge-Gildewart, and the Arps, for example—were given shelter in the Bills' own home. All these activities enabled Bill to keep his finger firmly on the pulse of the international art scene, while at the same time establishing himself as an artist and theoretician in his native Switzerland.

São Paulo and Buenos Aires

The end of World War II opened up new opportunities for Bill to expand his network still further. He had been spotted by Pietro Maria Bardi and his wife, the architect Lina Bo Bardi, as one of the participants in the Milan Triennale in 1936. The highly innovative exhibition architecture of the Swiss pavilion at that event was all Bill's doing and won him the Triennale Grand Prix—along with the opportunity to exhibit some of his most recent Concretist sculptures alongside his own posters and furniture. But it was not until the Primo Congresso Nationale per la Riconstruzione Edilizia in Milan in December 1945 that the Bardis actually met Bill in person. The following year they emigrated to Brazil, where Bardi became the founding director of the Museu de Arte de São Paulo (MASP) that opened in 1947. Together with his wife and with Jacob Ruchti, Bardi also opened an Instituto de Arte Contemporânea inside the MASP. This was to be Brazil's first ever Bauhaus-inspired school of design, and Bardi had already set his sights on Bill as one of its lecturers.[15] The major Max Bill retrospective at the MASP happened to coincide with the opening of the new school and featured not only sculptures, prints, posters, and paintings, but also documentary photographs of Bill's design work. While the show met with interest among those in the art and architecture scene, it went all but unnoticed in the local press.[16] The numerous letters exchanged between Bardi, his assistant Wolfgang Pfeiffer, and Bill during those years tell us that Bill had wanted the exhibition to travel on to Buenos Aires—a plan that ultimately had to be dropped owing to prohibitive customs formalities and political considerations.[17] Bardi tried to find alternative ports of call within Brazil and even put out feelers to the Museo de Santiago in Chile, though without success.[18] Bill also inquired about the planned exhibition catalog, which was never actually published. At least the journal *Habitat* published a write-up of the show, which it flanked with a translation of Bill's essay "schönheit aus funktion und als funktion."[19] The exhibition in Buenos Aires having had to be postponed until 1952, Bill gave his consent to the inclusion of his work *dreiteilige einheit* at the first São Paulo Art Biennial in the autumn of 1951. There it was championed by Argentinian jury member Jorge Romero Brest, and after winning the first prize was acquired by the Museu de Arte Moderna São Paulo (MAM-SP), although it now belongs to the collection of the Museu de Arte Contemporânea da Universidade de São Paulo. Brest himself visited Zurich the following year and there met Bill in person. The Brazilian artist Mary Vieira was already living in Zurich by then and visited Bill and other Zurich natives in his studio together with the Brazilian art critic Mário Pedrosa and the Paris-based artist Almir Mavignier.[20] That same year Bill also received a visit from Niomar Monis Sodré, Director of the Museu de Arte Moderna in Rio de Janeiro (MAM-RJ), who purchased two works of his for the collection of his museum.[21]

Alongside Brest, the person who did most to make Bill famous in Argentina was Tomás Maldonado, who first mentioned the Swiss Concretist in his 1946 essay, "Lo abstracto y lo concreto en el arte moderno," which appeared in the very first issue of *Arte Concreto-Invención*. This journal, launched by Maldonado himself, doubled as the mouthpiece of the group Asociación Arte Concreto-Invención, which numbered Lidy Prati, Alfredo Hlito, Claudio Girola, Enio Iommi, Nélida Fedullo, and others among its members. In June 1948 Maldonado visited Bill in Zurich and there met Bill's fellow Concretists Lohse, Loewensberg, and Camille Graeser. The close professional friendship that developed between Bill and Maldonado would ultimately lead to their collaboration at the HfG Ulm. Both believed in Concretism and were convinced that its application not just in art, but also in architecture and design, would benefit all humanity. Bill's theoretical writings on Concretism as well as his works of art were publicized in numerous books and journals throughout Argentina. Bill himself published several essays in *Nueva Visión*, a journal that Maldonado had founded together with Méndez Mosquera and Hlito. In 1955 Maldonado devoted a monograph to Bill, as part of the *Nueva Visión* series of books.[22] Maldonado's enthusiasm for Bill also shines through in his letters, in which he assures his friend: "[H]ere we consider you a major contributor to the theoretical basis of our movement."[23] Concrete Art, which by then had had to yield to gestural painting in postwar Europe, seemed to have found a new platform in Latin America.[24] This latest advance in modern art that Bill was so anxious to propagate was very much in tune with the prevailing zeitgeist, South America having embarked on a program of modernization that was receptive to avant-garde approaches such as this. In 1953 Bill accepted an invitation to Brazil to give a series of lectures, in the course of which he provoked controversy by being rather too candid about his views on contemporary Brazilian architecture. Without actually naming Oscar Niemeyer, he criticized the playful—or what he called "excessively Baroque"—character of Niemeyer's buildings and complained that for all the architect's communist sympathies, his architecture lacked a social function.[25] Those remarks led to Bill being expelled from the architecture jury of the second São Paulo Art Biennial and asked to adjudicate the fine arts instead. Yet the attention that his theories and art attracted, especially in Brazil and Argentina, was definitely to his advantage and inspired many young artists eager to find new methods of form-creation to follow Bill to the HfG Ulm.[26]

Ulm to Zurich

In 1950 Inge Aicher-Scholl and Otl Aicher invited Bill to become involved in the founding of the HfG Ulm. Bill took over as rector in 1953 and the campus designed by him was inaugurated in 1955. The school was to be a place where young people from all over the world would come together to learn from each other and so foster a democratic society. The project was financed by the Allies, first and foremost the United States.[27] Bill demanded that half the faculty and half the students should be foreigners so as to expedite the social and cultural changes that Germany needed in order to put the period of Nazi rule firmly behind it. Thus he presented himself as the perfect candidate for the job of rector, since not only did he have teaching experience, but he was also extremely well connected. His first step was to have letters sent out to former colleagues, inviting them to join the international board of trustees that would oversee the school. His contacts to those former Bauhaus students and teachers who had emigrated to the USA provided his American paymasters with the necessary political reassurances,[28] as Walter Gropius, Josef and Anni Albers, Ludwig Mies van der Rohe, Walter Peterhans, and Sibyl Moholy-Nagy were all building on their work at the Bauhaus as teachers at American universities by then. Bill regarded the HfG Ulm as the "direct continuation of the dessau bauhaus"[29] and in its early years invited several Bauhaus alumni to Ulm, notably Walter Peterhans, Albers, Johannes Itten, and Helene Nonné-Schmidt. He also recruited his Argentinian friend Maldonado as a teacher, as well as Hans Gugelot, an Indonesian-born Dutchman who had trained in the Netherlands, the German Vordemberge-Gildewart, and the Austrian Walter Zeischegg—to name but a few. The school's student body was cosmopolitan right from the start, with thirty-one of the sixty-five students who enrolled in the first three years coming from outside Germany.[30] Several young Brazilian artists such as Mary Vieira, Almir Mavignier, and Alexandre Wollner had followed Bill to Ulm after seeing his exhibition at the MASP, where Wollner had helped with the installation. While for this young generation Bill's Concrete Art was a revelation, for other artists already working with geometric forms—Geraldo de Barros, for example—it was an affirmation. The HfG Ulm was avowedly not an art school, yet Bill was convinced "that the fine arts are the primary formative influence on all design," and that "it has always been the truly revolutionary painter and sculptor who have wrought the works of art that first mirrored the spirit of his age, thereby setting free that hitherto-imprisoned spirit to reverberate throughout every branch of the arts and crafts."[31] His styling of artistic license as the greater good was derived from the Bauhaus, as was the practice of requiring students to complete a one-year preliminary course consisting of exercises in "purposeless aesthetics."[32] In Ulm, as previously in Dessau, there was a lot of discussion about the direction the school should take. Especially controversial were the debates of the relationship between design, science, and technology. The younger teachers believed scientific criteria should carry ever more weight in everyday life, whereas Bill still clung to the concept of beauty—and even began combining his "mathematical approach" with sentiment. This conflict led to a breakdown in the friendship between Bill and Maldonado, and in 1957 Bill left the HfG altogether to devote himself to his own design projects. If Bill's international contacts had been crucial to the school's success, so, too, had his personal charisma and powers of persuasion. As so often in Bill's life, his compelling, forthright manner was well received by some, but rejected as insufferable arrogance by others.

In 1960 Bill organized a major exhibition on the international development of Concrete Art to be held at the Helmhaus Zurich. The list of artists who took part in *konkrete kunst. 50 jahre entwicklung* reads like Bill's own address book, taking in both established artists and several young newcomers from Latin America. Having as a young man promoted his own career by taking part in group shows alongside famous artists, he now paved the way to prominence for as yet unknown artists by inviting them to participate in a wide-ranging historical review. At the same time, his list of artists was a way of persuading his Swiss audience that Concrete Art was one of the great global phenomena of the twentieth century and an influential art movement, first and foremost in Switzerland.

New York

Bill initiated numerous publication and exhibition projects in the course of the 1960s and 1970s. Among these was his first solo exhibition on American soil, the opportunity for which finally presented itself in 1963, when the Staempfli Gallery in New York organized the first of several shows. The Minimalist Donald Judd wrote a review of that event in which he singled out Bill's sculptures for special praise.[33] Bill later bought two works by Judd from an exhibition at the gallery owned by Annemarie and Gianfranco Verna, but was not to meet Judd in person until the 1980s. Bill's quest for reduction also aroused the interest of other adherents of Minimal Art, such as Carl Andre and Richard Serra, who even created a two-part steel sculpture for Bill's house in Zumikon near Zurich. From now on, Bill was a frequent visitor to the States, where he gave lectures and kept abreast of his many contacts there. In 1974/75 his tireless networking again bore fruit in a touring exhibition at the Albright-Knox Art Gallery in Buffalo, the Los Angeles County Museum, the San Francisco Museum of Art, and the Corcoran Gallery of Art in Washington, DC.

Bill was to be given many more such exhibition opportunities right up to his death in 1994, just as he won several prizes and commissions for sculptures in the public space both in Switzerland and abroad. His decades of networking and unflagging efforts to popularize Concrete Art appeared to have paid off.

[1] Hans Fischli in *Hans Fischli. Malerei Plastik Architektur*, exh. cat., Zurich: Kunsthaus Zurich 1968, pp. 5–86, here p. 49.

[2] Letter from Max Bill to Dr. Wartmann, Kunstverein Zurich, January 7, 1928, Archiv Kunsthaus Zurich.

[3] Bill submitted an entry, as is proven by a letter from him of September 29, 1929 to the conservator of Kunsthaus Zurich, Dr. Wartmann, Archiv Kunsthaus Zurich.

[4] Thomas 2008, p. 298.

[5] Letter from Max Bill to the exhibitions committee of Kunsthaus Zurich, December 3, 1929, Archiv Kunsthaus Zurich.

[6] Thomas 2008, p. 201.

[7] Thomas 2008, pp. 326–327.

[8] Max Bill's articles on contemporary artists in *Das Werk* were as follows: "Paul Klee," no. 8 (1940); "Sophie Taeuber-Arp," no. 6 (1943); "Wassily Kandinsky," no. 4 (1946); "Frank Kupka," no. 9 (1946); "Antoine Pevsner," no. 1 (1947), "Piet Mondrian," no. 4 (1947), and "Josef Albers," no. 4 (1958).

[9] For a more detailed account, see Rudolf Koella: "Die Künstlergruppe 'Allianz' und die Zürcher Konkreten," in Winterthur 1981, pp. 36–40.

[10] On the exhibition history of Allianz, see Martin Pauli: "Die 'Allianz' und ihre Ausstellungen," in Winterthur 1981, pp. 41–43.

[11] Bill 1938. On the various reactions to this, see Mariuccia Sprenger: "Die 'Allianz' im Spiegel der Presse," in Winterthur 1981, pp. 46–49.

[12] Jörg Stürzebecher: "Die Zürcher Konkreten – ein Mythos," in Ingolstadt 2012, pp. 31–43, here p. 38.

[13] Markus Zehentbauer: "Der konkreteste Konkrete? Max Bill," in Ingolstadt 2012, pp. 45–52, here p. 47.

[14] Bill 1944, pp. 9–10.

[15] Ethel Leon: "A Bauhaus Domesticated in São Paulo," www.bauhaus-imaginista.org/articles/5684/a-bauhaus-domesticated-in-sao-paulo (accessed August 12, 2020).

[16] Letter from Pietro Maria Bardi to Max Bill, March 28, 1951, Archiv MASP, São Paulo.

[17] Letter from Pietro Maria Bardi to Max Bill, December 29, 1949, Archiv MASP, São Paulo. On the failure of the plan to take the exhibition to Buenos Aires, see the letter from Pietro Maria Bardi to Max Bill, July 2, 1951, Archiv MASP, São Paulo, and the letter from Wolfgang Pfeiffer to Max Bill, July 25, 1951, Archiv MASP, São Paulo.

[18] Letter from Pietro Maria Bardi to Luis Vargas Rosas, Director of the Museo Nacional de Bellas Artes, Santiago de Chile, January 9, 1950, Archiv MASP, São Paulo.

[19] Published in Portuguese as "beleza provinda da funçao e beleza como funçao," in *Habitat*, no. 2 (January-March 1951), pp. 61–64.

[20] Aracy Amaral: "almier mavignier—chronology," in São Paulo 2000, p. 19.

[21] Juan Manuel Bonnet: "bill-brazil: a trans-atlantic history," in Cohn 2010, p. 11.

[22] Mónica Amor: *Theories of Nonobject: Argentina, Brazil, Venezuela 1944–1969*, Oakland 2016, p. 241, note 19.

[23] Letter from Tomás Maldonado to Max Bill, Bibliothek Max Bill, quoted in García 2019, p. 121.

[24] García 2019, pp. 107–147.

[25] Bachmann 2019, pp. 50–59, and Varela 2012.

[26] For a more detailed account of Bill's activities in Latin America, see María Amalia García: "max bill in argentina and brasil. south american episodes in concrete art," in Madrid 2015, pp. 242–250.

[27] For a more detailed account of how the HfG Ulm was founded, see Spitz 2002 and Spitz 2014.

[28] Gillermo Zuasnambar and Neus Moyano: "bill and the hfg ulm: lines of division," in Madrid 2015, pp. 47–61, here p. 51.

[29] Max Bill: "Bauhaus-Chronik. Vom Bauhaus in Weimar zur Hochschule für Gestaltung in Ulm," in Weimar 2007, pp. 5–9, here p. 7. English translation *the bauhaus idea from weimar to ulm*, published in Madrid 2015, pp. 286–287.

[30] René Spitz: "10,000 Kilometers as the Crow Flies. How Young Brazilian Students Found Their Way to the Ulm School of Design," in Frankfurt a. M. 2013, pp. 28–43, here p. 30.

[31] Cf. Madrid 2015, see note 29, here p. 287.

[32] Max Bill in conversation with Michael Erlhoff in Lindinger 1987, p. 67.

[33] Judd 1963, p. 88.

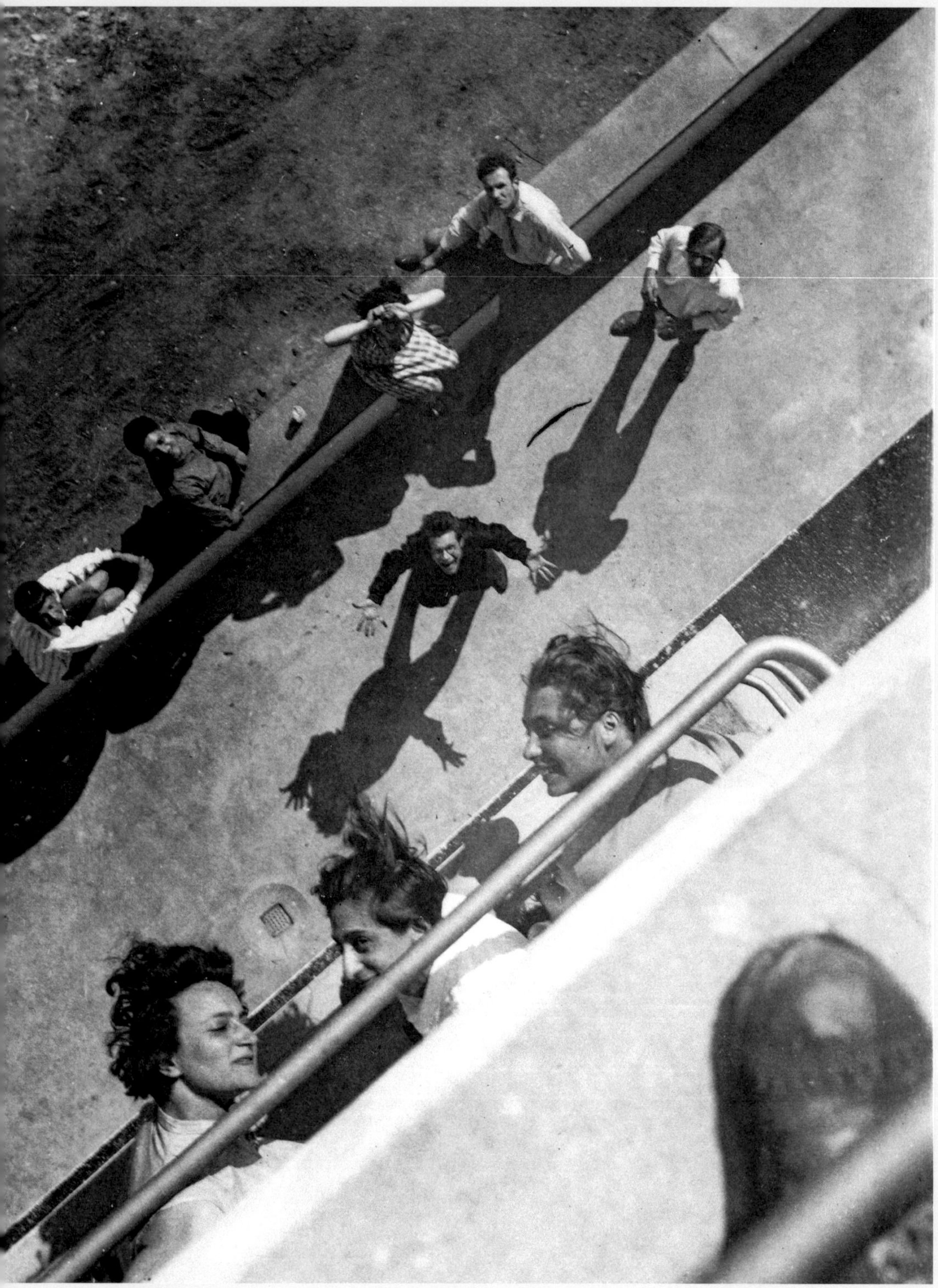

1927

Max Bill, dressed in dark clothing, in the midst of a group of Bauhaus members in 1927. On the studio's balcony: Anni Albers (center) and Gunta Stölzl (right). Bill would remain in touch with both of them.

Bauhaus-Archiv Berlin

Intent on becoming an architect, Max Bill enrolled at the Bauhaus in Dessau in 1927. There he was taught by Josef Albers, Oskar Schlemmer, László Moholy-Nagy, Wassily Kandinsky, and Paul Klee. On completing the preliminary course, he worked first in the metal workshop and then switched to the theater workshop. He also played the banjo in the Bauhaus band. Bill befriended two other members of the theater workshop, Clemens Röseler and Xanti Schawinsky.

Two female students, Hilde Rantzsch and Katt Both, also belonged to his circle of Bauhaus friends. Both were students in the architecture department. Despite not having been admitted there, Bill still attended some of the lectures, including those given by Mart Stam. He also entered several architecture competitions, developing one of his three submissions in collaboration with the Swiss Hans Fischli, with whom he shared lodgings in Dessau. Another fellow student, Takehiko Mizutani, assisted him with a design he was working on for a building in Osaka, Japan.[1]

1928

Group photo with members of the Bauhaus troupe, from left to right: Clemens Röseler, Lux Feininger, Max Bill, Joost Schmidt, Roman Clemens, Xanti Schawinsky.

Bauhaus-Archiv Berlin

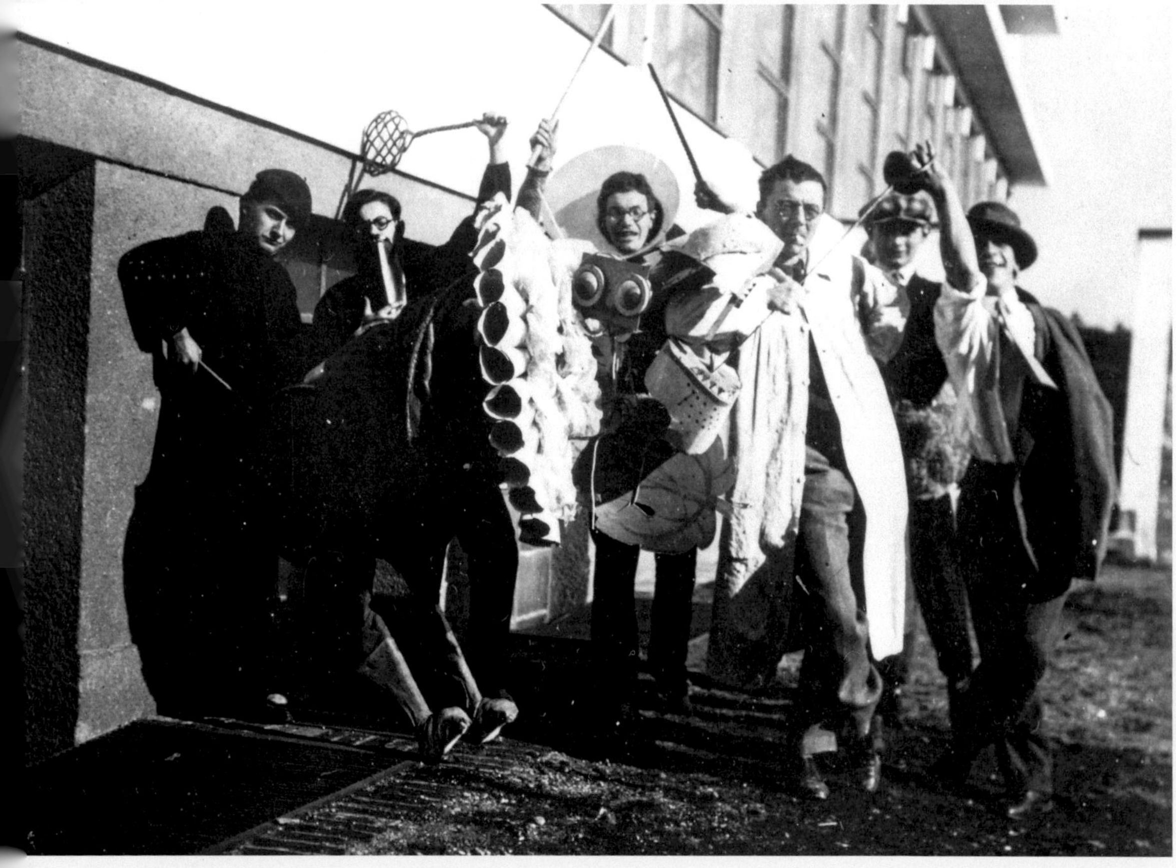

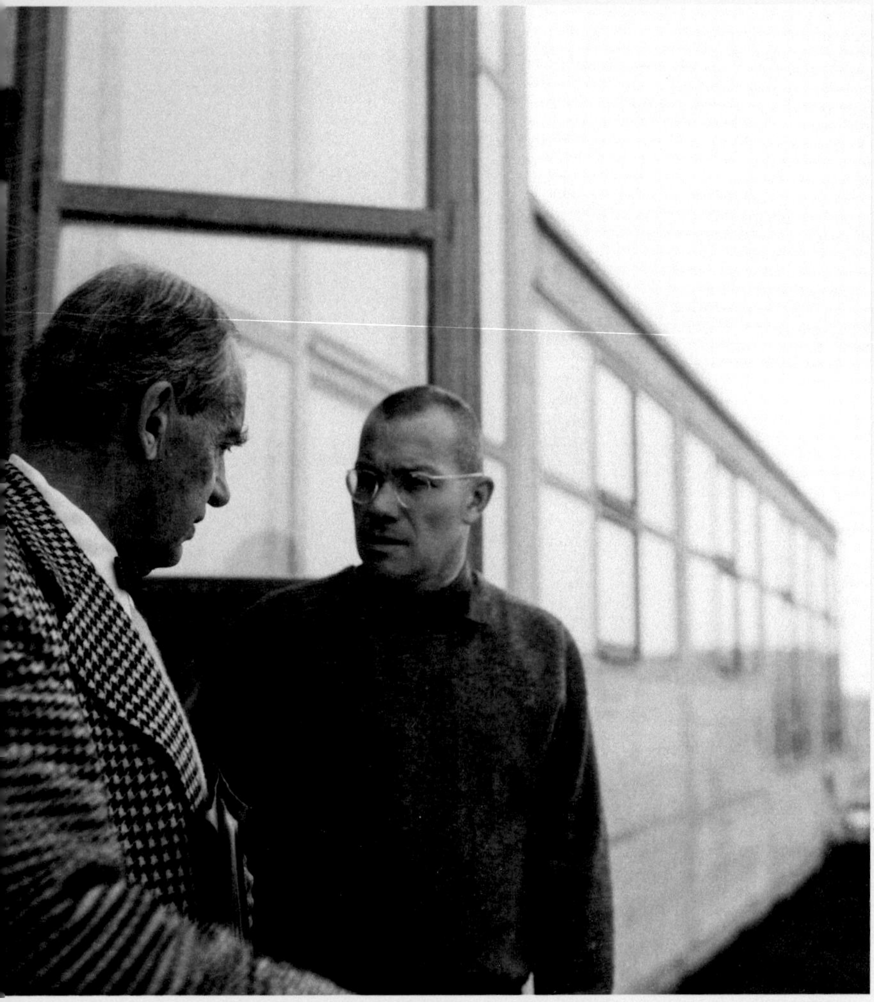

1955

Max Bill and Walter Gropius, photographed in front of the HfG Ulm. Bill, in the meantime a founding member and rector of the HfG Ulm, recruited the Bauhaus founder to join the board of trustees and invited him to give the opening speech in 1955.

HfG-Archiv Museum Ulm, photo: Sigrid von Schweinitz

Believing that young artists would be in a much stronger position if they joined forces, Bill and Fischli founded the Dessau-based gruppe z, neue malerei, plastik etc. Its members, alongside Bill and Fischli, were Röseler, Rantzsch, Annemarie Hennings, Alfredo Bortoluzzi, Lou Scheper, and Margaret Leiteritz.[2]

Although Bill was in Dessau for only two years, after which he settled in Zurich, his time at the Bauhaus was crucial to the career he had thereafter. Not only had the school's ideas and ideals left their stamp on him, but the network of friends and associates that he began developing there, coupled with his status as a Bauhaus alumnus, would later be an important factor in his success. Bill put his contacts to good use. After Kandinsky died, for example, he edited new editions of many of the painter's writings; he also wrote articles about the art of the Bauhaus artists, and initiated exhibitions of their works to raise awareness of what the school had accomplished. In the postwar period, his contacts to former Bauhaus students and teachers helped him in establishing the HfG Ulm.

1 Cf. Bill 2008, p. 23, and Thomas 2008, p. 137.

2 Cf. Thomas 2008, pp. 229 f.

1954

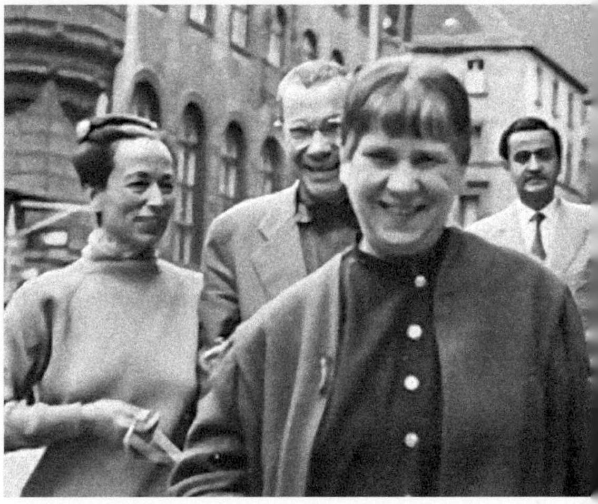

Binia and Max Bill with Helene Nonné-Schmidt and Tomás Maldonado. Along with Josef Albers, the former Bauhaus members Nonné-Schmidt, Walter Peterhans, and Johannes Itten were also among the HfG Ulm's early faculty.

HfG-Archiv Museum Ulm, photo: Sigrid von Schweinitz

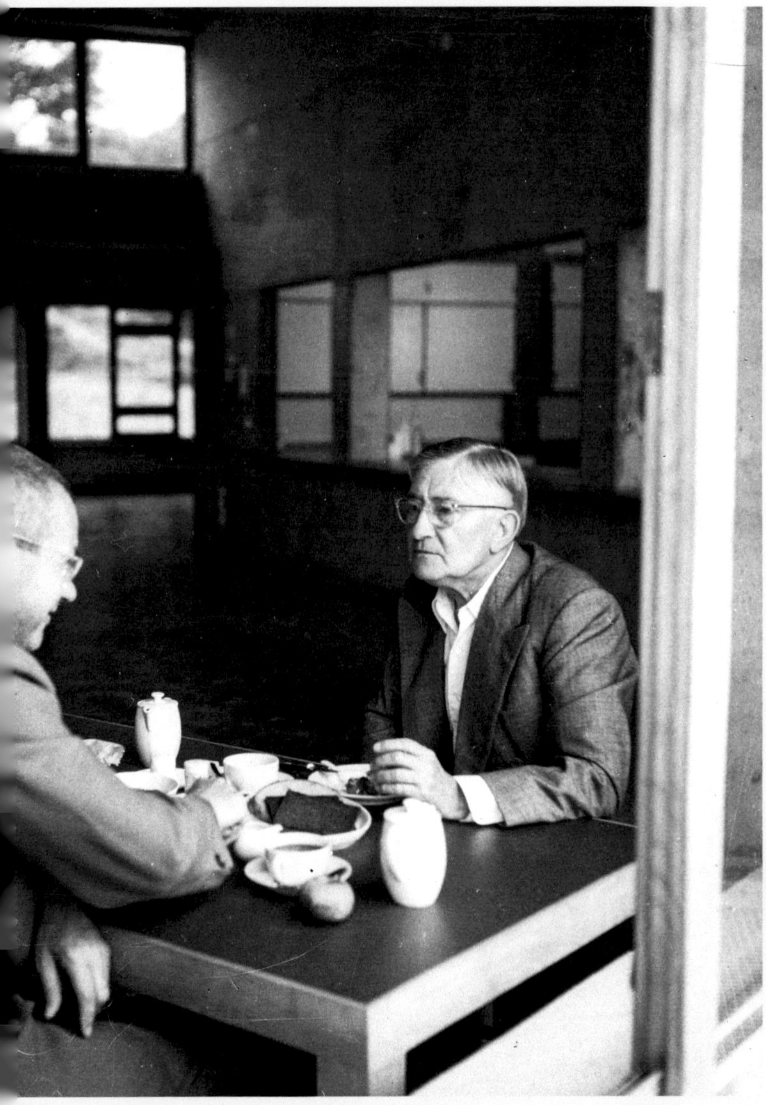

1955

Max Bill and Josef Albers having breakfast at the HfG Ulm. Albers, Professor at Yale University in New Haven, traveled to Ulm several times to teach there.

max bill georges vantongerloo stiftung, photo: Margit Weinberg-Staber

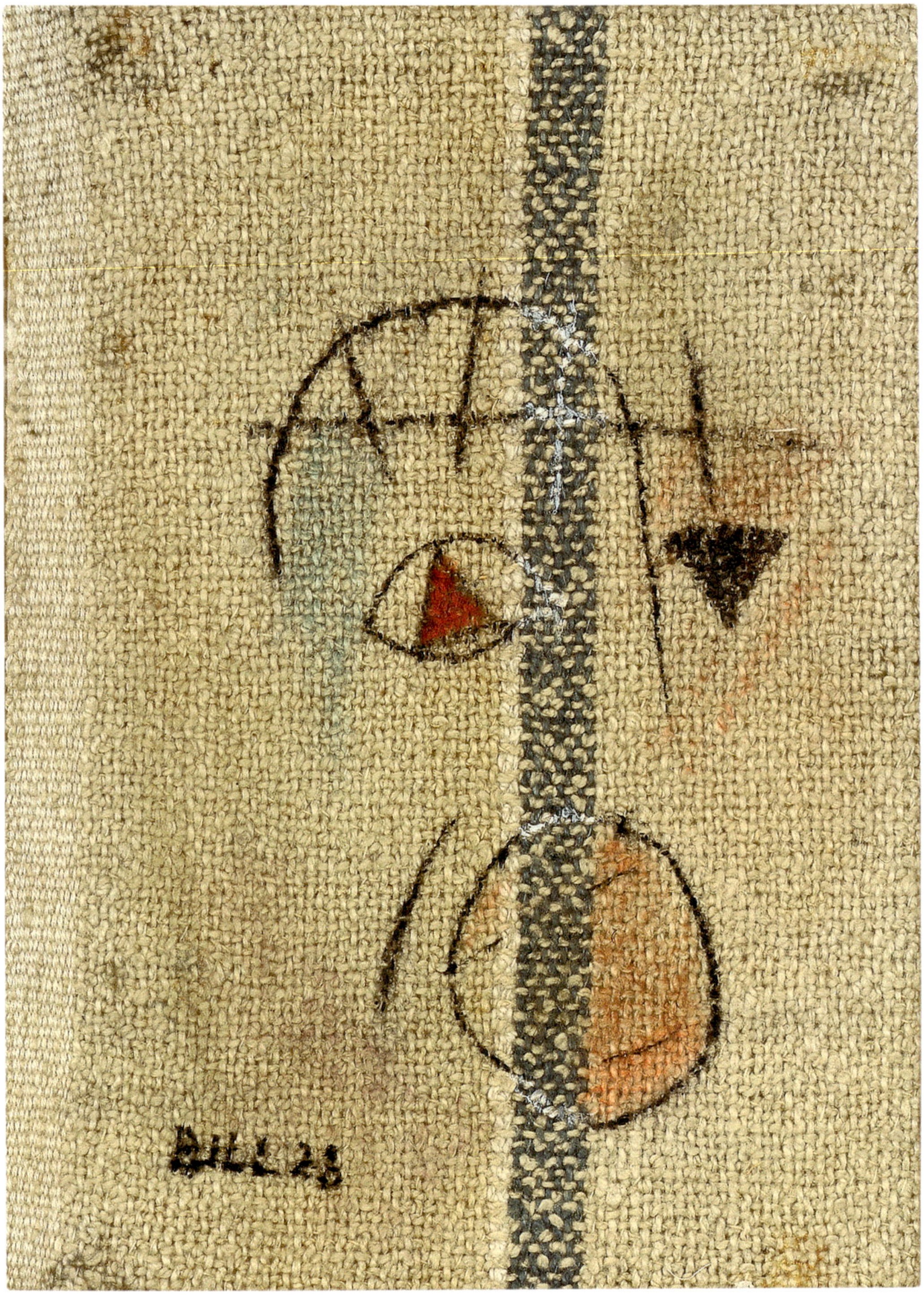

Max Bill
Was man nur auf dem Bilde sieht, 1928

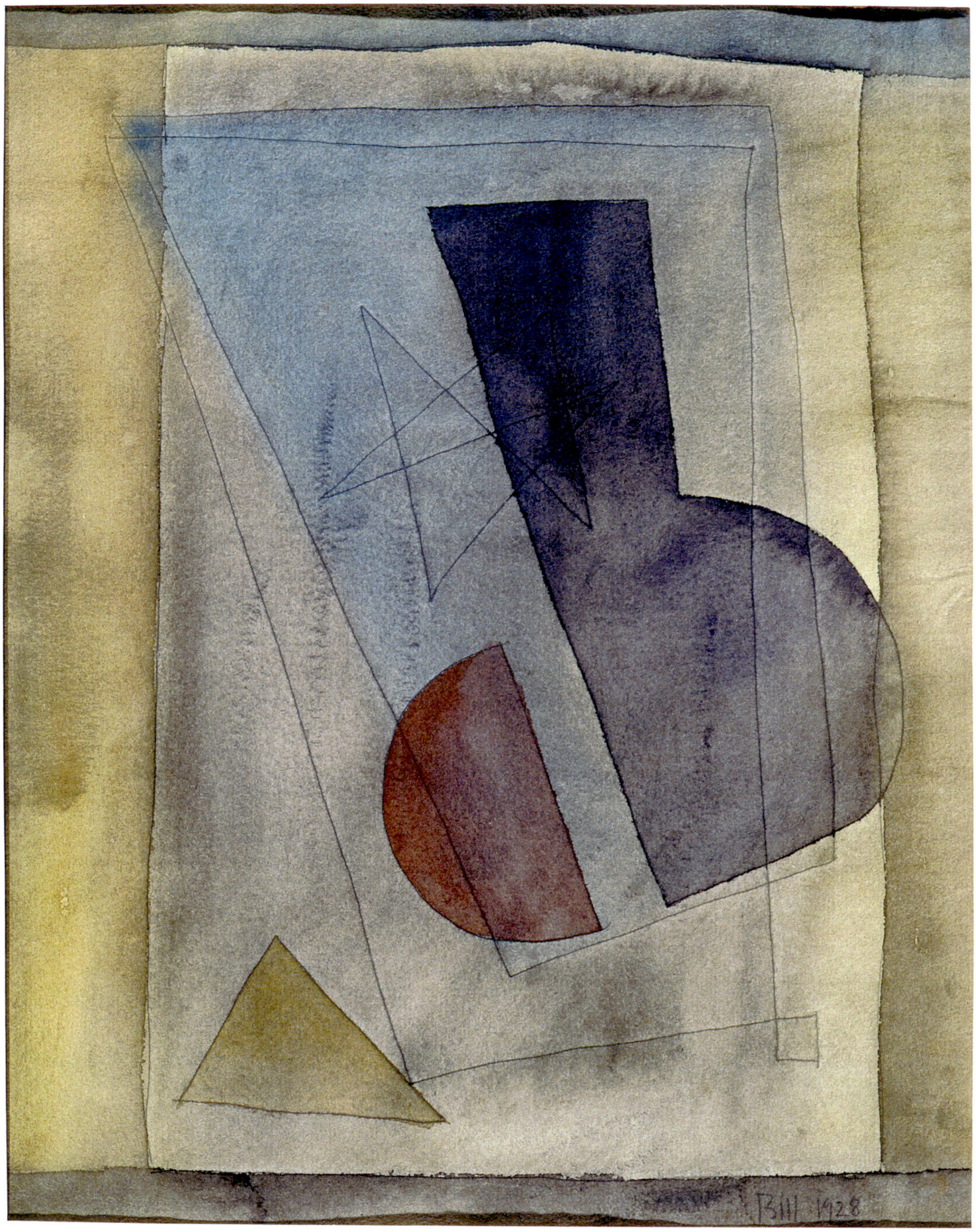

Max Bill
Düstere Bewegungen (Stilleben), 1928

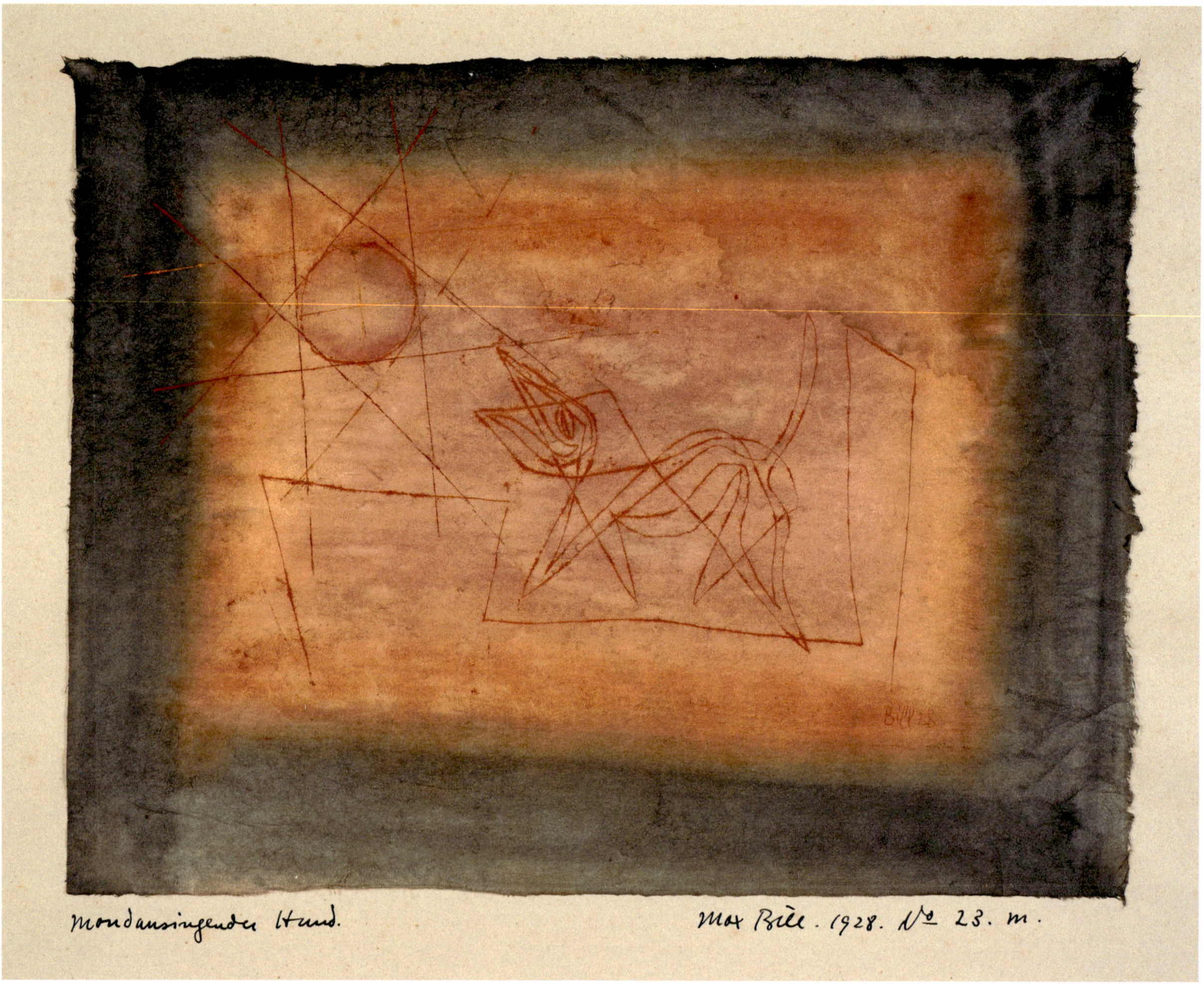

Max Bill
Mondansingender Hund, 1928

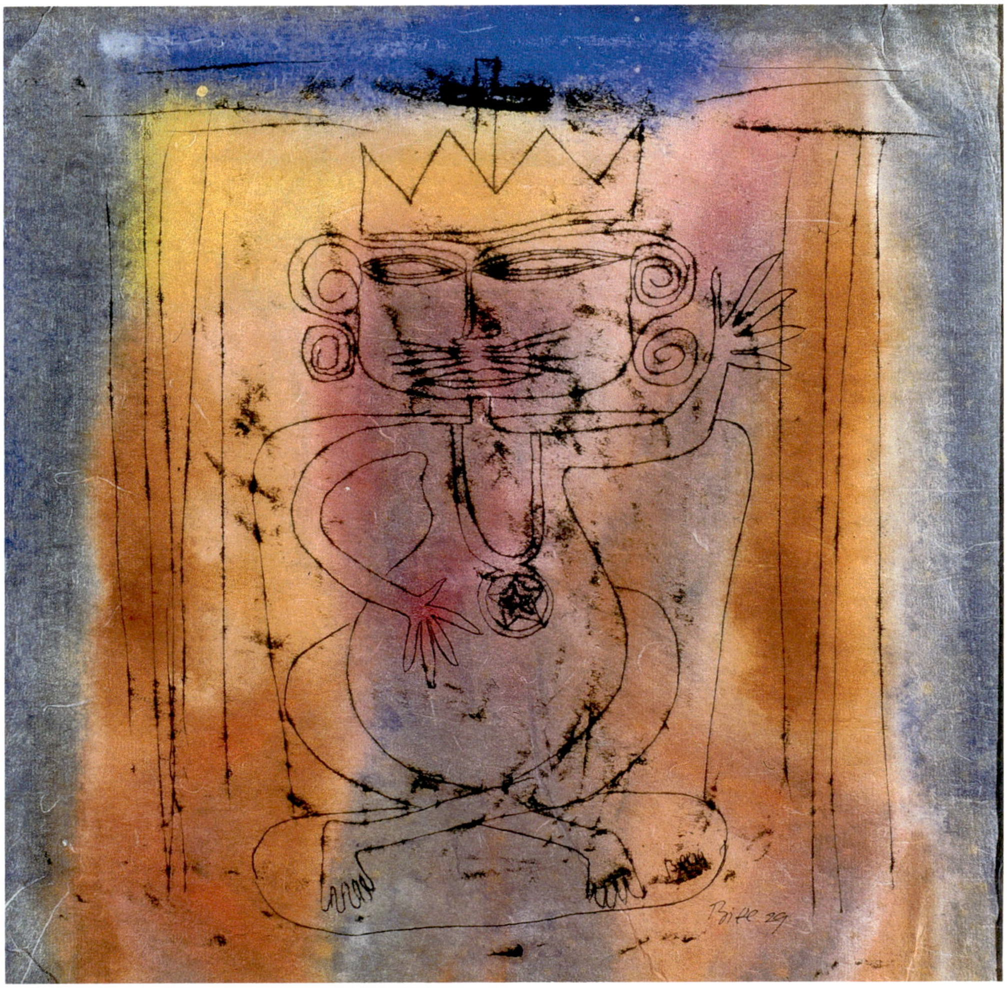

Max Bill
Der kleine Jammer König, 1929

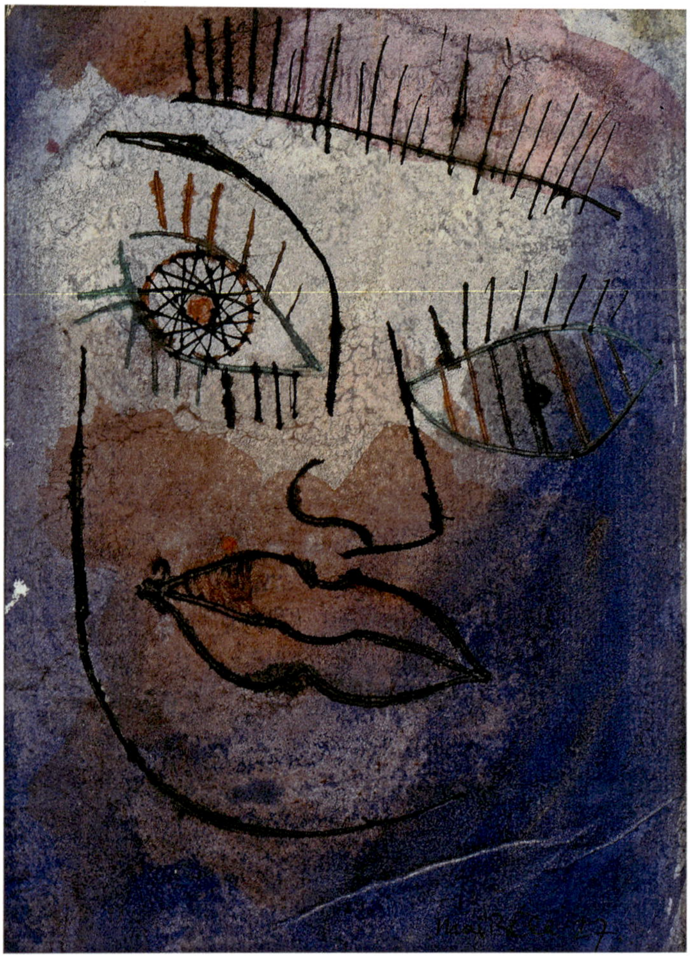

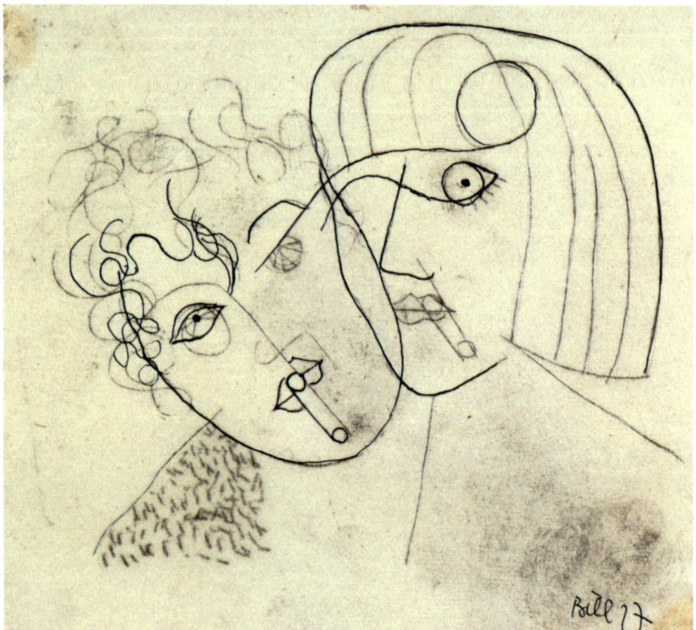

Max Bill
Ich, ein Katzenmensch, 1927

Max Bill
Zwei Freundinnen, Katt und Hilde, 1927

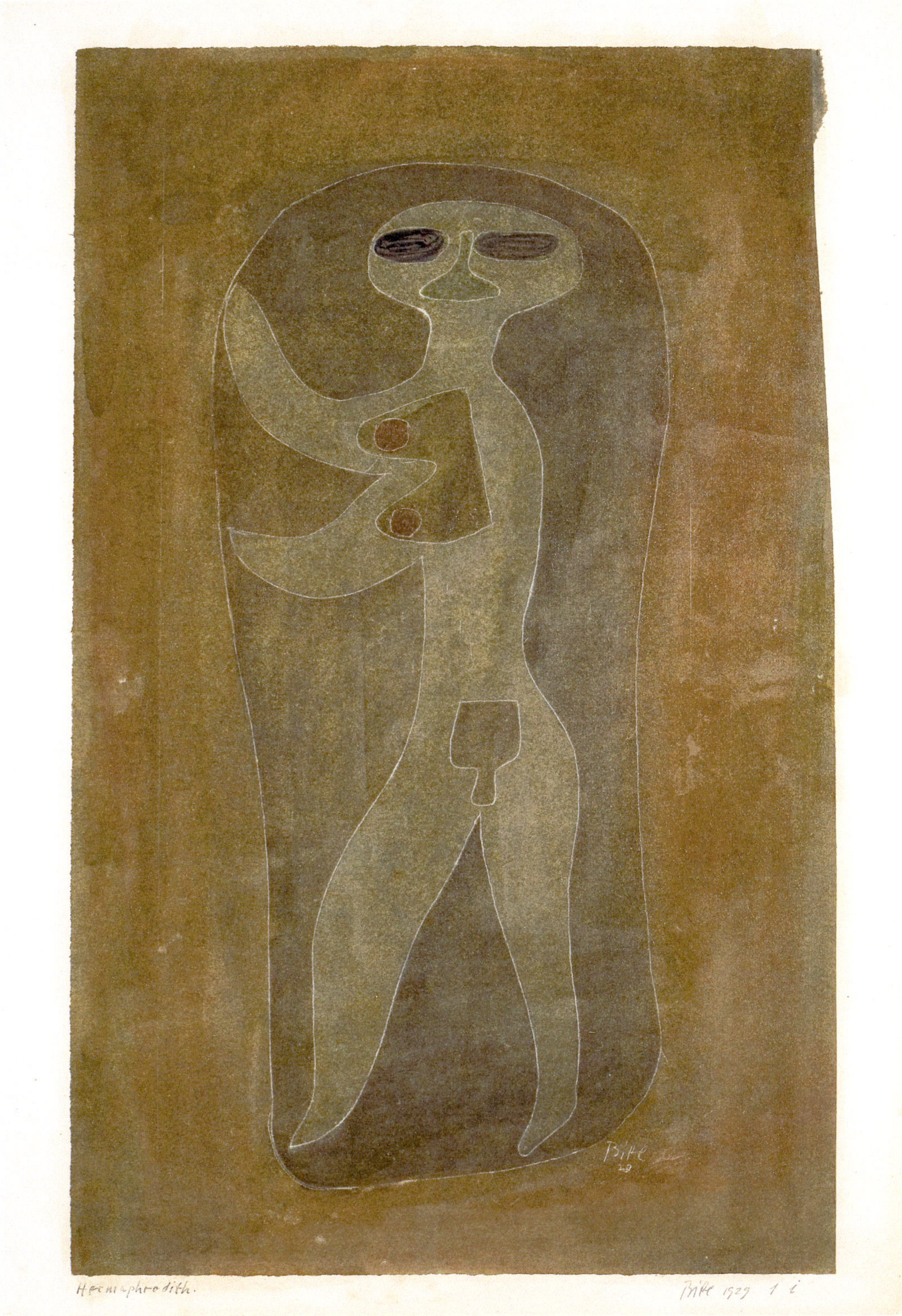

Max Bill
Hermaphrodith, 1929

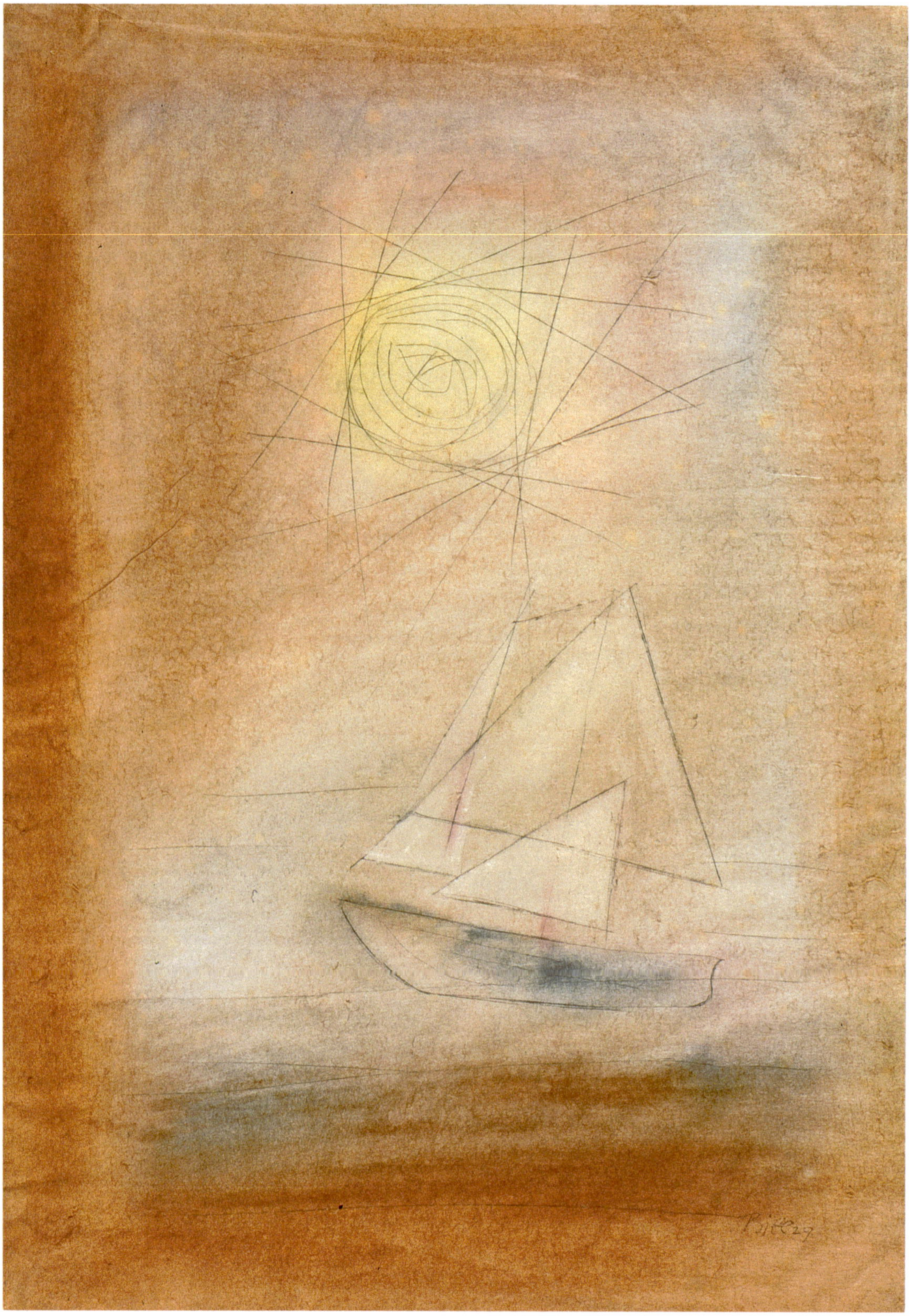

Max Bill
Ein Schiff unter der Sonne, 1929

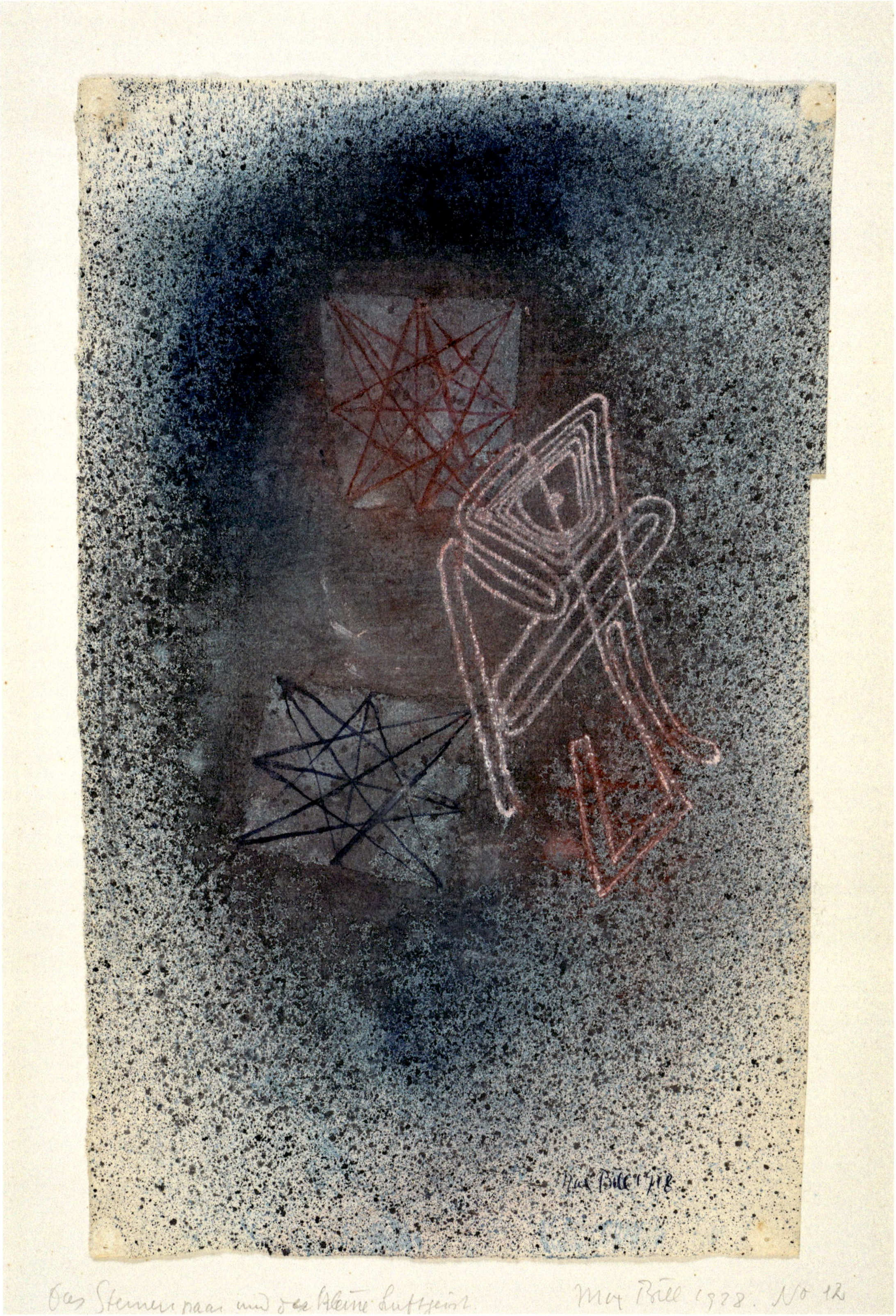

Max Bill
Das Sternenpaar und der kleine Luftgeist, 1928

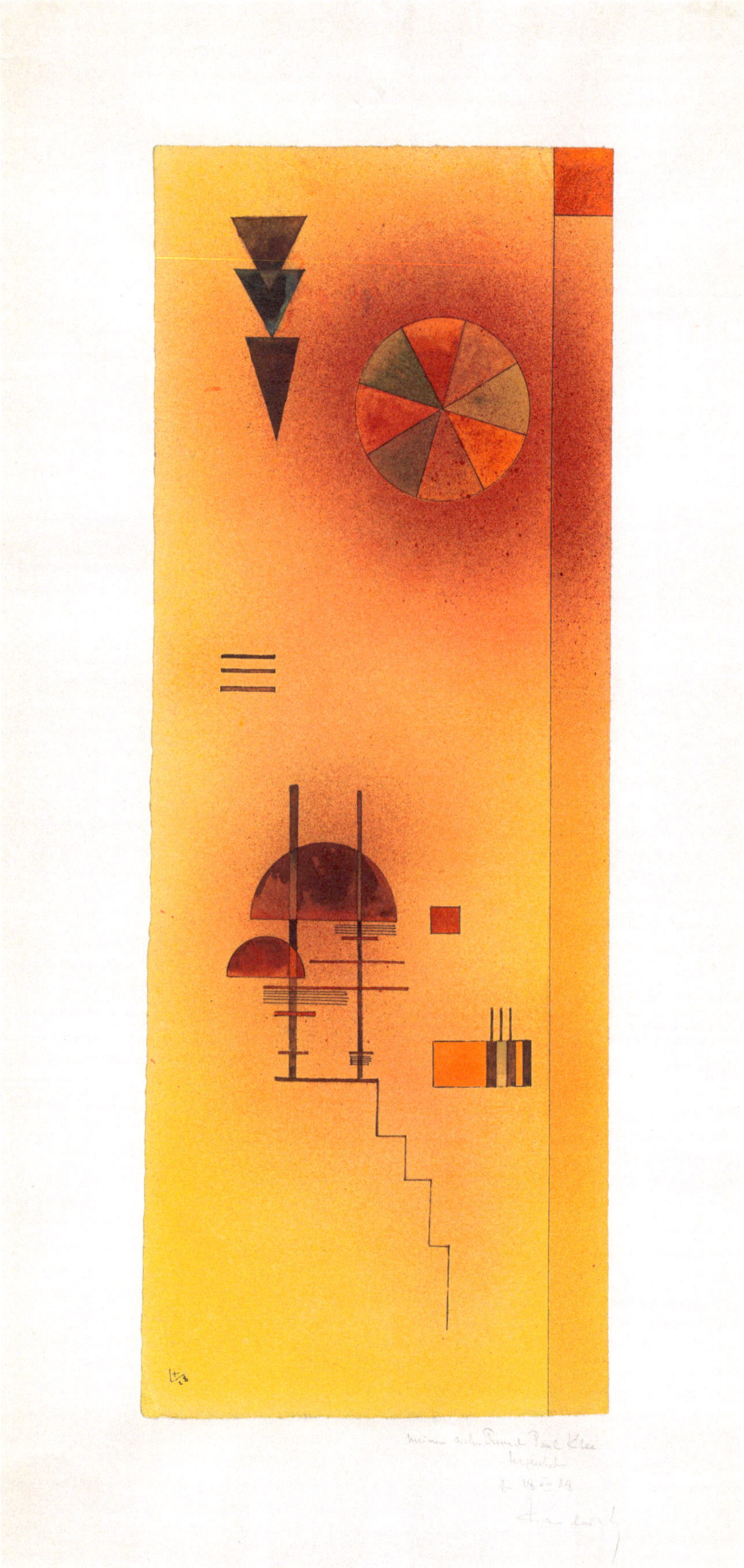

Wassily Kandinsky
Untitled (Circle and Stairs), 1928

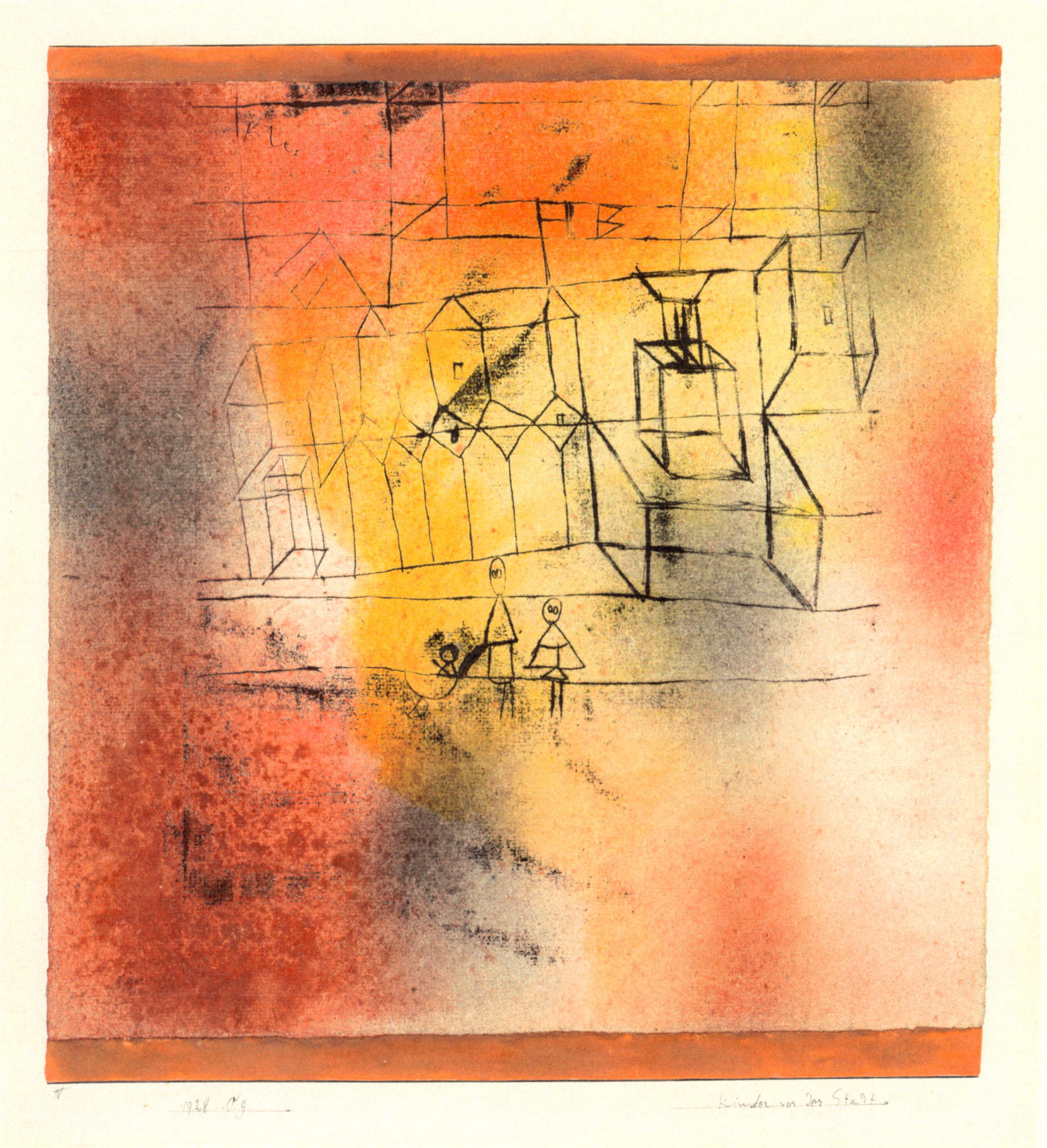

Paul Klee
Kinder vor der Stadt, 1928, 59

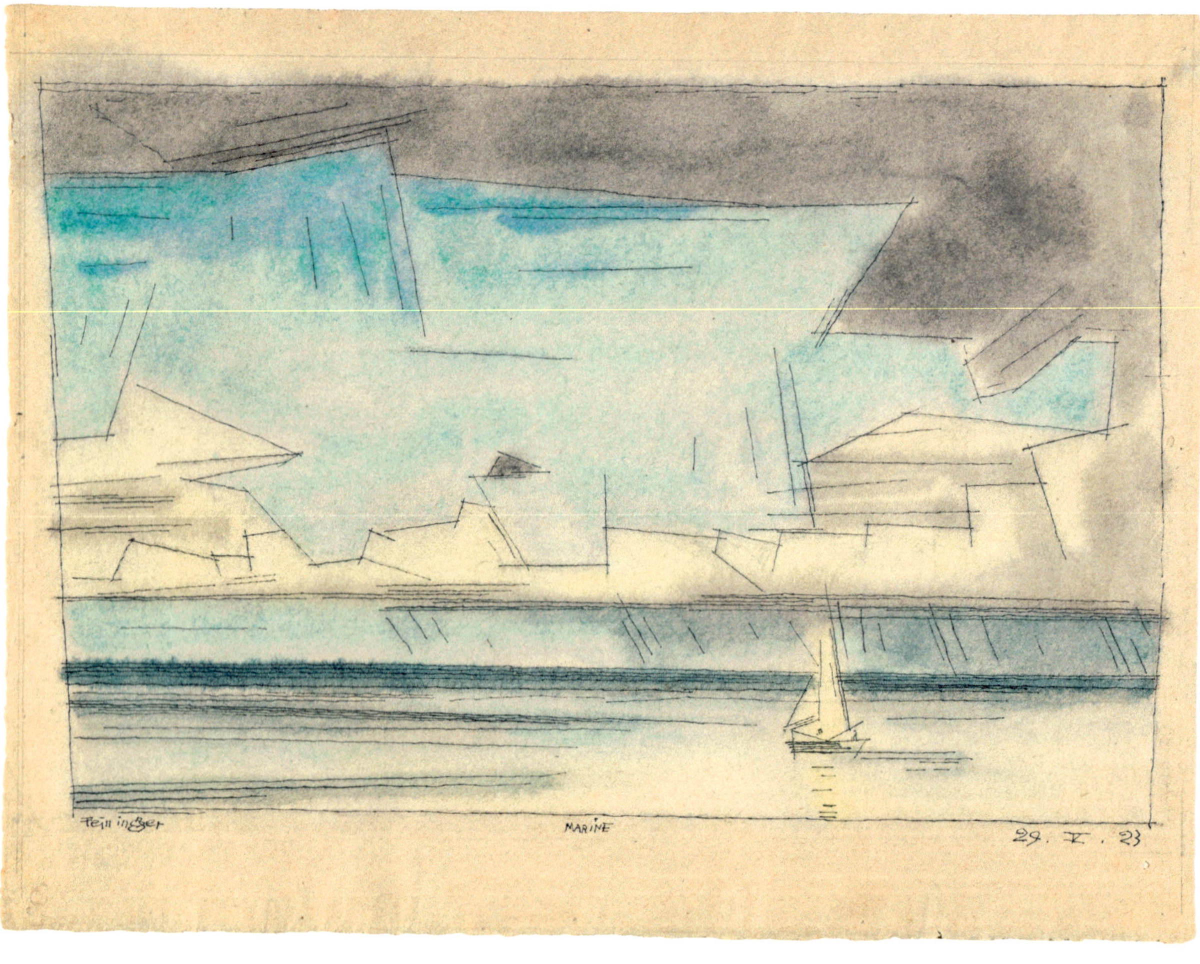

Lyonel Feininger
Marine, 1923

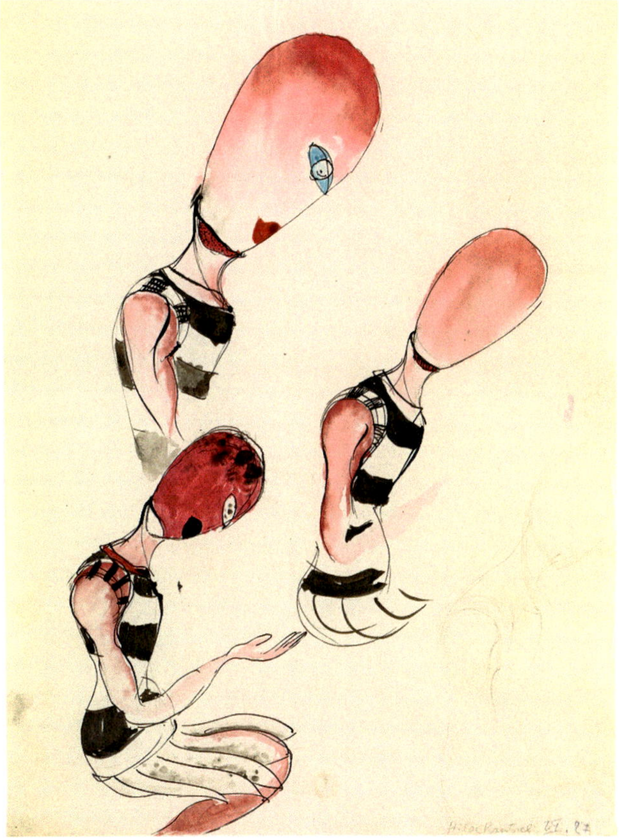

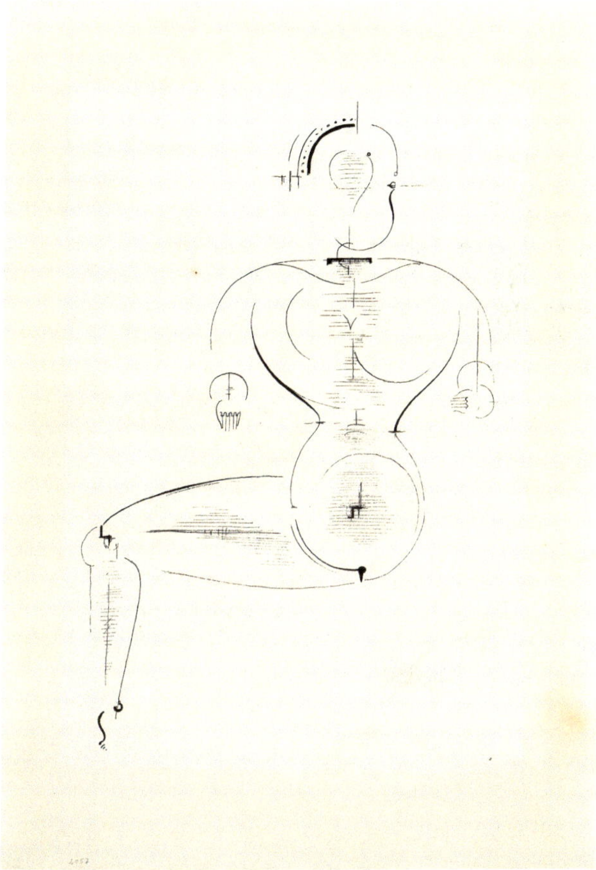

Hilde Rantzsch
Untitled, 1927

Oskar Schlemmer
Untitled, 1922

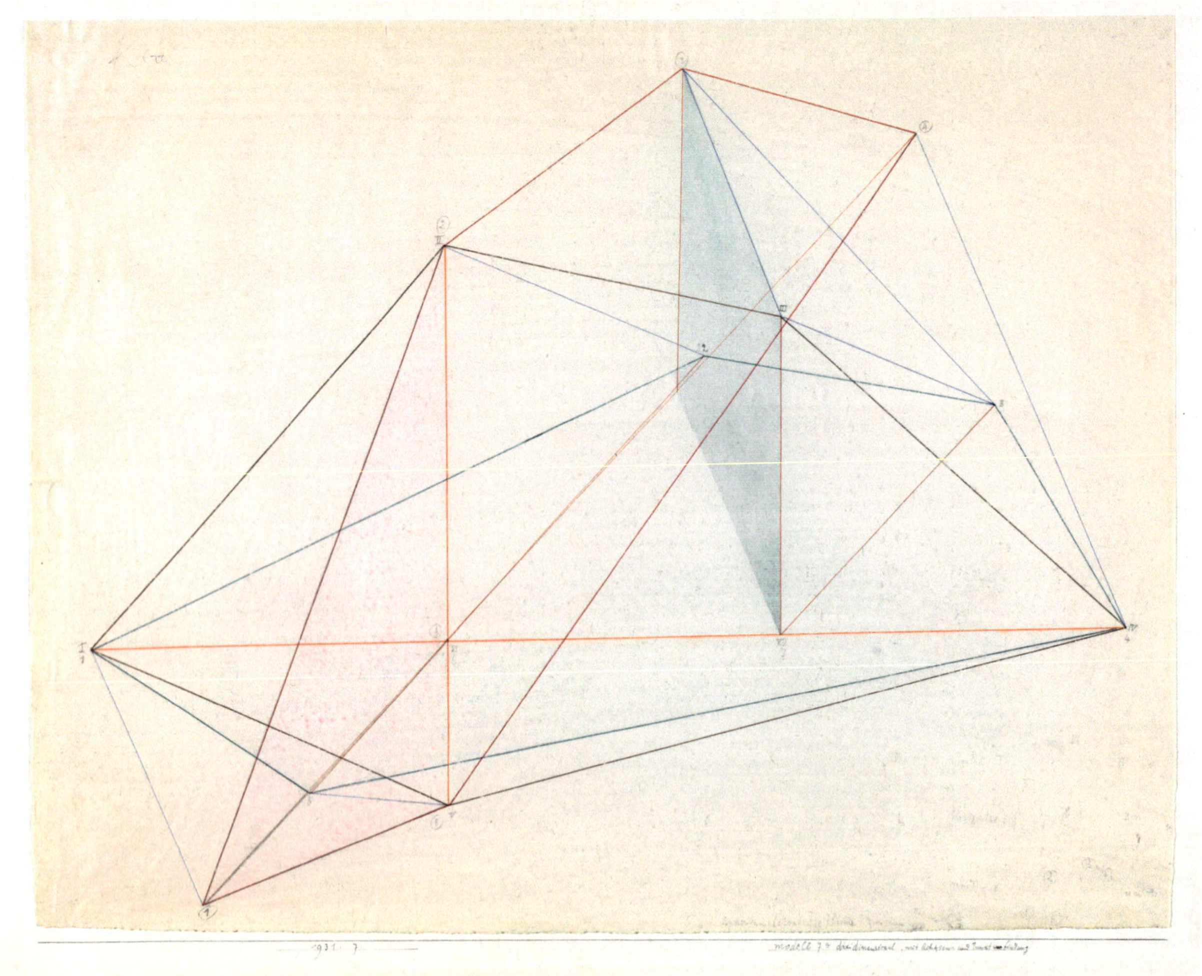

Paul Klee
modell 7a dreidimensional,
mit Achsen= und Punktbindung, 1931, 7

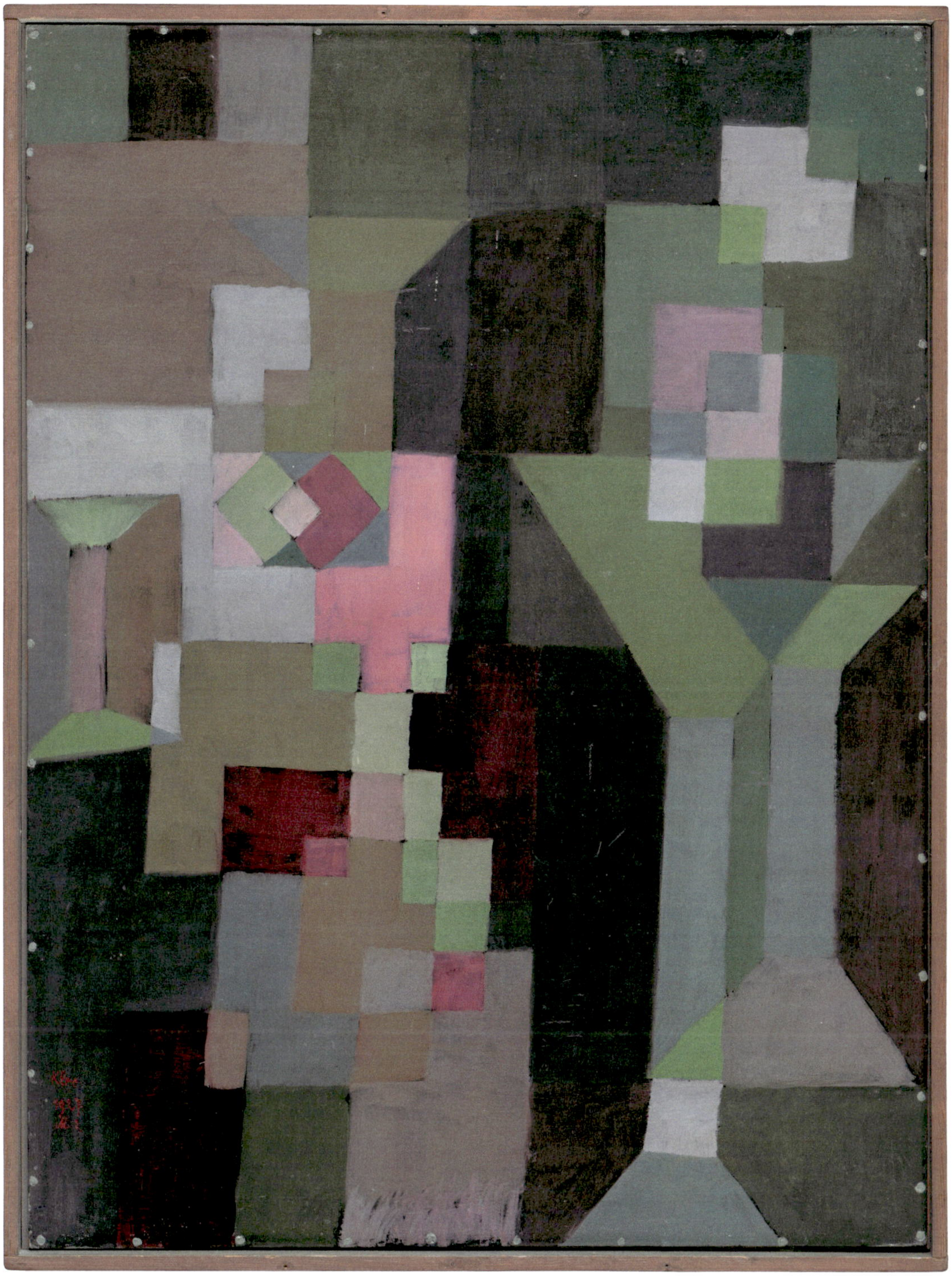

Paul Klee
Constructiv-impressiv, 1927, 32

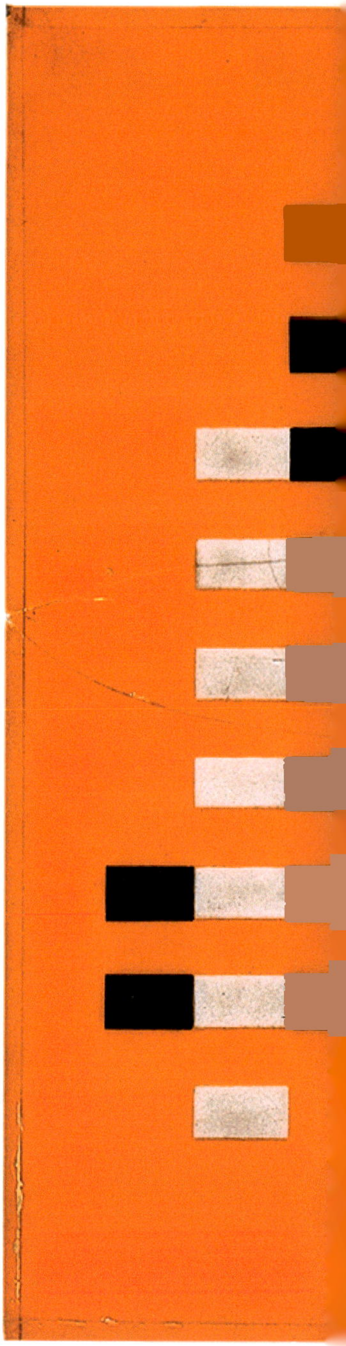

Josef Albers
Tectonische Gruppe, 1925

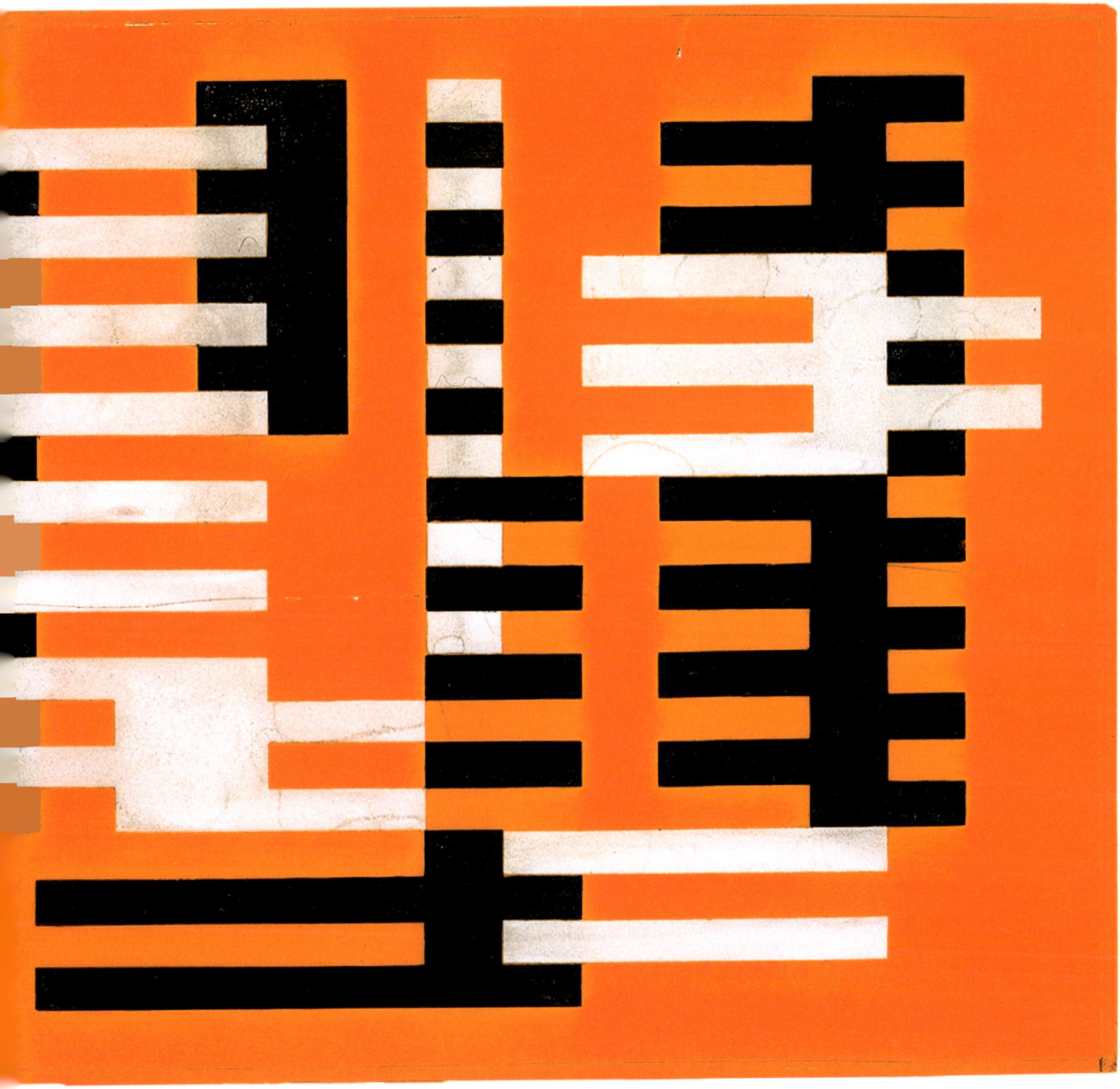

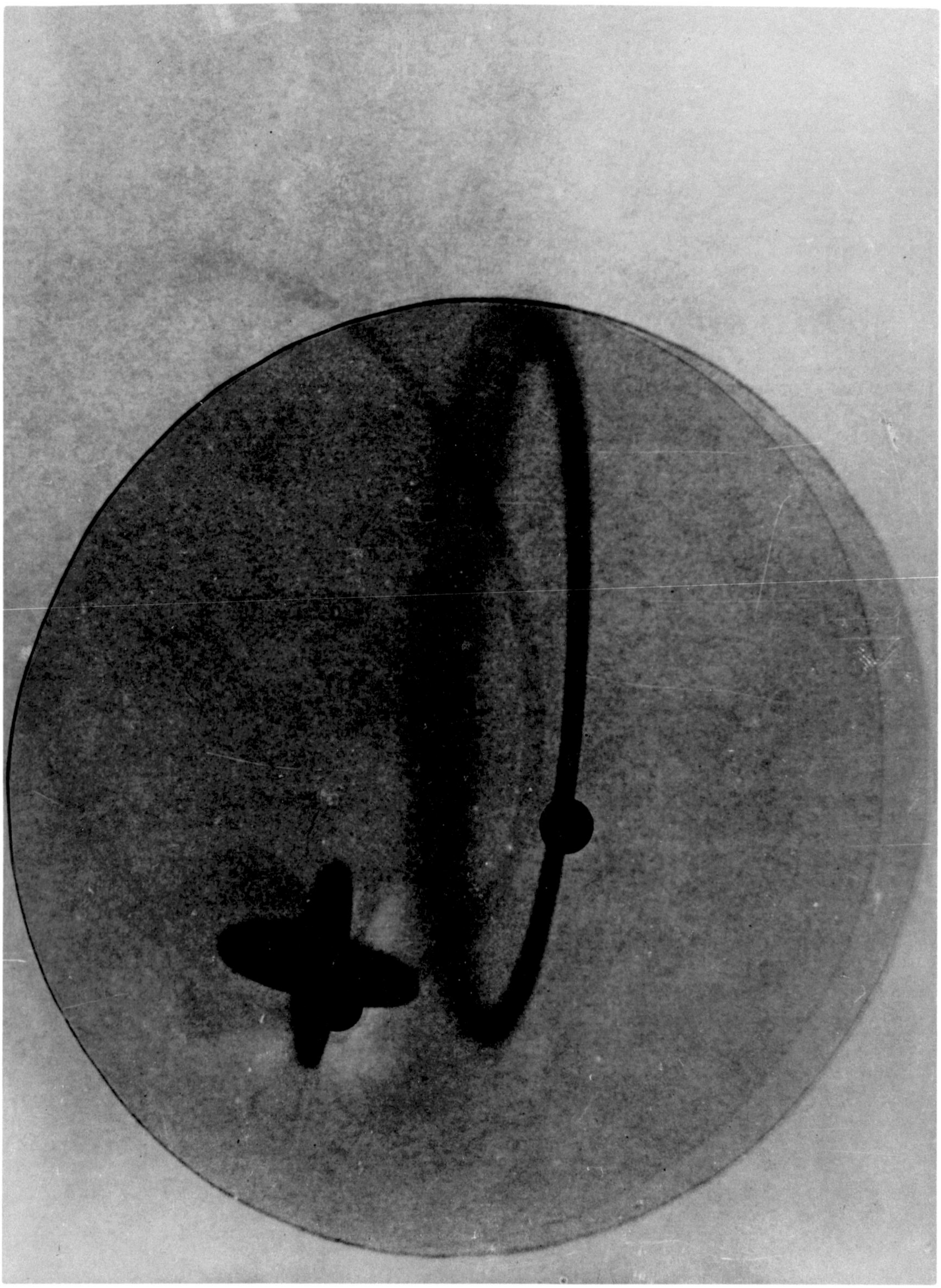

László Moholy-Nagy
Fotogramm (positiv), 1924

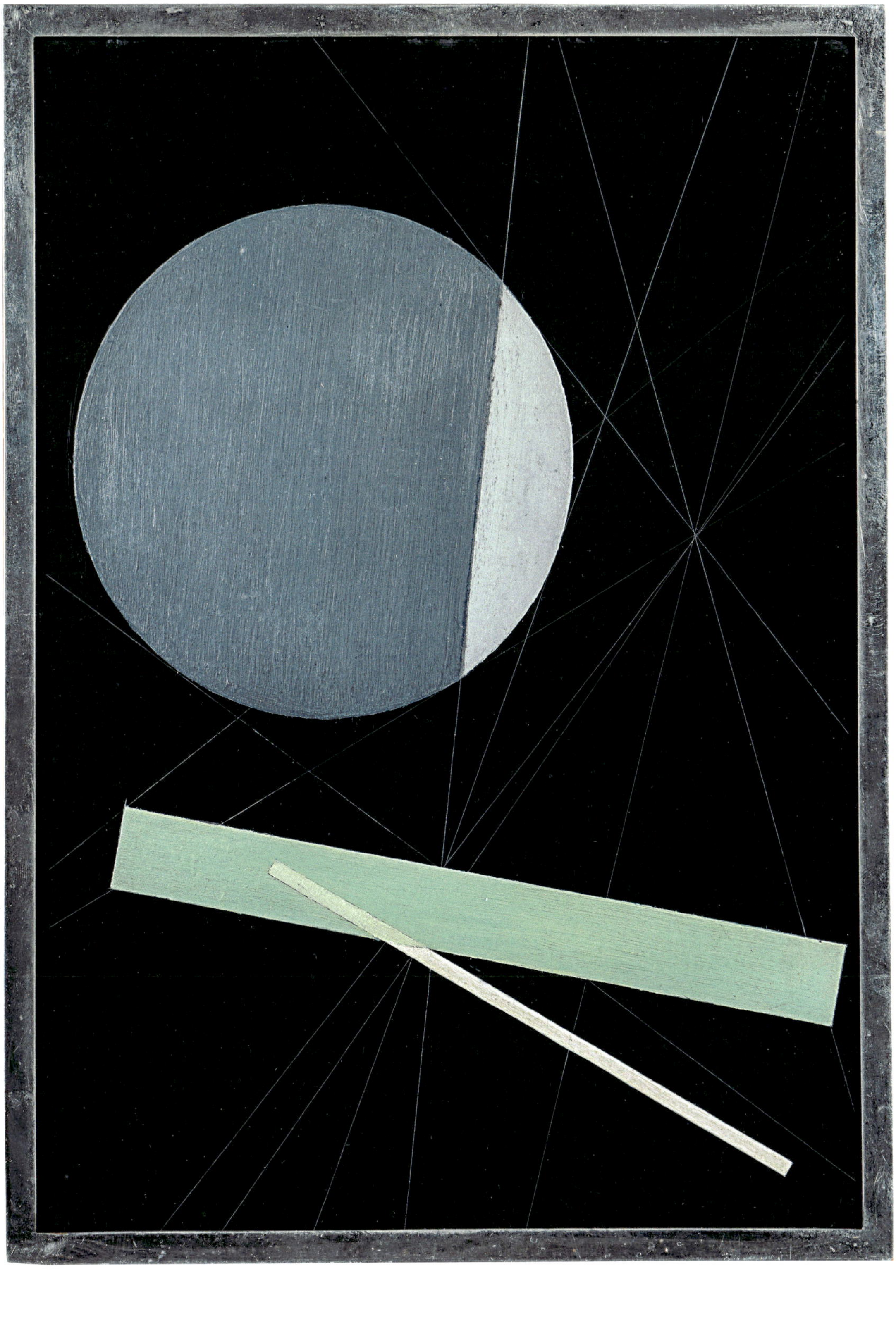

László Moholy-Nagy
Komposition TP 5, 1930

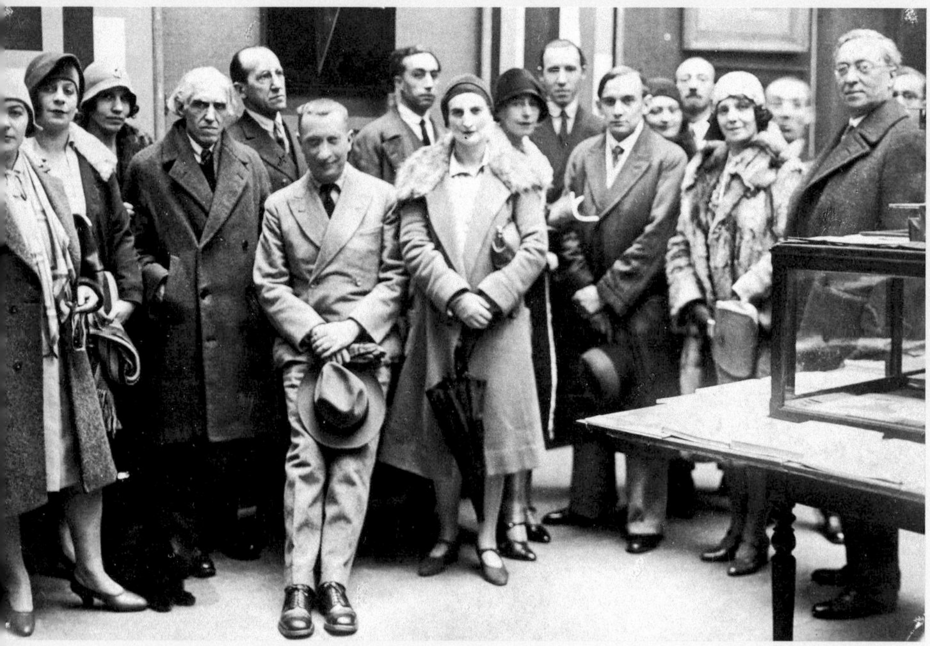

1930

Group shot of the artists' group Cercle et Carré at the opening of an exhibition at Galerie 23 in Paris. From left to right: Francisca Clausen, Florence Henri, Mañolita Pina de Torres, Joaquín Torres-García, Piet Mondrian, Hans Arp, Pierre Dura, Marcelle Cahn, Sophie Taeuber-Arp, Michel Seuphor, Friedrich Vordemberge-Gildewart, Vera Idelson, Luigi Russolo, Nina Kandinsky, Georges Vantongerloo, Wassily Kandinsky, and Jean Gorin. Many of them were also members of the group Abstraction Création, founded in 1931, which Bill joined in 1933.

Museum Wiesbaden, Archiv Vordemberge-Gildewart, photo: Ed Restle

1950s

The friendship with Vantongerloo was one of the most formative relationships Bill established in Paris. Vantongerloo often came to visit Bill in Zurich, here with Adrien Turel (center) in the studio house in Höngg.

Stiftung Ernst Scheidegger Archiv, Zurich, photo: Ernst Scheidegger

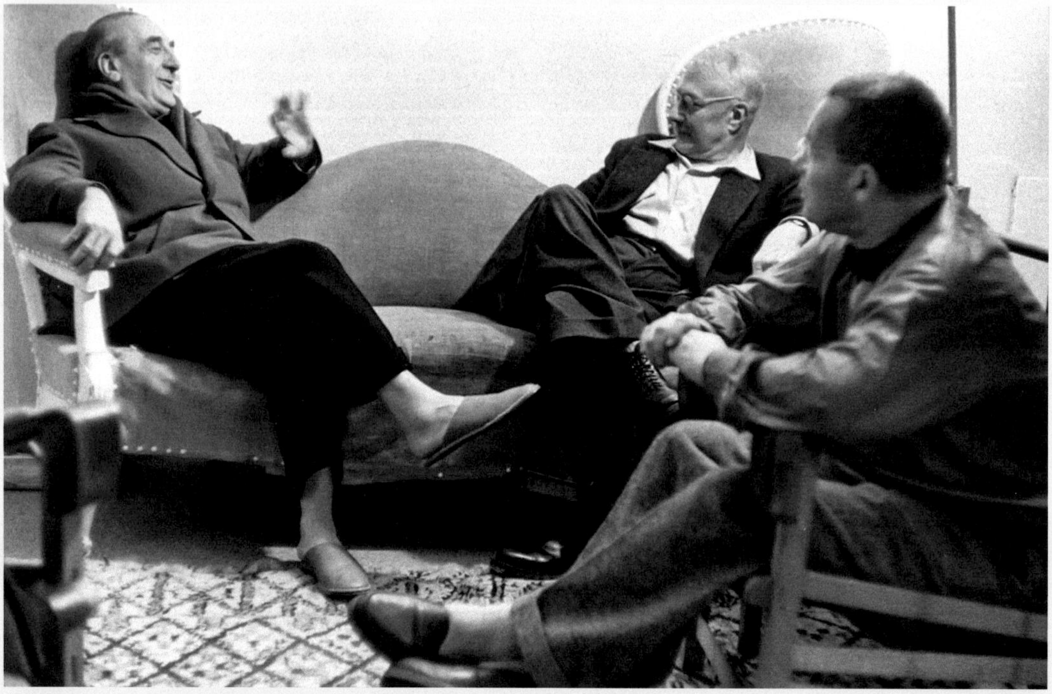

The 1930s saw Max Bill frequently making the journey from Zurich to Paris. On one such trip undertaken in 1930 with his architect friend Ernst F. Burckhardt he made a point of meeting artists who subscribed to various forms of abstract and non-representational art. Among these was Joaquín Torres-García, a co-founder of the Cercle et Carré group, whom Bill sought out in his Paris studio, and Joan Miró, Jacques Lipchitz, and Serge Brignoni, whom he met at Jeanne Bucher's gallery.[1]

At the recommendation of Sophie Taeuber-Arp and Hans Arp, Bill was invited to join Georges Vantongerloo's group Abstraction Création, and later that same year, 1933, was able to exhibit his *lange plastik* at the group's gallery in Paris. Besides Taeuber-Arp, Arp, Wassily Kandinsky, Josef Albers, and Theo van Doesburg, Abstraction Création also numbered Auguste Herbin, Antoine Pevsner, František Kupka, Marlow Moss, Piet Mondrian, and Friedrich Vordemberge-Gildewart among its members. Another important Paris-based group was Art Concret, founded by Van Doesburg in 1929. Its manifesto, published in the group's magazine Art Concret in 1930, laid the foundations for Bill's "konkrete gestaltung" of 1936, a text that set the

1949

View of the exhibition *pevsner, vantongerloo, bill* at the Kunsthaus Zurich. In 1947 Max Bill was appointed to the exhibition commission of the Zürcher Kunstgesellschaft as successor to Hans Fischli. After his letters to the Kunsthaus in the 1930s had been met with little response, he was able to realize a number of exhibition projects starting in the 1940s that featured his own works and those of artist friends, and which he often curated himself. From among the Parisian circle, Pevsner and Vantongerloo as well as Mondrian in 1955 featured prominently in a solo exhibition, while Vordemberge-Gildewart's work was shown in the 1956 exhibition *josef albers, fritz glarner, friedrich vordemberge-gildewart.*

max bill georges vantongerloo stiftung

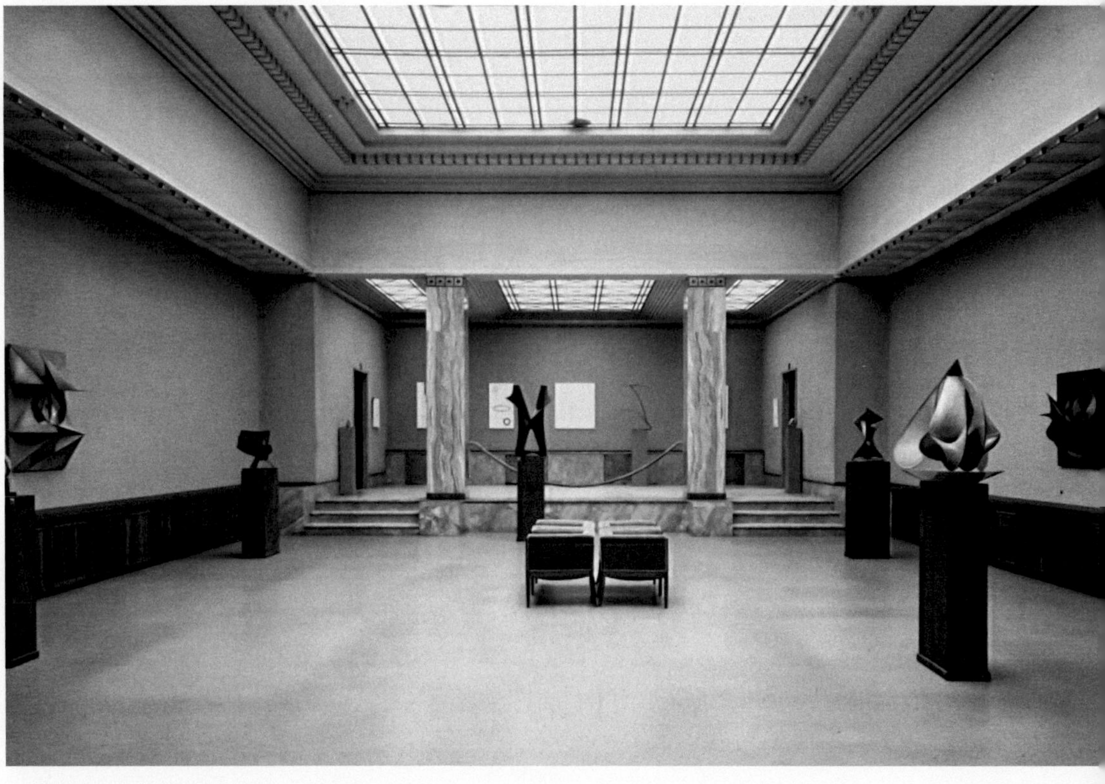

course for the development of abstract art in Switzerland. As Van Doesburg died in 1931, however, the two artists never met.

It was during another long stay in Paris in 1938 that Bill printed his series *quinze variations sur un même thème*, while at the same time working on volume three of his catalog of the works of Le Corbusier and Pierre Jeanneret. Pevsner invited him to tea—along with Vantongerloo and Mondrian—and took the opportunity to introduce him to Marcel Duchamp.[2]

All of these artists would figure in Bill's later exhibition projects and publications. Bill and Vantongerloo were to remain lifelong friends and, at the latter's death in 1965, it was Bill who took over the administration of his estate.

1 Cf. Thomas 2008, pp. 316–323.

2 Max Bill, in *dokumentation über marcel duchamp*, exh. cat. Zurich: Kunstgewerbemuseum der Stadt Zürich, Zurich 1960, p. 5.

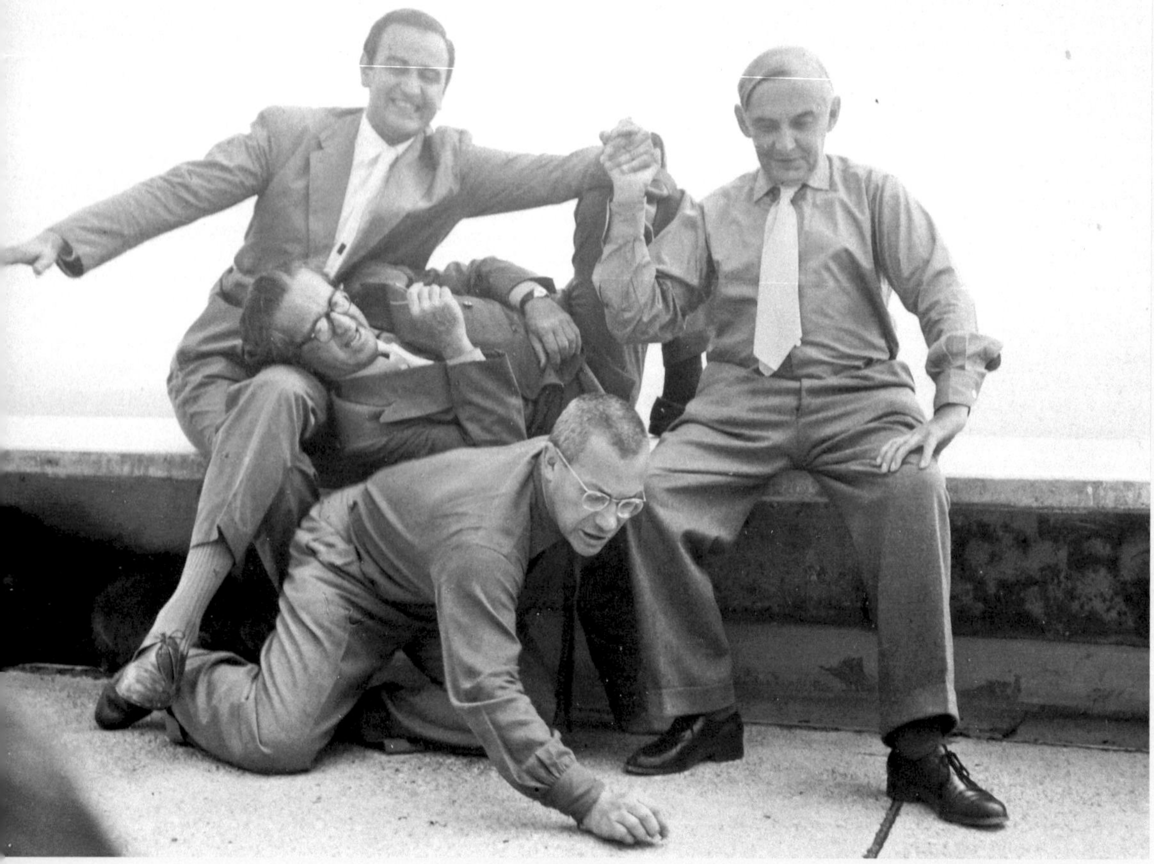

c. 1954/57

From left to right: Tomás Maldonado, Konrad Wachsmann, Max Bill, and Friedrich Vordemberge-Gildewart in Ulm. The faculty that Bill assembled at the HfG Ulm included Vordemberge-Gildewart, an acquaintance from Paris. He taught visual communication from 1954 until his death in 1962.

Museum Wiesbaden, Archiv Vordemberge-Gildewart, photo: Ed Restle

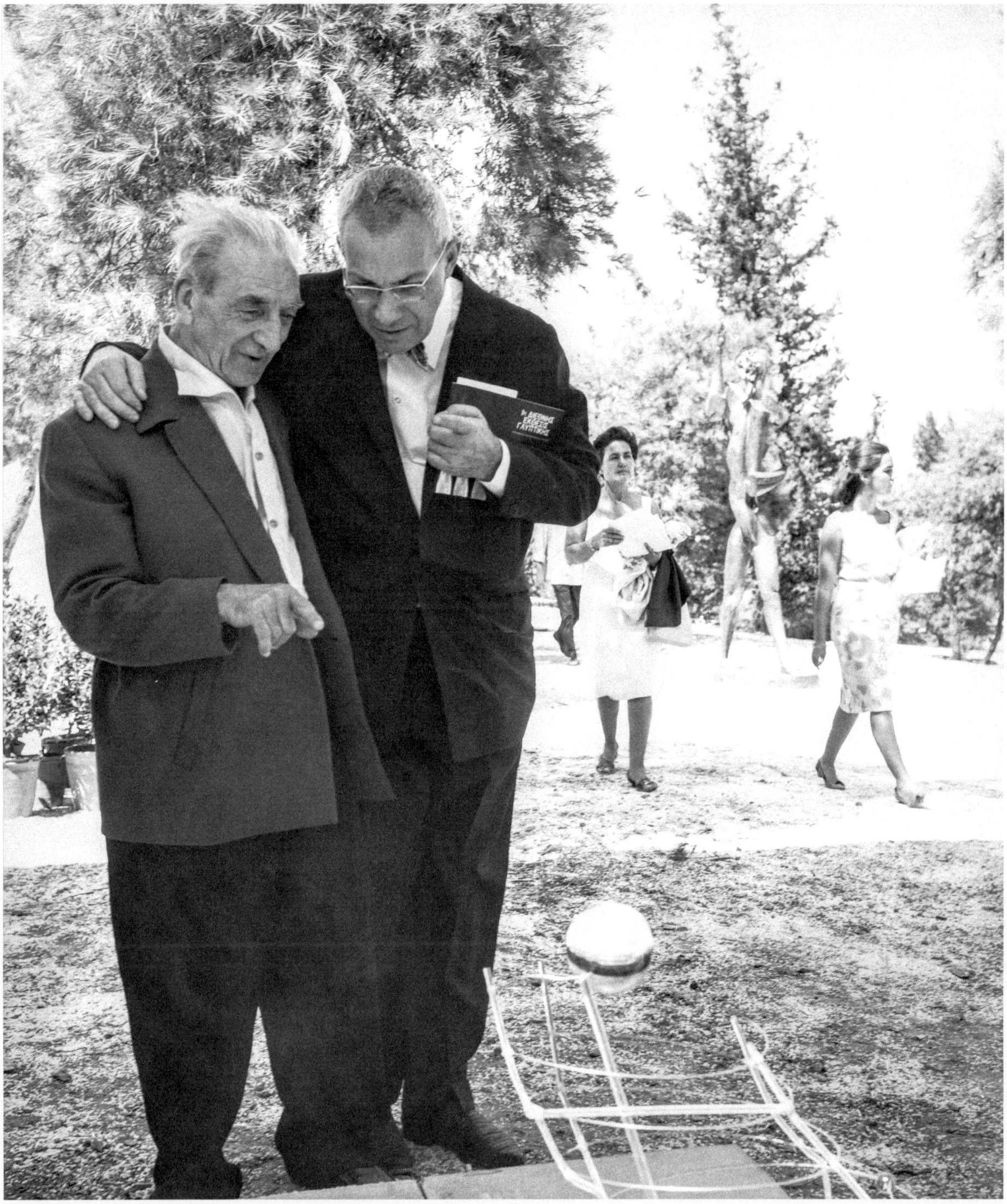

Georges Vantongerloo and Max Bill at the first Sculpture Biennial in Athens, September 18, 1965. After Vantongerloo's death in 1965, Bill worked hard to ensure that the artist's name would not be forgotten. In the 1980s Bill organized a retrospective of Vantongerloo's work with several stops in the USA, followed in 1981 by exhibitions in Brussels and Zurich, and in 1986 by a retrospective shown in Milan, Berlin, and Bottrop.

Angela Thomas Schmid,
photo: Carmen Martinez

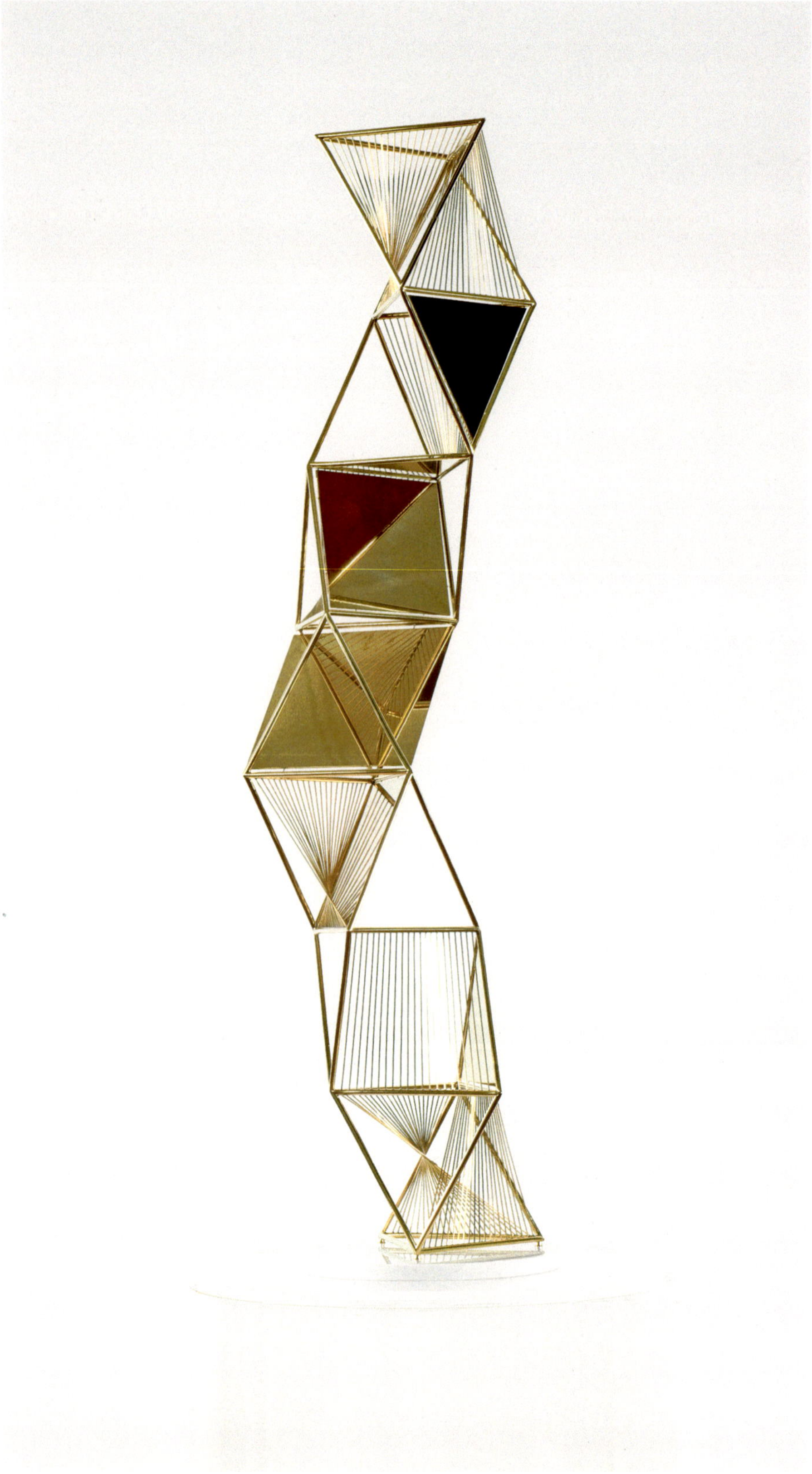

Max Bill
konstruktion in messing , 1939

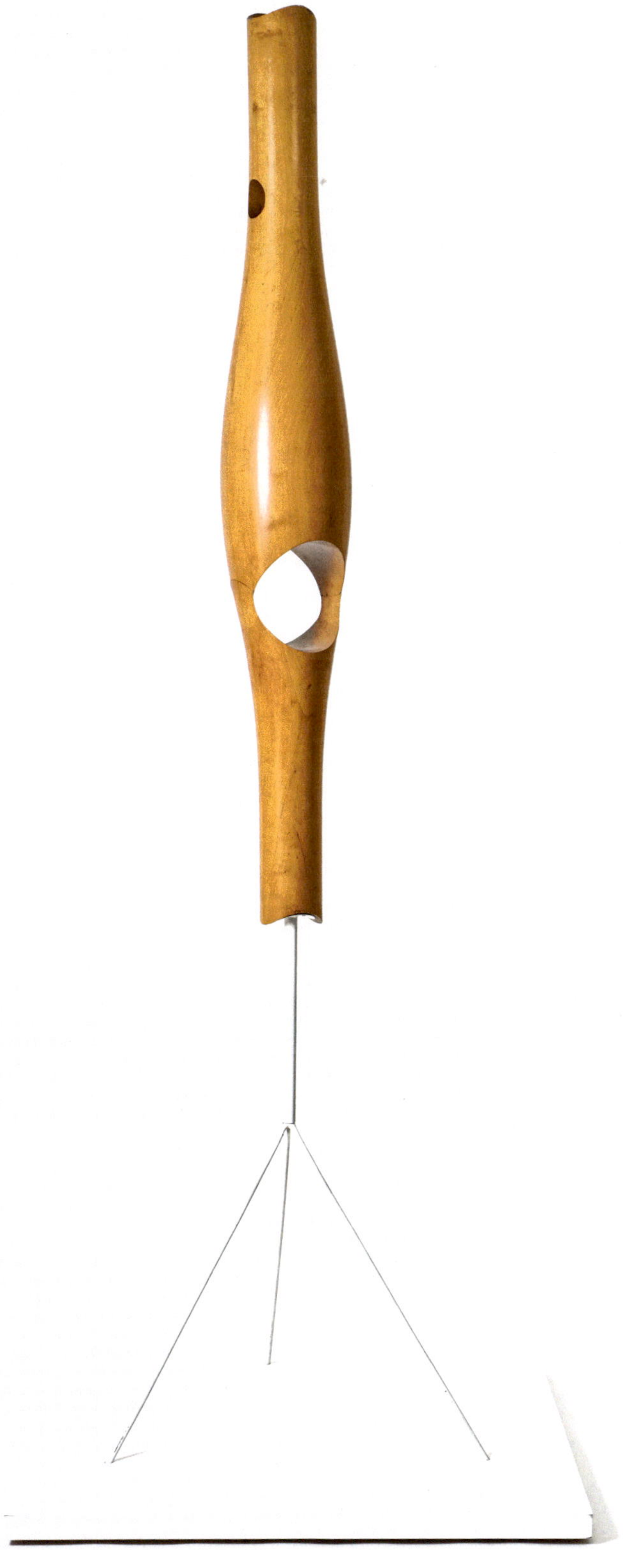

Max Bill
lange plastik, 1933

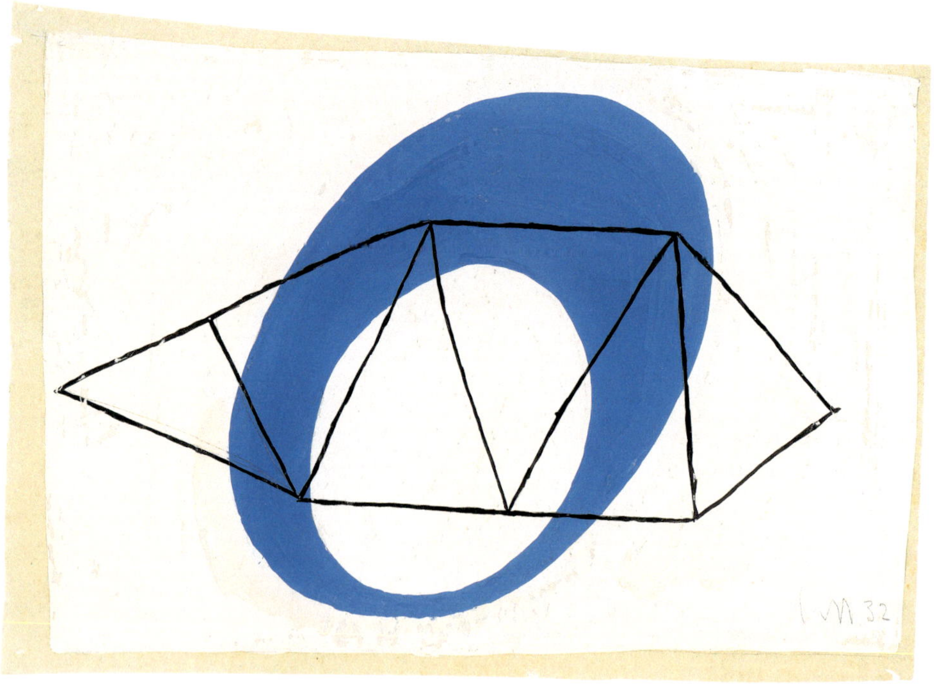

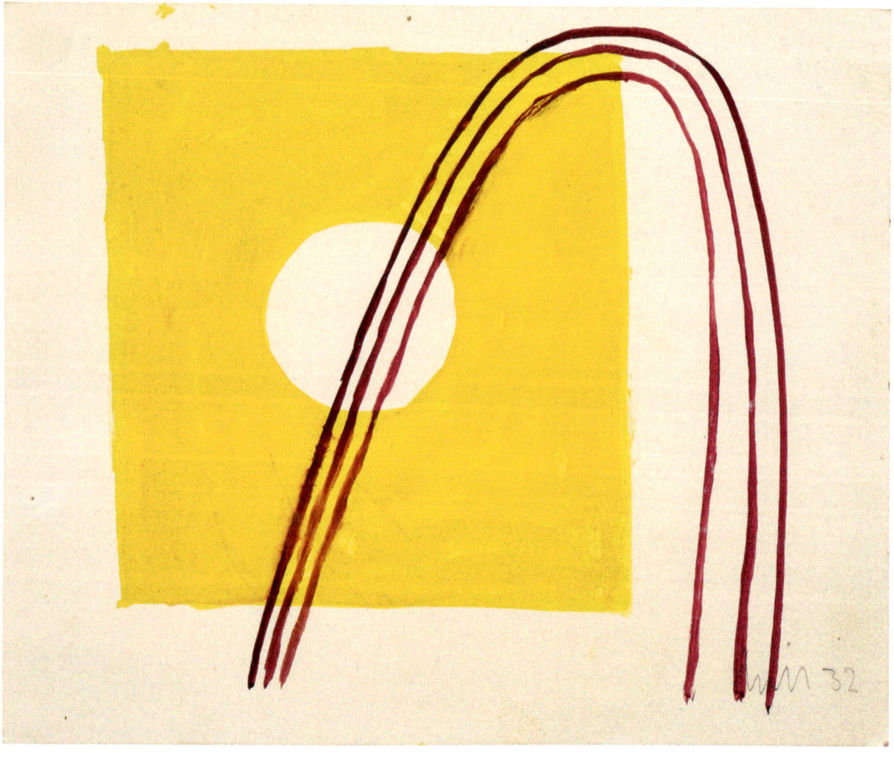

Max Bill
Untitled. Sketch for a mural with large O, 1932

Max Bill
Untitled, 1932

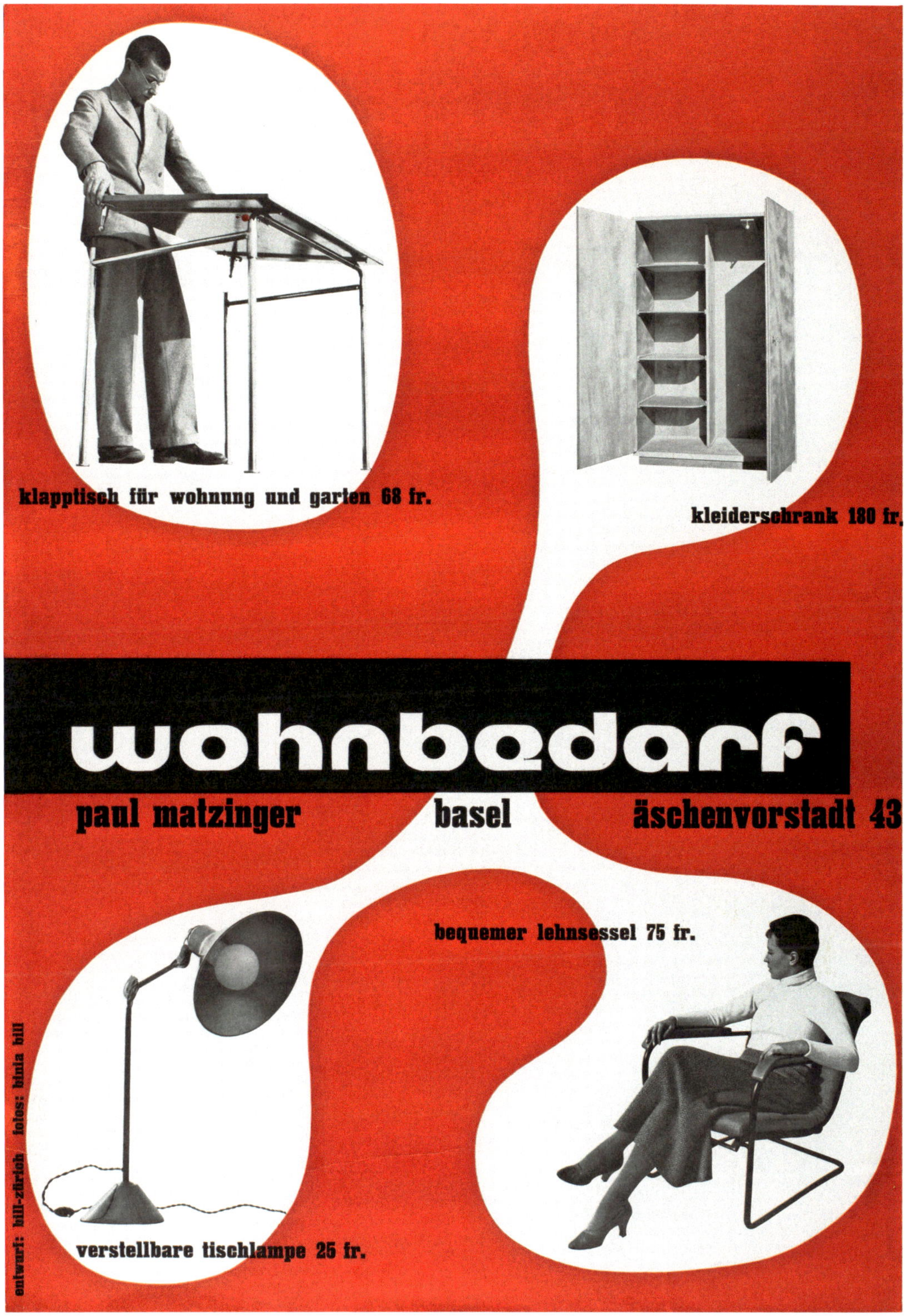

Max Bill
Poster: wohnbedarf—paul matzinger—basel, 1932

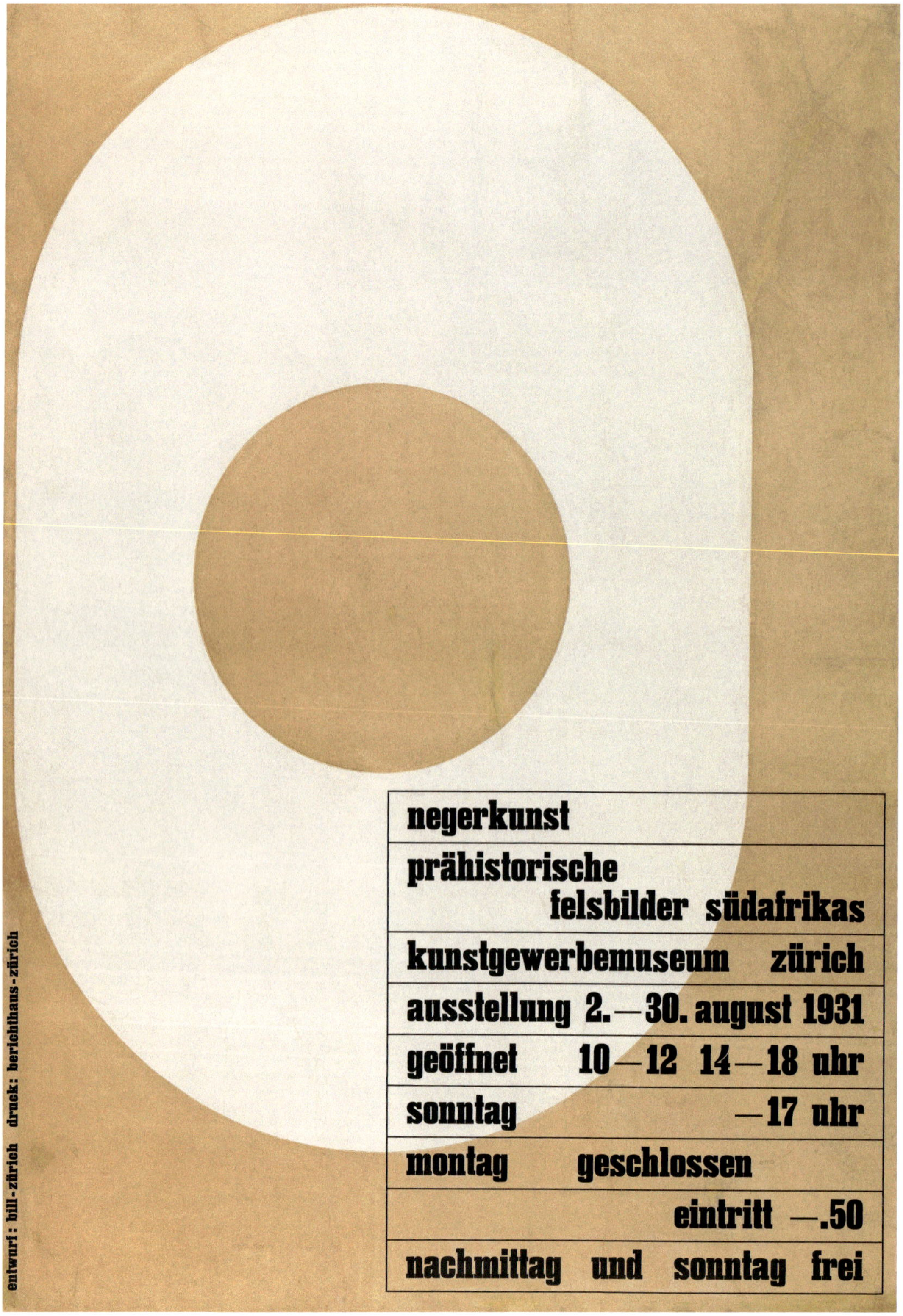

Max Bill
Poster: n****kunst—prähistorische felsbilder südafrikas—kunstgewerbemuseum zürich, 1931

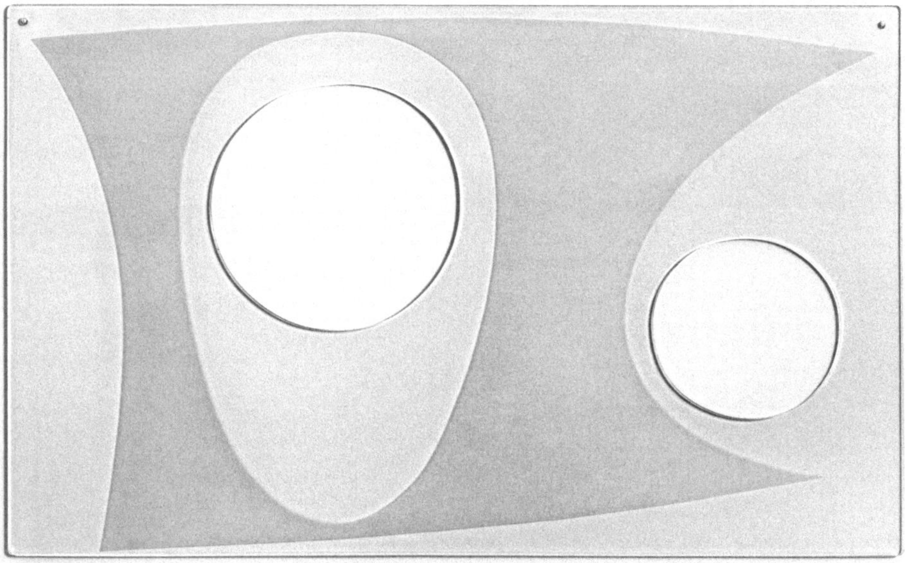

Max Bill
glasbild, 1930–1931

Max Bill
well-relief, 1931–1932

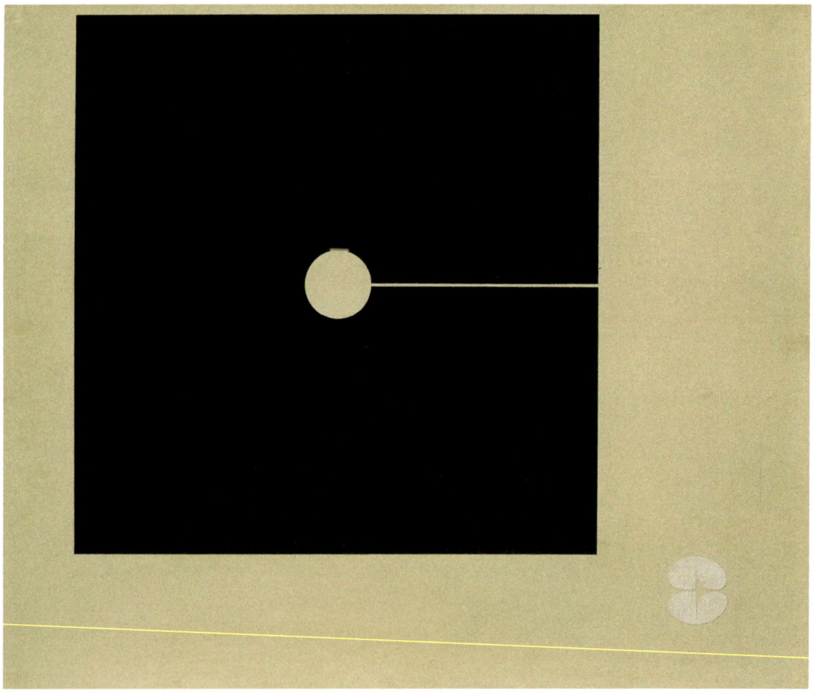

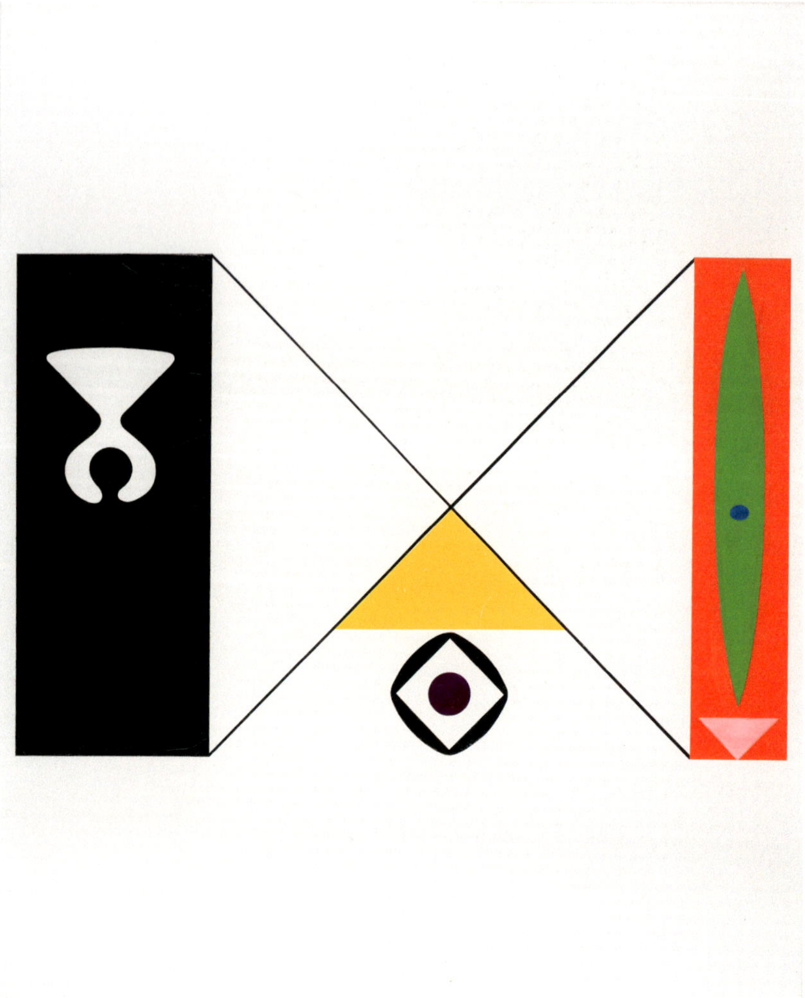

Max Bill
konstruktion, 1934

Max Bill
3 variations, 1935

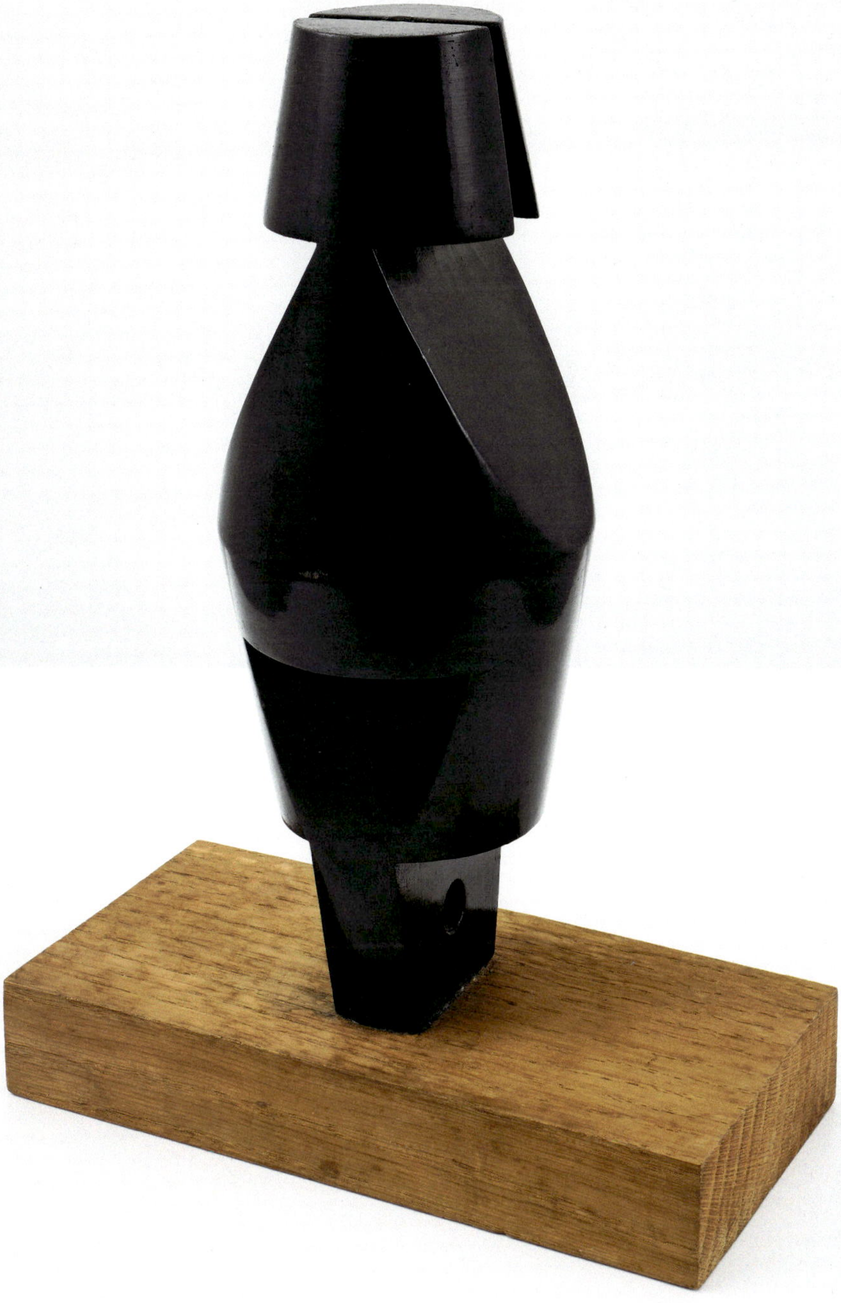

Max Bill
schwarze plastik, 1934

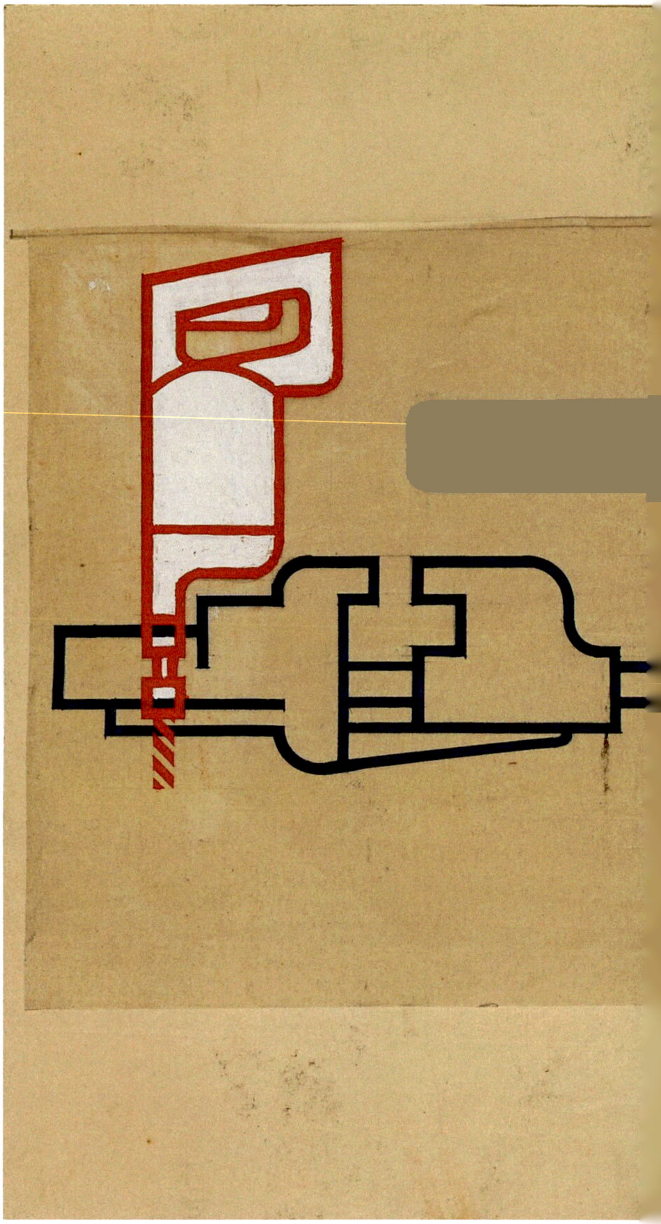

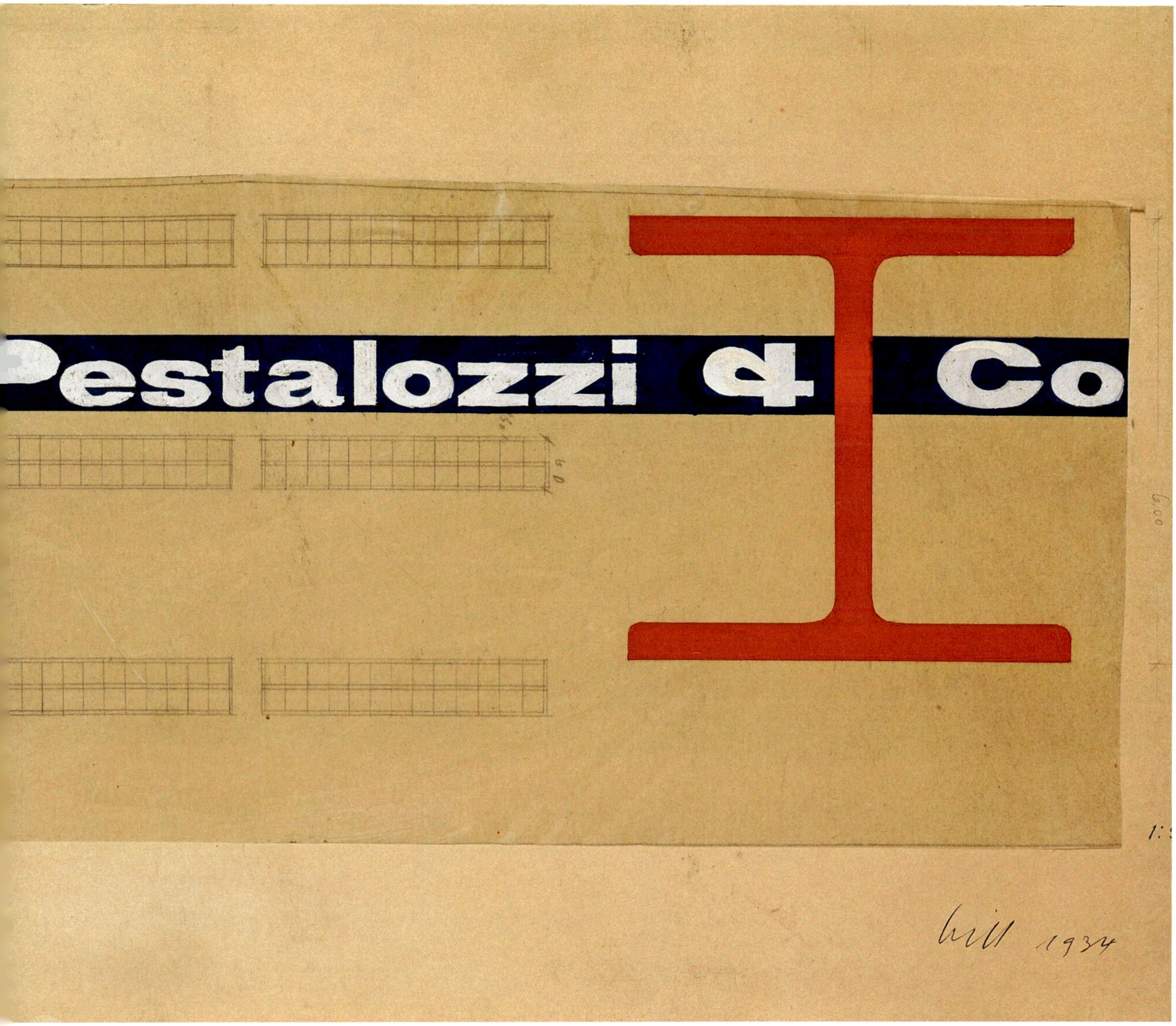

Max Bill
Design for a facade drawing for Pestalozzi & Co, 1934

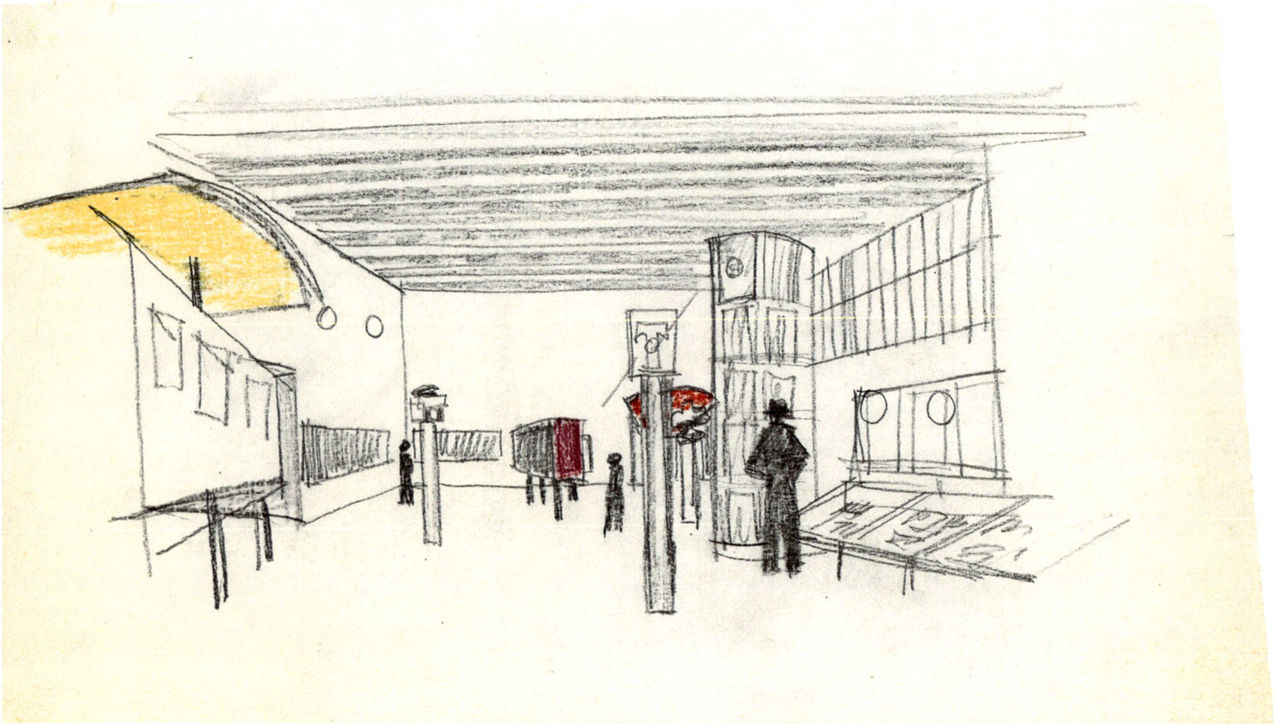

Max Bill
Design sketches for the Swiss Pavilion,
IX. Milan Triennale, 1936

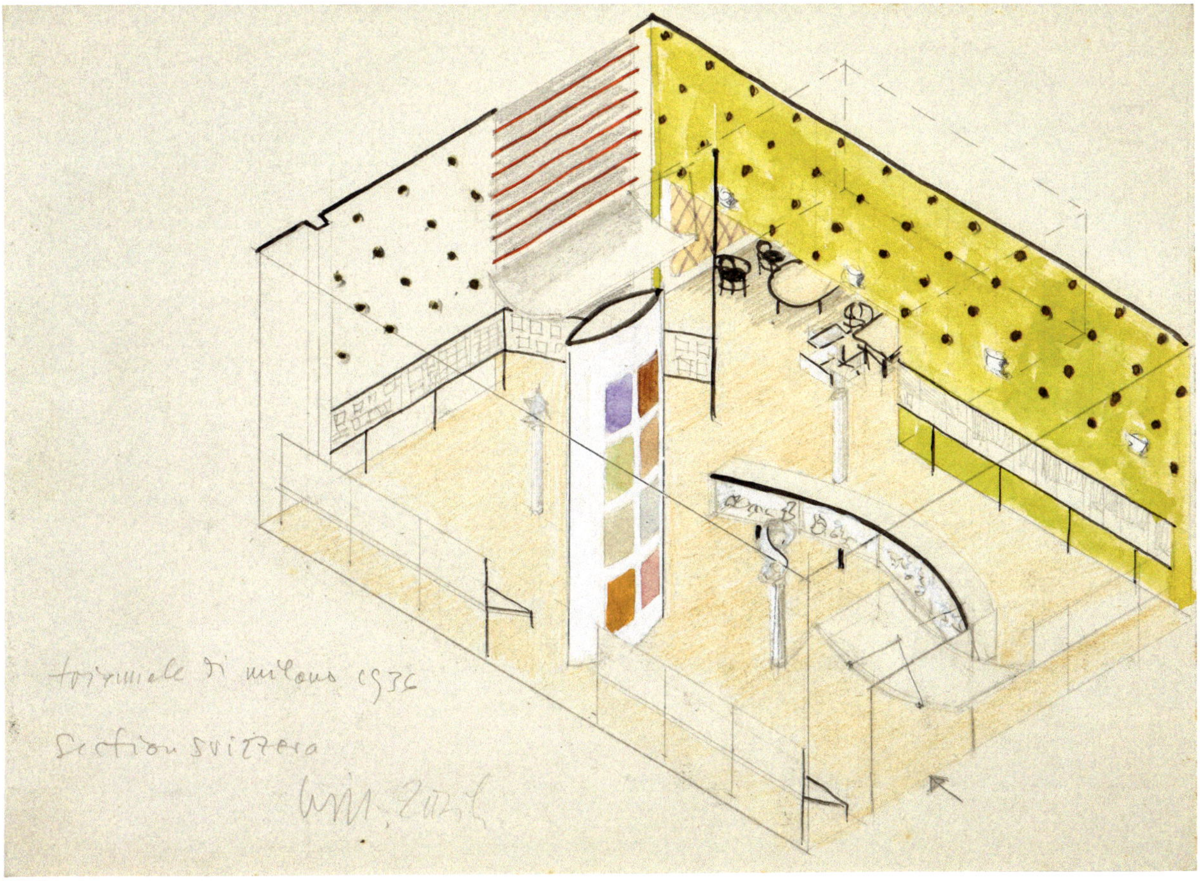
triennale di milano 1936
sezione svizzera

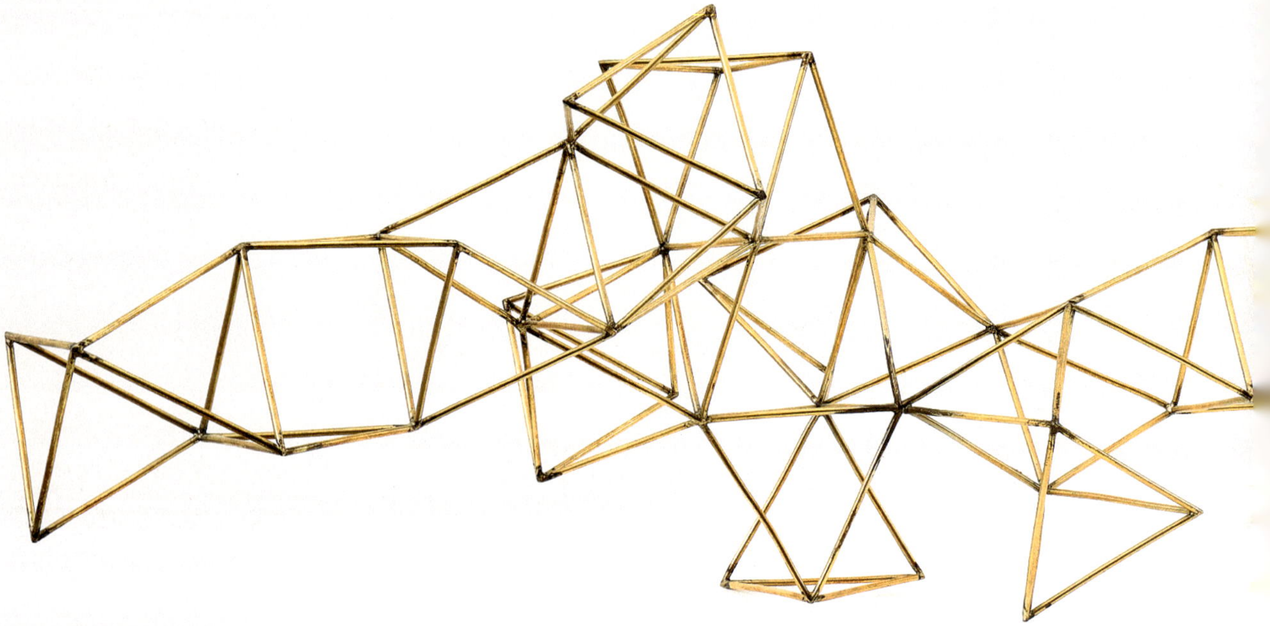

Max Bill
konstruktion aus 30 gleichen elementen, 1938–1939

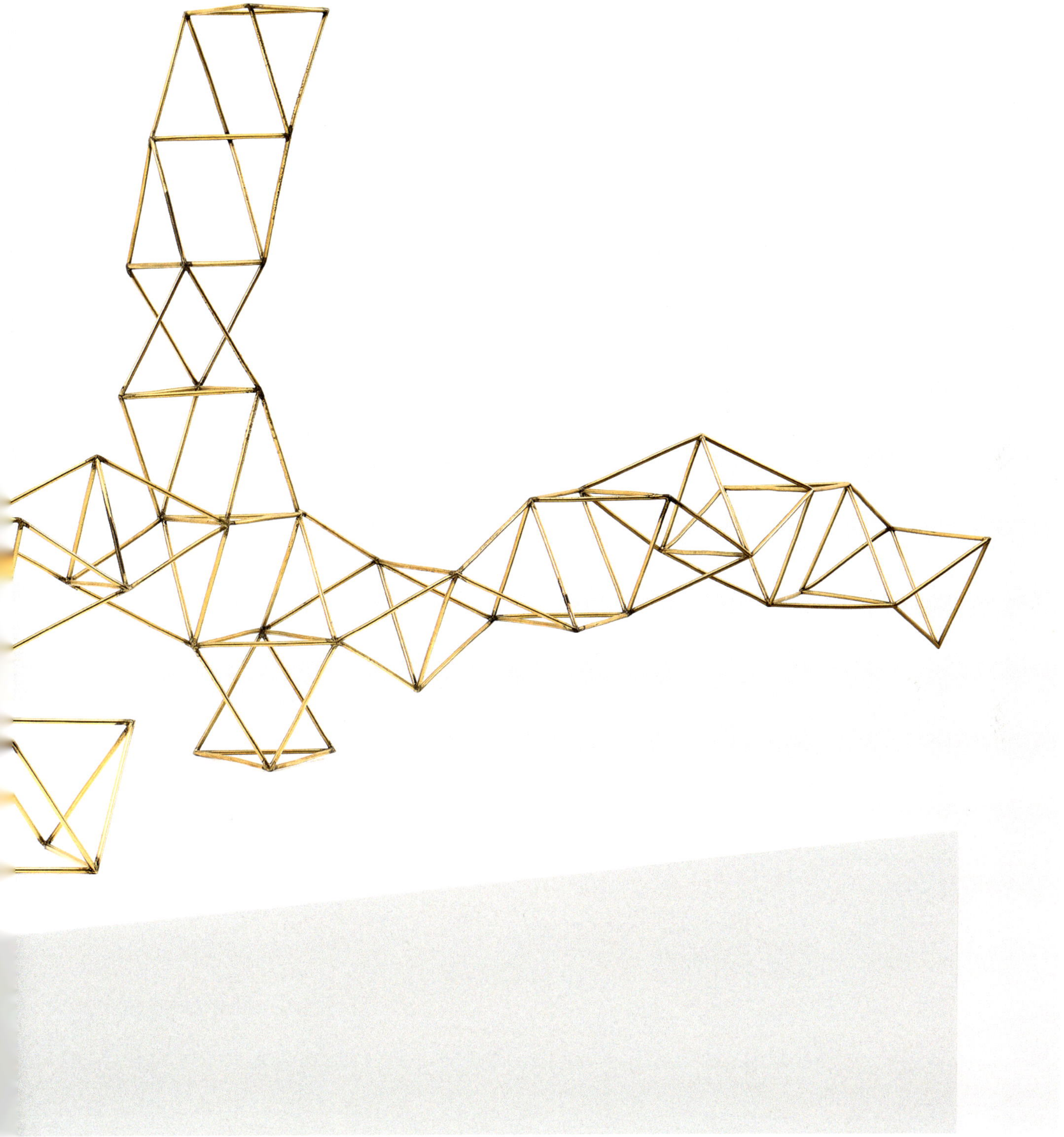

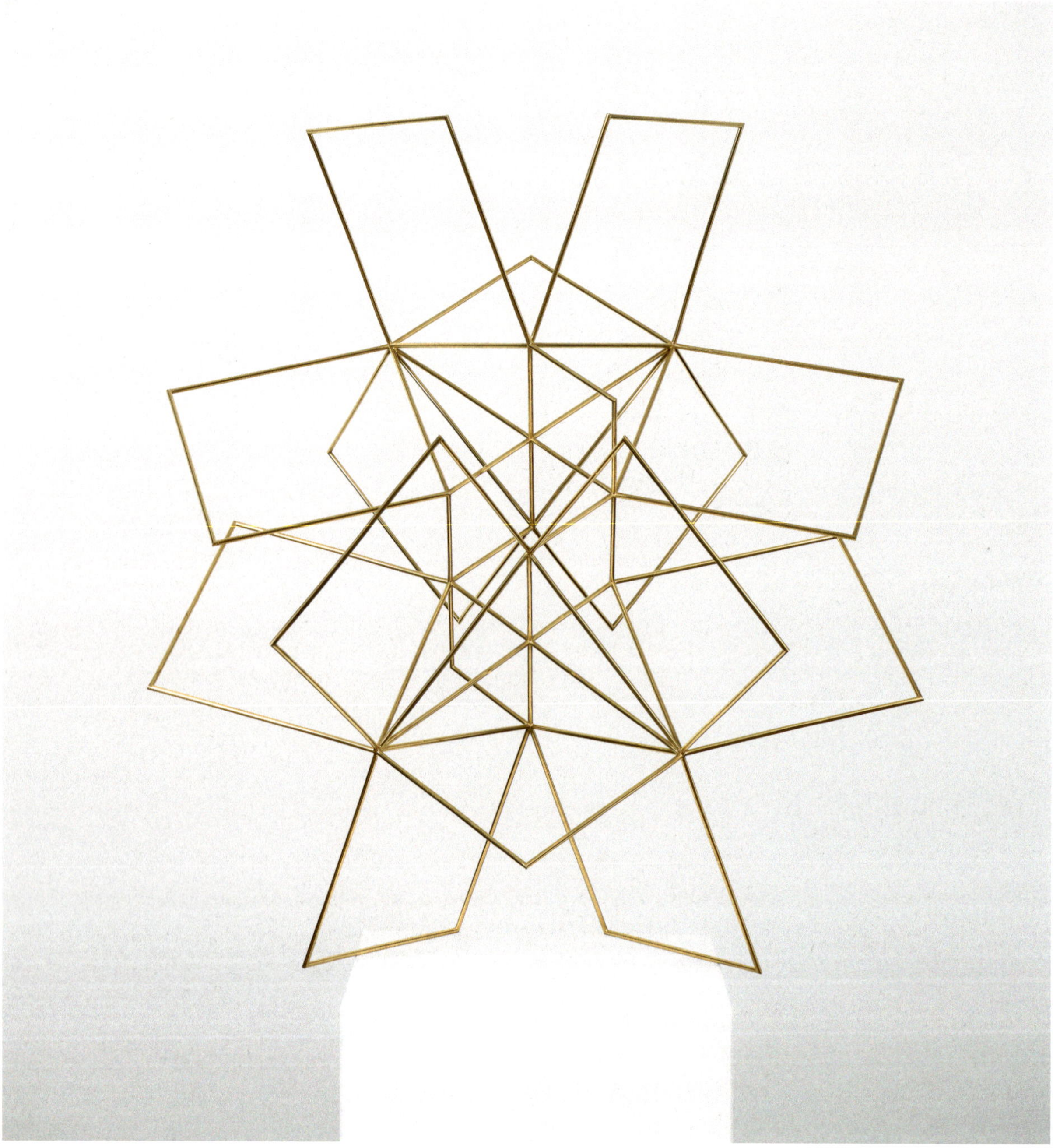

Max Bill
konstruktion aus drei quadratgrössen
(denkmal für pythagoras), 1939–1941

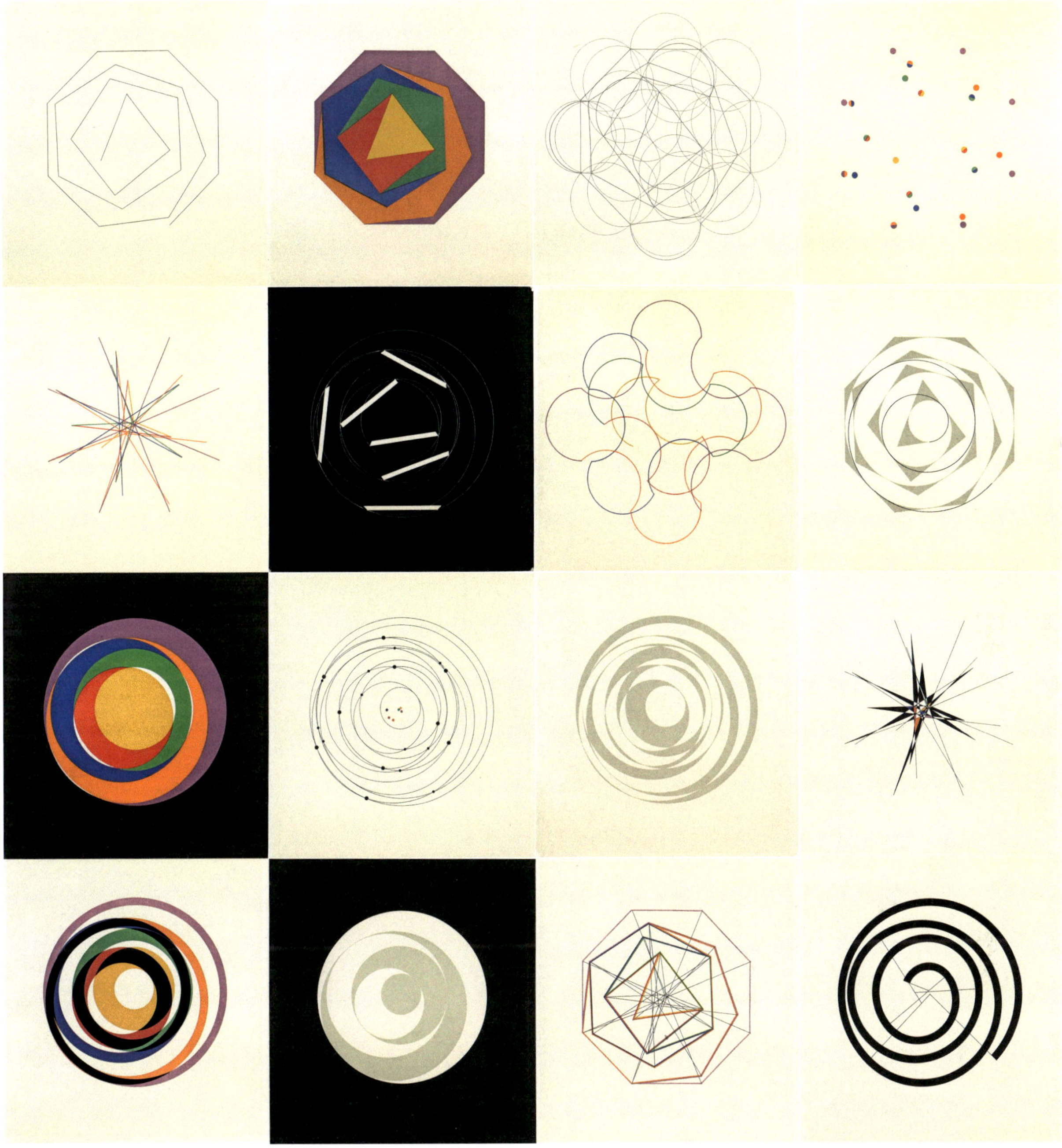

Max Bill
quinze variations sur un même thème, 1935–1938

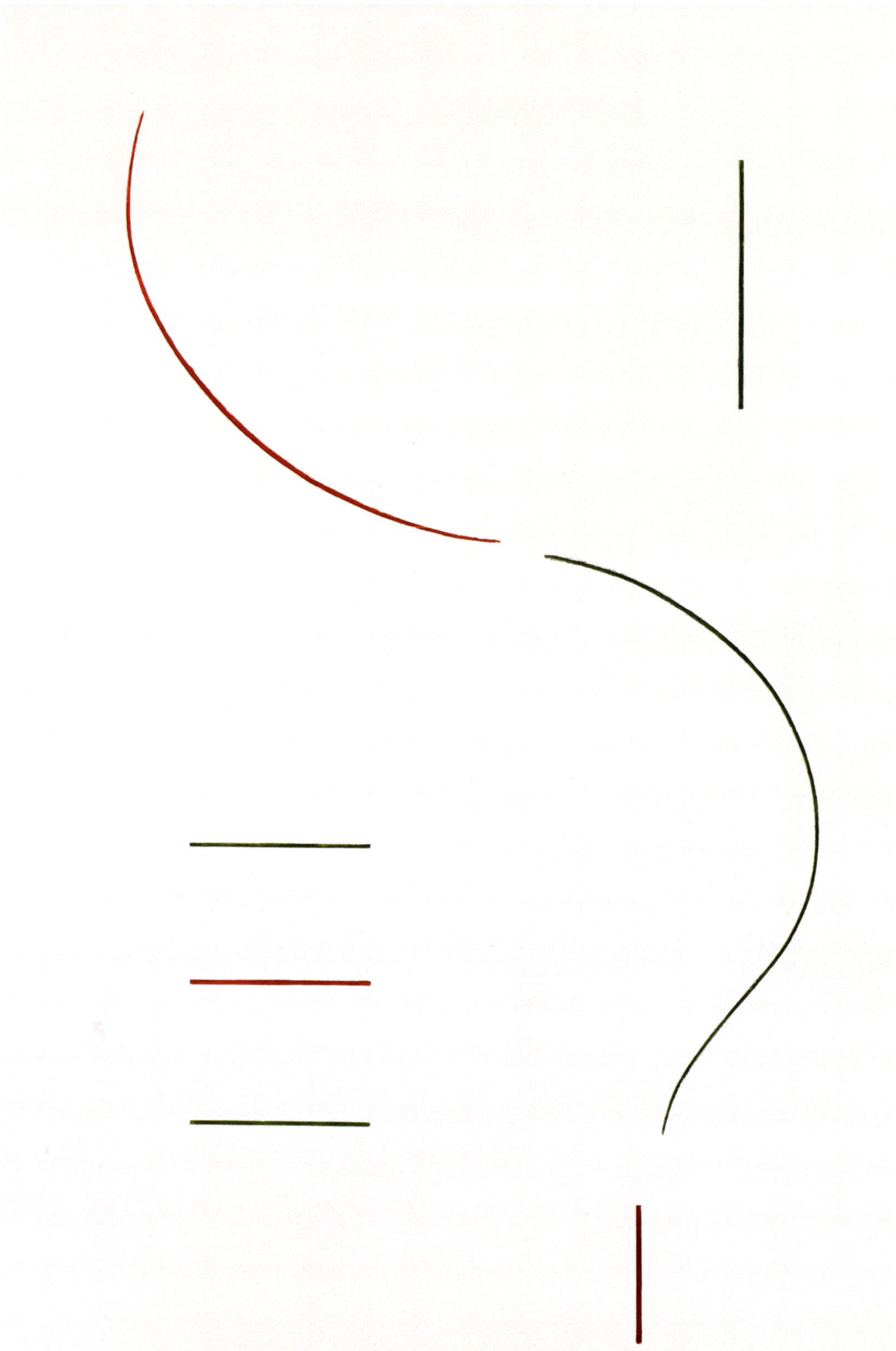

Georges Vantongerloo
Courbes, 1939

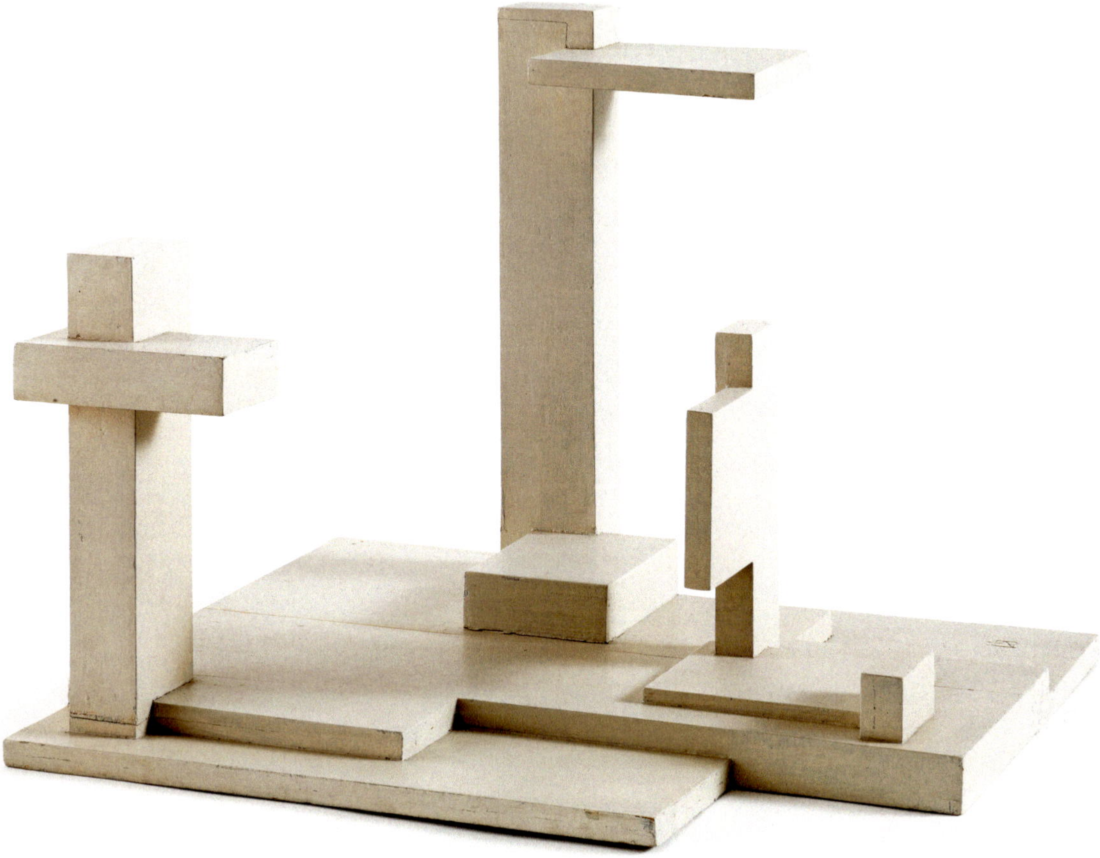

Georges Vantongerloo
Groupe y = -ax2 + bx + c y'= -2ax + b y'=-ax2 + bx + c / -2ax + b, 1931

Joaquín Torres-García
Formas animicas en rojo y negro, 1938

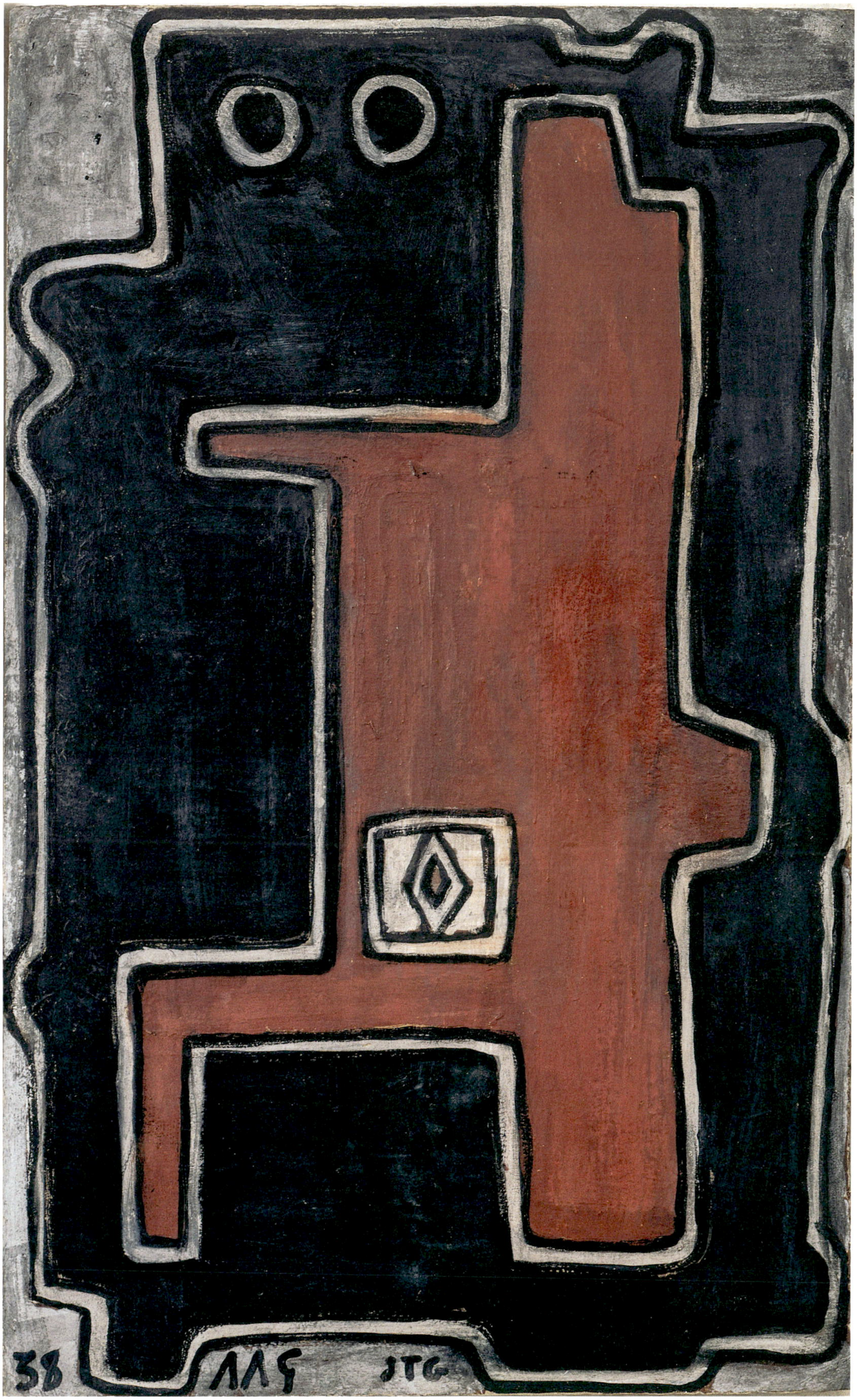
38
115
JTG

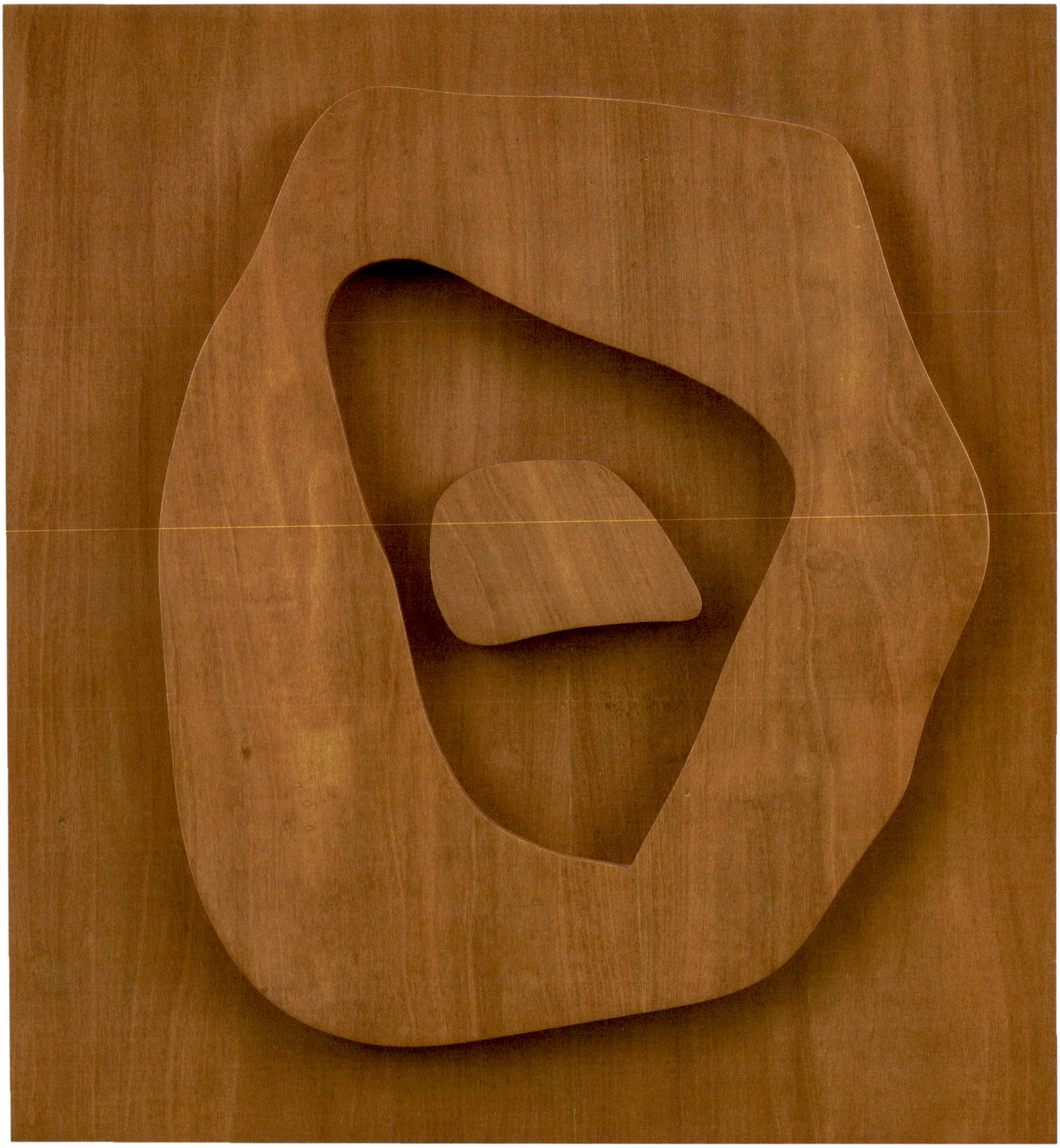

Hans Arp
Formes préadamites, 1945

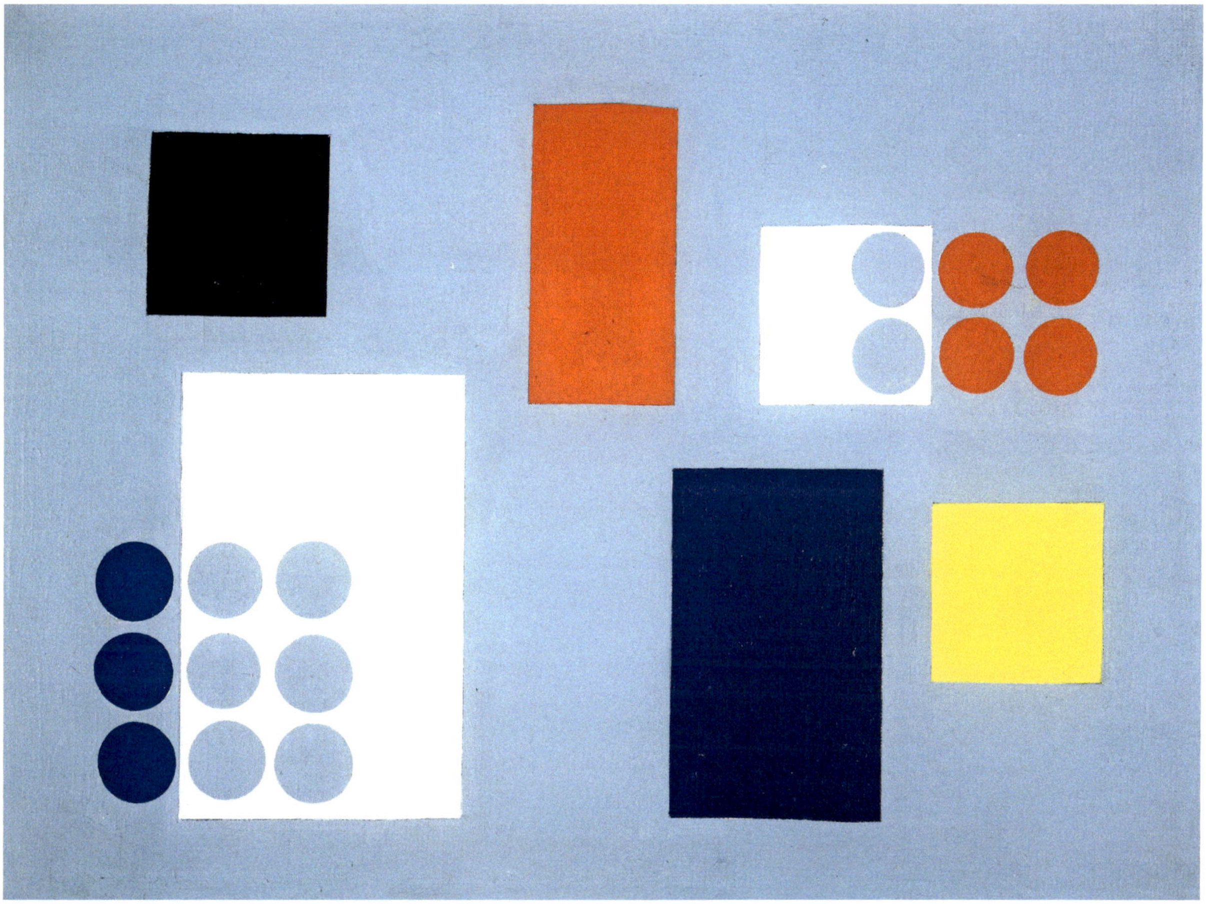

Sophie Taeuber-Arp
Composition à rectangles, et carrés pavés de cercles, 1939

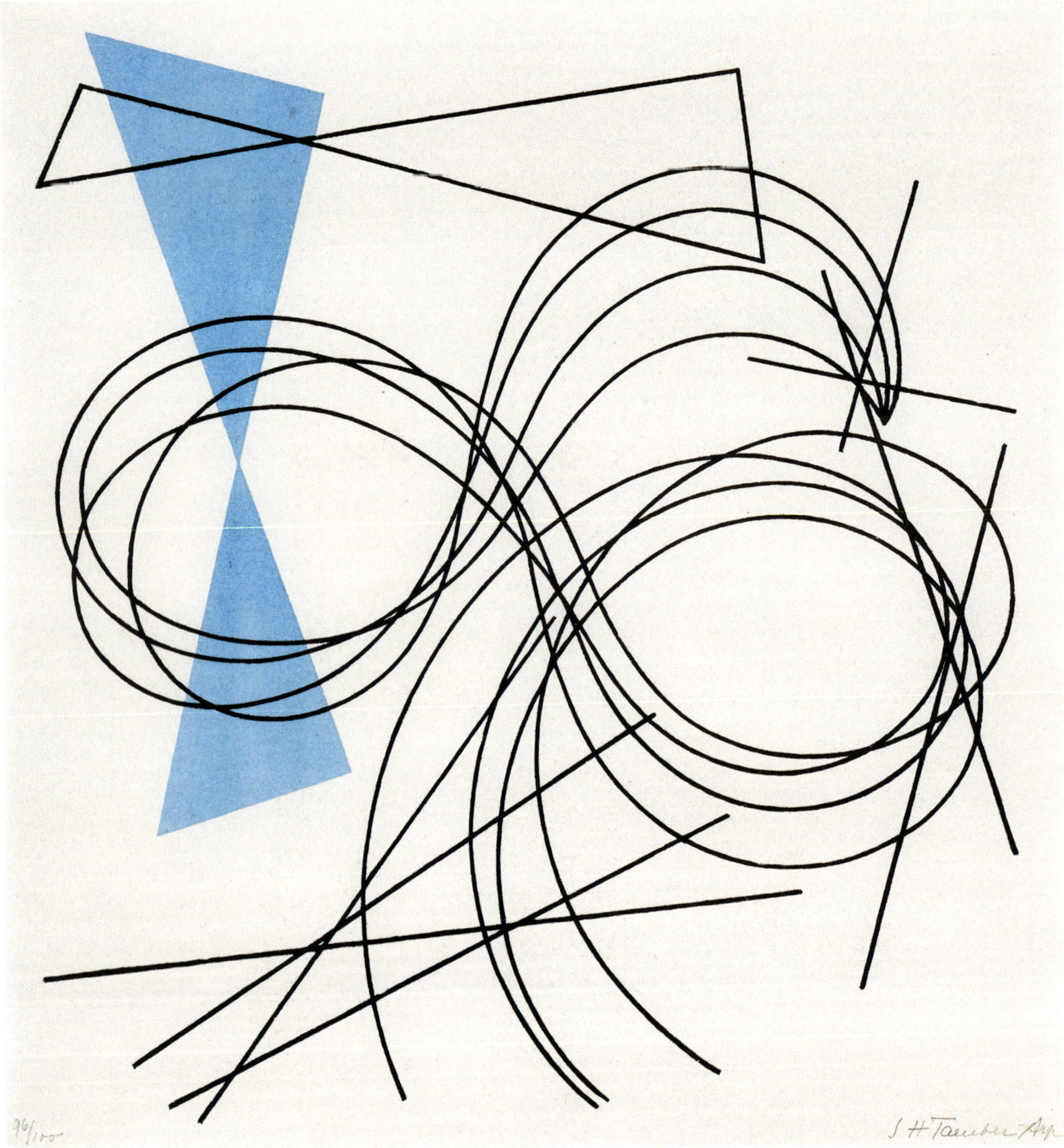

Sophie Taeuber-Arp
Untitled (from the portfolio "fünf konstruktionen"), 1941

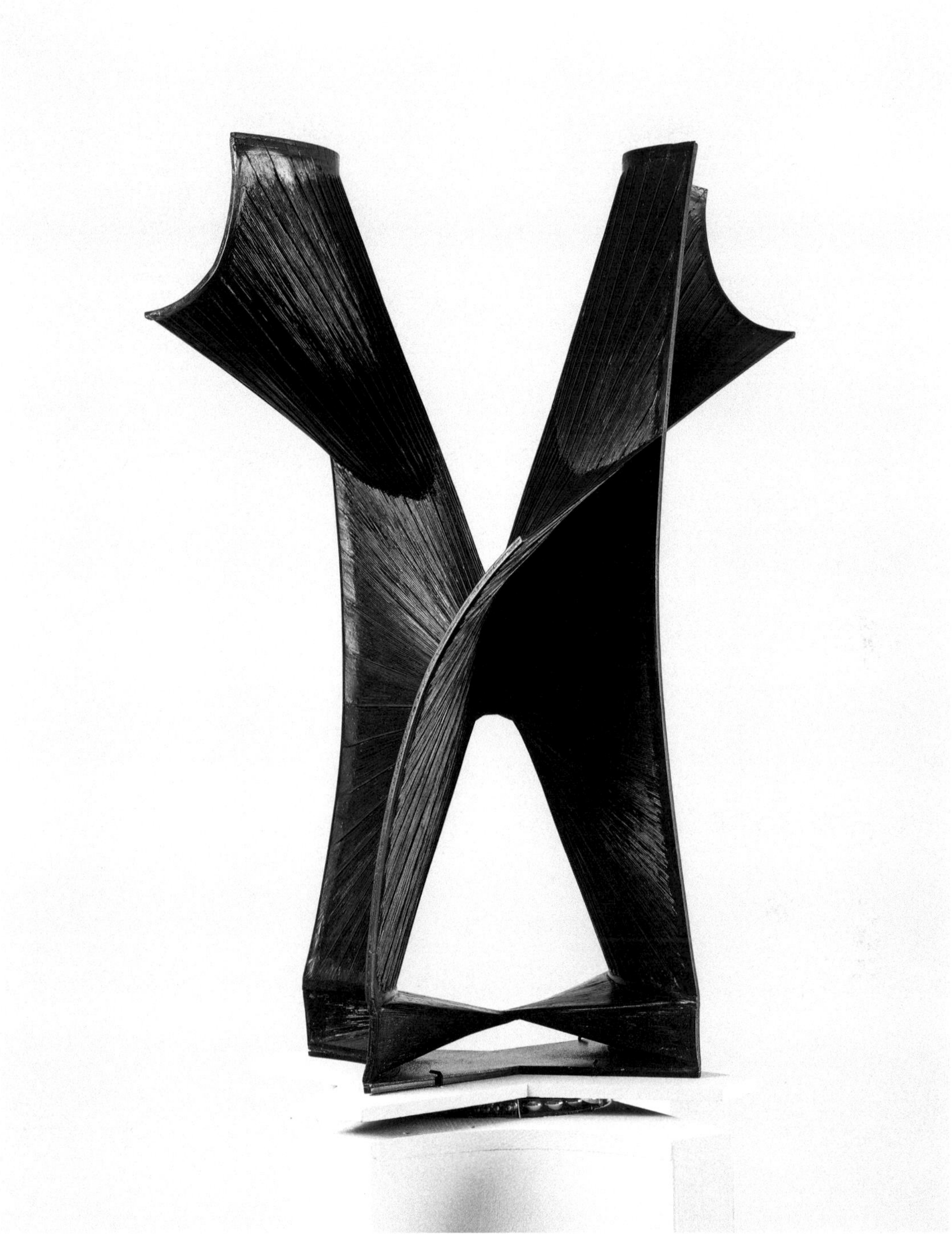

Antoine Pevsner
Colonne développable de la victoire, 1946

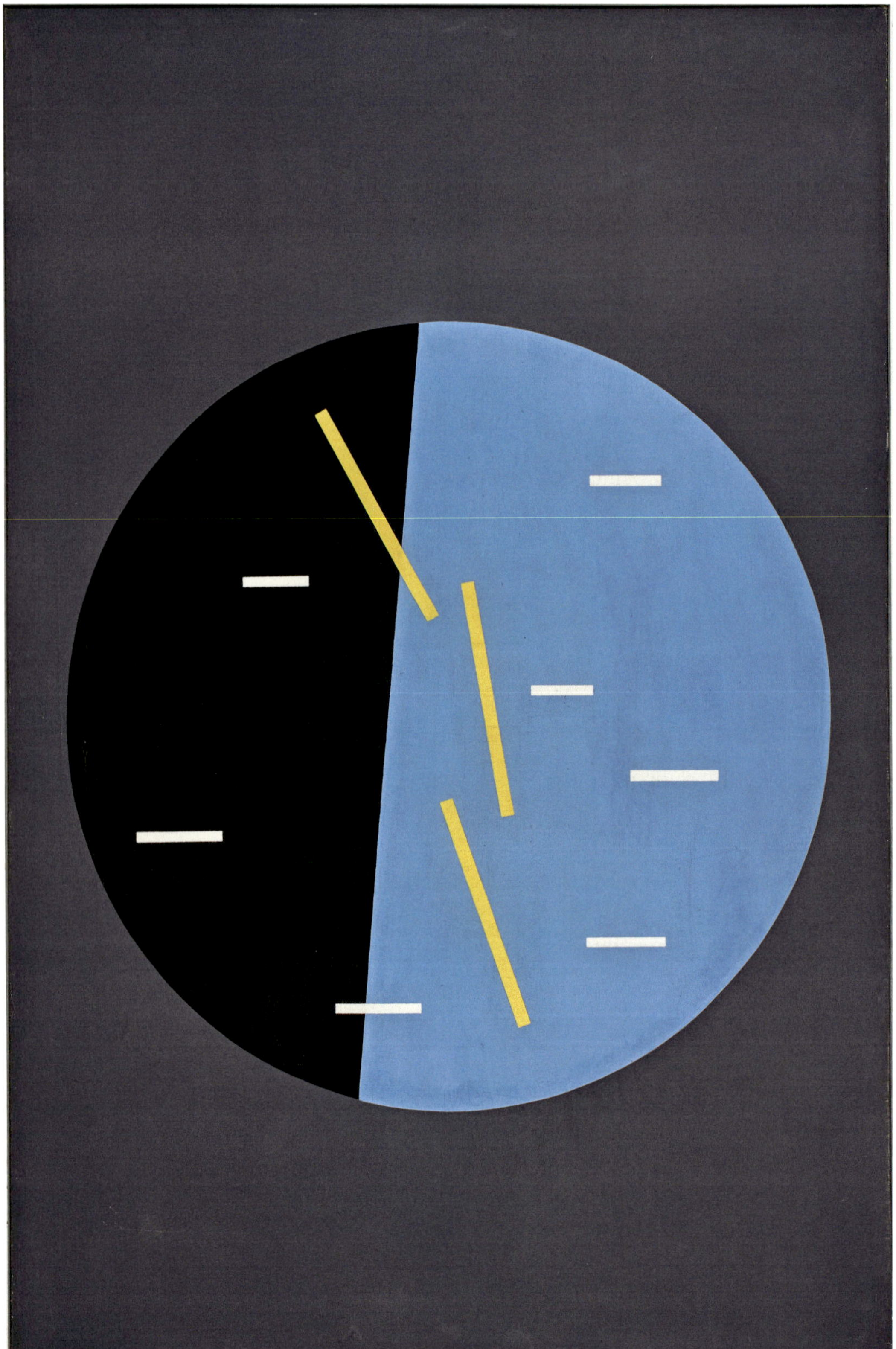

Friedrich Vordemberge-Gildewart
Untitled (composition no. 155), 1946

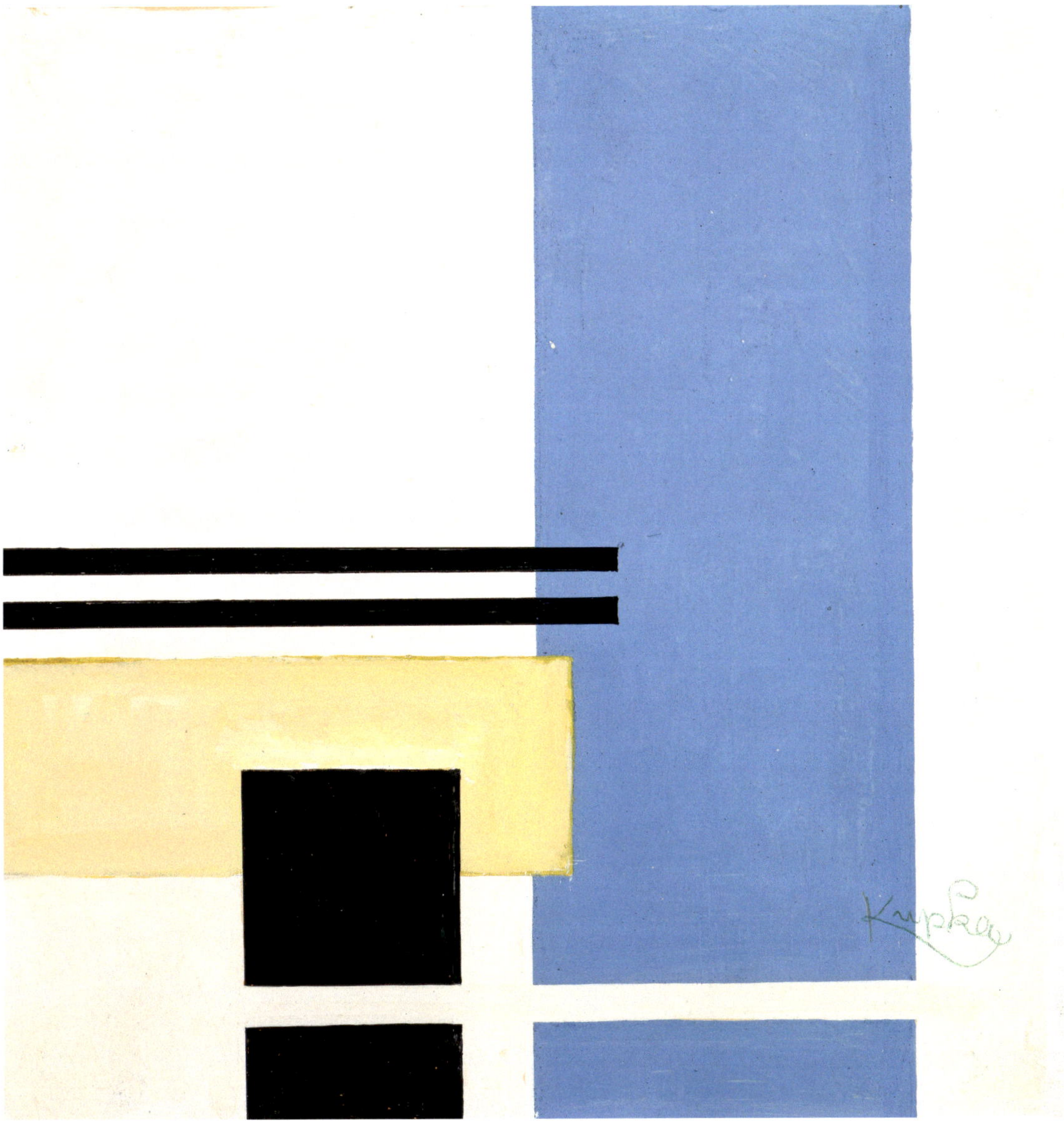

František Kupka
Composition néo-plastique, c. 1930

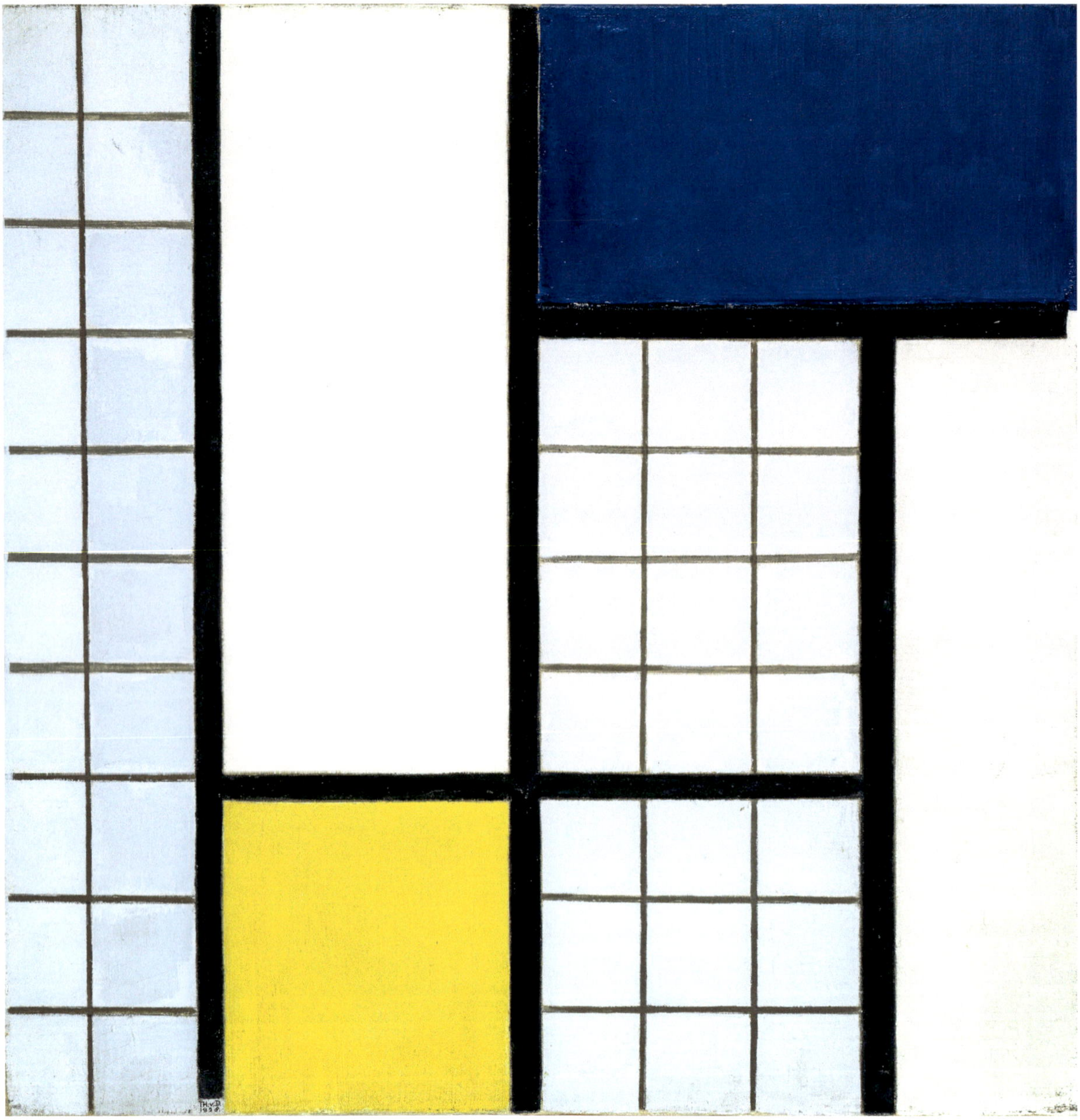

Theo van Doesburg
Komposition in Halbtönen, 1928

Piet Mondrian
Tableau no II (with grey and black), 1925

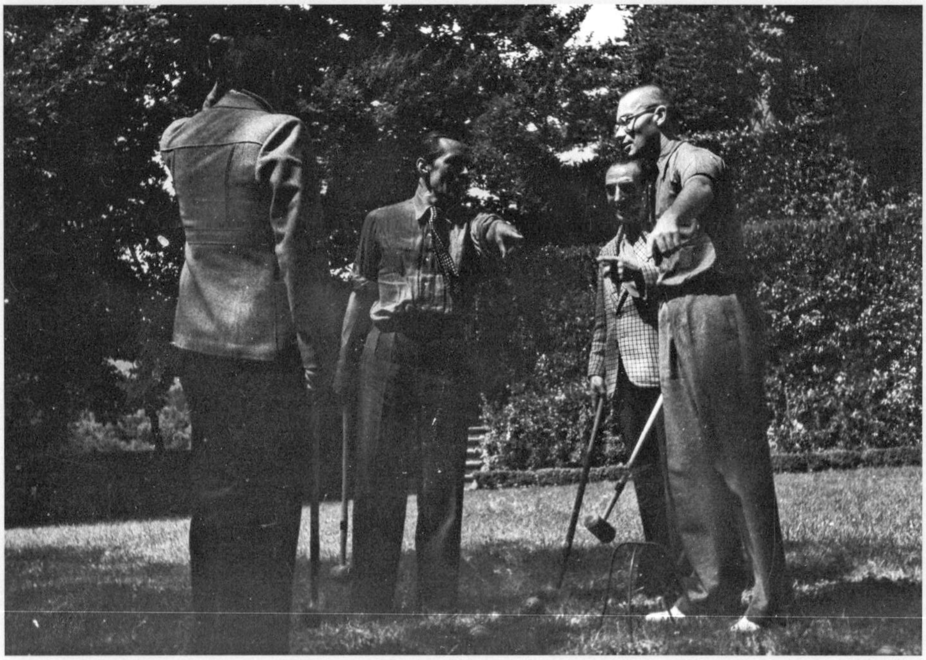

1939

Alfred Roth, Georges Vantongerloo, and Max Bill on La Sarraz. In the same year that Bill joined the Congrès Internationaux d'architecture moderne (CIAM), he was invited by its co-founder, Hélène de Mandrot, to her chateau La Sarraz. At that time, she would each year gather an illustrious company of exponents of the avant-garde to meet there.

gta Archiv / ETH Zürich, Alfred Roth

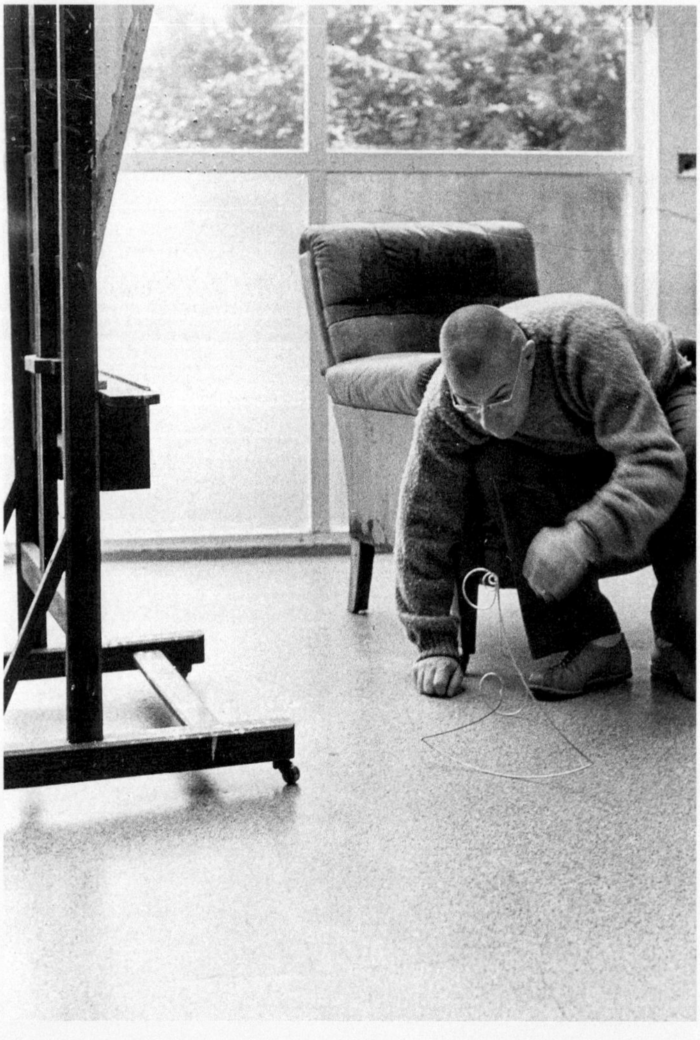

c. 1950

Bill returned to Switzerland from Dessau in 1929. In 1932/33, he built himself the so-called studio house in Zurich's Höngg district. Bill saw himself primarily as an architect, but his success in that discipline failed to materialize and he earned his money mainly as a commercial designer and typographer. He considered the production of art works a leisure activity.

Stiftung Ernst Scheidegger Archiv, Zurich, photo: Ernst Scheidegger

Max Bill met Hanns Robert Welti in Zurich in 1929. Both artists felt snubbed by Kunsthaus Zurich, which had not invited either of them to take part in the exhibition *Abstrakte und surrealistische Malerei und Plastik*. In protest at their exclusion, Bill and Welti founded a society called die augen, which Willi Eidenbenz, Heiri Steiner, and Anton Stankowski also joined.[1] Like Bill, most of these artists were earning their living as graphic designers.

Bill joined the Schweizerischer Werkbund, a progressive organization with a mission to promote collaboration between art and industry, in 1930, and nine years later became a member of the Zurich chapter of CIAM (Congrès internationaux d'architecture moderne).

Exhibition opportunities in Switzerland for artists who subscribed to Concrete Art were nevertheless sorely lacking in those years. This changed in 1936, when Welti and Leo Leuppi initiated a show at Kunsthaus Zurich called *Zeitprobleme in der Schweizer Malerei und Plastik* that featured works by both aspiring and established Swiss artists. Bill had a hand in the selection of works and included some of his own; he also designed the

1936

In the 1930s Bill participated in numerous competitions. His design for the Swiss section at the Triennale in Milan in 1936 was realized and won the Grand Prix. This success earned Bill widespread recognition. Participating as both artist and publicist that same year in the exhibition *Zeitprobleme in der Schweizer Malerei und Plastik*, he began to definitively insert his voice into the discourse about Swiss art.

Triennale Milano—Archivio Fotografico, photo: Crimella

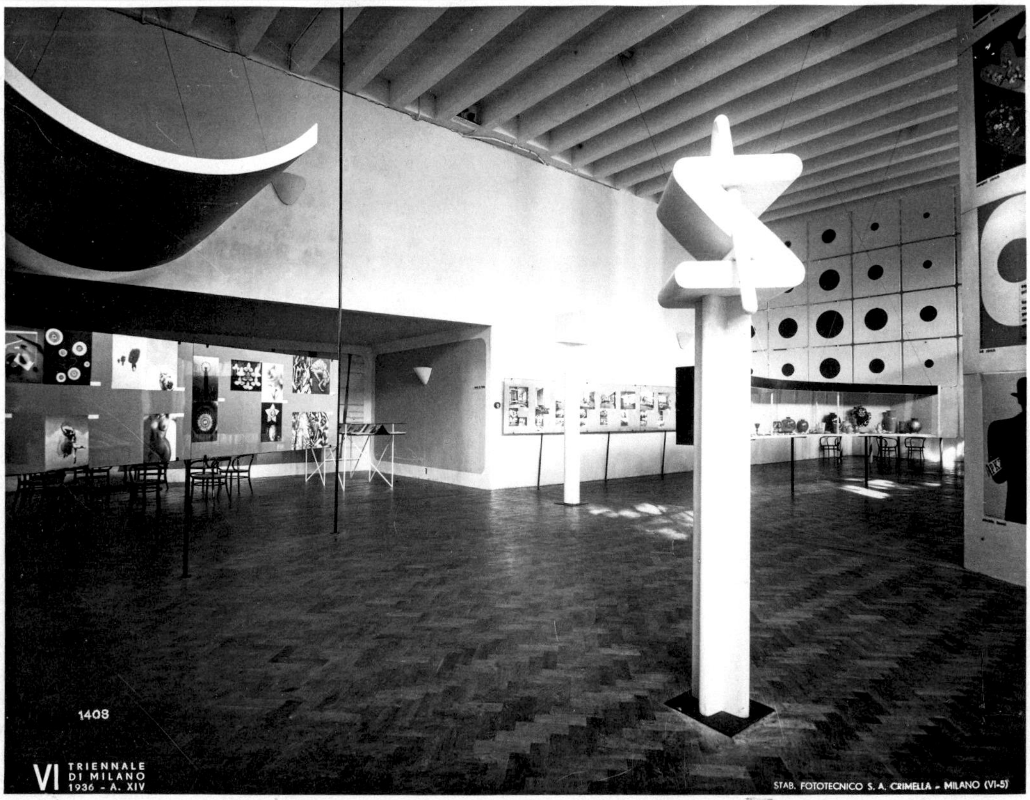

exhibition poster and catalog, in which he published his controversial essay "konkrete gestaltung." The show prompted Leuppi and Richard Paul Lohse to found the artist group Allianz, which Bill joined in 1937, taking over as head of its publishing arm in 1941. Starting in 1943, Allianz members were able to exhibit their works at Hansegger's Eaux-vives gallery in Zurich. This connection came about through Camille Graeser.[2] Graeser, Bill, Lohse, and Verena Loewensberg would later become internationally known as the Zurich Concretists. While Bill's relationship with Lohse was shaped largely by rivalry, Loewensberg became a close friend.

Bill stayed in touch with a number of Bauhaus people even after his return to Switzerland. He designed printed matter for S-P-H Stoffe in Zurich, a hand-weaving business co-owned by Gunta Stölzl, the former head of the Bauhaus weaving workshop, and in 1936 he invited Stölzl to exhibit some of her fabric designs at the Milan Triennale. Similarly, when Roman Clemens from the theater workshop fled Nazi Germany, Bill gave him temporary shelter in Switzerland.[3]

1 Cf. Thomas 2008, pp. 292–294.

2 Cf. Vera Hausdorff: "Camille Graeser und die Formierung der Zürcher Konkreten – Entwicklung einer konstruktiv-konkreten Formensprache," in *Camille Graeser. Vom Werden eines konkreten Künstlers*, exh. cat. Zurich: Museum Haus Konstruktiv 2020, Cologne 2020, pp. 88 f.

3 Cf. Thomas 2008, p. 179.

1944

View of the exhibition *konkrete kunst. klee, kandinsky, lohse, vantongerloo, bodmer, leuppi, bill, sophie täuber, arp, mondrian*, which Max BIll organized at the Kunsthalle Basel. There, he not only exhibited members of the Allianz, but also chose works by numerous international artists. Works by Arp can be seen in the foreground, and some by Bill in the adjoining room.

Fotoarchiv Kunsthalle Basel, photo: Atelier Eidenbenz

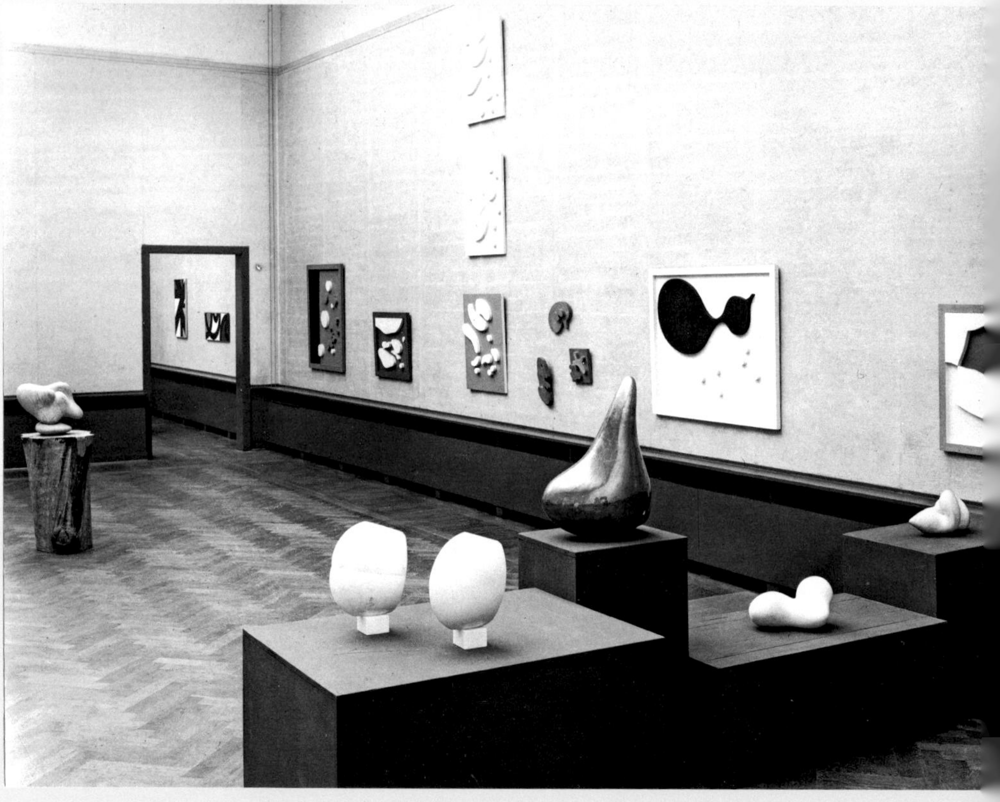

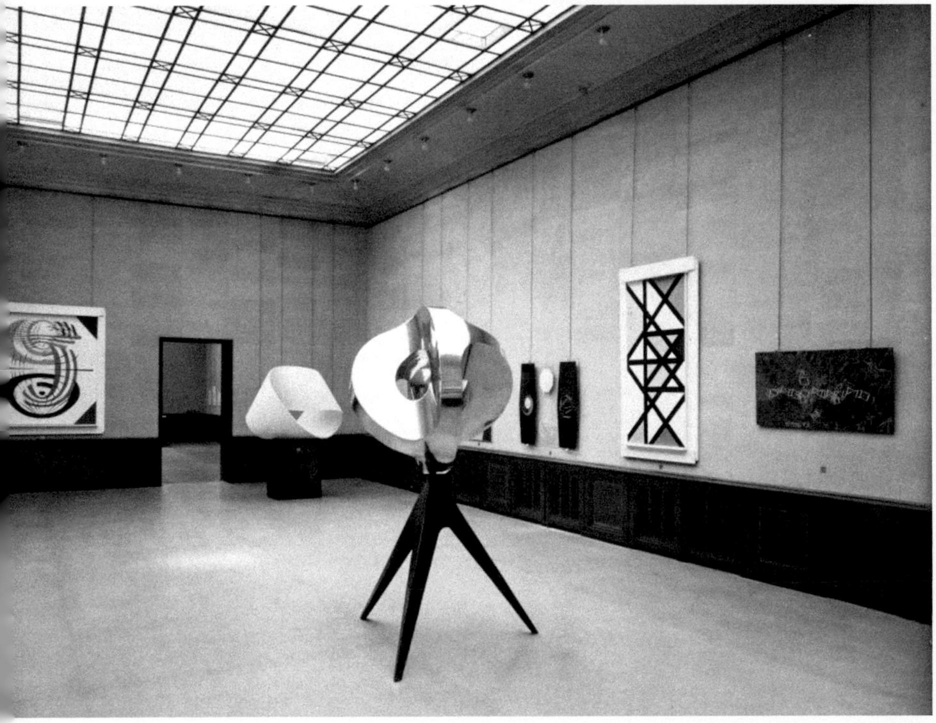

1942

View of Max Bill's works in the Allianz exhibition of 1942 at the Kunsthaus Zurich. The Allianz had the ambitious goal of organizing a comprehensive exhibition every year. In 1938 it succeeded with the exhibition *New Art in Switzerland* at the Kunsthalle Basel; and after that in 1942 and 1947 at the Kunsthaus Zürich and, finally, in 1954 at the Helmhaus Zurich. In the 1940s Concrete Art was still met with rejection, but was able to establish itself in the canon of Swiss art and subsequently even became the figurehead of it.

max bill georges vantongerloo stiftung, photo: Hans Finsler

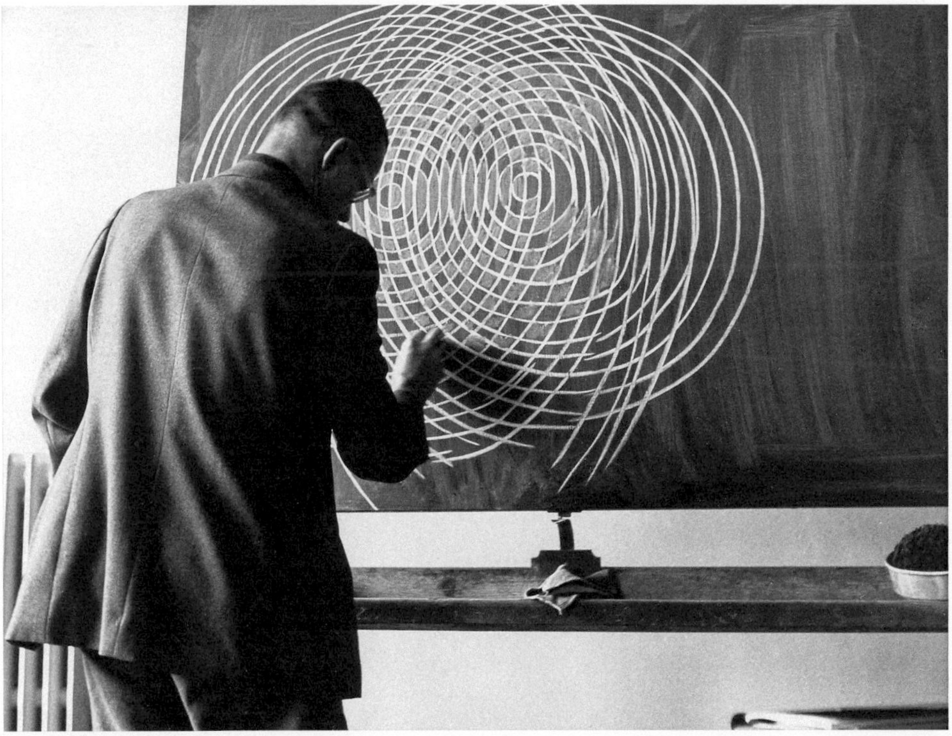

1944/45

In 1944/45 Max Bill was appointed as teacher at the School of Applied Arts in Zurich.

Stiftung Ernst Scheidegger Archiv, Zurich, photo: Ernst Scheidegger

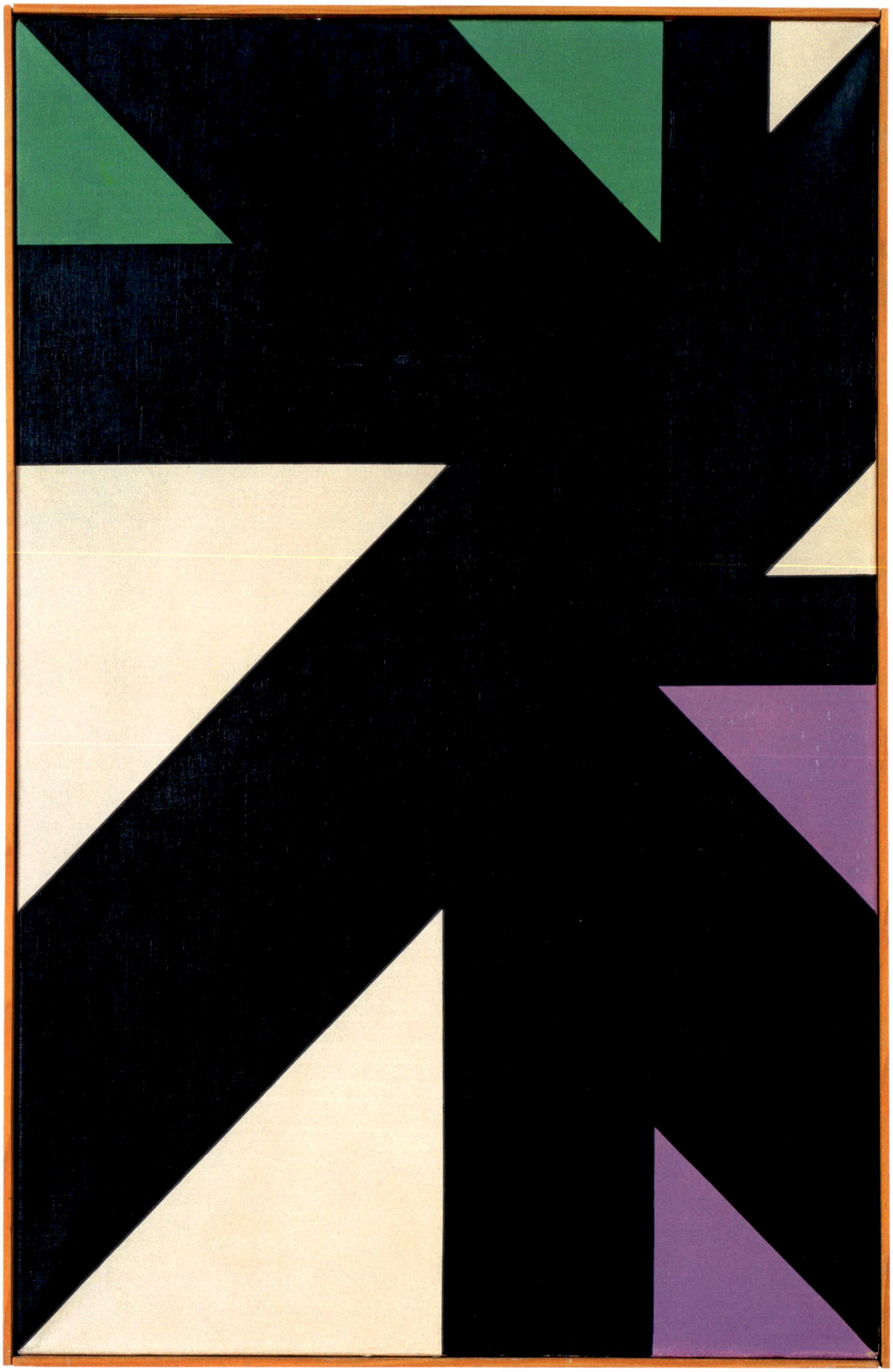

Max Bill
acht-teiliger rhythmus, 1942

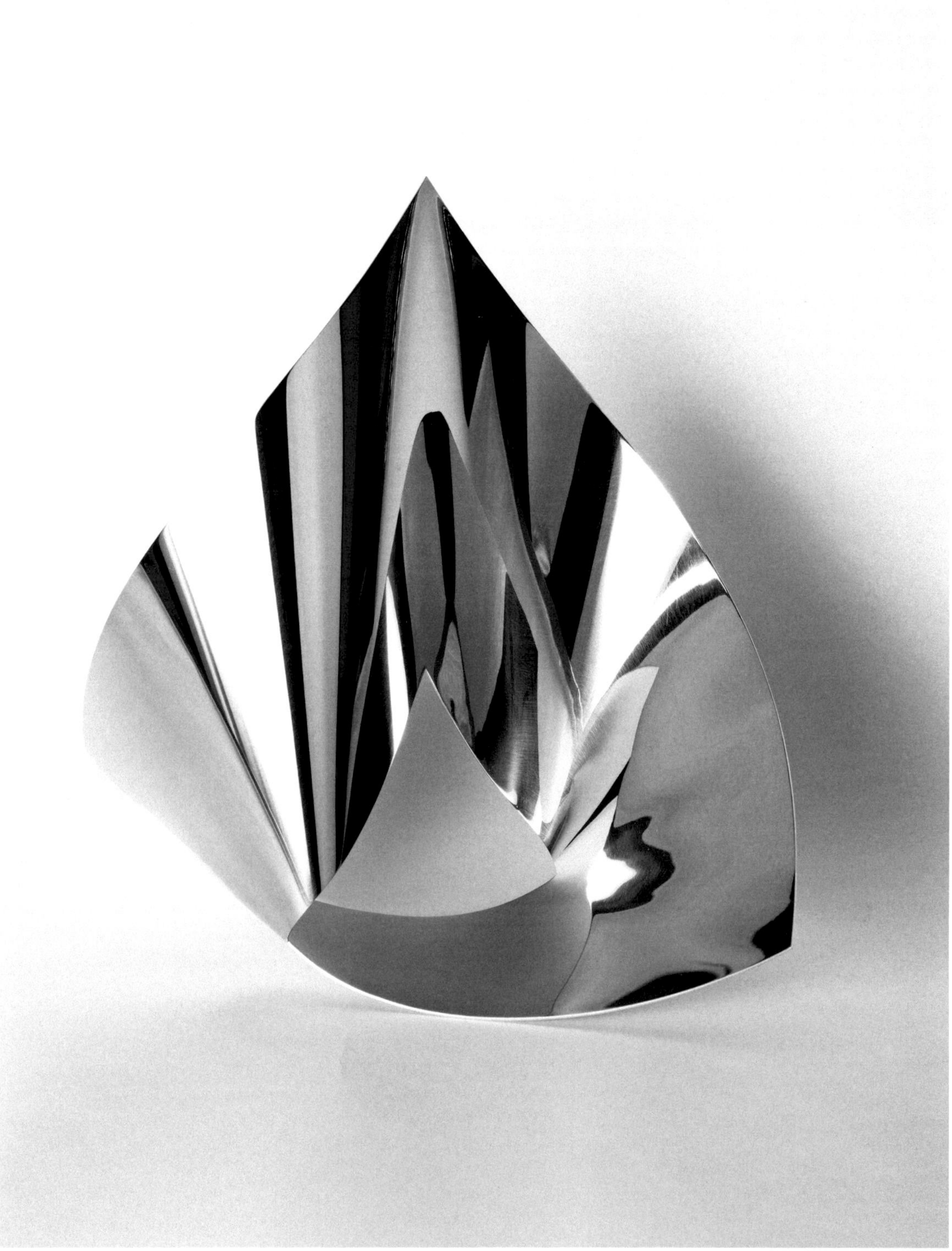

Max Bill
sechseckfläche im raum, 1948

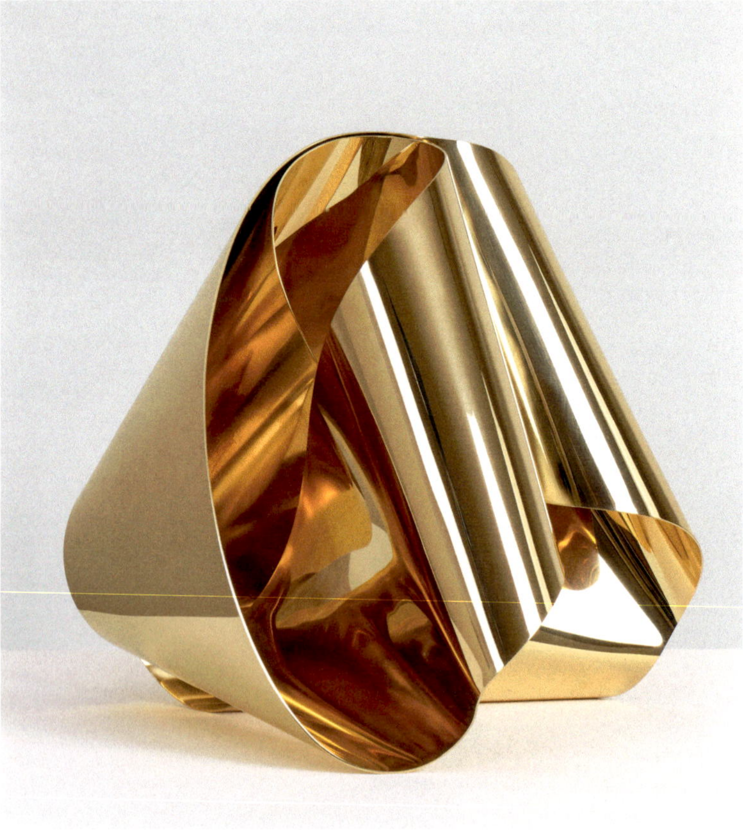

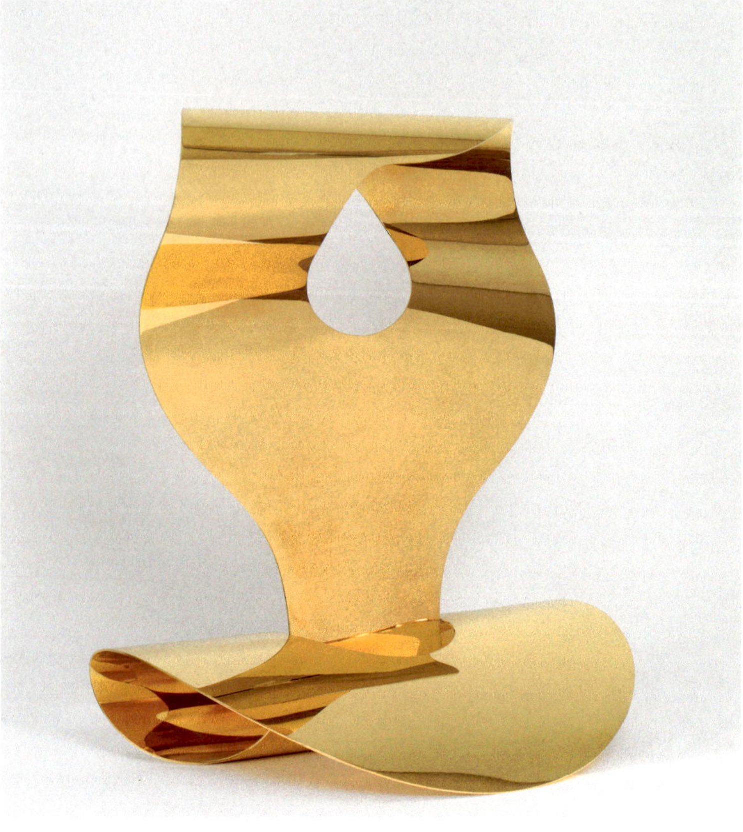

Max Bill
kontinuität, 1946/1982

Max Bill
fläche im raum, 1948/1971

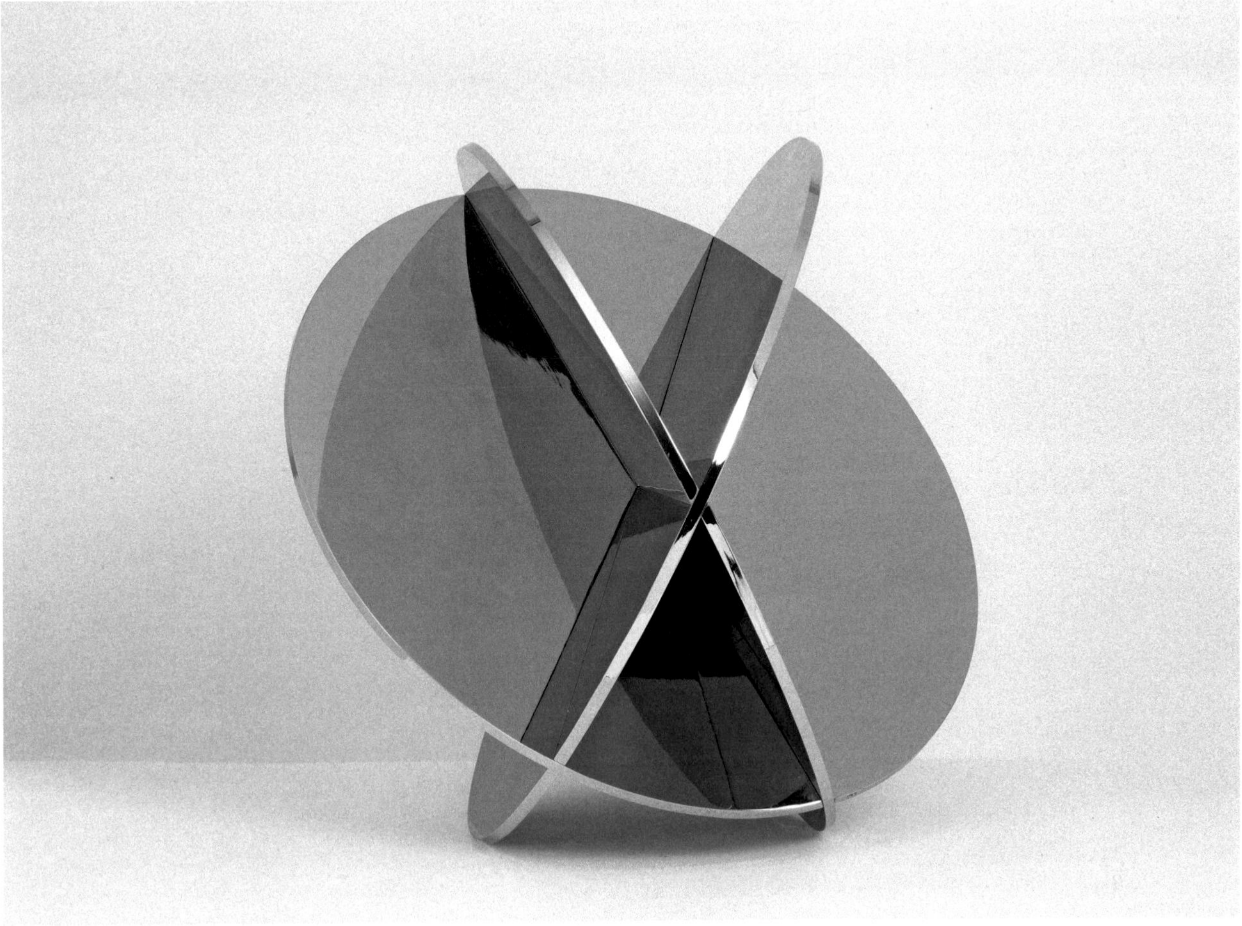

Max Bill
konstruktion aus drei kreisscheiben, 1945–1946

Max Bill
konstruktion mit 10 vierecken, 1940–1943

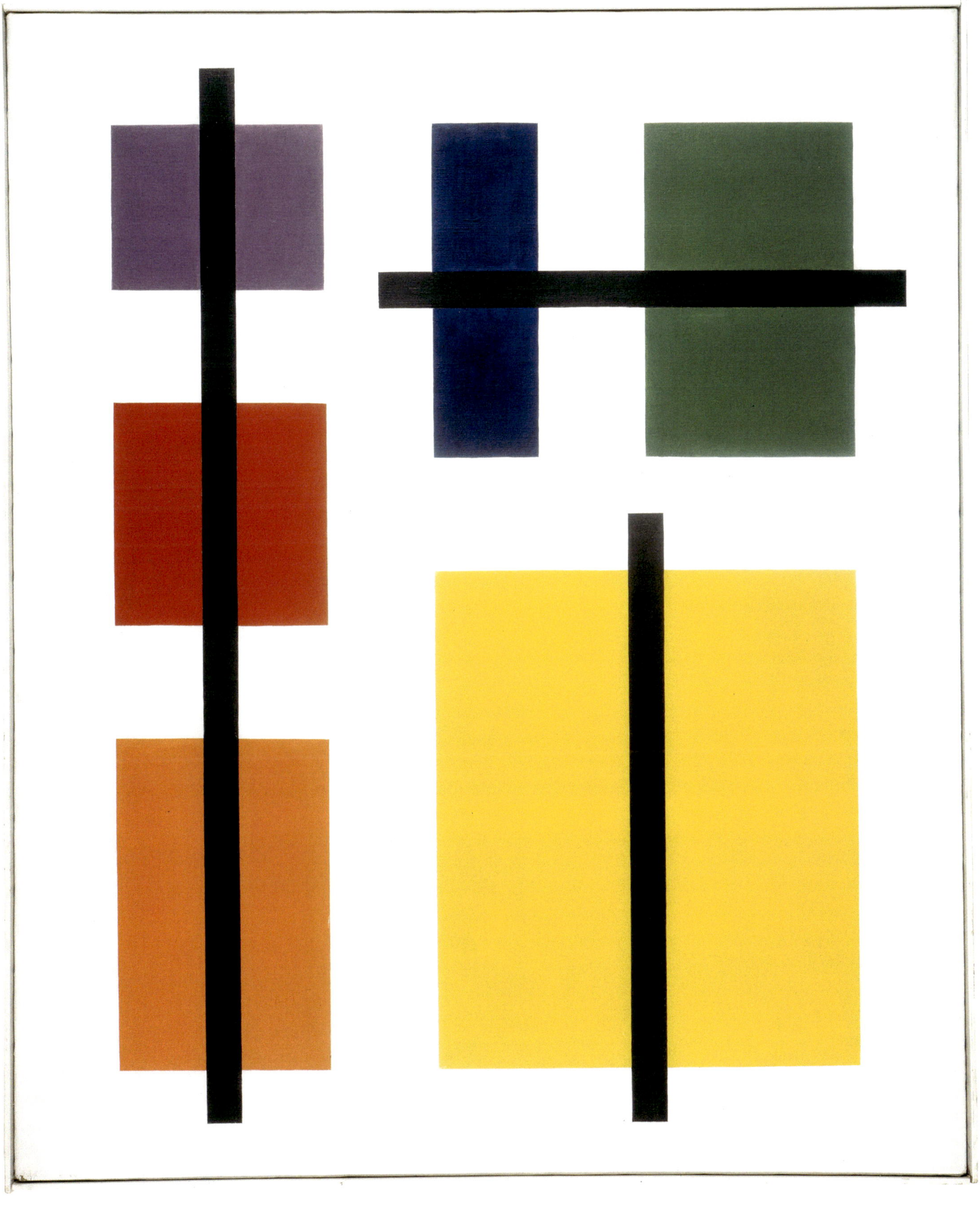

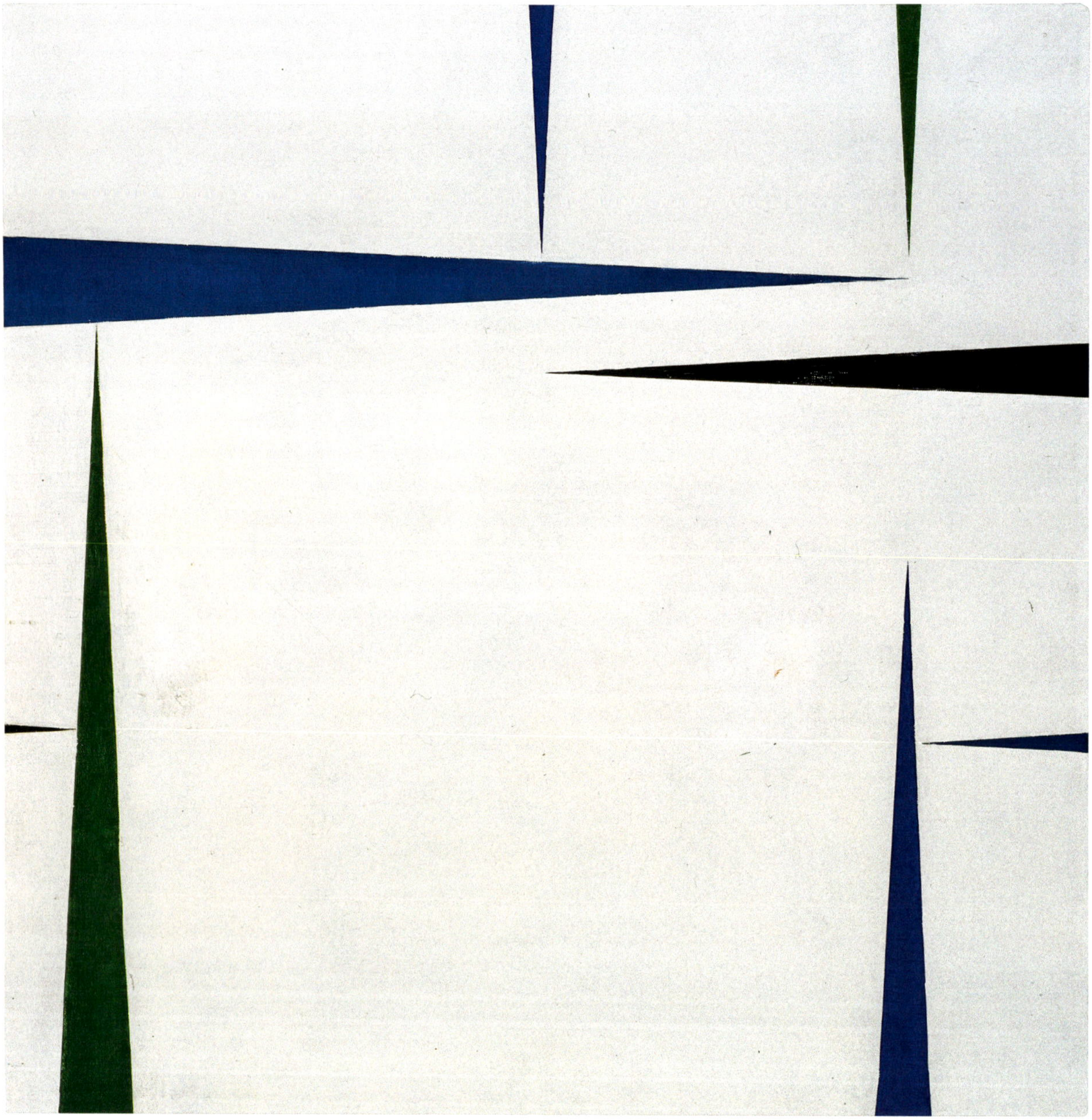

Max Bill
kühle teilung, 1943

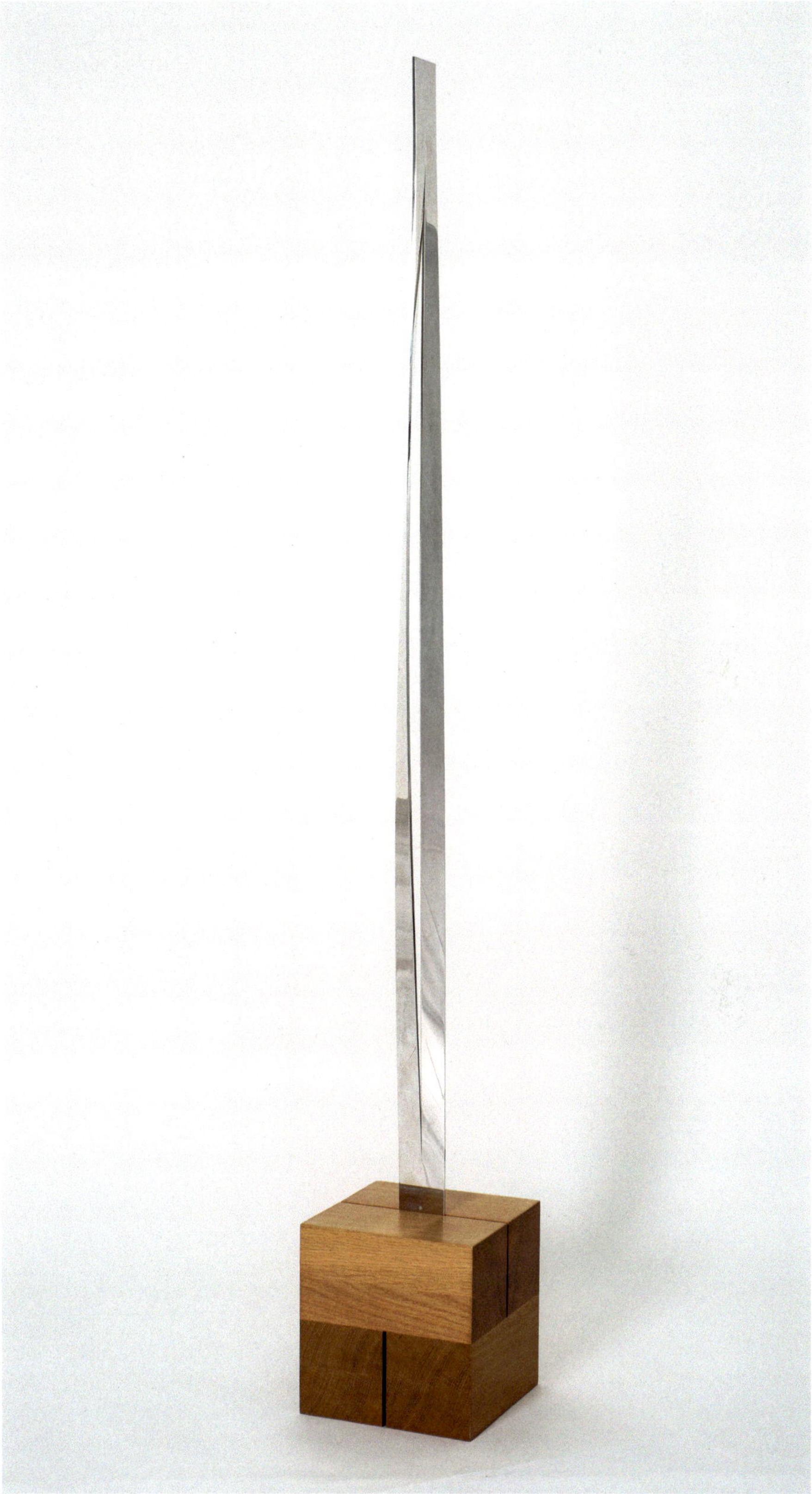

Max Bill
unendliche fläche in form einer säule, 1953/1993

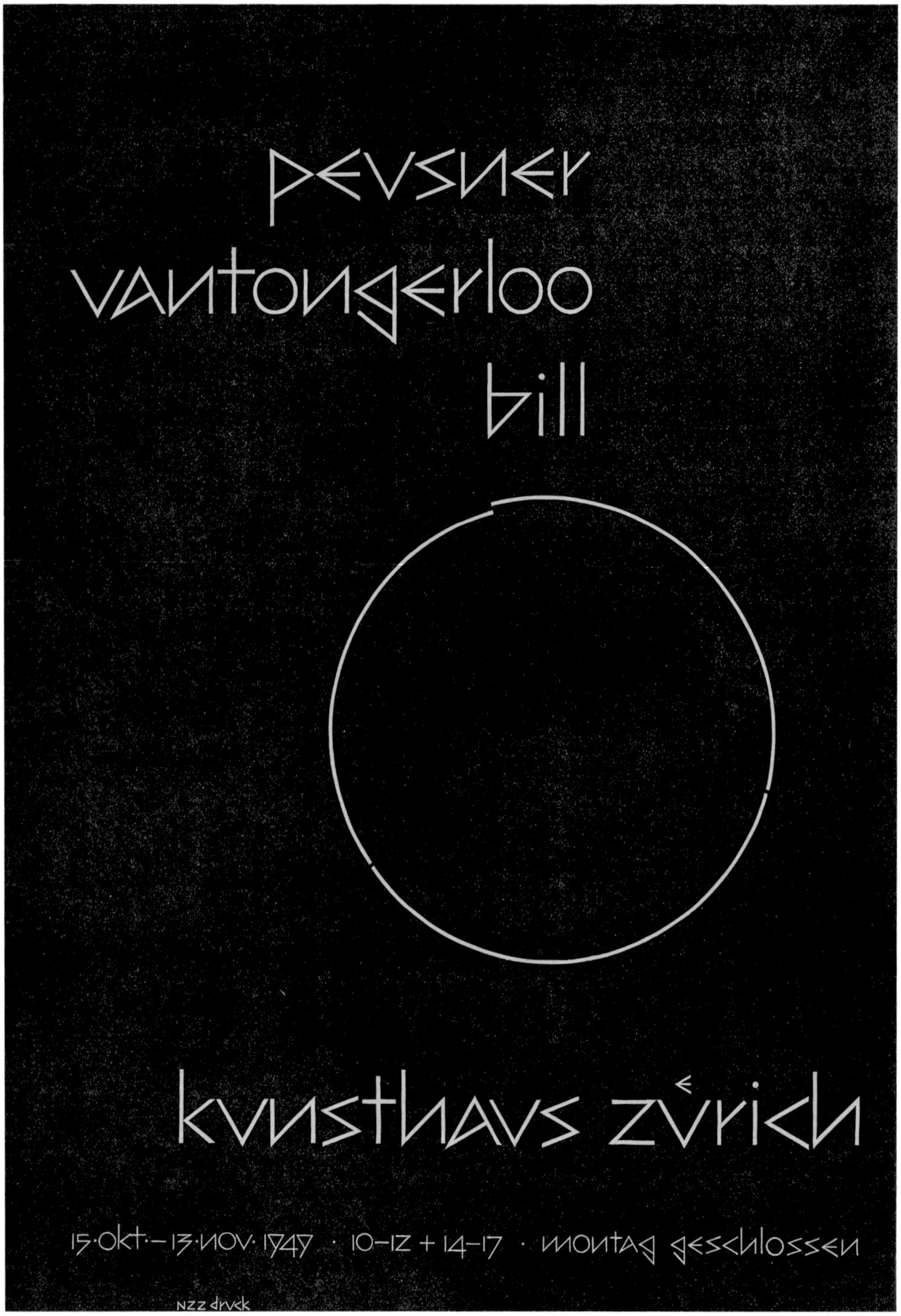

Max Bill
Poster: pevsner—vantongerloo—bill—kunsthaus zürich, 1949

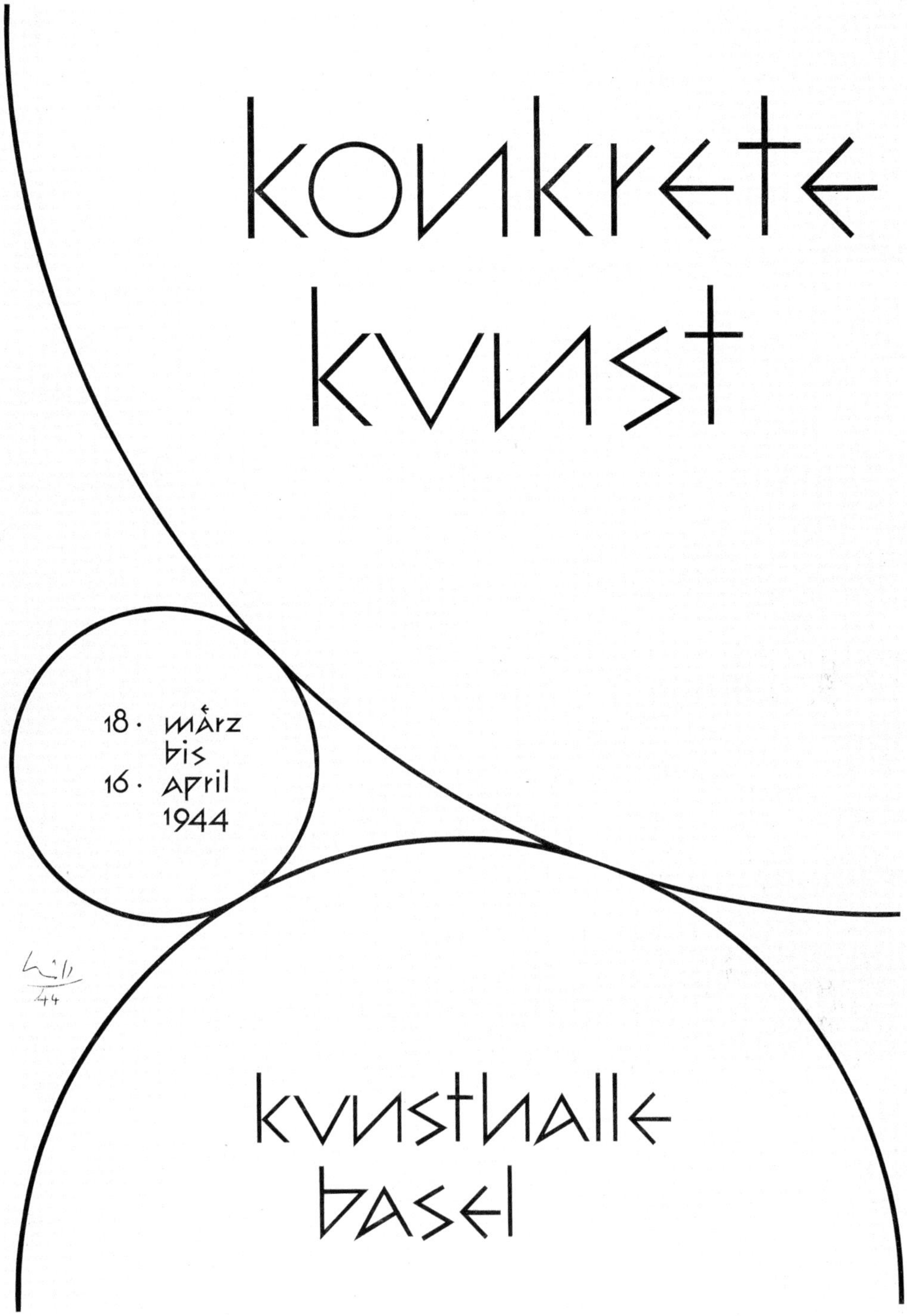

Max Bill
Poster: konkrete kunst—kunsthalle basel, 1944

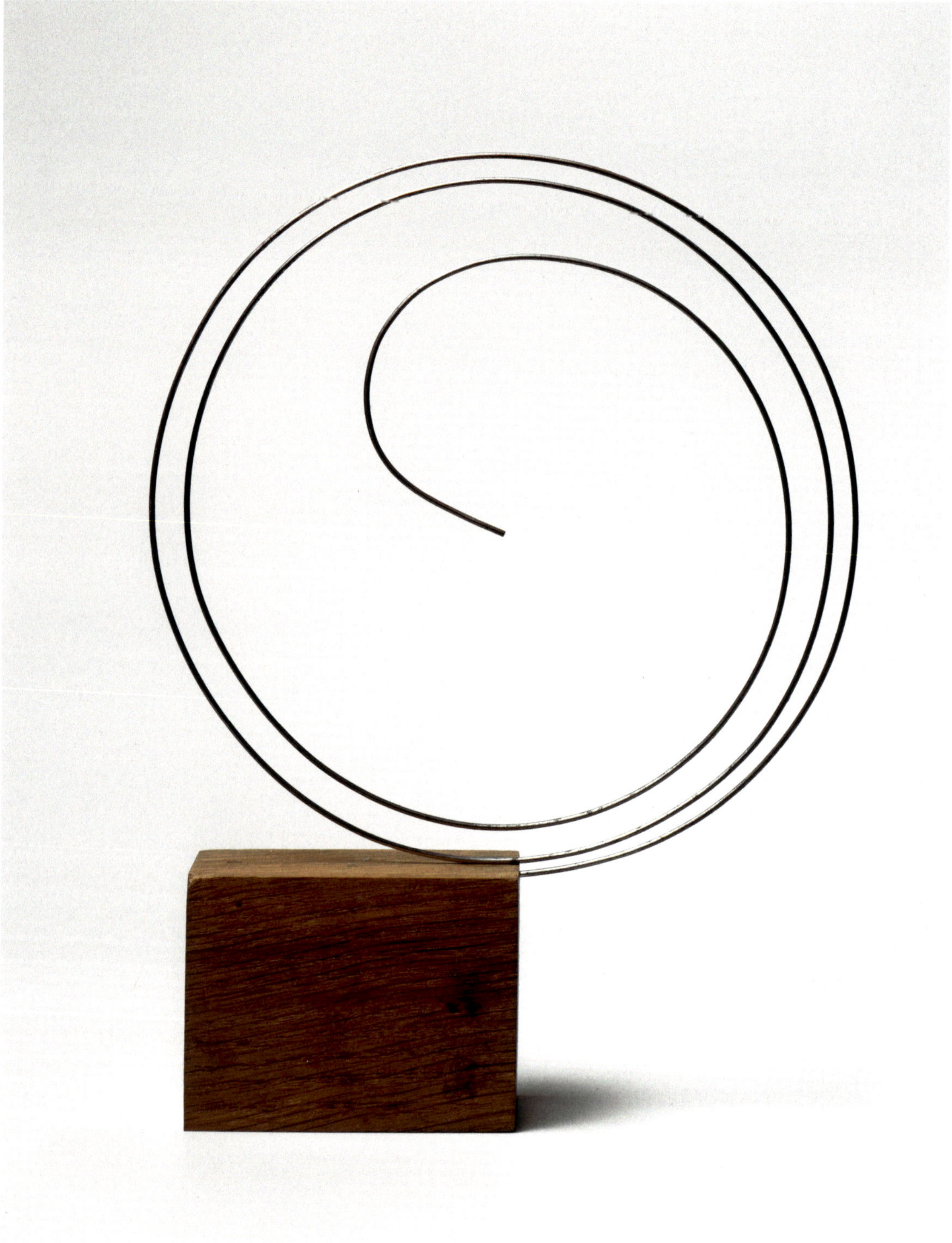

Max Bill
umgekehrt laufende spirale, 1944

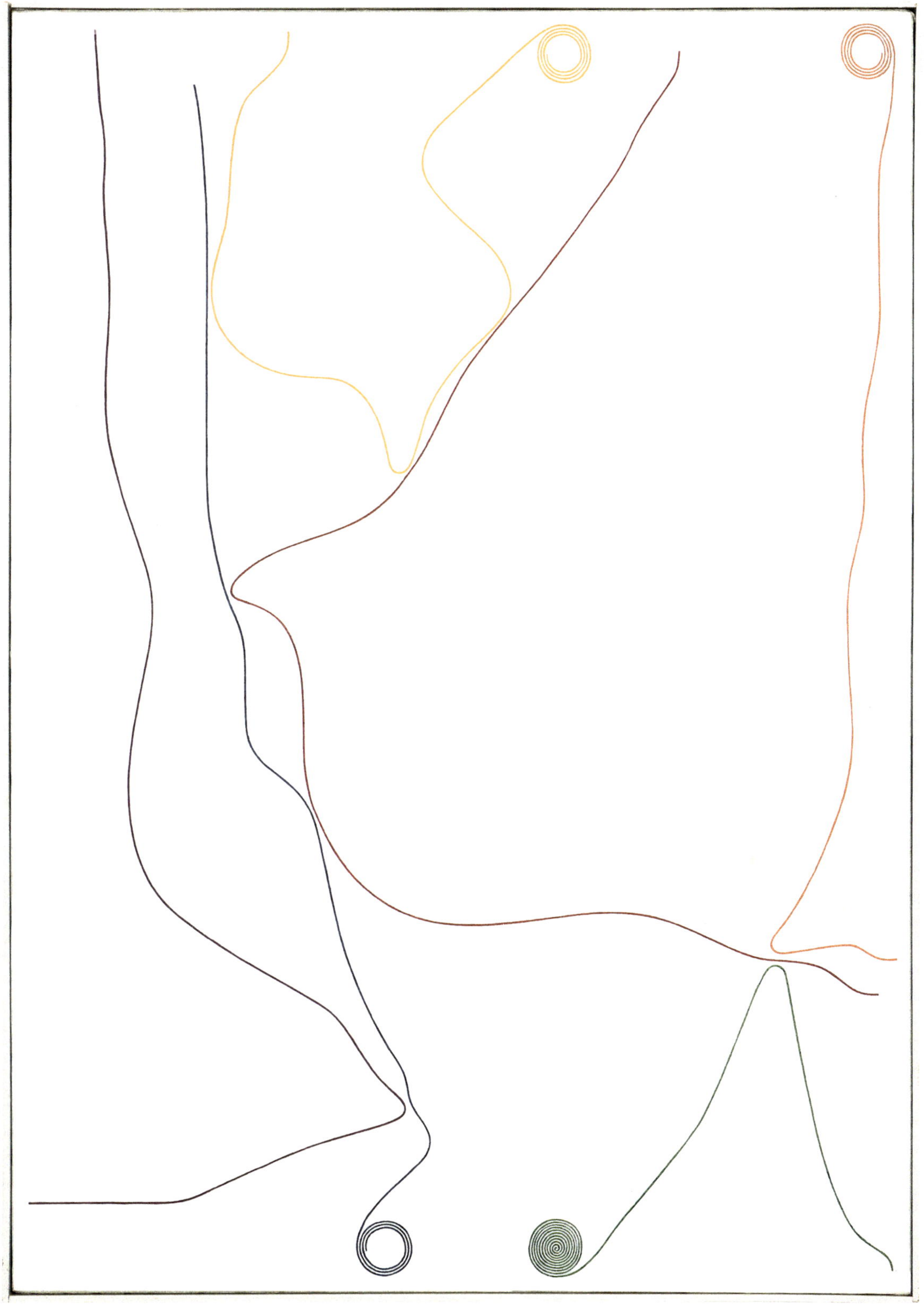

Max Bill
sechs gleichlange linien, 1947

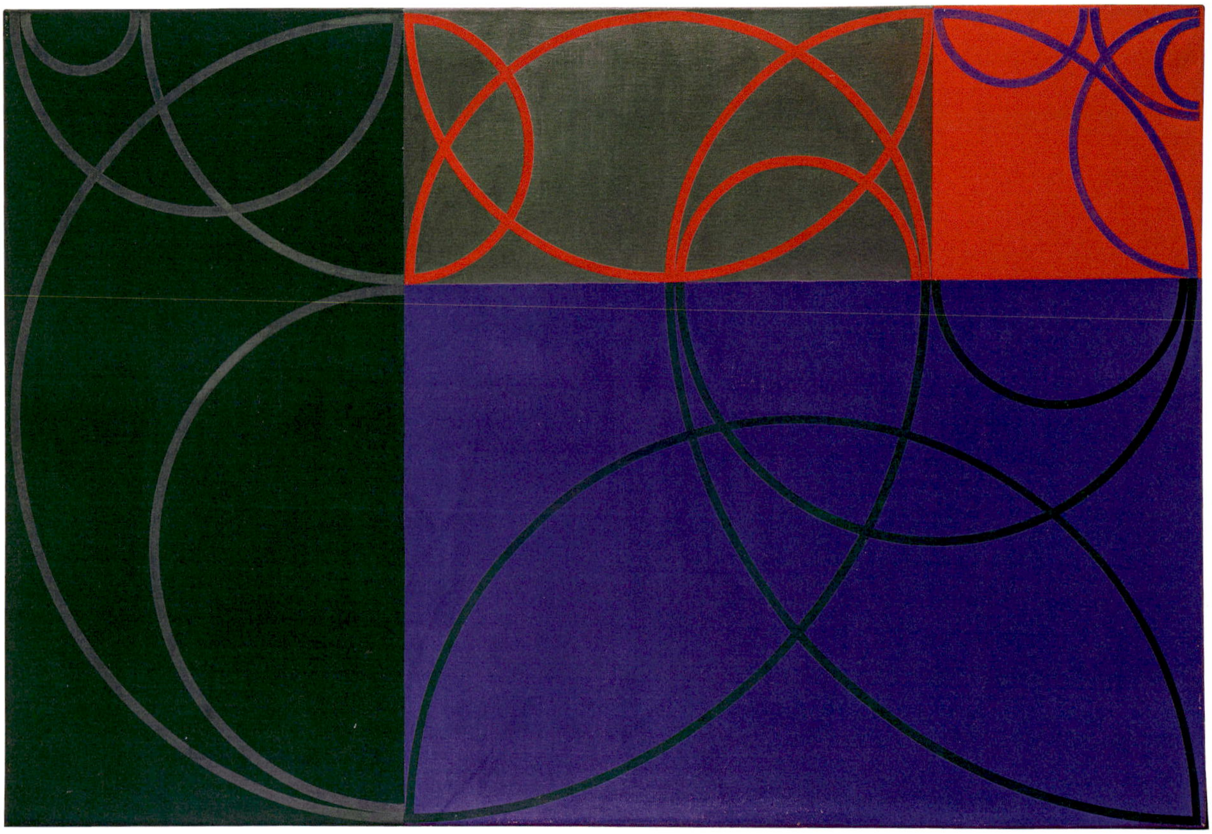

Max Bill
magische chromographie, 1944–1946

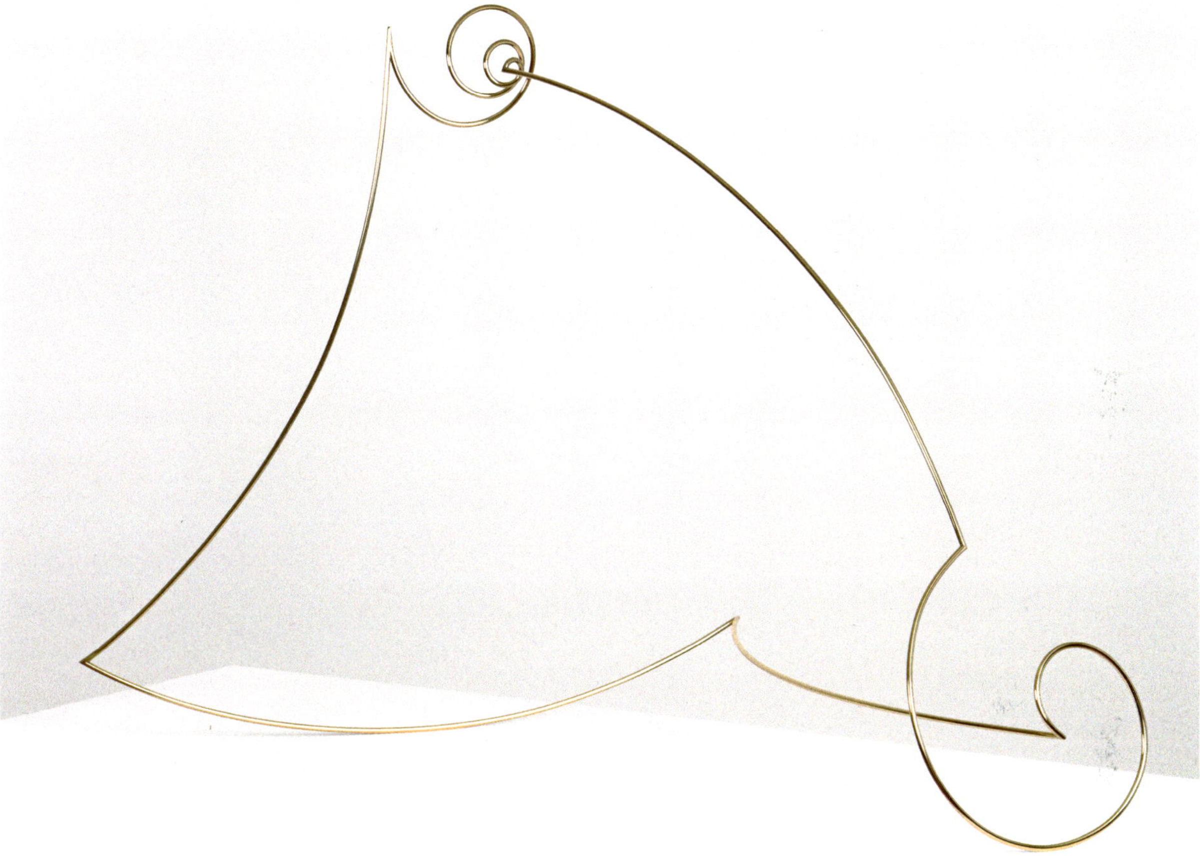

Max Bill
sechseck im raum mit gleichen seitenlängen, 1947/1965

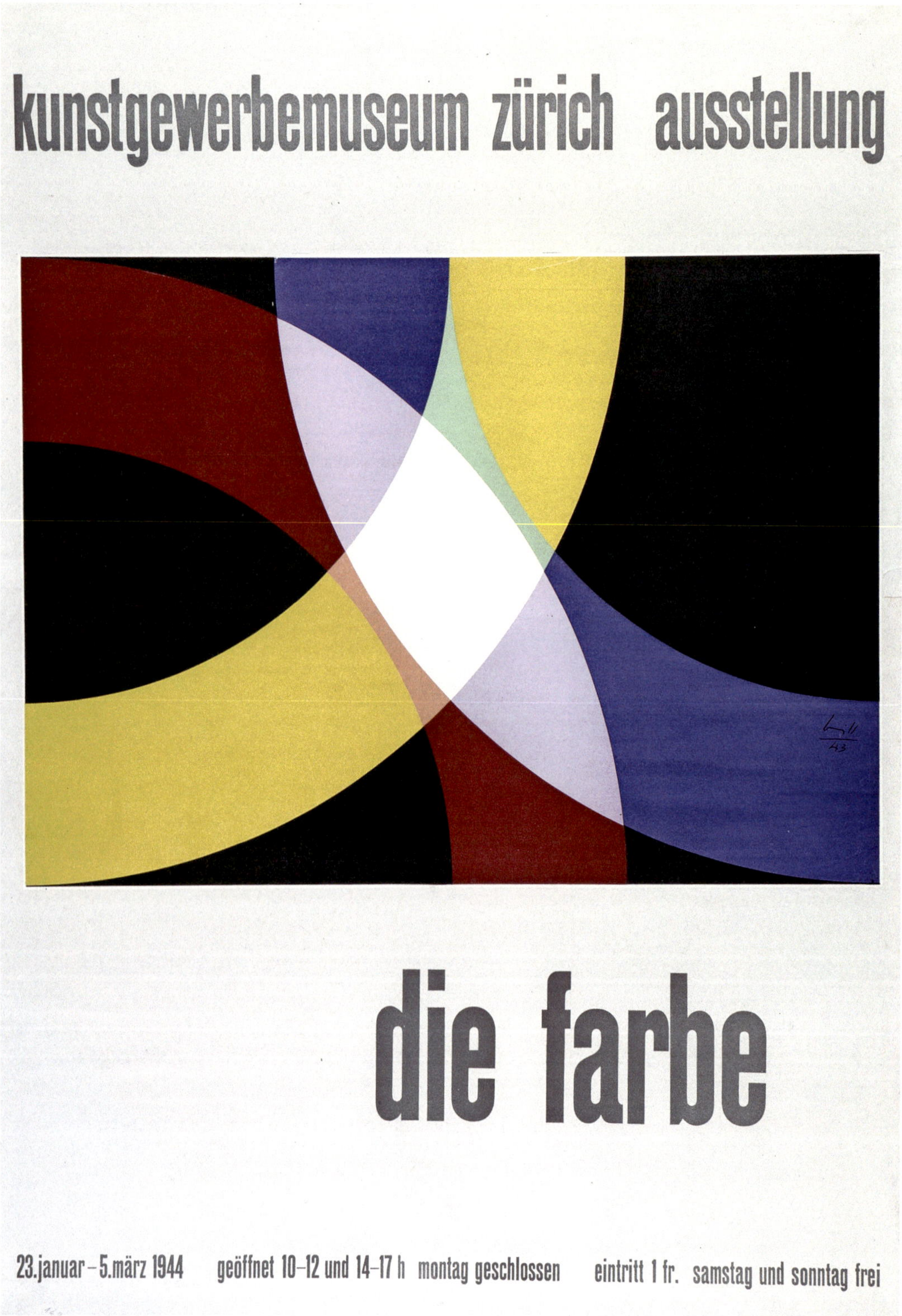

Max Bill
Poster: die farbe—kunstgewerbemuseum zürich, 1944

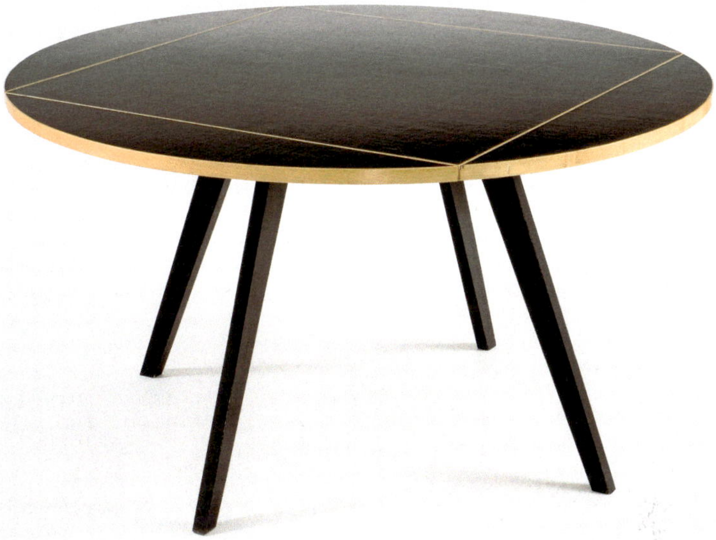

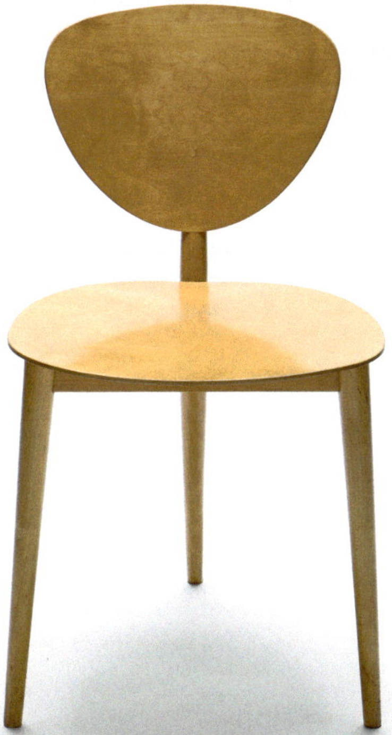

Max Bill
Quadratrundtisch, design: 1949

Max Bill
Dreibeinstuhl, design: 1949

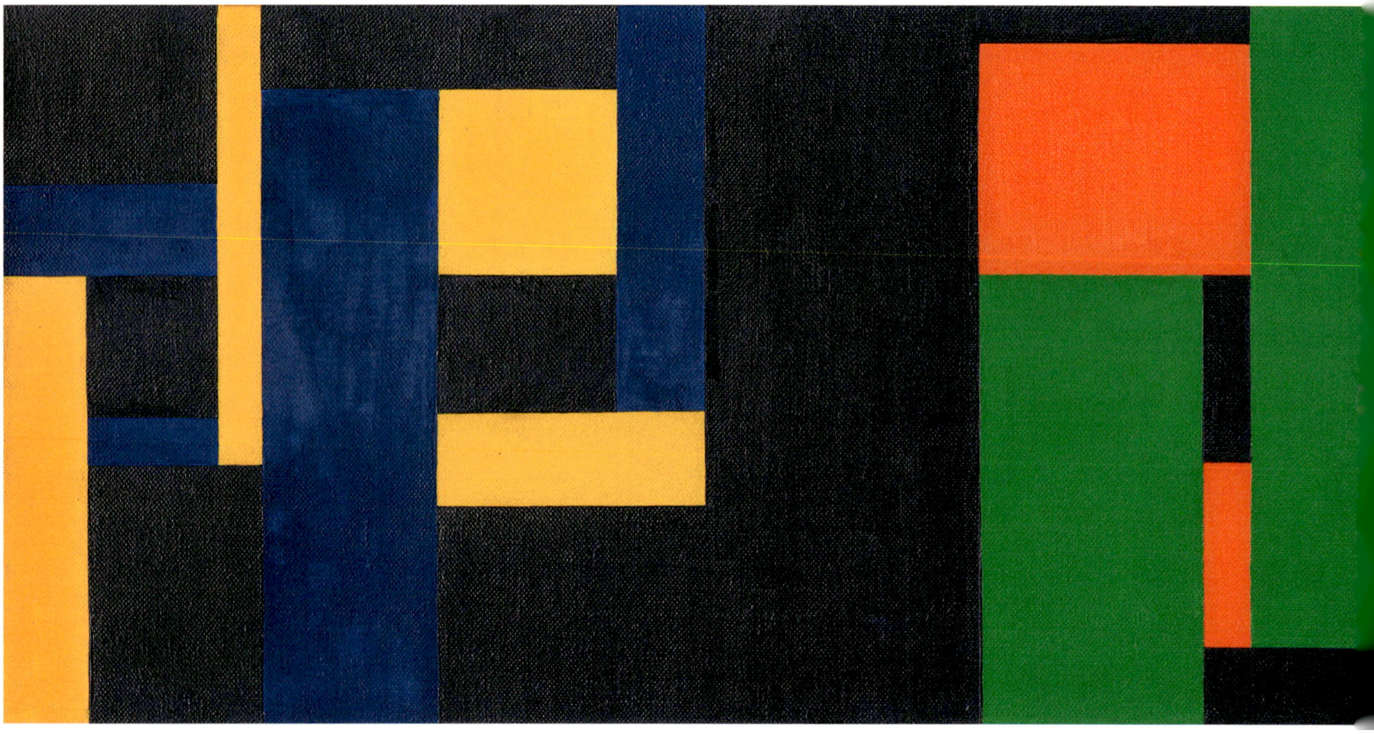

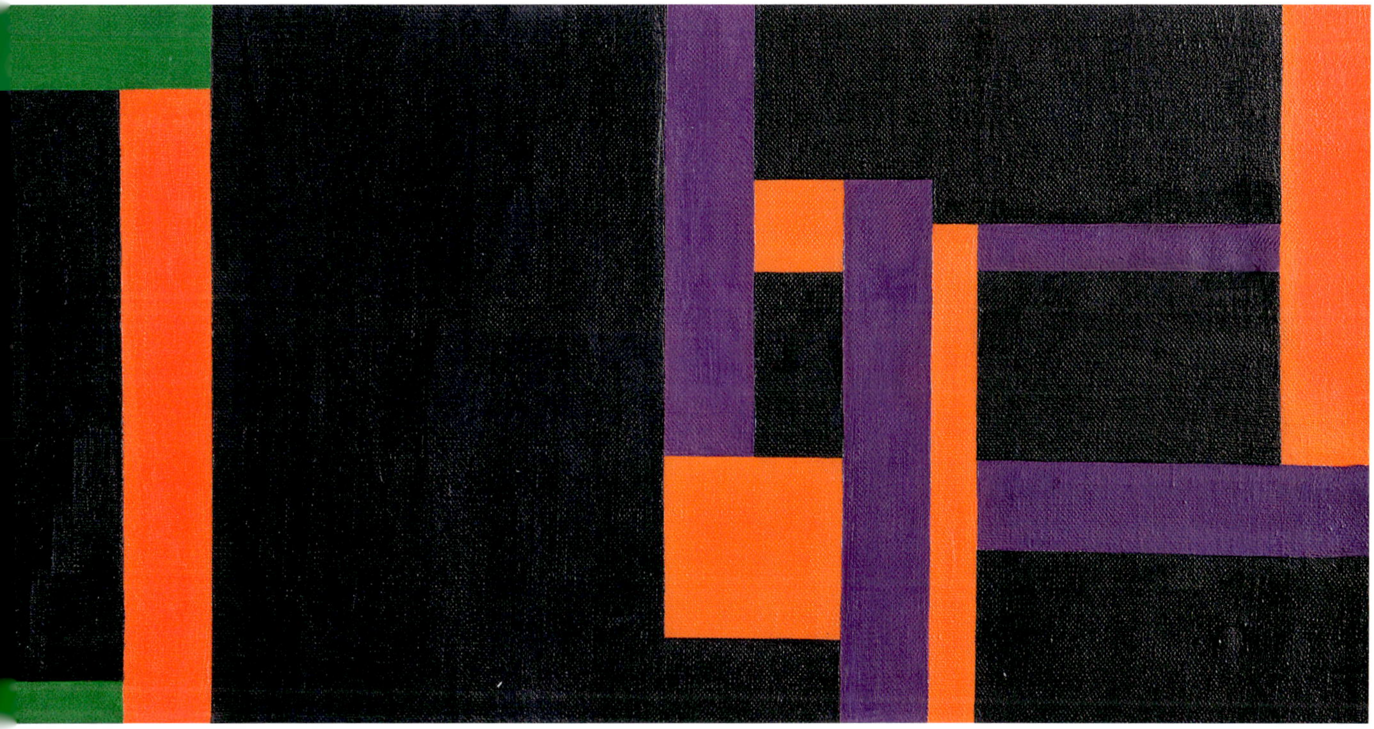

Max Bill
rhythmus in vier quadraten, 1943

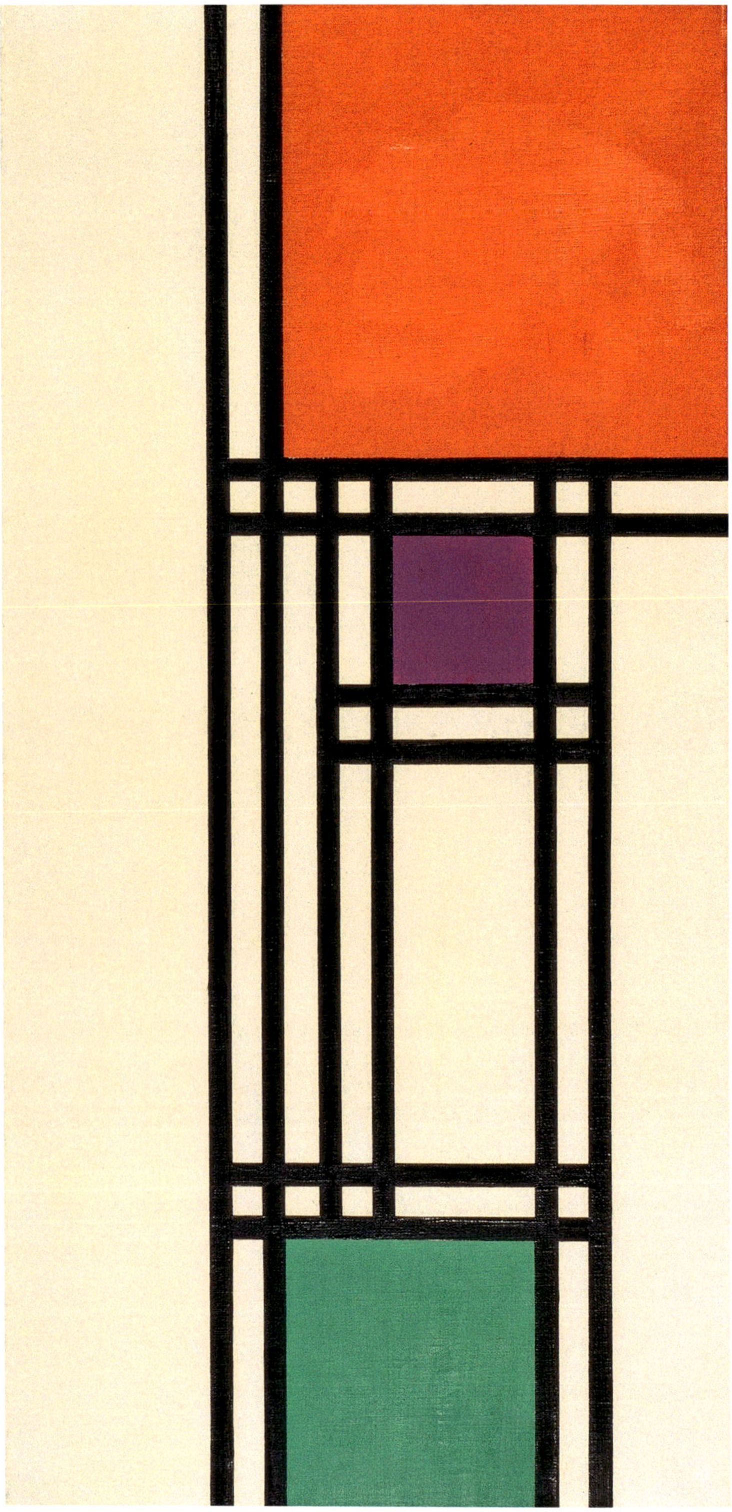

Max Bill
konstruktion mit 3 quadraten, 1942

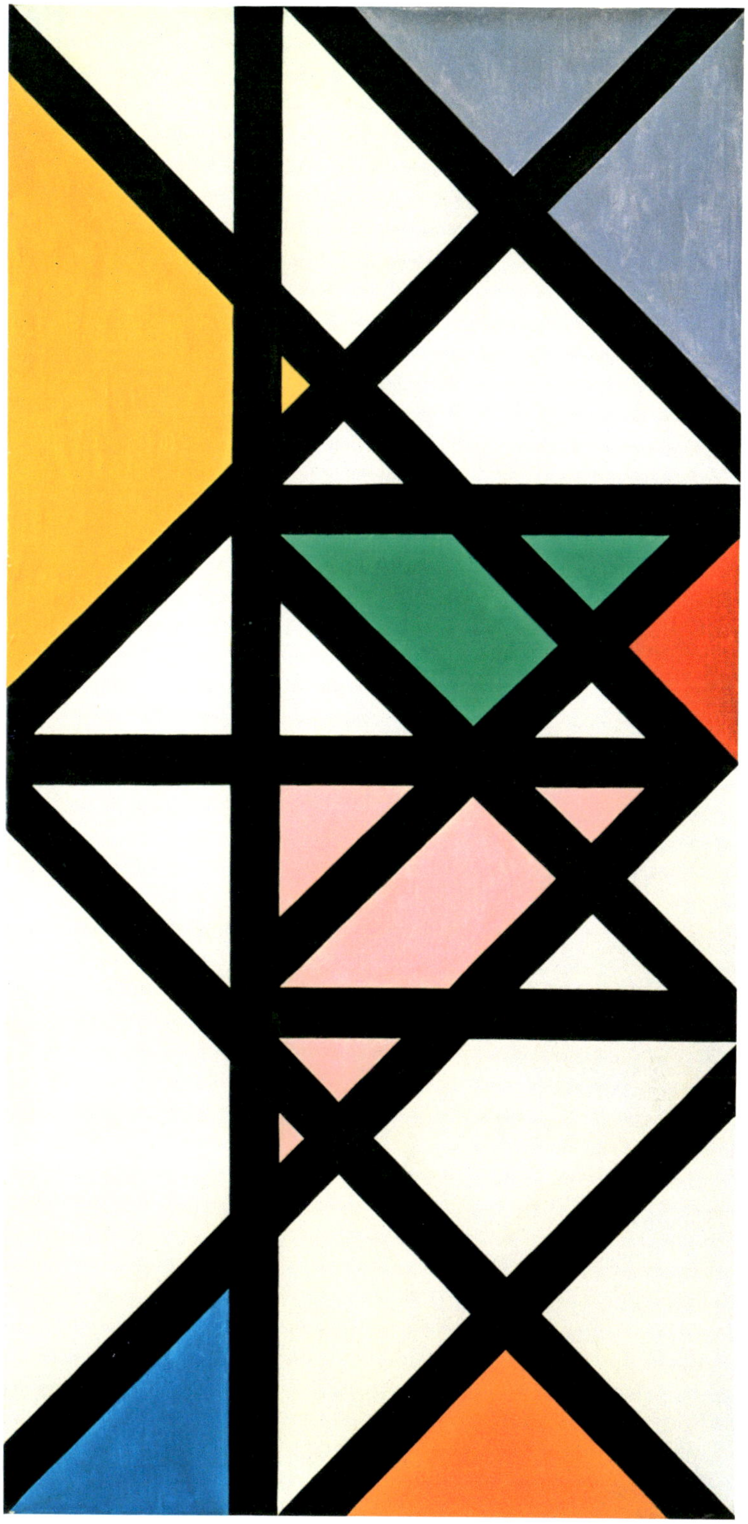

Max Bill
horizontal-vertikal-diagonal-rhythmus, 1942

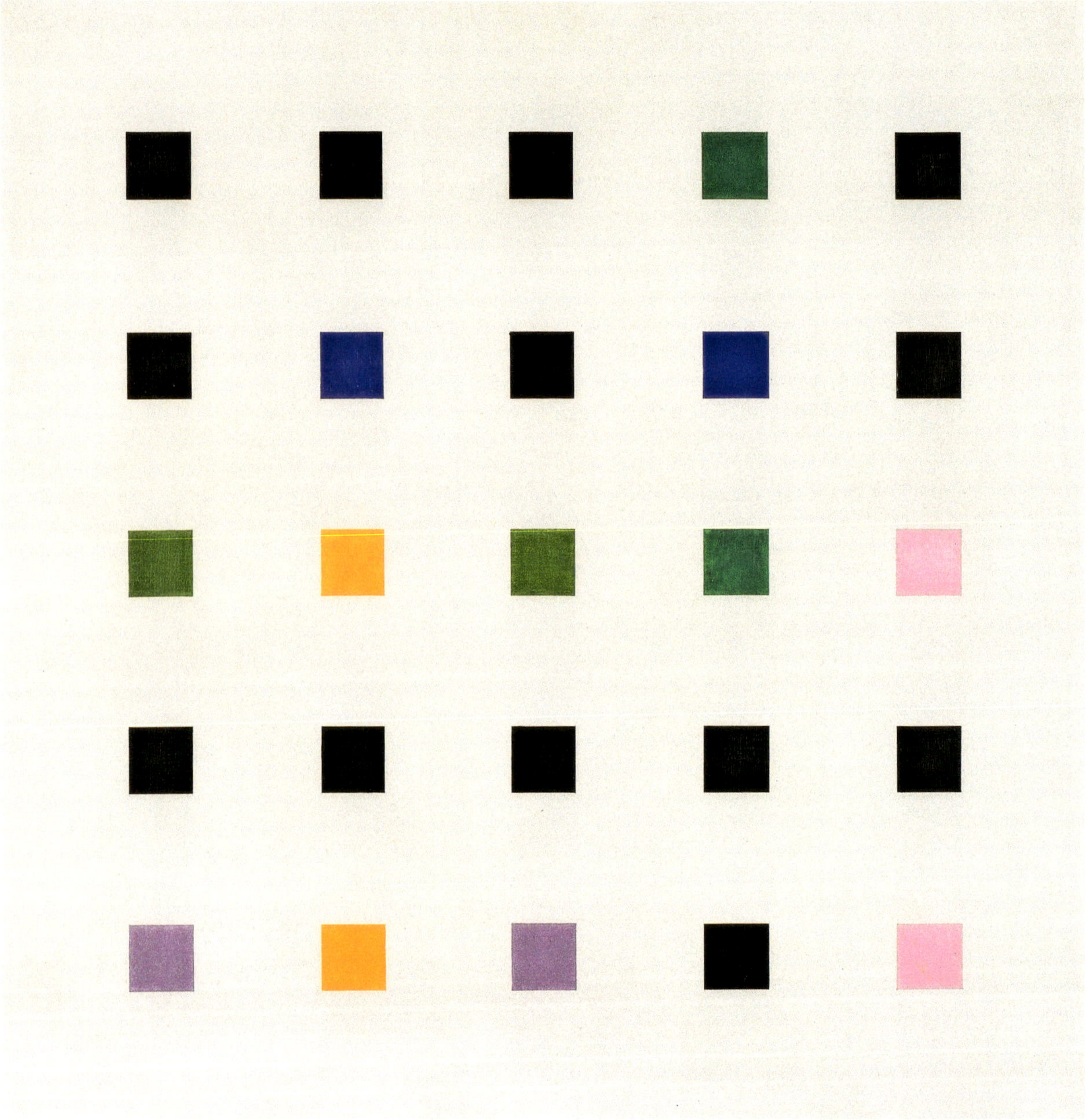

Max Bill
kühles gleichgewicht, 1946

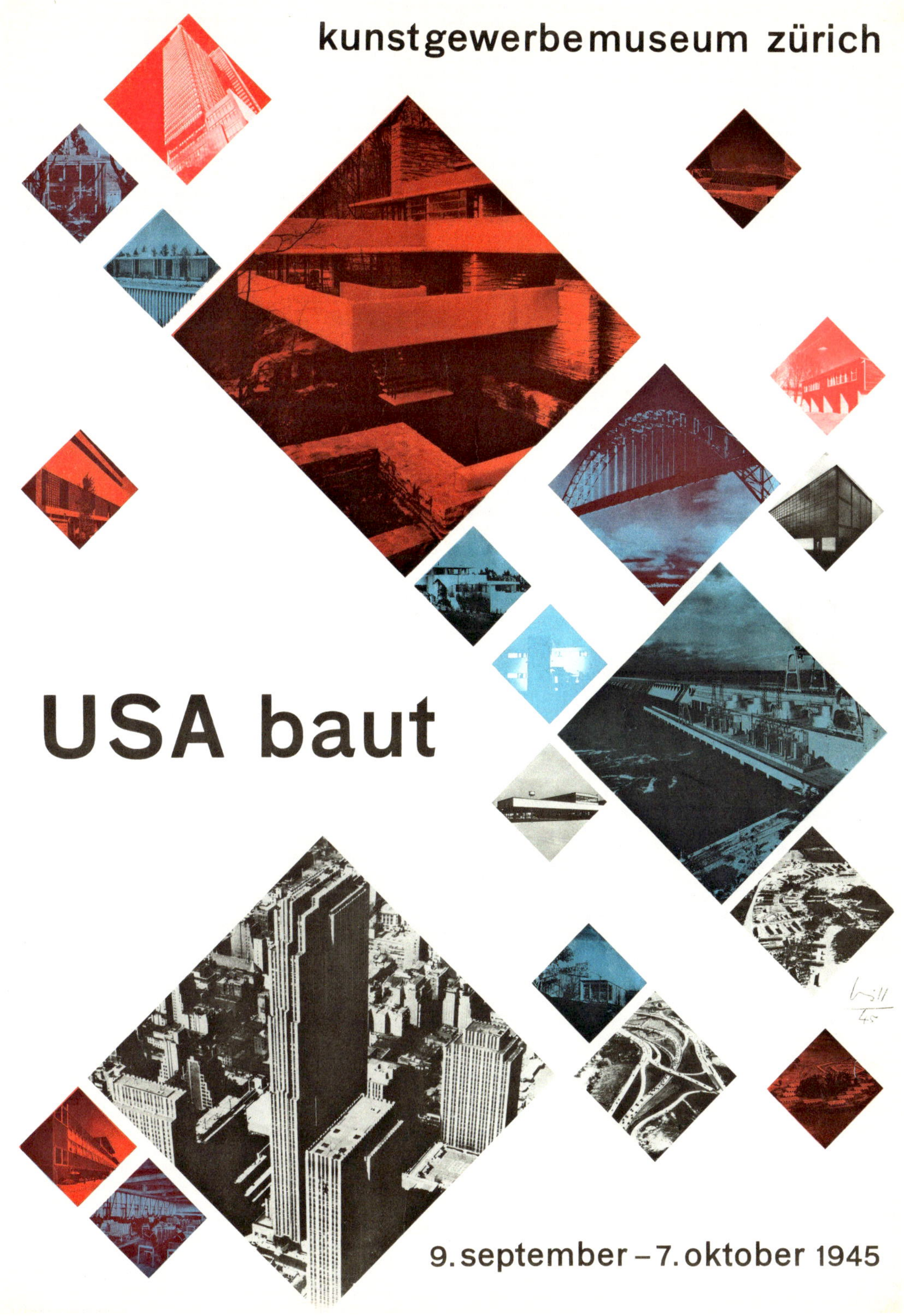

Max Bill
Poster: USA baut—kunstgewerbemuseum zürich, 1945

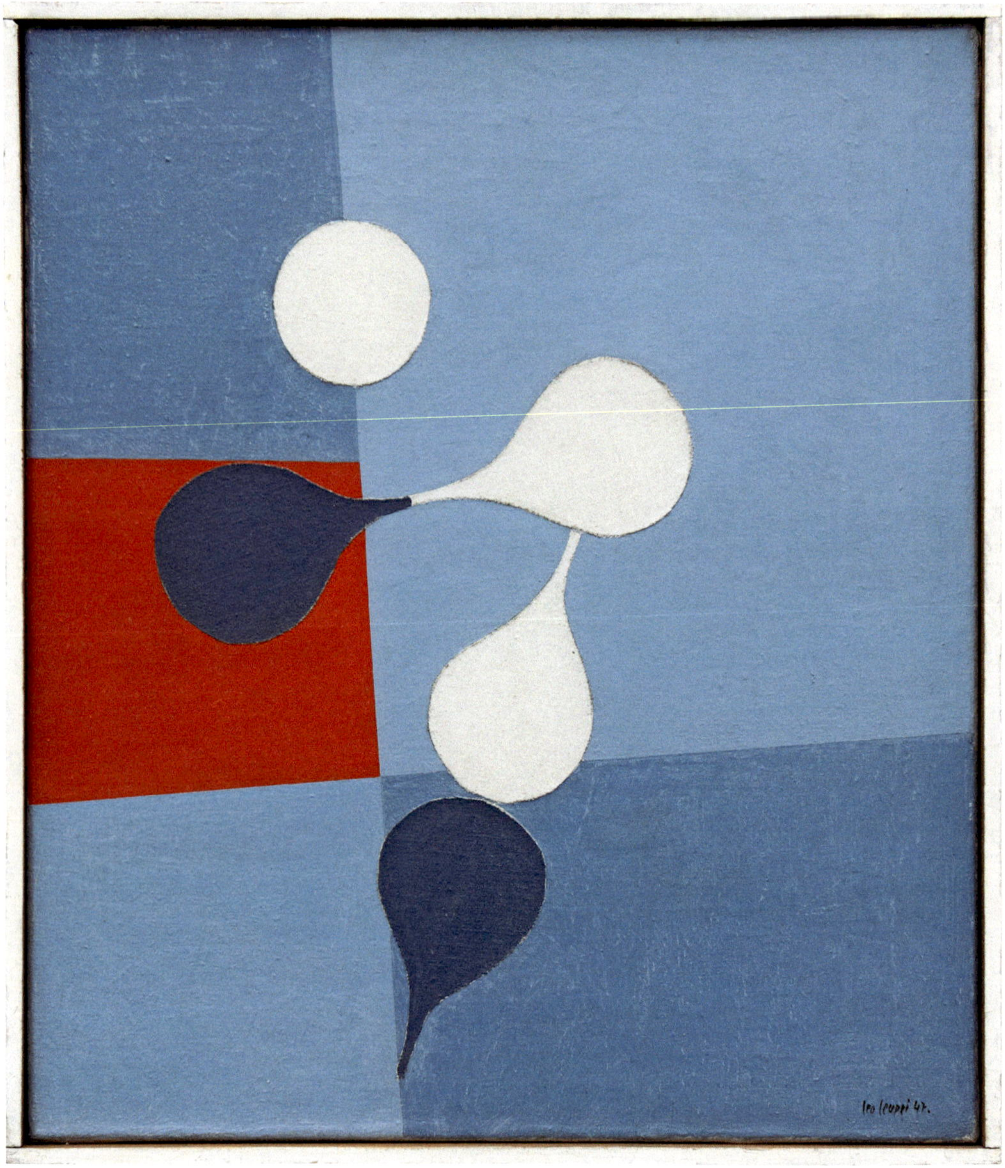

Leo Leuppi
Variation VI, 1947

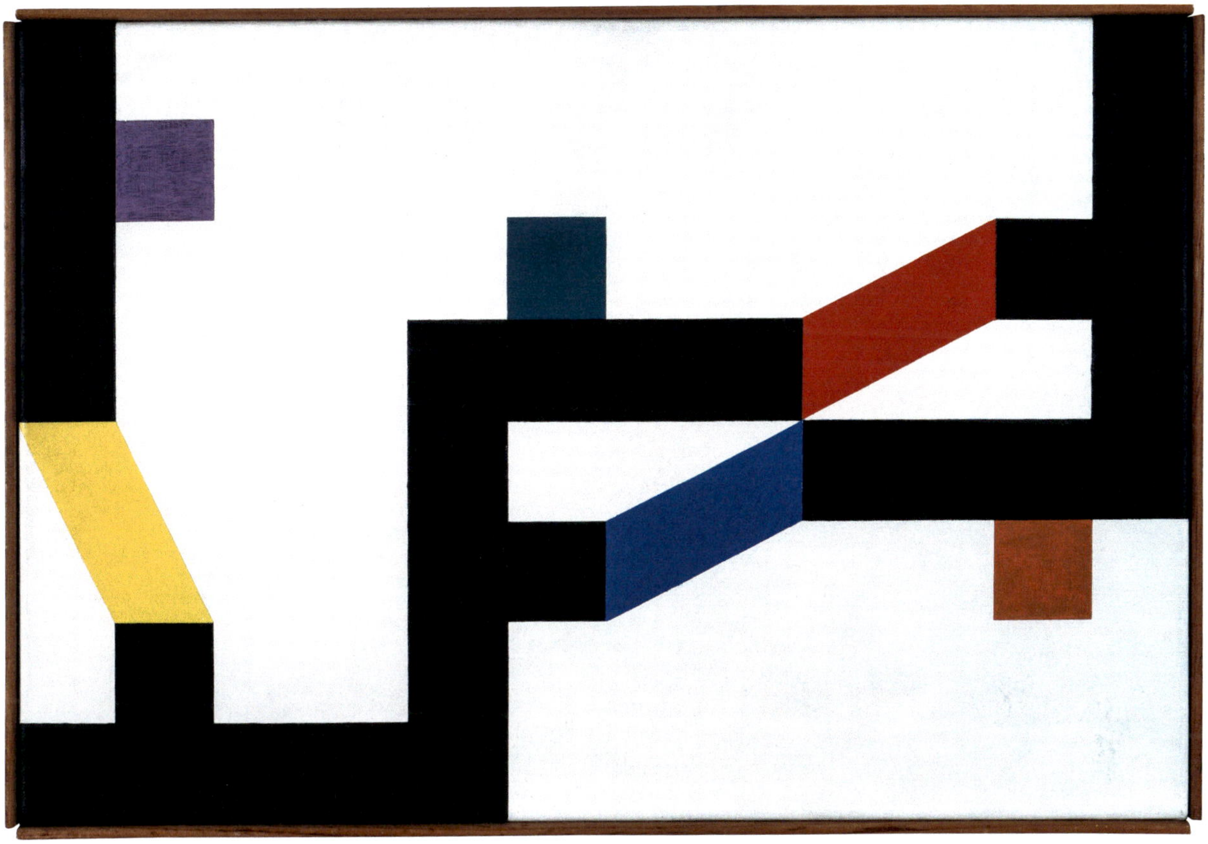

Camille Louis Graeser
Konstruktion mit sechs Farbakzenten, 1949

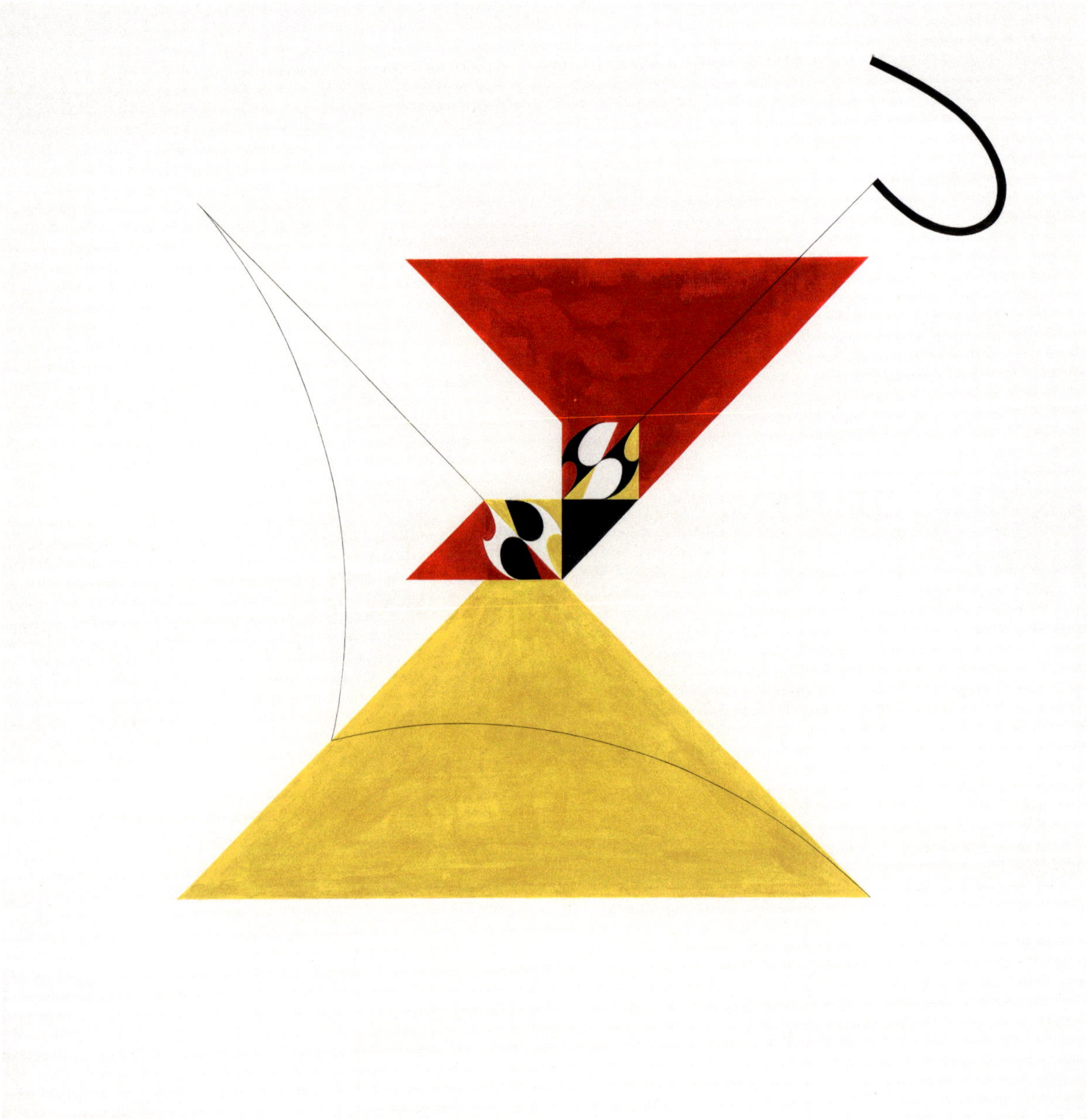

Richard Paul Lohse
Dynamische Konstruktion, 1942

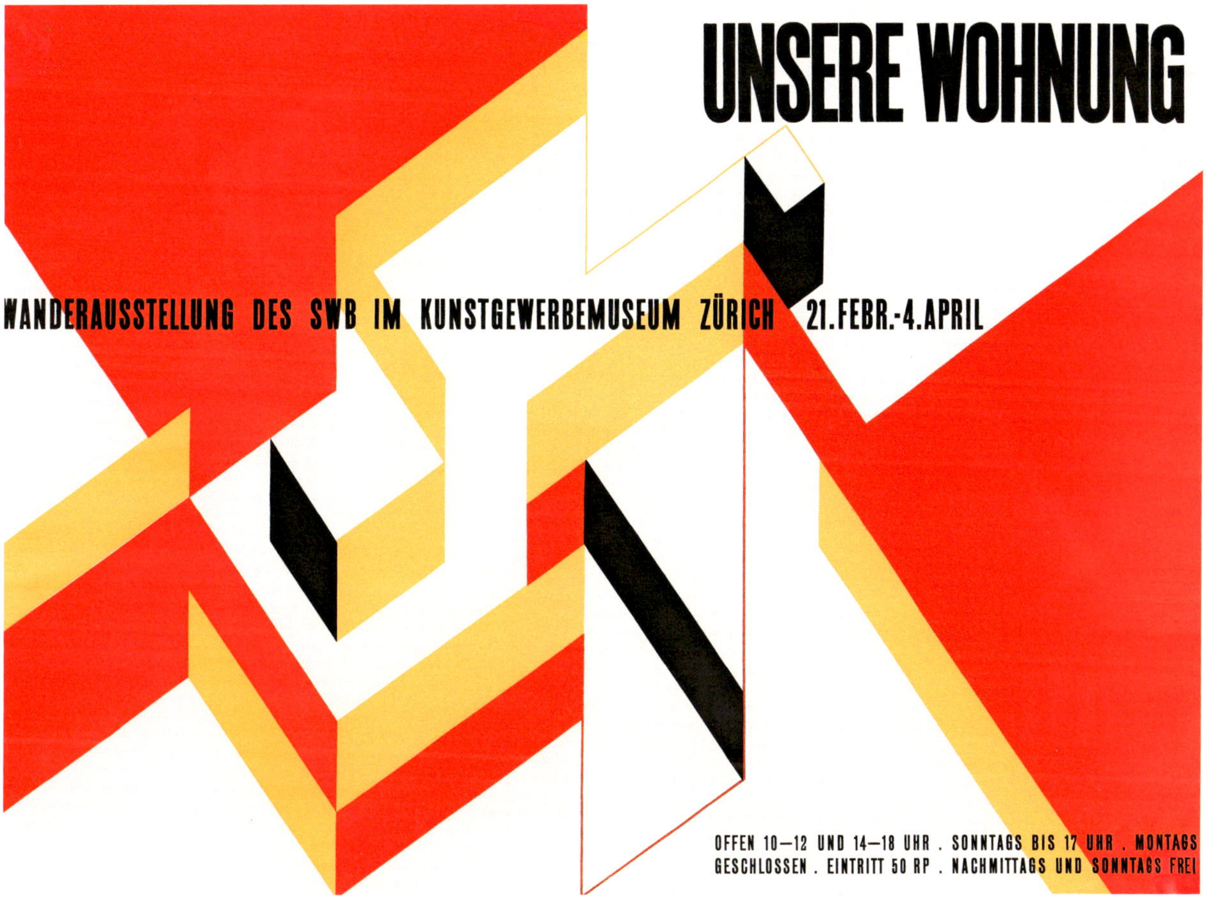

Richard Paul Lohse
Poster: Unsere Wohnung—Wanderausstellung
des SWB im Kunstgewerbemuseum Zürich, 1943

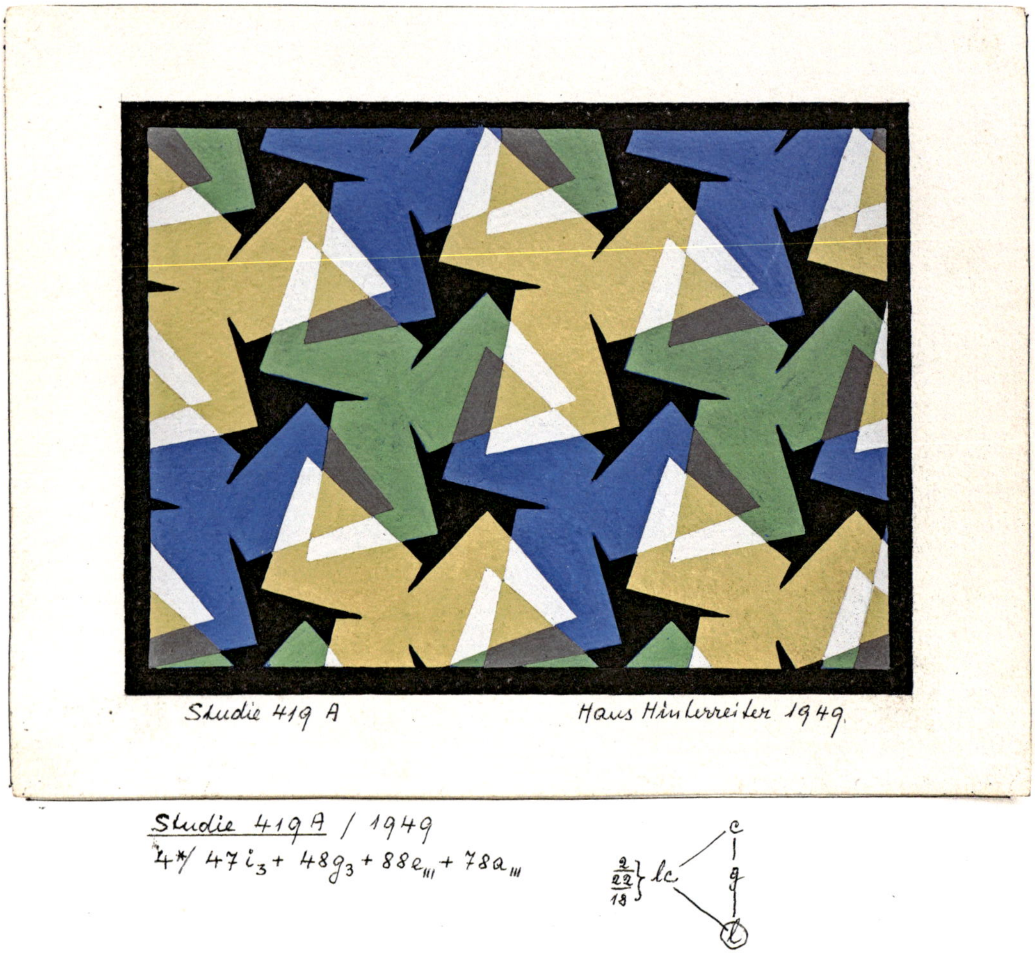

Hans Hinterreiter
Studie 419A, 1949

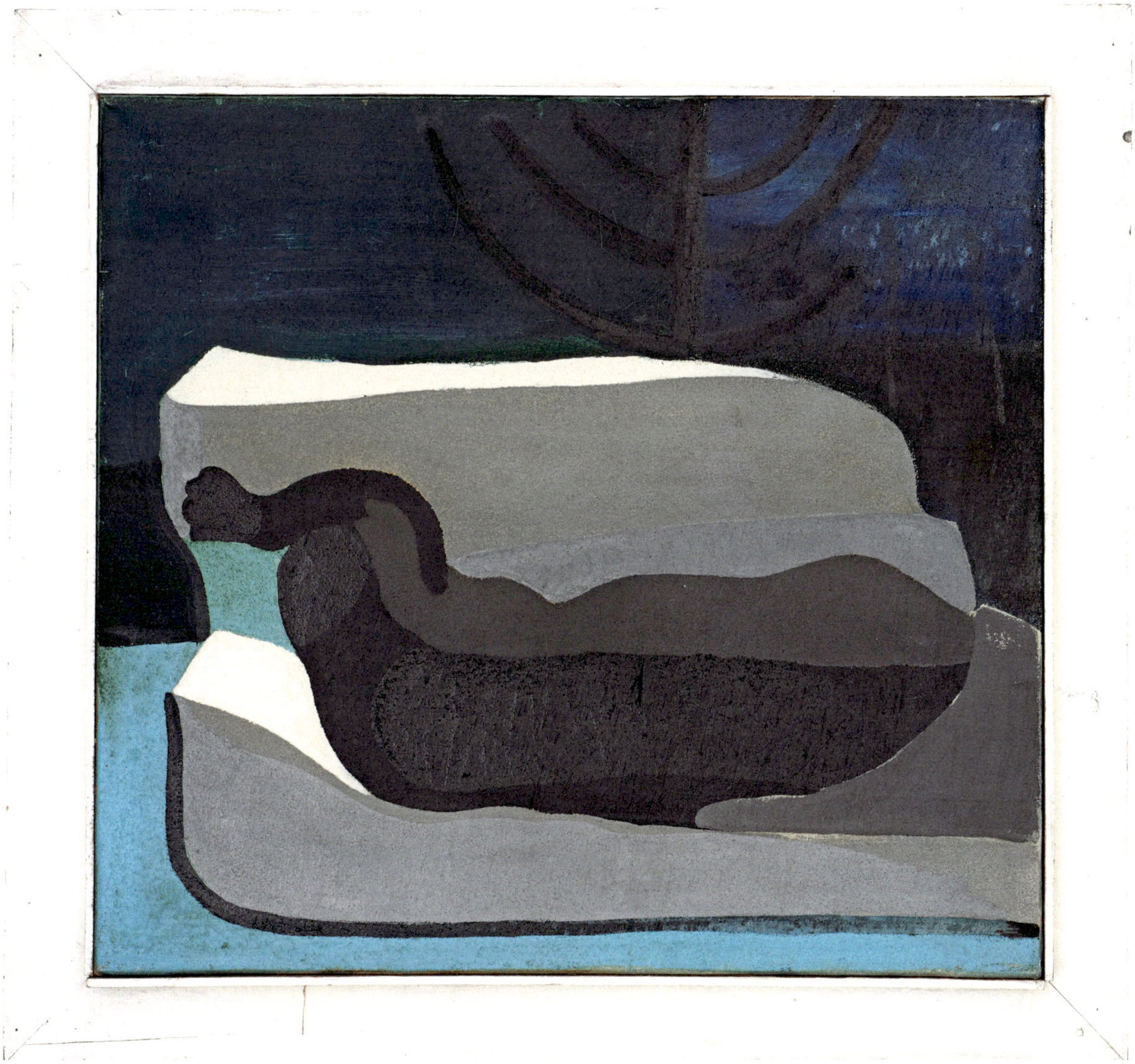

Hanns Robert Welti
Untitled (surrealistic composition with sevenbranched chandelier), n. d.

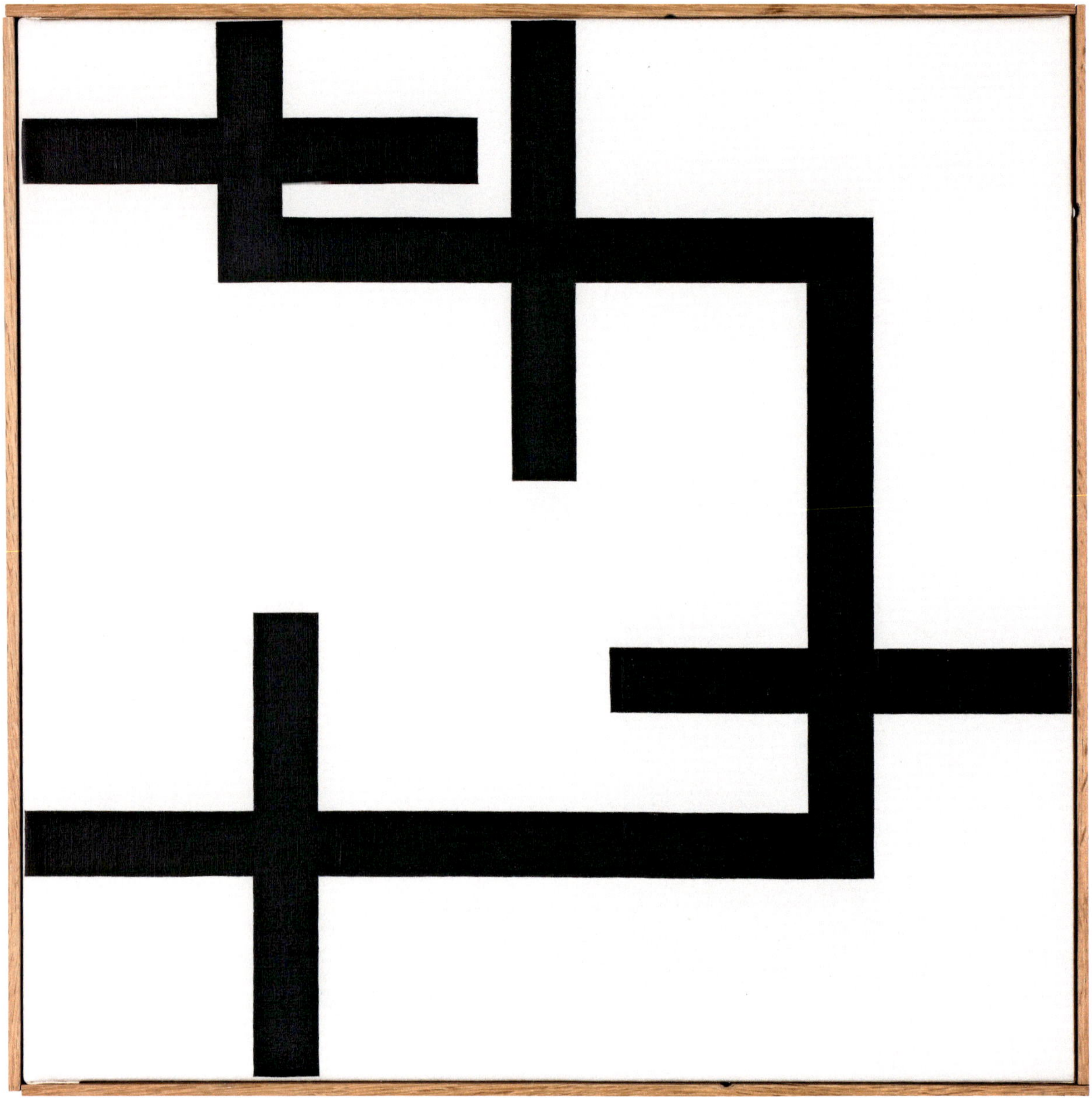

Verena Loewensberg
Untitled, 1947

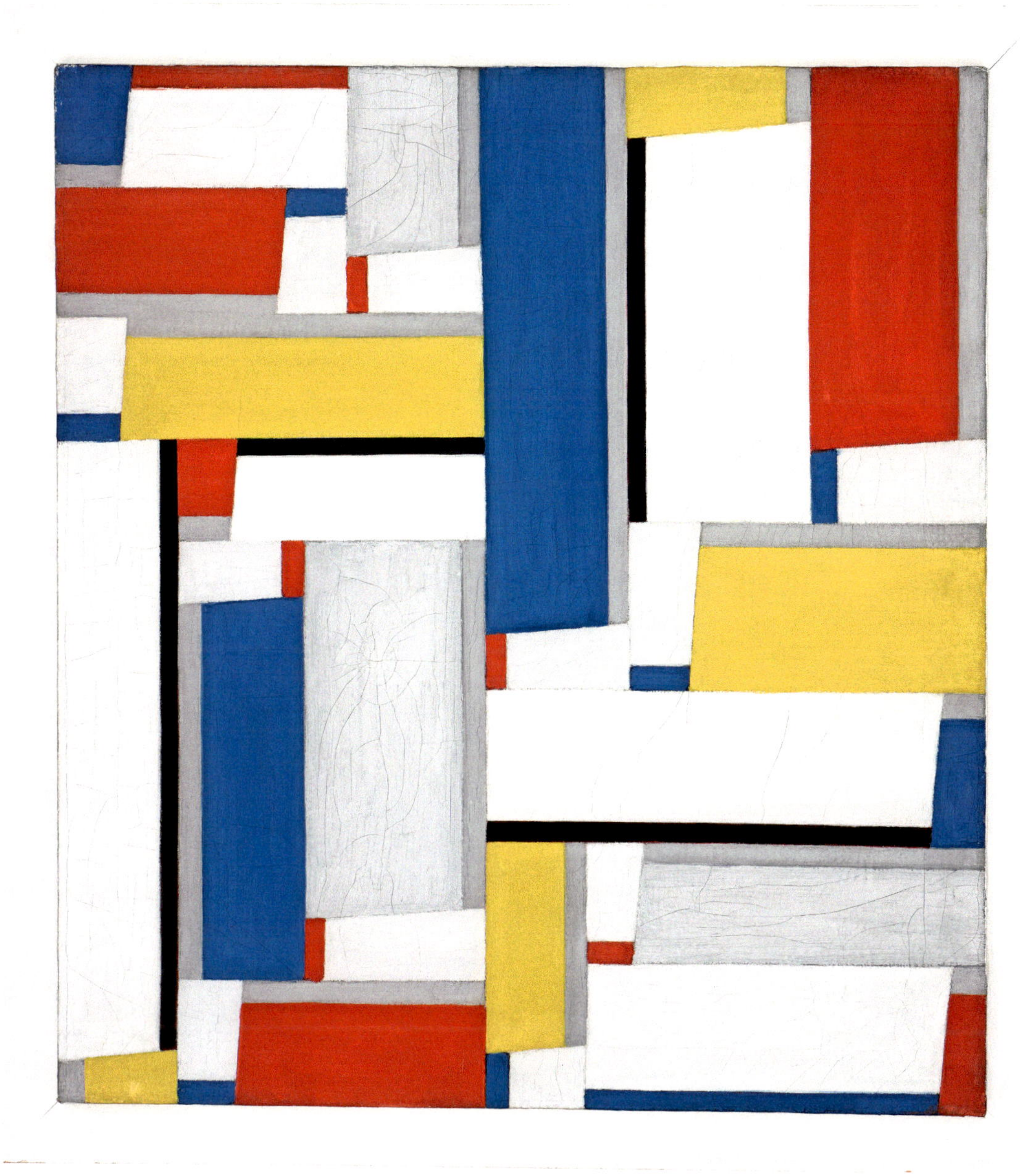

Fritz Glarner
Relational Painting No. 101, 1959

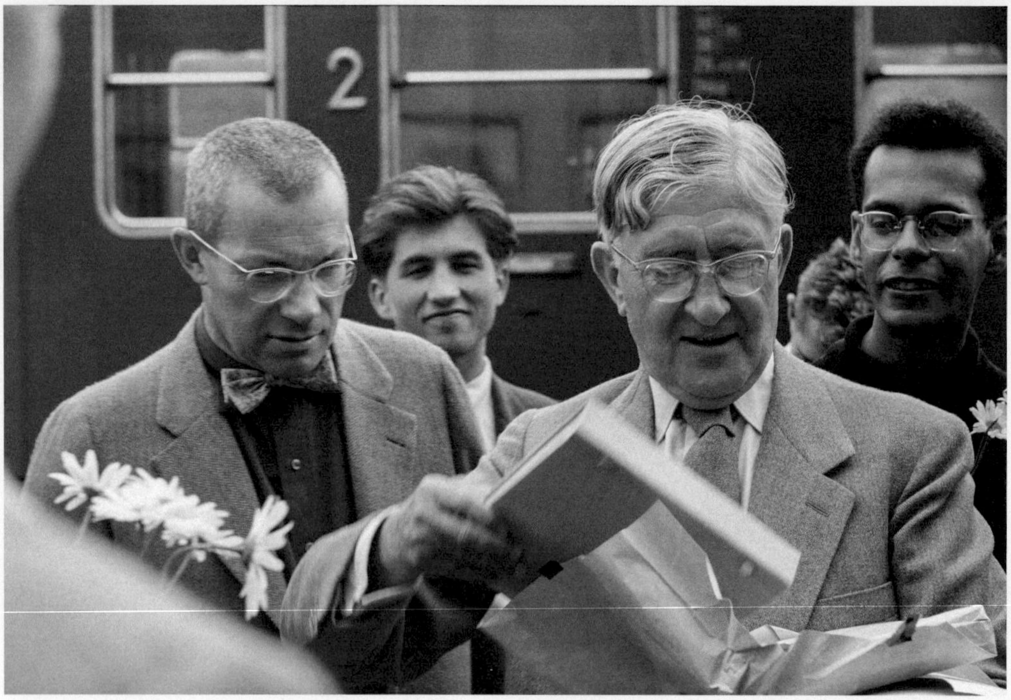

1955

From among the former Bauhaus members, Bill maintained the closest ties with Josef Albers. Bill visited him when he came to the USA, and following Bill's Brazil trip, the two met up in Peru. Albers also traveled to Ulm several times to teach at Bill's school. Following his second basic course, he received a ceremonial farewell at the Ulm train station on August 2, 1955. Students behind Bill and Albers, left: Herbert Lindinger, right: Almir Mavignier.

Copyright: René Spitz, photo: Hans G. Conrad

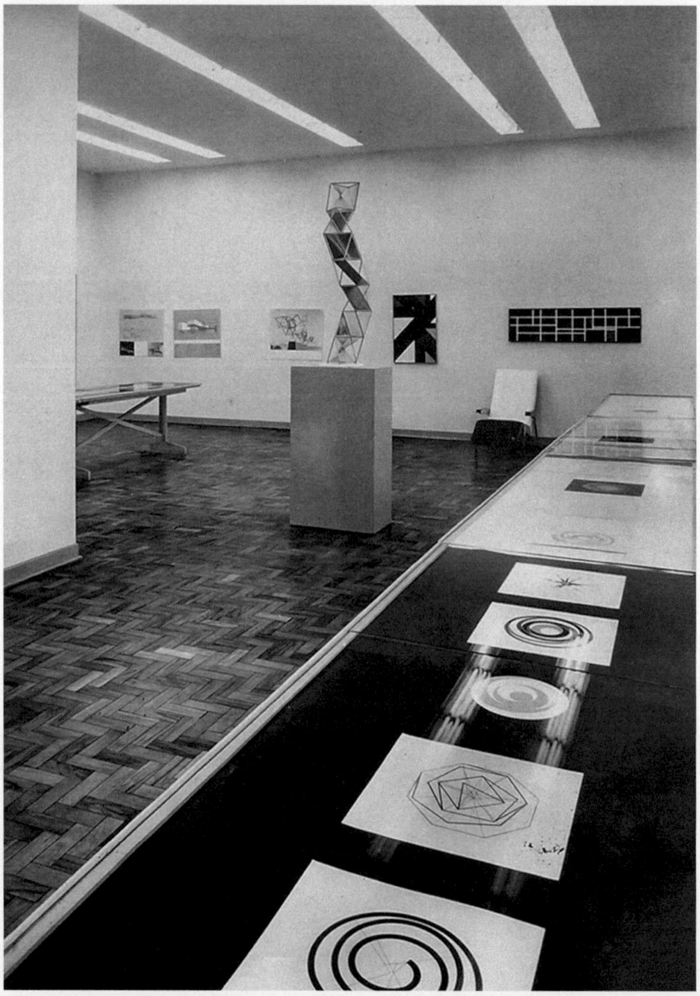

1951

View of the Max Bill exhibition that Pietro Maria Bardi organized in 1951 at the MASP. Aside from paintings, prints, and sculptures, the exhibition also showed Bill as an architect and graphic designer.

Instituto Moreira Salles Collection, photo: Peter Scheier

After World War II Inge Scholl enlisted Max Bill to assist with the founding of the Hochschule für Gestaltung Ulm (HfG), a design school project that had the support of the American high command as the occupying power. Eager to perpetuate the Bauhaus, Bill persuaded several former Bauhaus professors and students to come to Ulm, even though many of them had long since emigrated to the United States. Josef Albers twice visited Ulm as a guest lecturer, while Helene Nonné-Schmidt and Walter Peterhans were on the permanent faculty there. Walter Gropius, as a member of the board of trustees, held an inaugural address, and Johannes Itten, who left the Bauhaus long before Bill's time there, but who in the 1940s hired Bill to teach at Zurich School of Arts and Crafts, was also a visiting lecturer in Ulm.

Thanks to his global network, Bill was able to attract a host of teachers and students from all over the world.[1] Many came from Latin America, where Bill had become a figurehead for many young artists and designers, especially in Brazil and Argentina. This was in part due to the major exhibition of his work organized

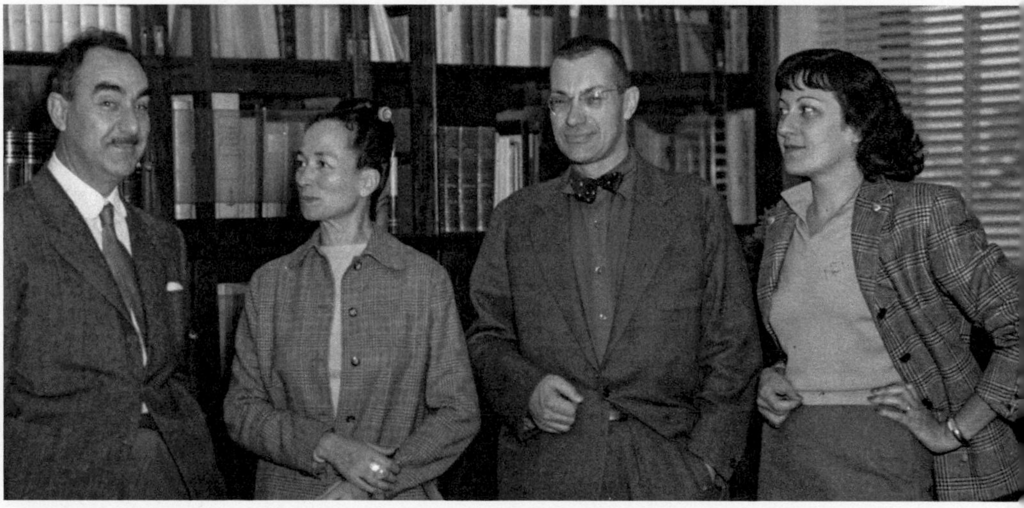

1953

Italian couple Pietro Maria Bardi and Lina Bo Bardi played a central role in bringing contemporary European art to Brazil and fostered the exchange between artists from both continents. Binia and Max Bill (center) visited them in São Paulo in 1953.

MASP Research Center

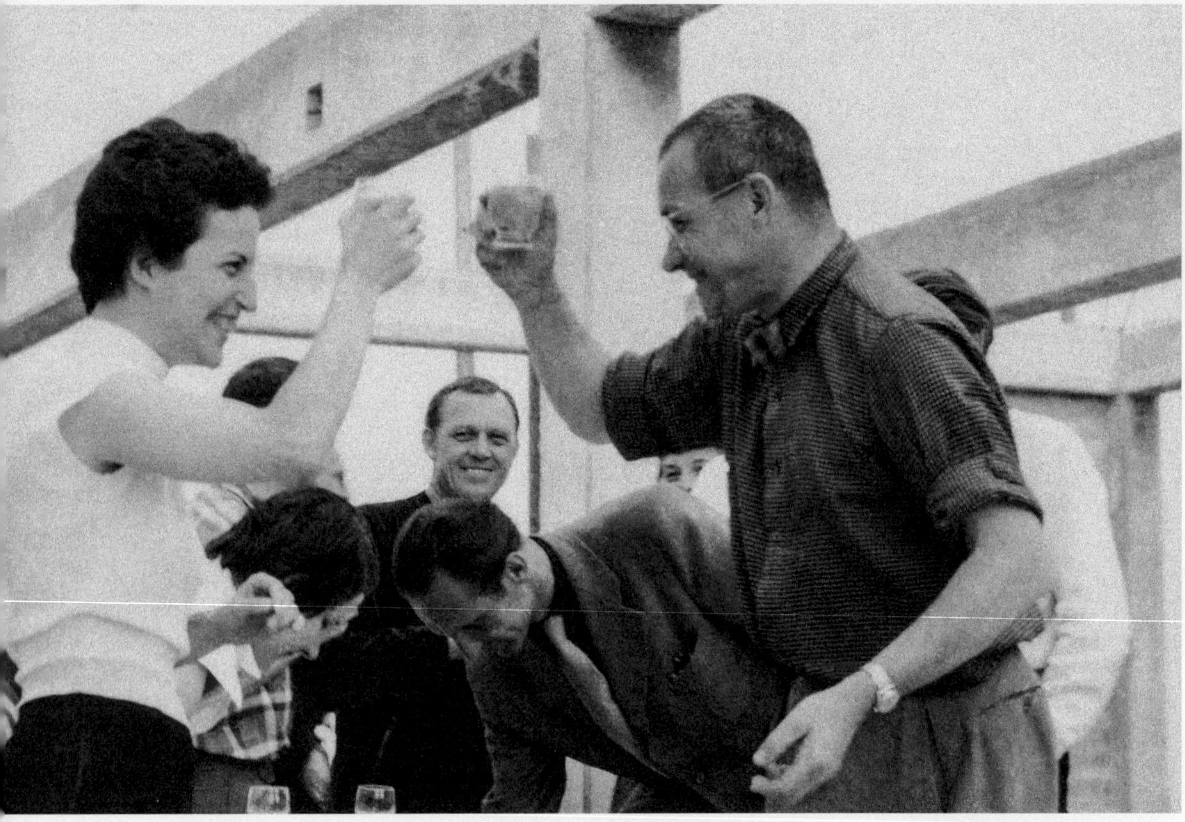

1955

Max Bill and Mary Vieria during the closing celebration for the first basic course in the building shell of the HfG Ulm.

Copyright René Spitz, photo: Hans G. Conrad

by Pietro Maria Bardi at the Museu de Arte de São Paulo (MASP) in 1951, and in part a consequence of Bill's sculpture *dreiteilige einheit*, which won the first prize at the first São Paulo Art Biennial that same year. Bill traveled to Brazil in 1953 and asked Bardi to nominate some promising young artists whom he might invite to Ulm as students. Geraldo de Barros declined, but asked that his place be taken by Alexandre Wollner, who had assisted on the installation of Bill's exhibition in 1951.

Another student who came to Bill through the MASP show was Mary Vieira, who wrote to him directly. On receiving her letter, Bill invited her to Zurich, where she worked initially in his architect's office while waiting to join the Ulm School of Design's first intake. Bill would later exhibit her sculpture *Polyvolume : surface multidéveloppable* at Expo 1964 in Lausanne. Almir Mavignier, who was studying painting in Paris at the time, also had hopes of studying under Bill, though it was only at Vieira's urging that he was accepted, Bill having argued that the HfG was not the right place for a painter. The sisters Frauke and Elke Koch-Weser were also among the students from Brazil.

In Argentina it was Tomás Maldonado and Romero Brest who did most to spread Bill's theories and work. Maldonado had visited Bill in Zurich in 1948 and later became one of the most influential figures at the Ulm School of Design. Bill's texts met with an enthusiastic response in Buenos Aires and Maldonado sent Bill photos of the works of various Argentinian artists, among which it was those of Maldonado himself and of Alfredo Hlito, Lidy Prati, and Enio Iommi that interested Bill the most.[2] Prati met Max Bill in 1952 while traveling through Italy, Switzerland, and France. Like Vieira and Mário Pedrosa, she probably visited Georges Vantongerloo in his studio in Paris following Bill's recommendation.[3]

1 *alex wollner brasil. design visual*, cat. Frankfurt a. M.: Museum Angewandte Kunst 2013/14, ed. by Klaus Klemp, Julia Koch and Matthias Wagner K, Tübingen 2013, pp. 29 f., 65.

2 Cf. García 2019, pp. 120 f., 126.

3 Lidy Prati's travels through Europe are mentioned in *Nueva Visión: Revista de cultura visual*, no. 5 (1954), p. 45. I'm grateful to Angela Thomas Schmid for providing this information as well as telling me that Bill habitually recommended visiting Vantongerloo to his guests.

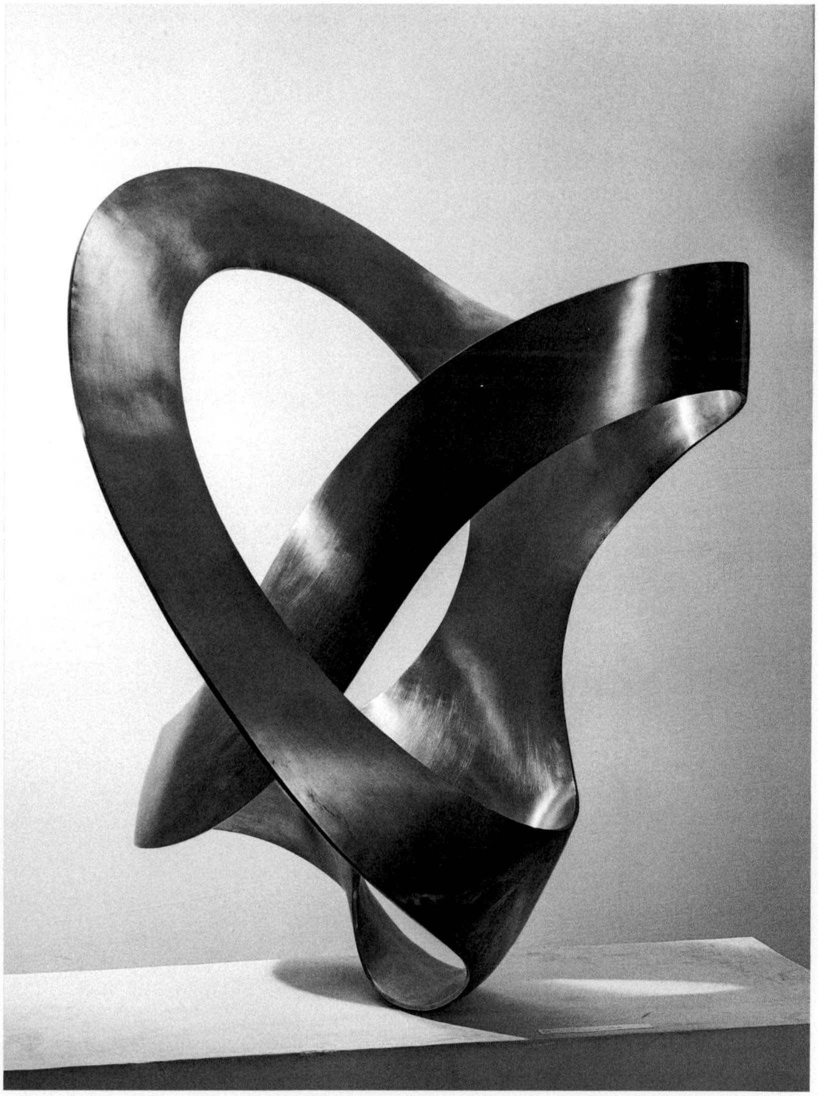

1951

Also in 1951, Max Bill won the first prize for sculpture at the First Biennial of Saõ Paulo with his 1947/48 piece *dreiteilige einheit*. While the exhibition at the MASP itself had attracted little attention, the award earned him greater renown in Brazil.

Instituto Moreira Salles Collection, photo: Hans Günter Flieg

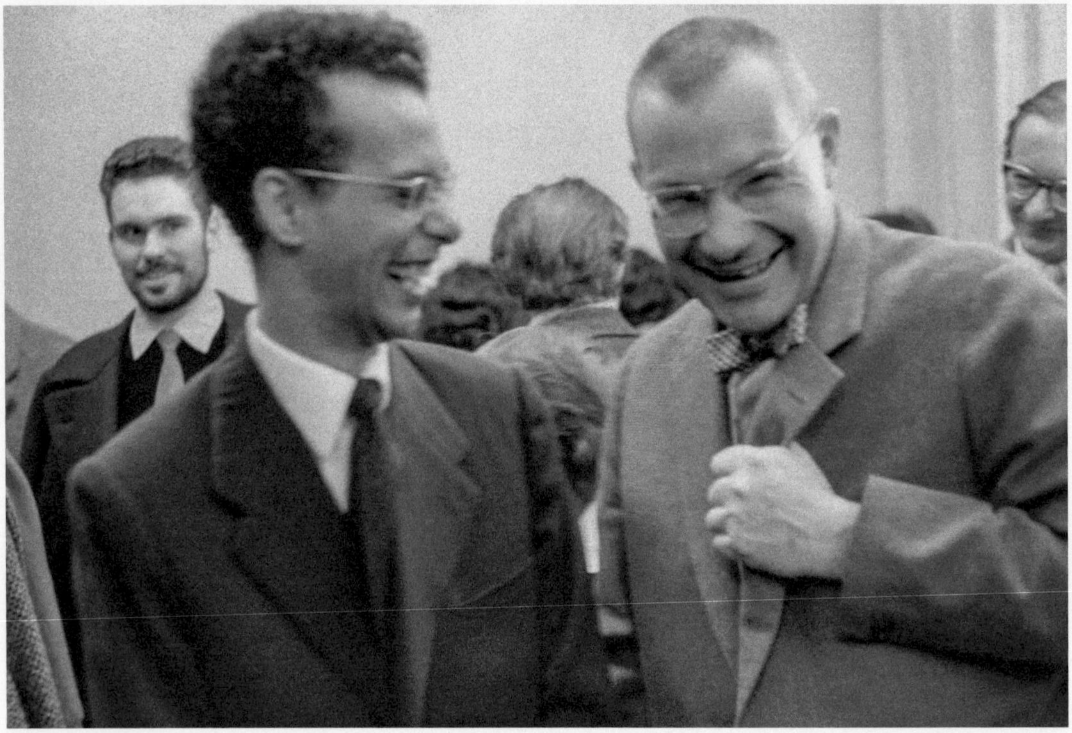

1955

Max Bill and Almir Mavignier during the opening of Bill's exhibition at the Museum Ulm.

Copyright: René Spitz,
photo: Hans G. Conrad

1956

Max Bill and Tomás Maldonado kept up a lively exchange of letters after meeting in 1948, and Bill invited him to Ulm as a lecturer. Due to their differing views on the direction of the school, their relationship subsequently cooled.

Copyright: René Spitz,
photo: Hans G. Conrad

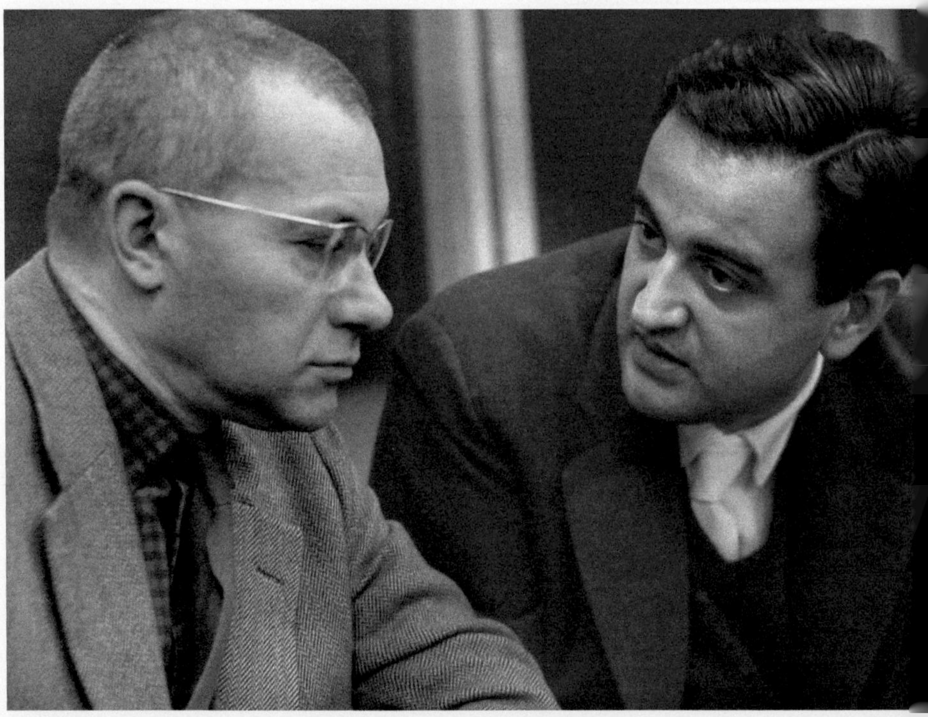

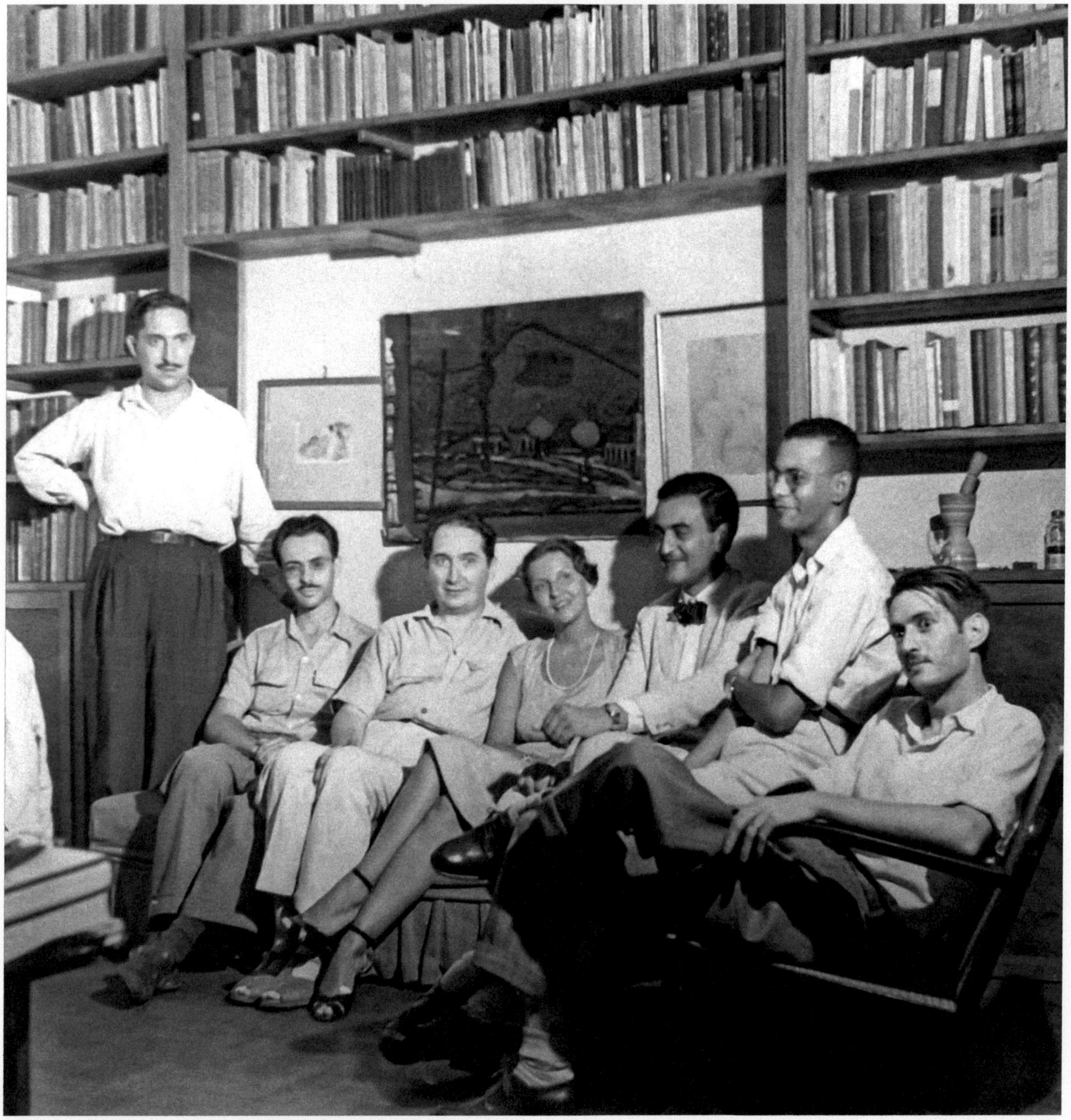

1951

People meeting at Mário Pedrosa's home in 1951; from left to right: Geraldo de Barros, Abraham Palatnik, Mário Pedrosa, Lidy Prati, Tomás Maldonado, Almir Mavignier, and Ivan Serpa.

Lidy Prati archive. Courtesy of the Polastri Prati family

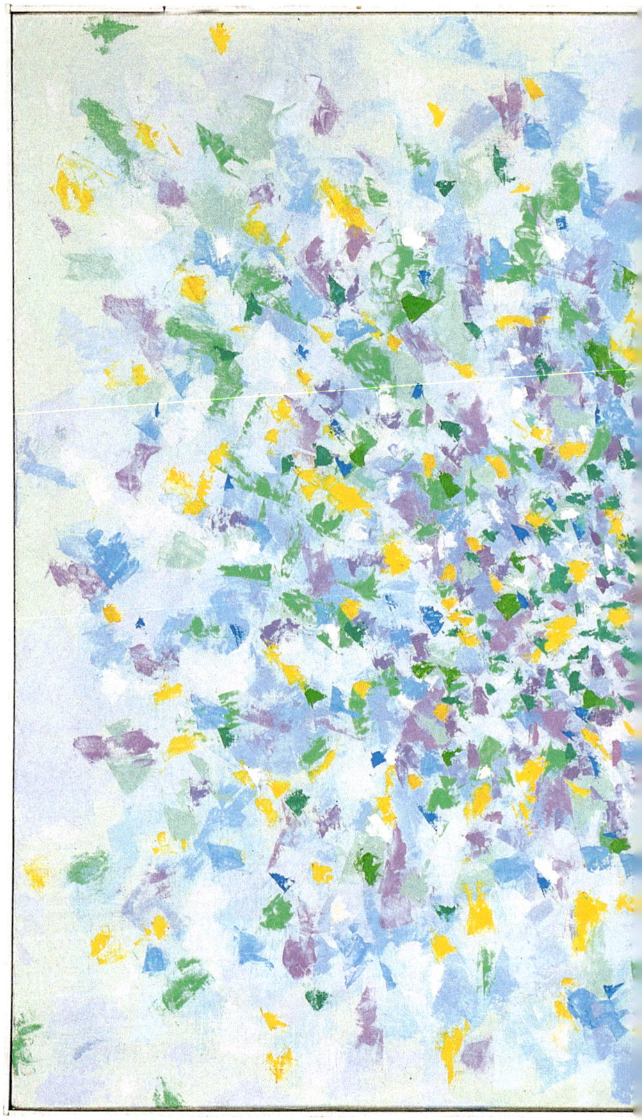

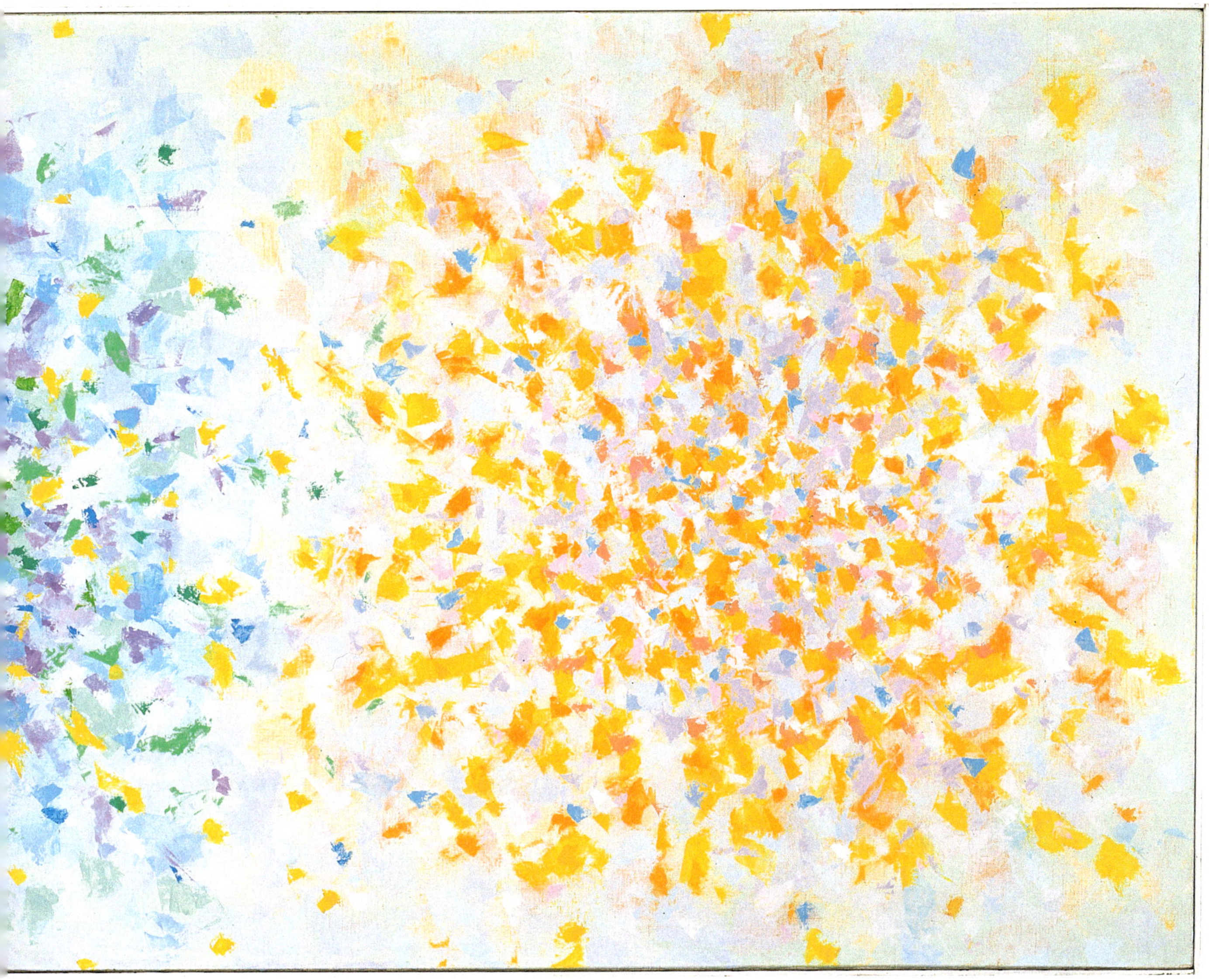

Max Bill
zwei zentren (grün + orange), 1956

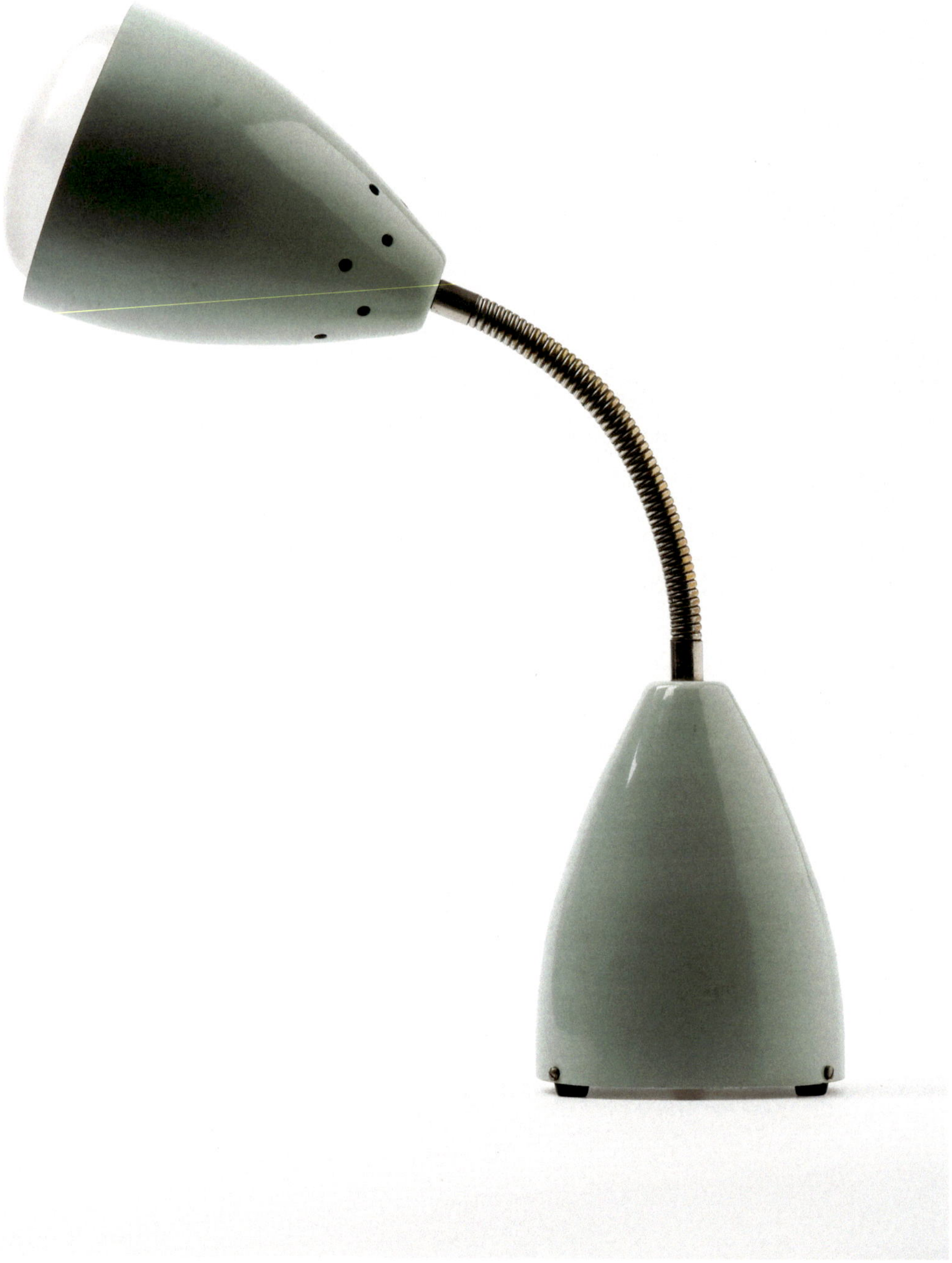

Max Bill
Höhensonne, design: 1951

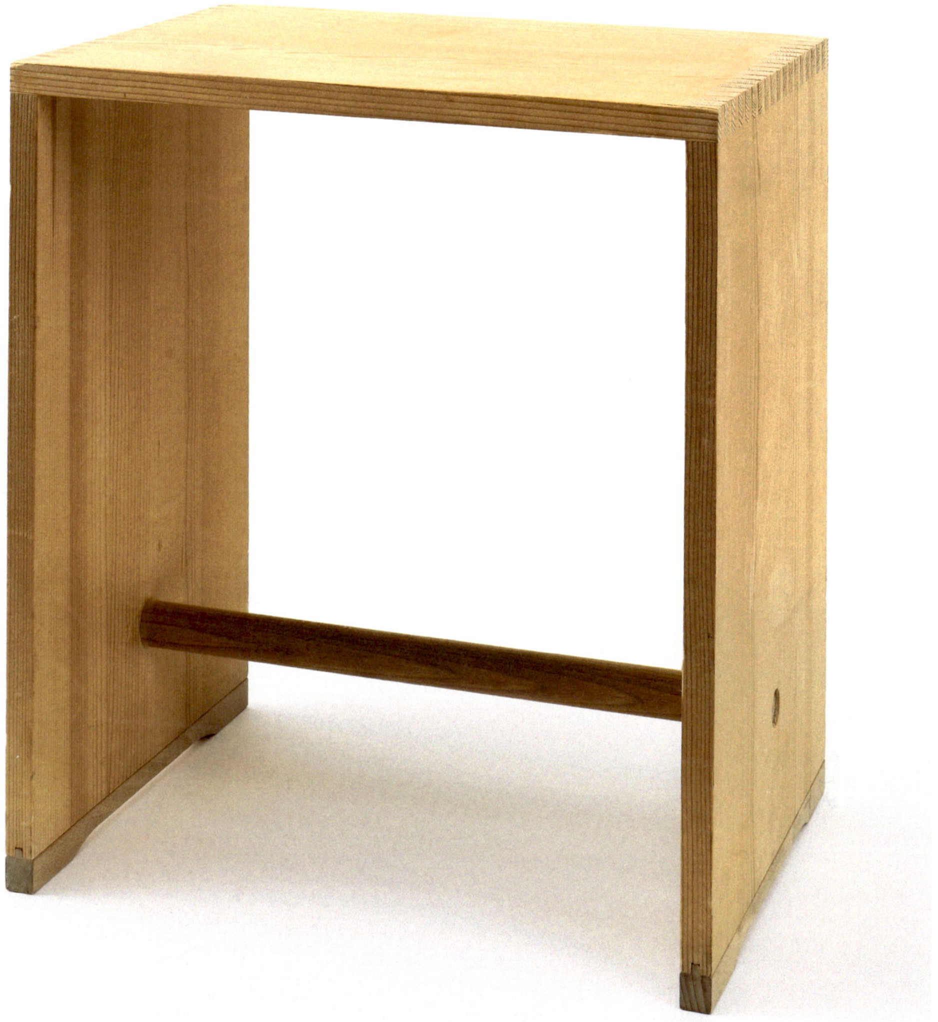

Max Bill and Hans Gugelot
Ulmer Hocker, 1954

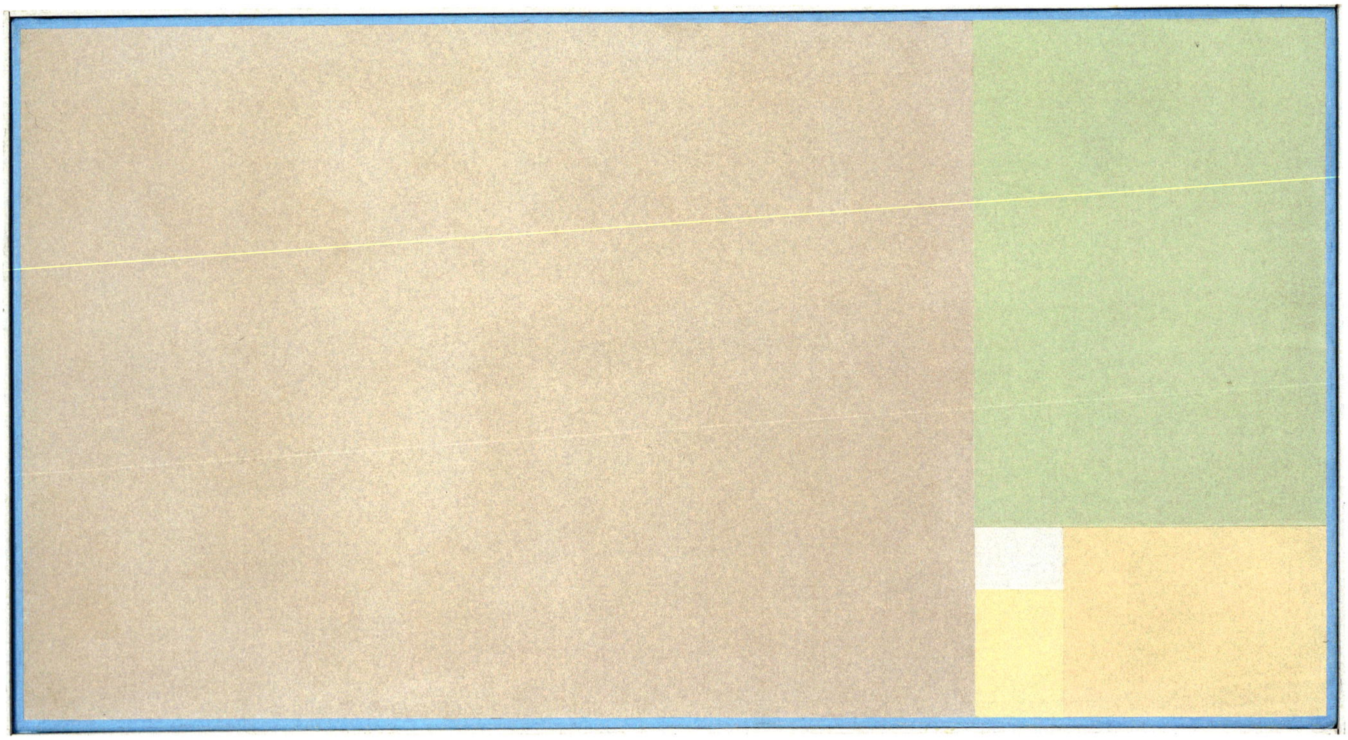

Max Bill
blau gefasst, 1956

Max Bill
22, 1953

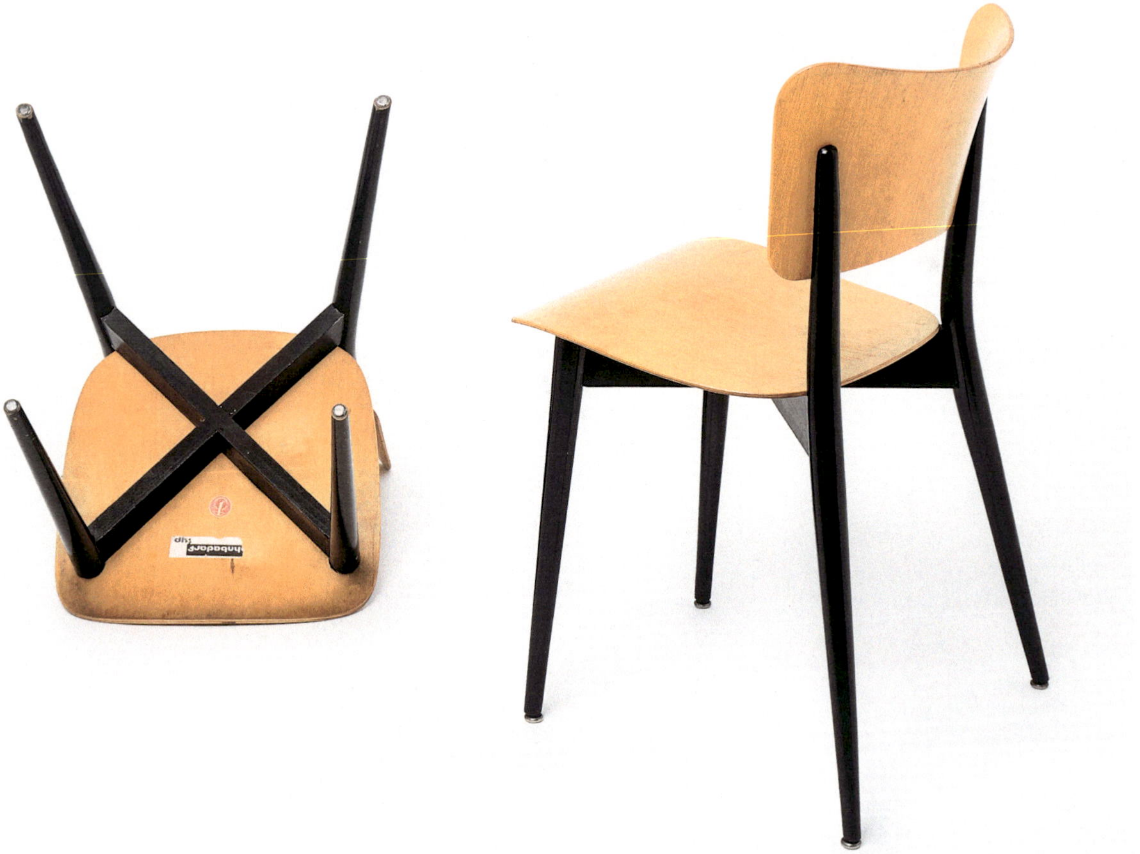

Max Bill
Kreuzzargenstuhl, design: 1951

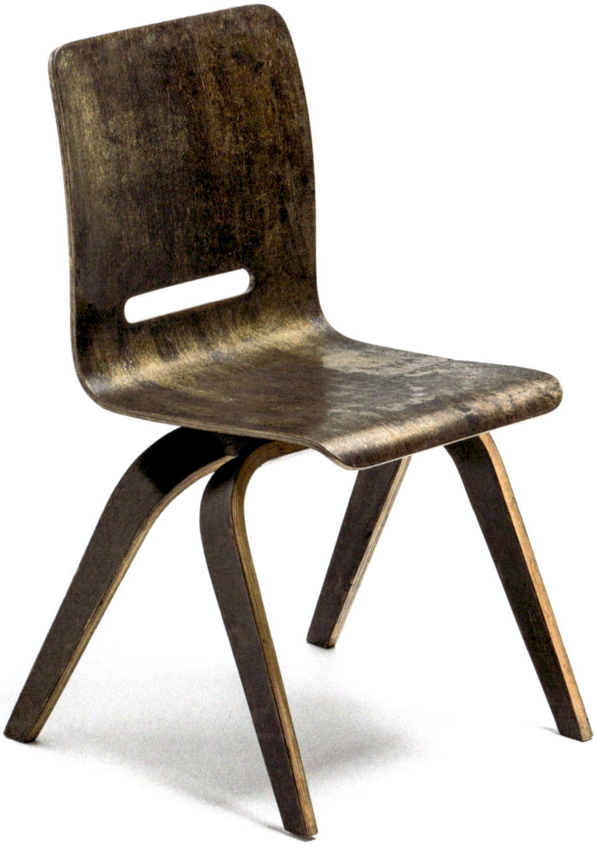

Max Bill
Chair for the Swiss pavilion, Milan Triennale, 1951,
design: 1951

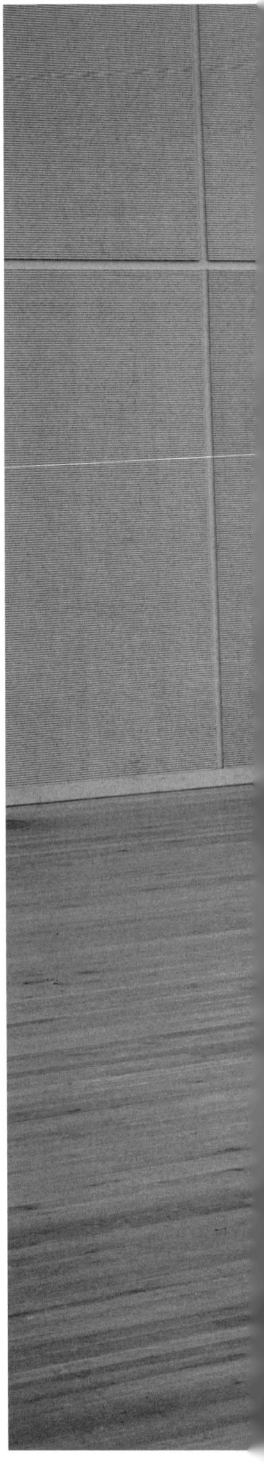

Max Bill
fläche im raum durch eine linie begrenzt, c. 1952/1994

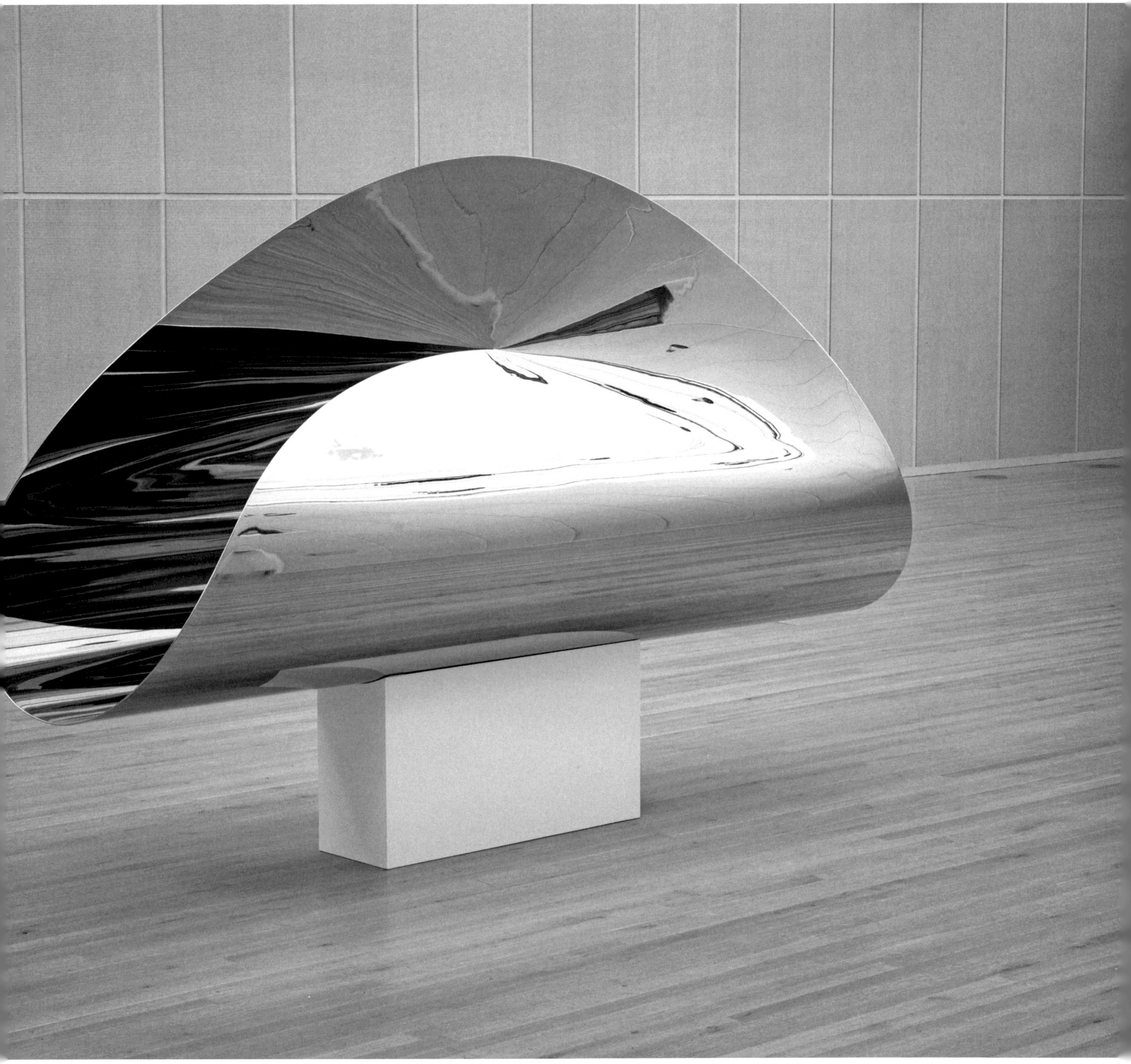

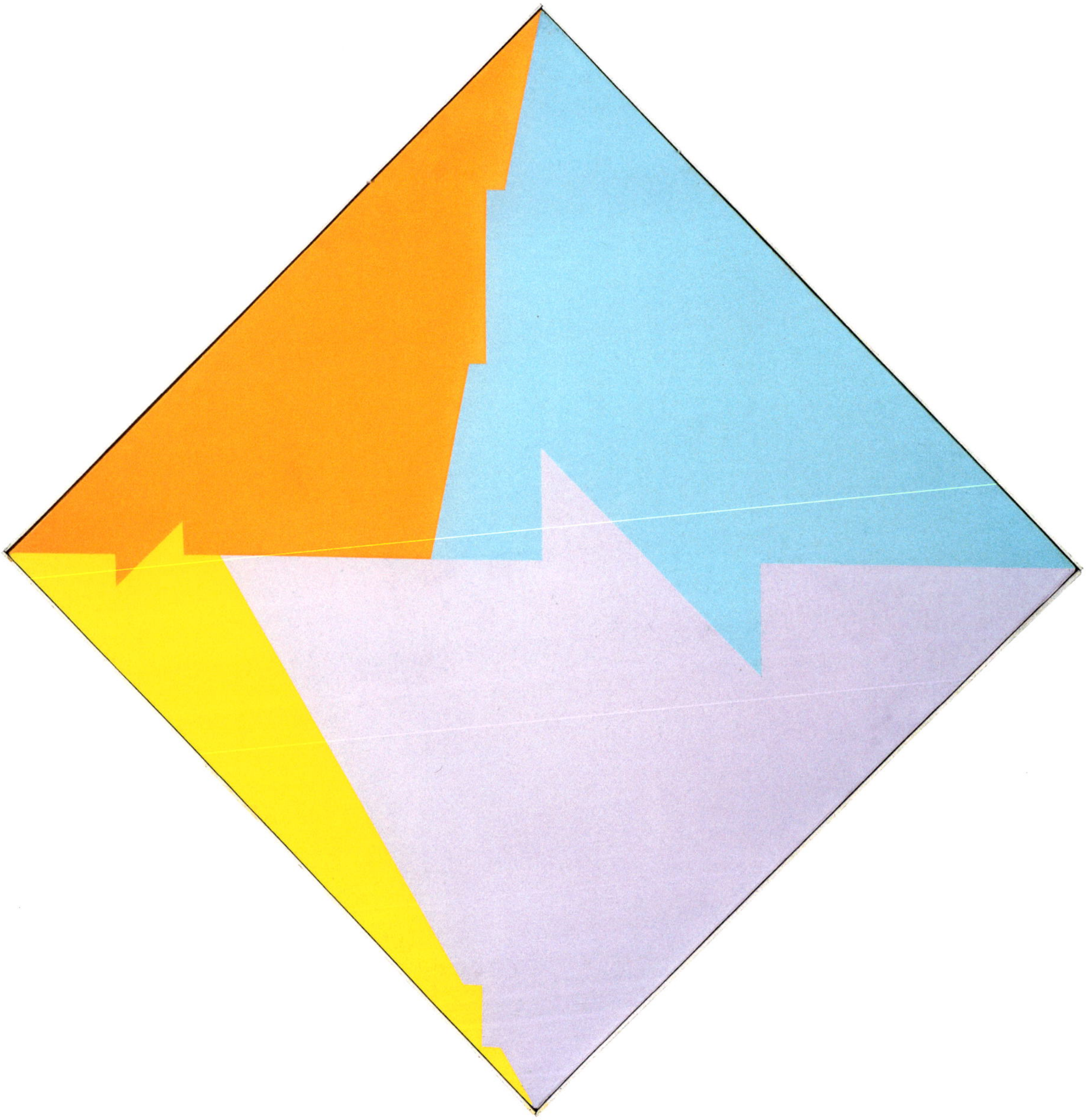

Max Bill
verteilung 4 : 3 : 2 : 1, 1960

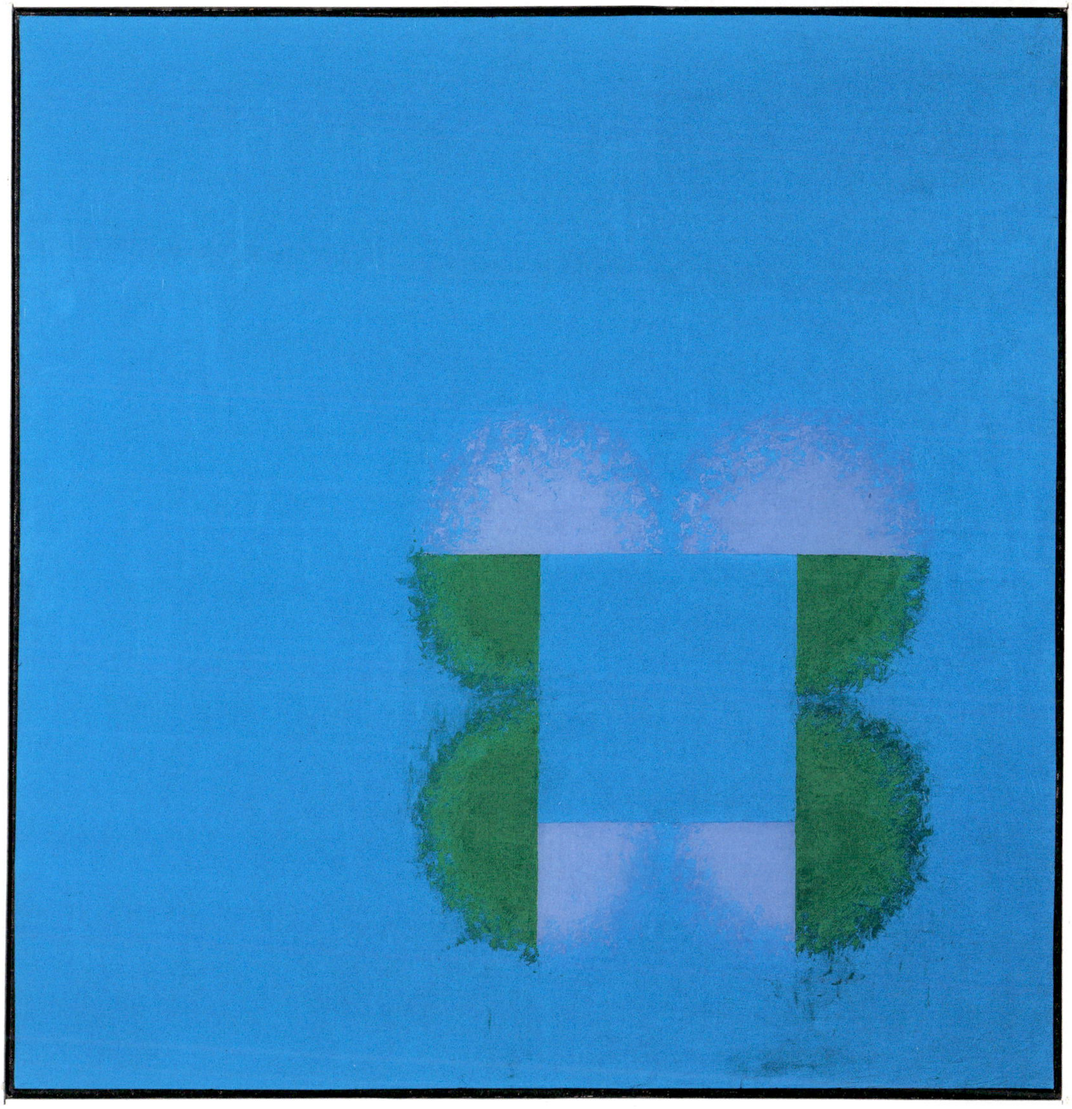

Max Bill
quadrat im quadrat, 1960

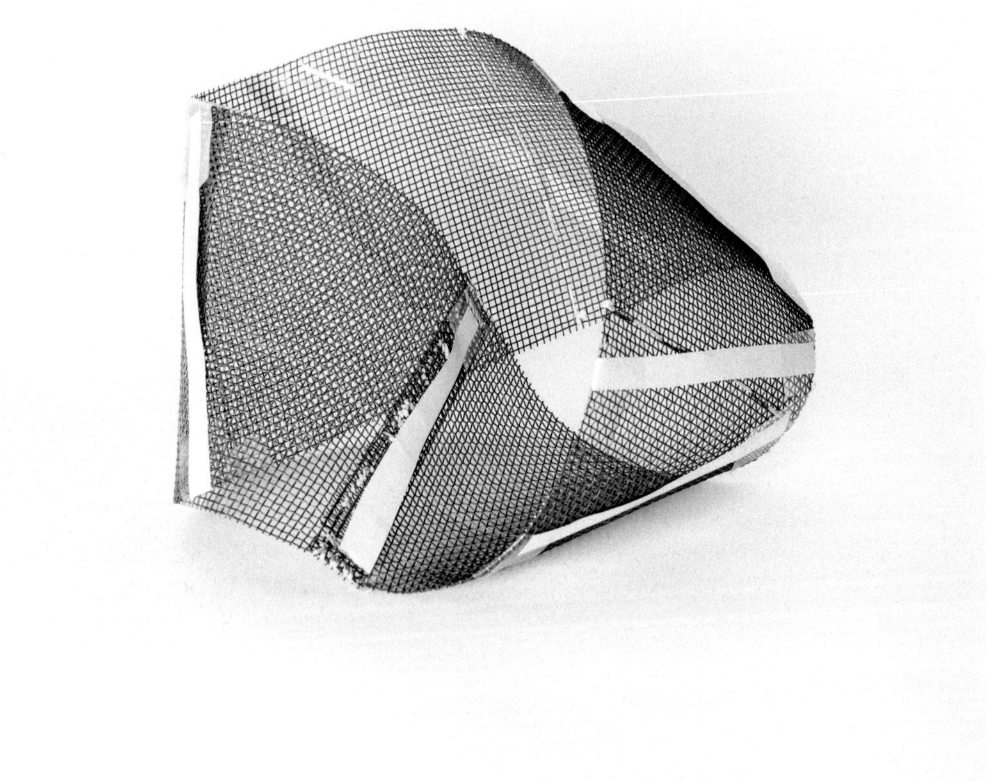

Mary Vieira and Max Bill
Wire model for Bill's sculpture "unendliche schleife" (HfG Ulm), 1953/54

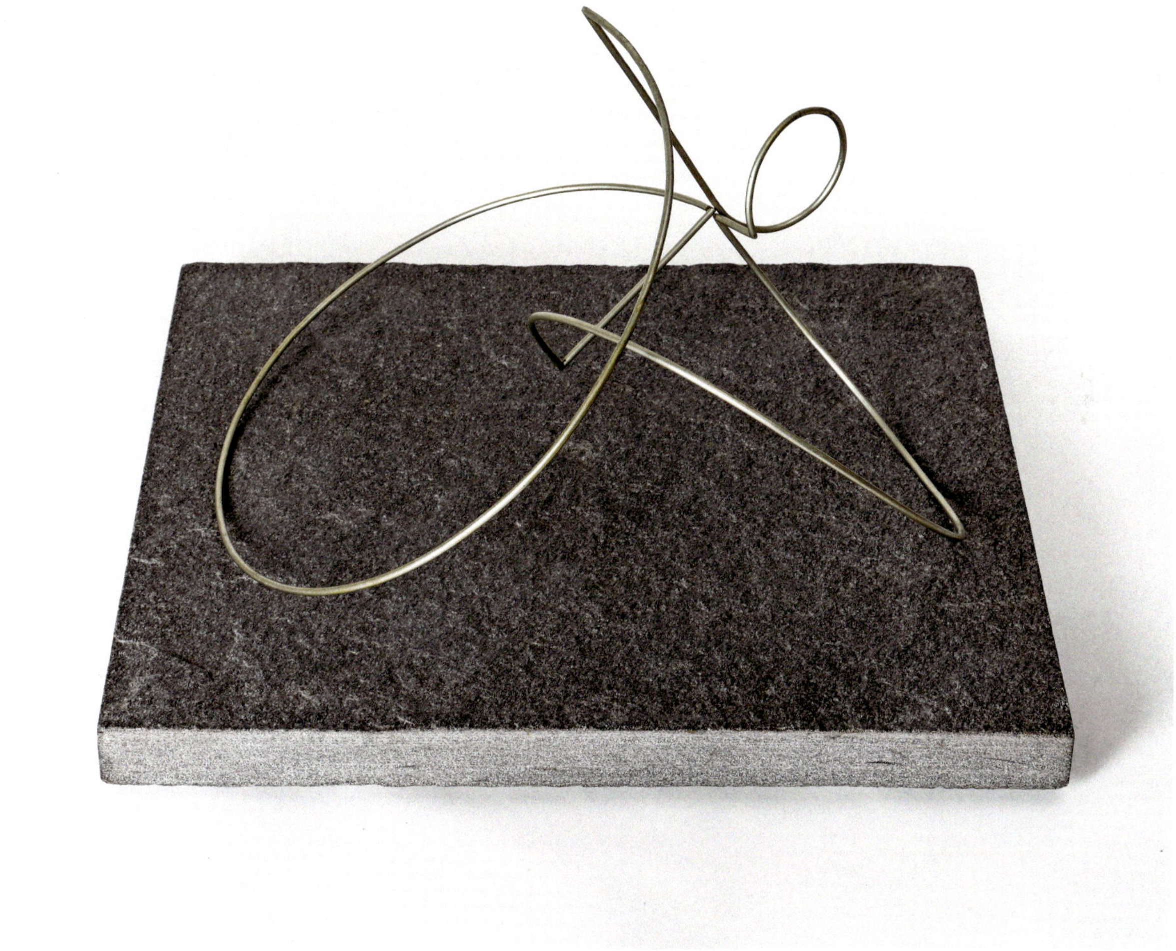

Mary Vieira
ritmo no espaço: 2: tensão-expansão (model), c. 1952

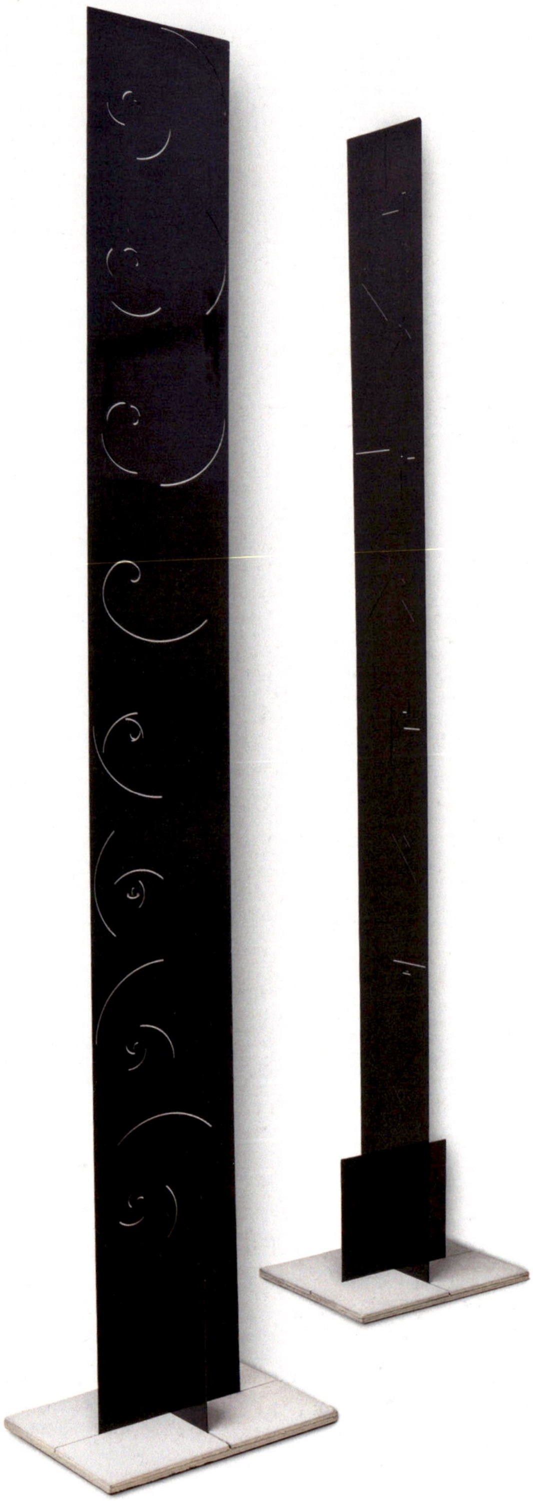

Mary Vieira
zeiten einer bewegung: a + b, 1952–1955

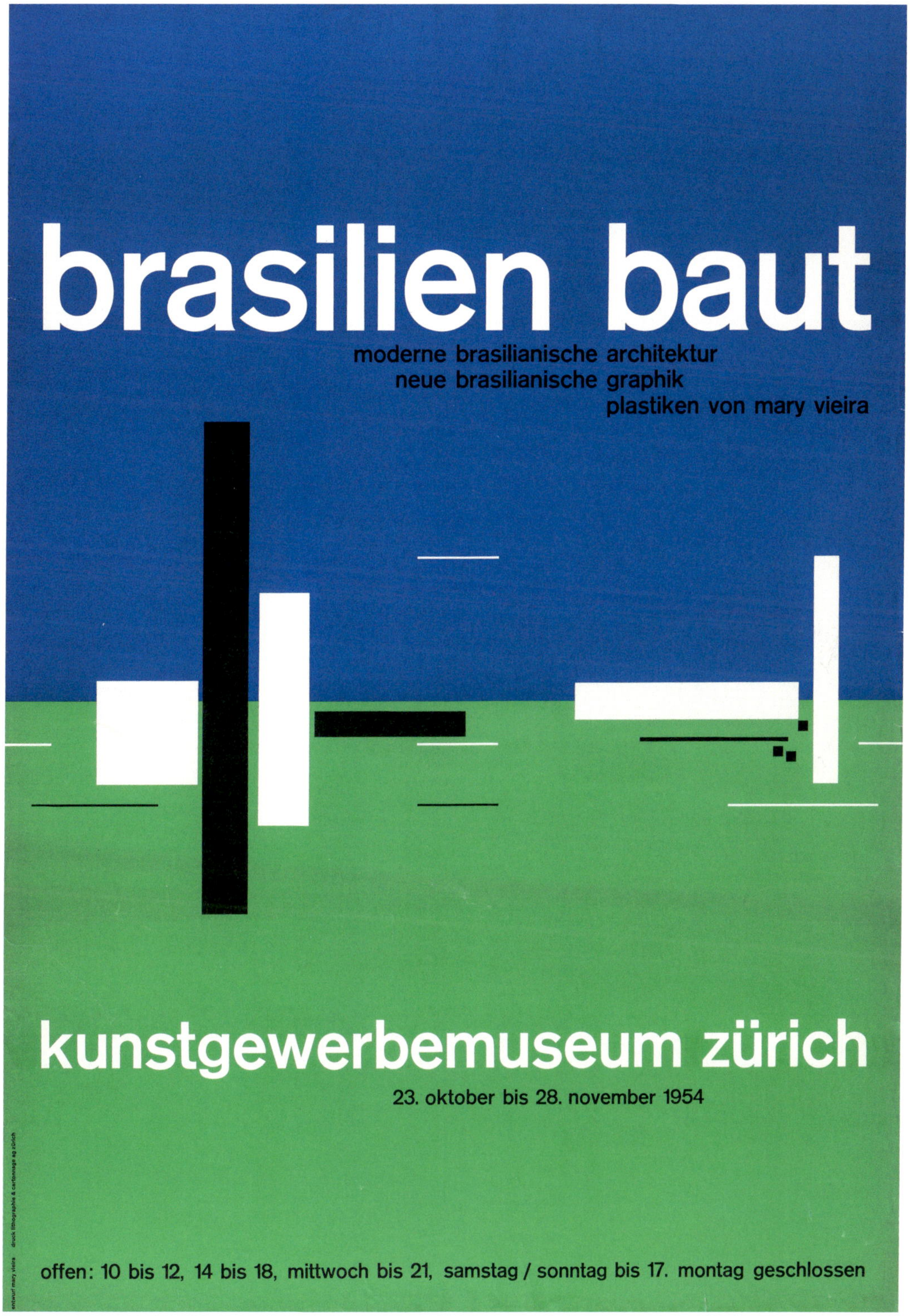

Mary Vieira
Poster: brasilien baut—kunstgewerbemuseum zürich, 1954

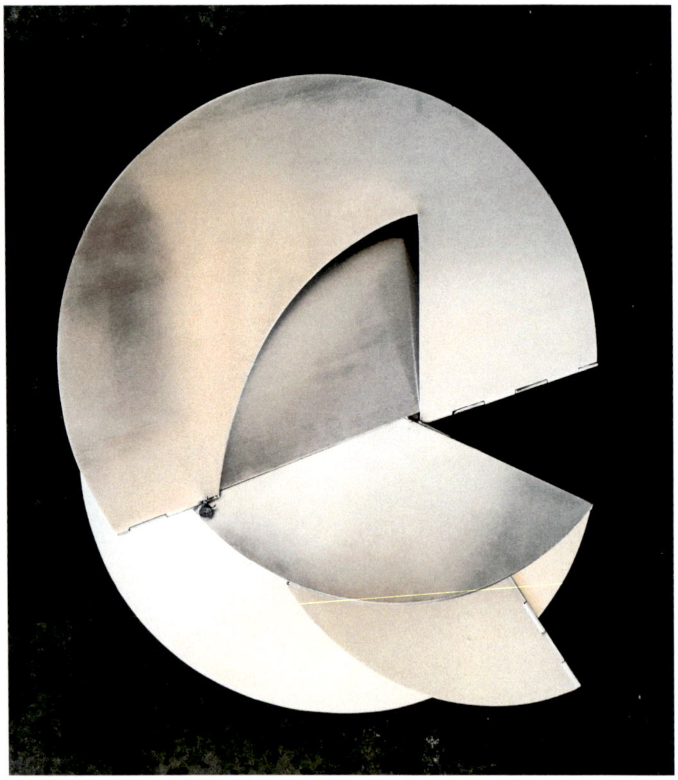
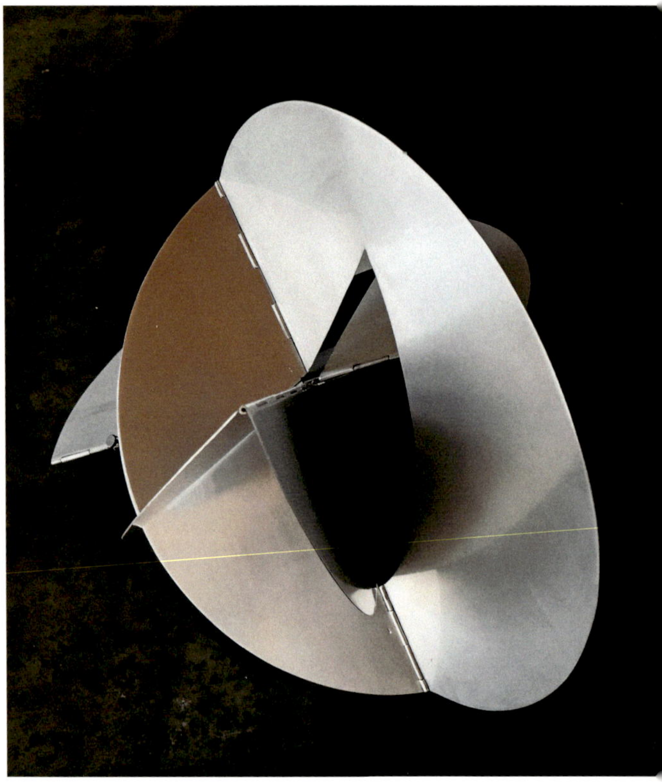
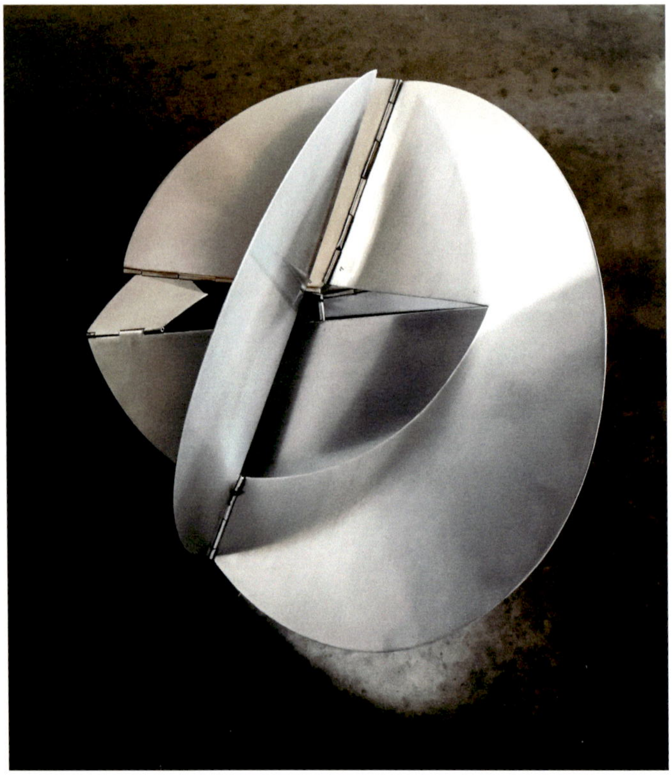

Lygia Clark
Bicho—Projecto para um Planeta, c. 1960

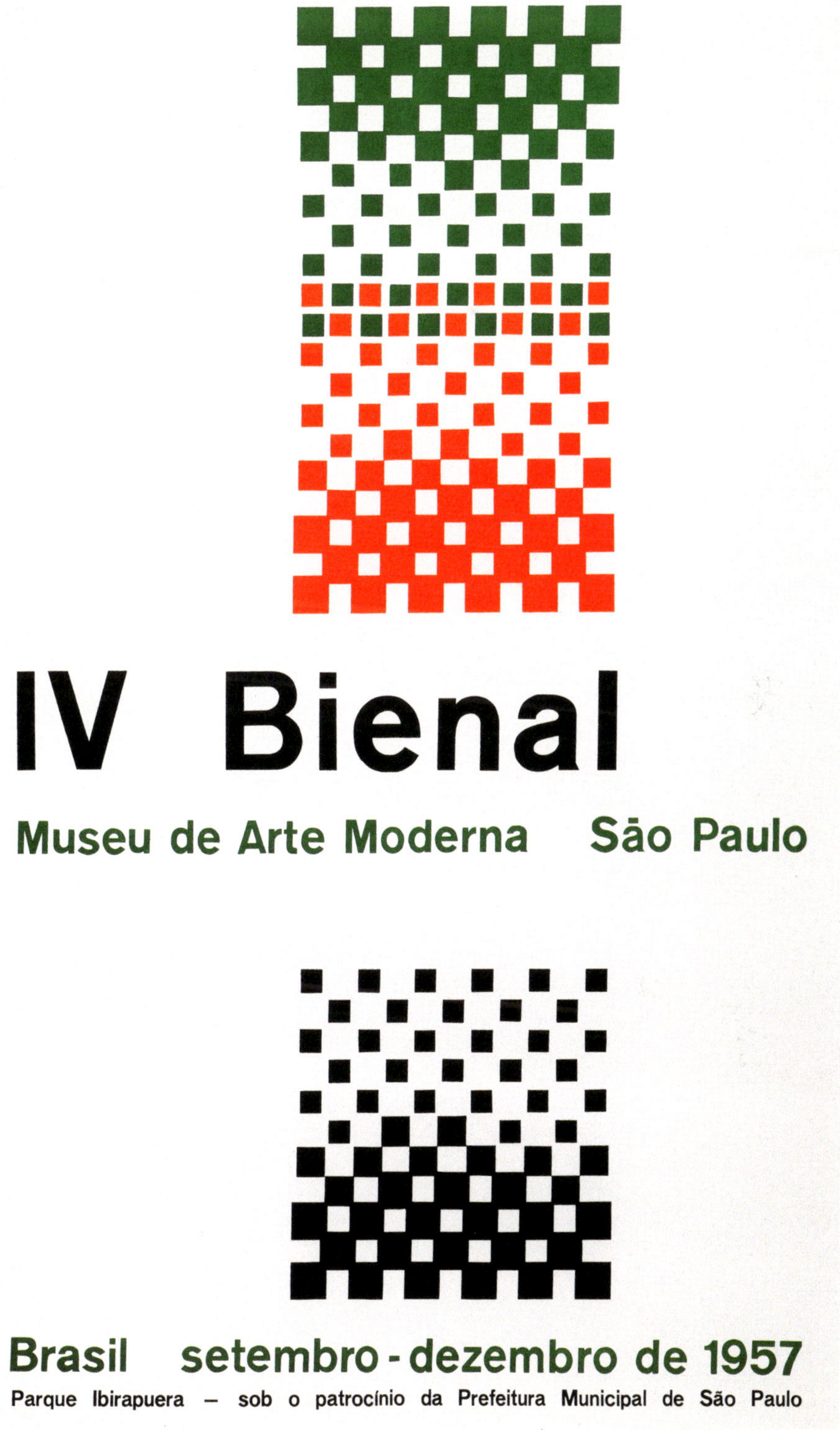

Alexandre Wollner
Poster: IV Bienal, Museu de Arte Moderna São Paulo, 1957

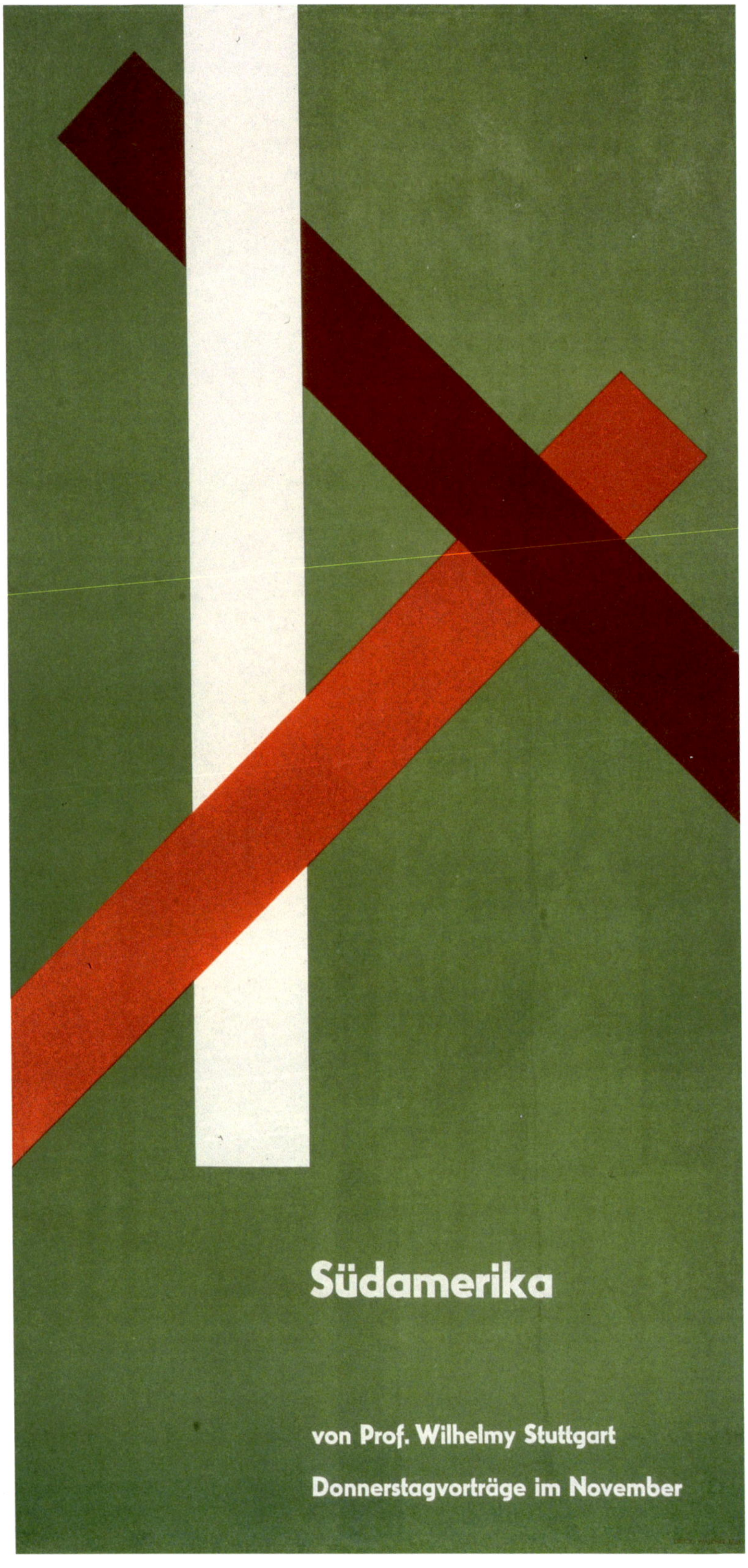

Almir Mavignier
Poster: Südamerika, c. 1953

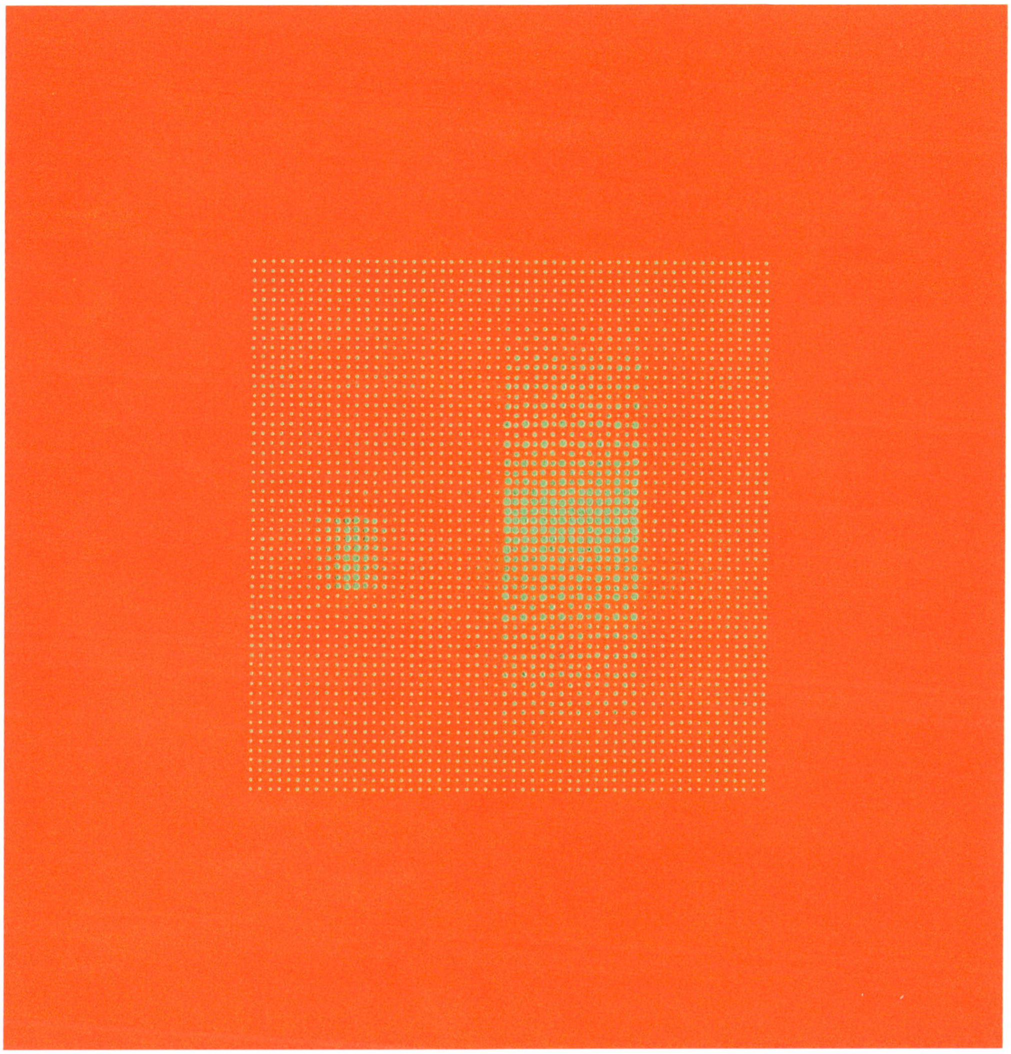

Almir Mavignier
flimmerndes quadrat, 1956

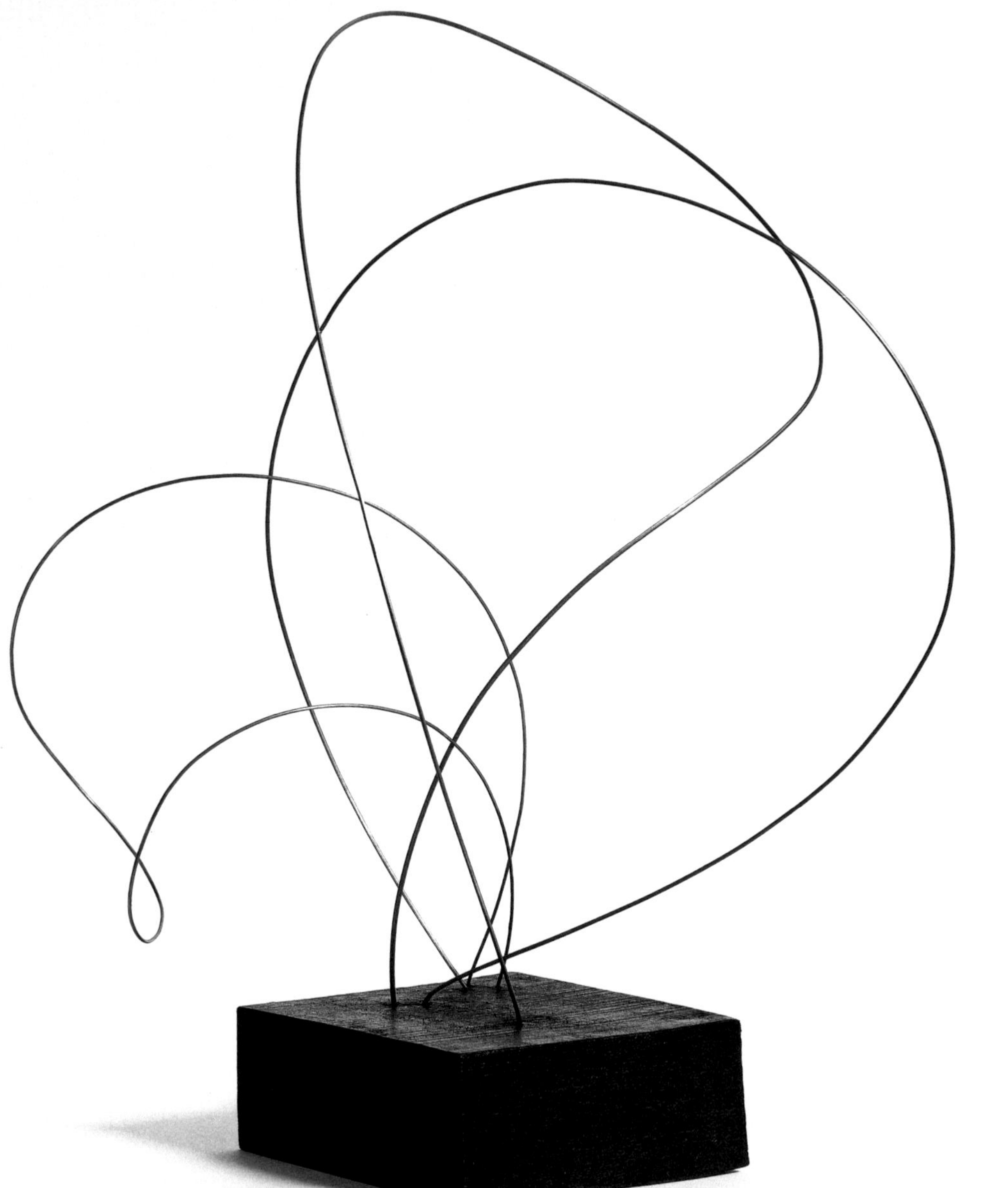

Enio Iommi
Ritmos espaciales, 1945

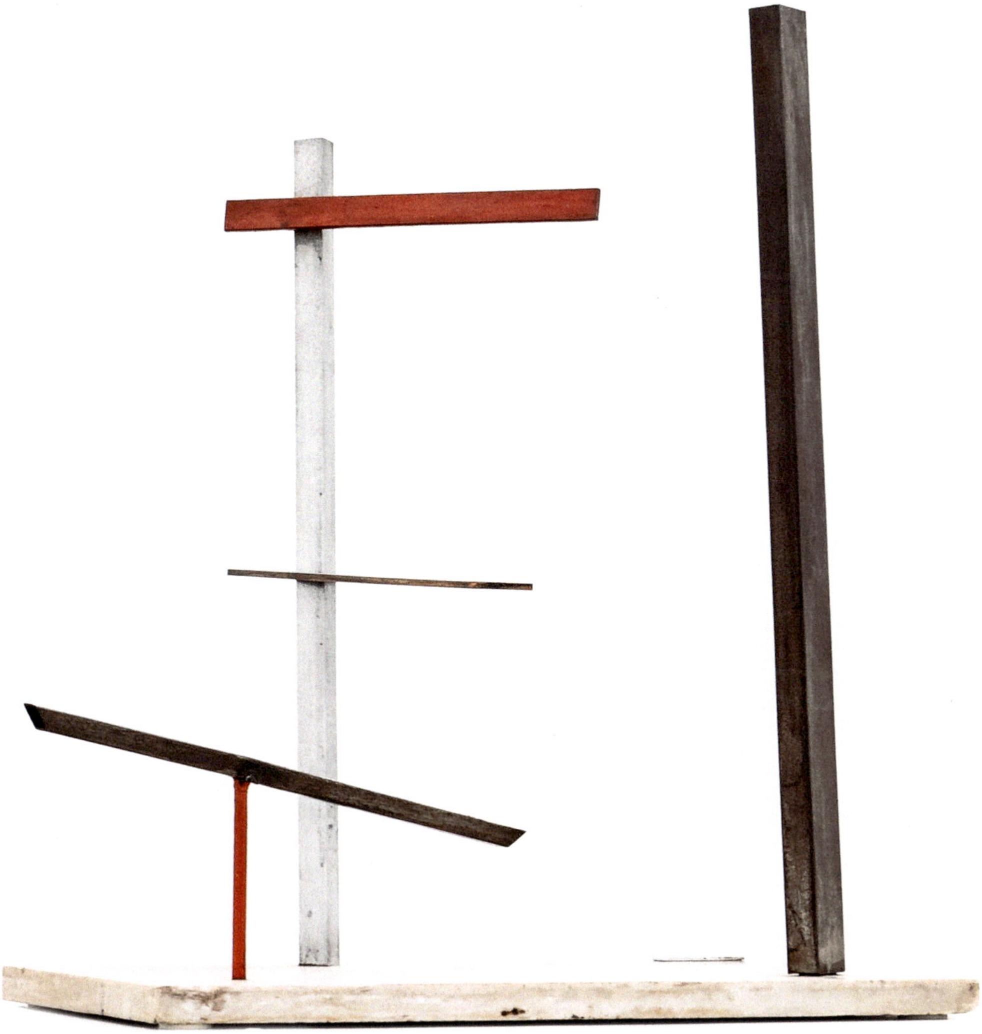

Enio Iommi
Construcción, 1945

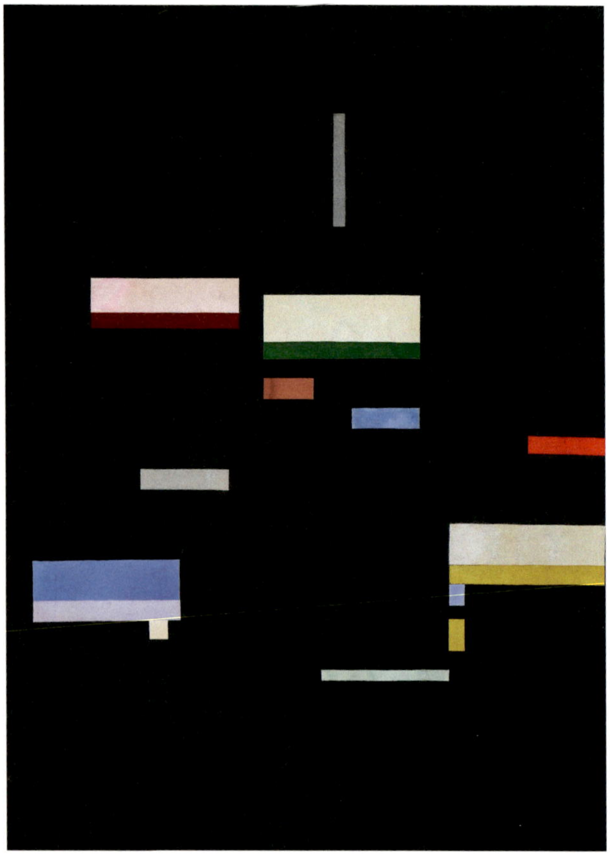

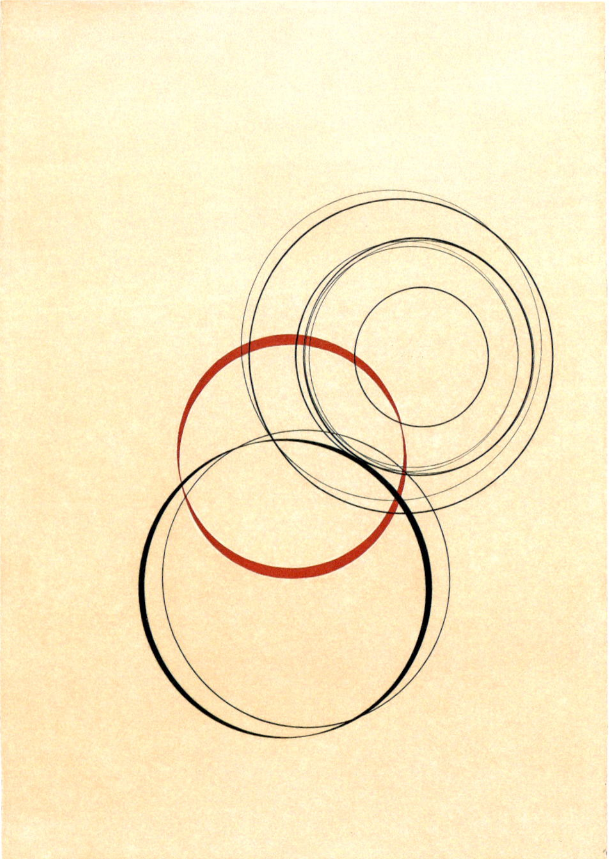

Nélida Fedullo
Untitled, 1950

Nélida Fedullo
Untitled, c. 1949

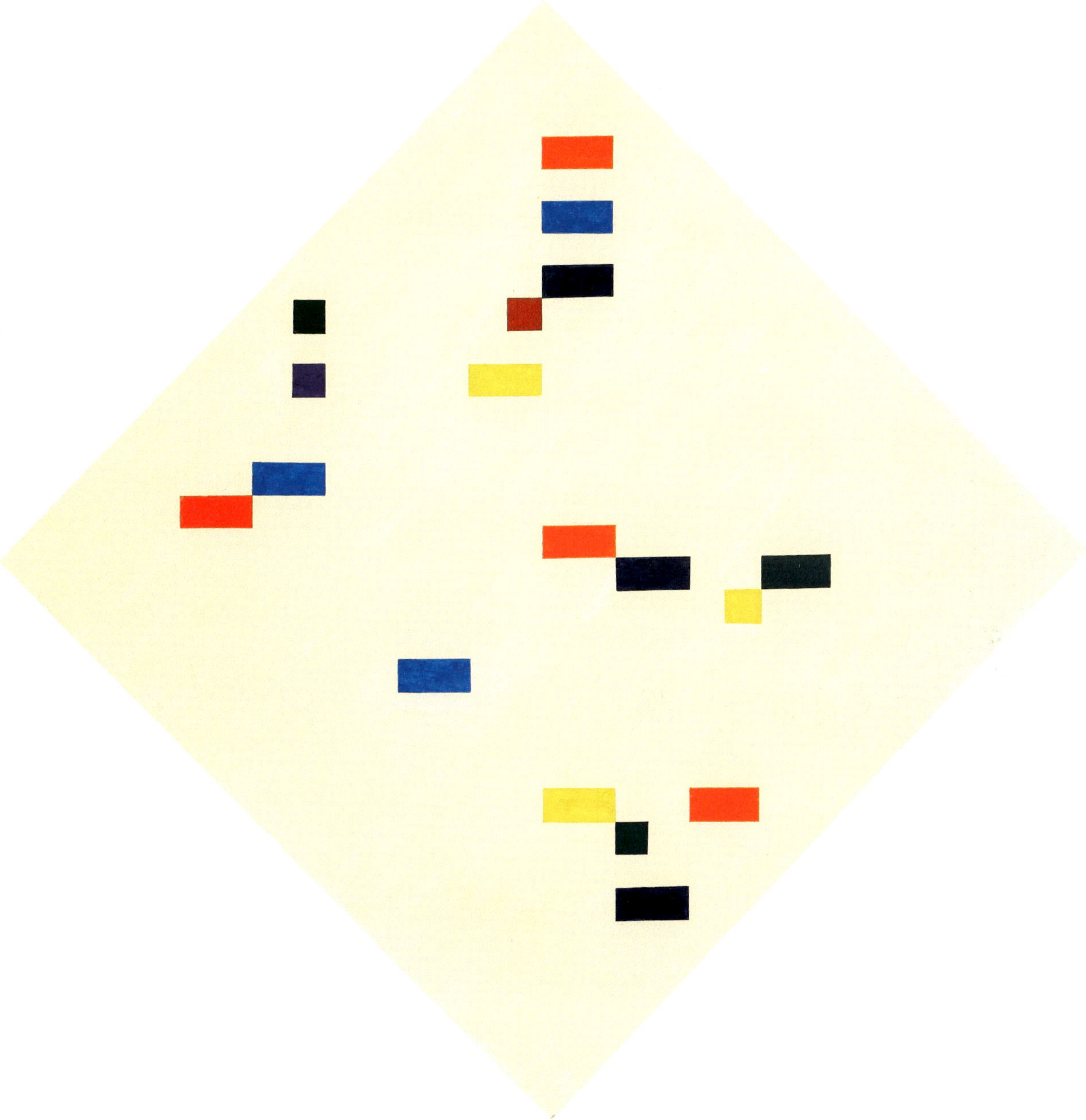

Lidy Prati
Concreta N° 2-B, 1948

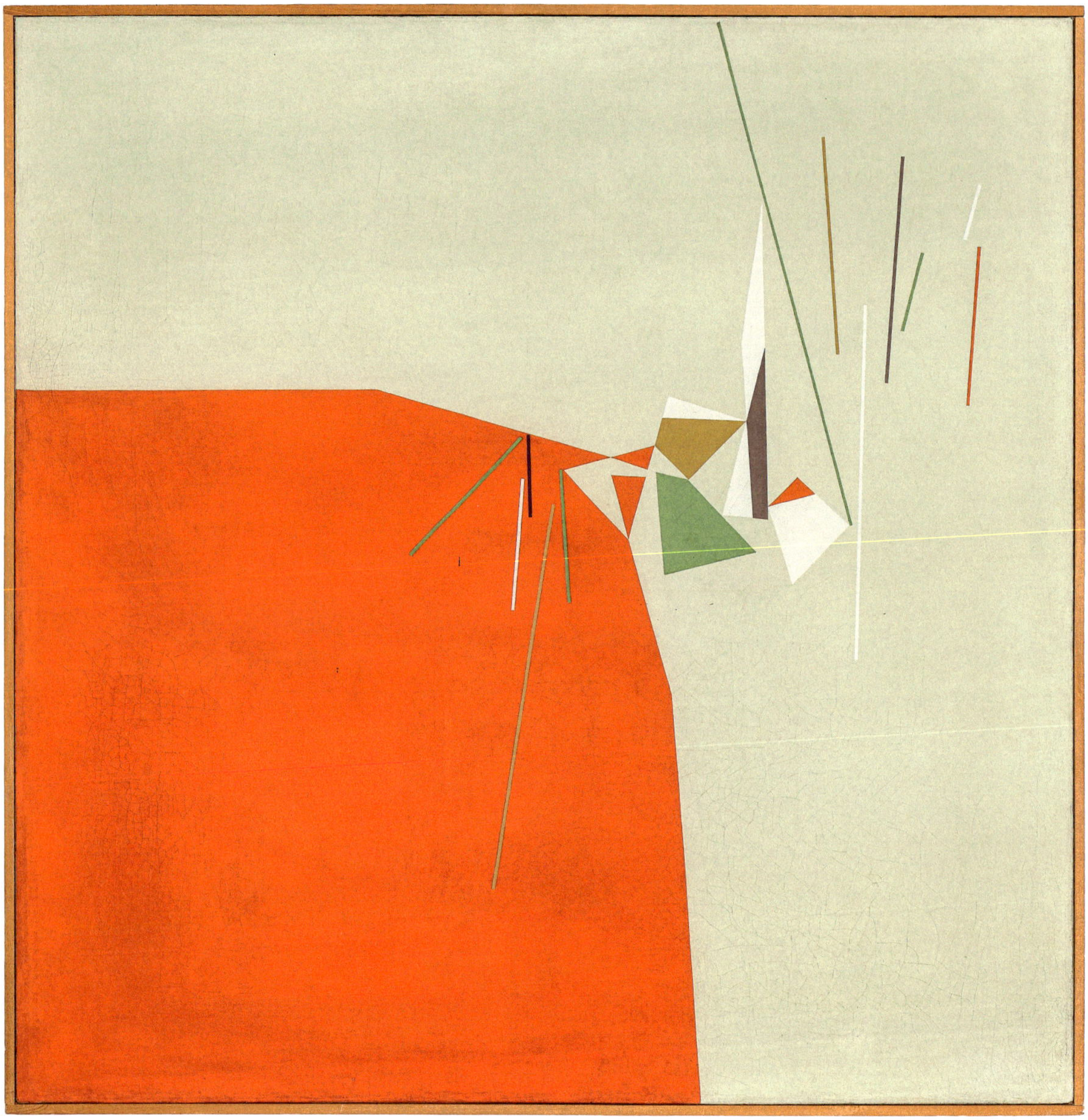

Alfredo Hlito
Formas y líneas en el plano, 1953

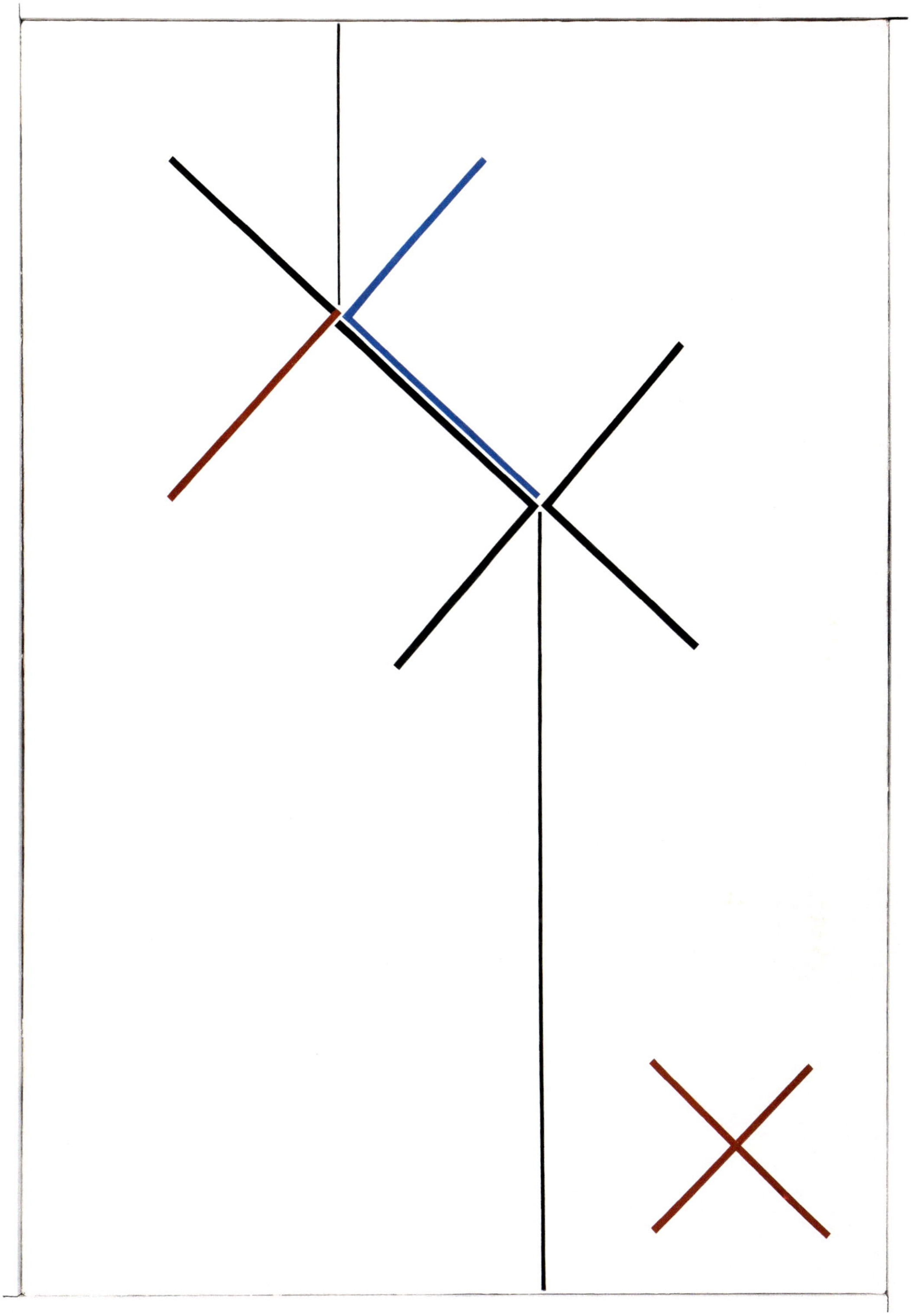

Tomás Maldonado
Construcción de 2 elementos, 1953

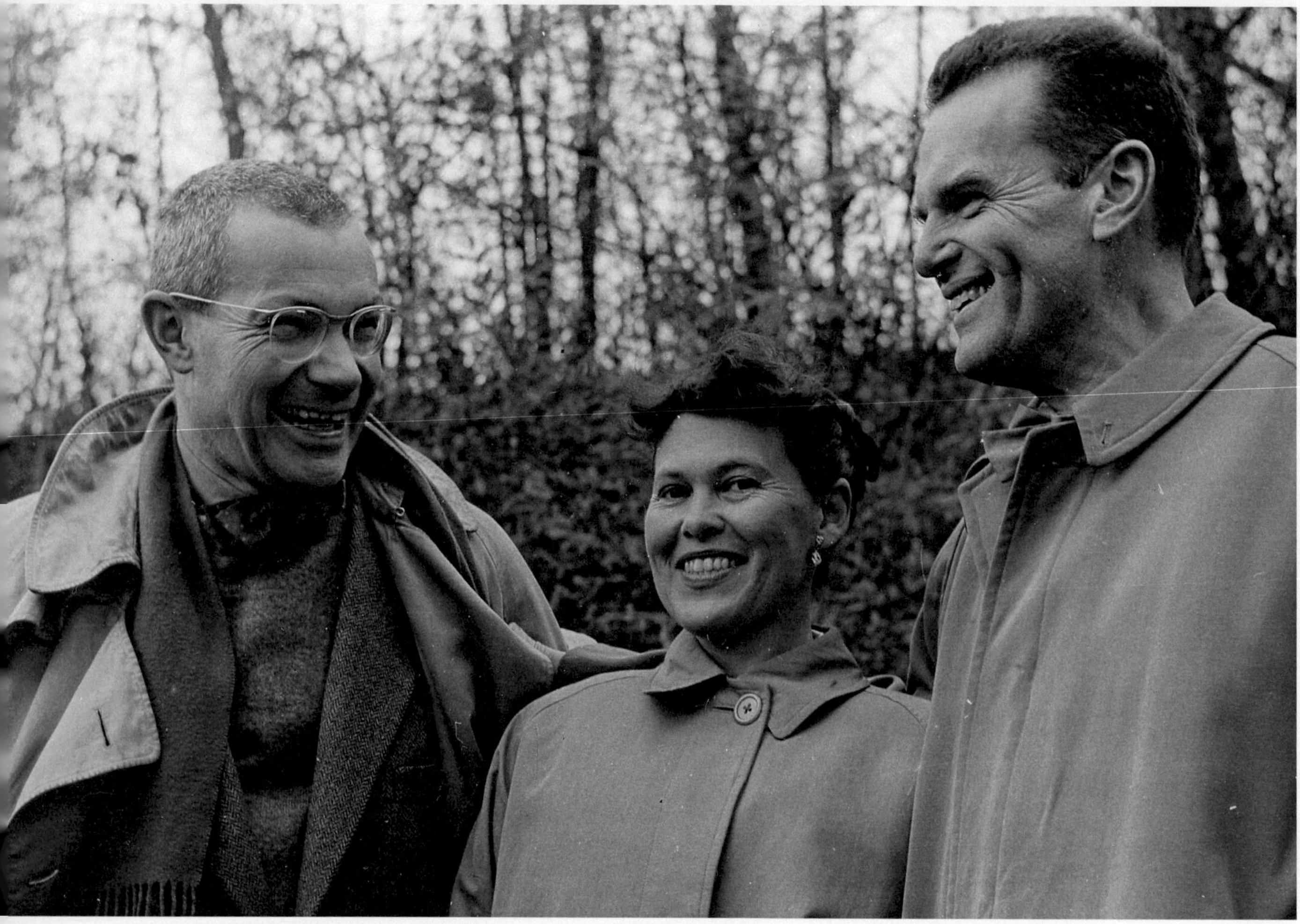

1958

Max Bill with American designer couple Ray and Charles Eames; the latter came to Ulm to teach at HfG in 1955 and again in 1958.

HfG-Archiv Museum Ulm

The rise of Nazism in Germany culminating in the outbreak of World War II induced numerous European artists to emigrate to the USA. By 1939 Bill was also entertaining the idea of emigrating, though he eventually elected to remain in Switzerland. The émigrés were instrumental in founding new art centers and innovative schools, where Bauhaus alumni might throw themselves into the work of cultural transfer. Josef Albers, Bill's most important contact from his Bauhaus days, made a name for himself at Black Mountain College, the experimental school in North Carolina to which he invited Xanti Schawinsky as a lecturer in 1936, and eventually became its rector in 1948/49. László Moholy-Nagy for his part founded the New Bauhaus in Chicago and even invited Bill to teach there, albeit without success. Walter Gropius, Walter Peterhans, Lyonel Feininger, Marcel Breuer, and Ludwig Mies van der Rohe all became influential teachers at American colleges. Bill paid regular visits to the USA from the 1950s onward. He gave

1990

Donald Judd and Max Bill only met personally in the 1980s, after Judd had written a review of Bill's exhibition in New York's Stämpfli Gallery in 1963 and Bill had bought some of Judd's works for his own collection in the 1970s.

max bill georges vantongerloo stiftung, photo: Thomas Cugini

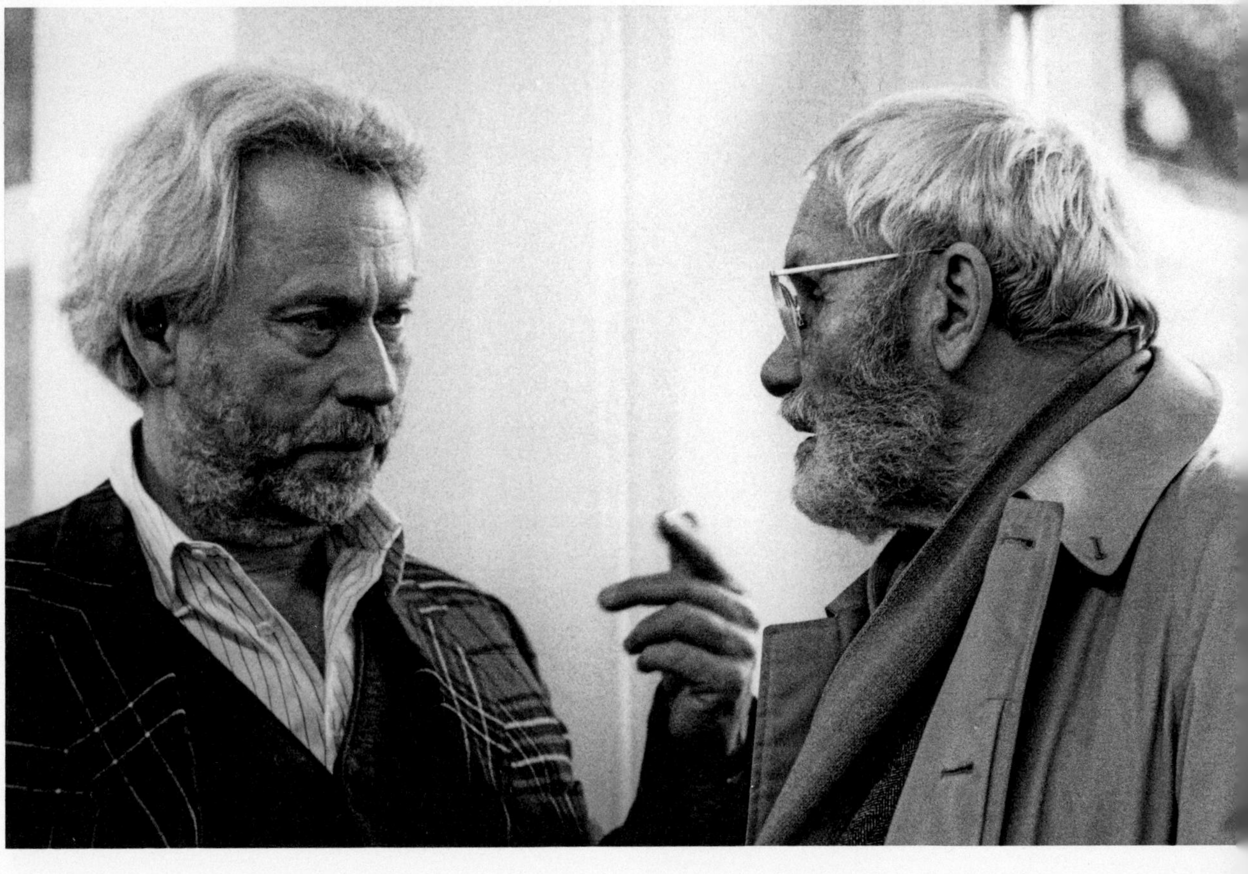

lectures there and whenever possible went to visit Albers, who having by then accepted a professorship at Yale was living in New Haven. In 1963, the Staempfli Gallery in New York City organized Bill's first solo exhibition in the USA. Among those to review that show was Donald Judd, who did at least write appreciatively of the sculptures. In 1969 the Arts Club of Chicago showed a solo exhibition of Bill's sculptures and paintings.

The years 1974/75 saw a Max Bill retrospective tour the United States, calling at the Albright-Knox Art Gallery in Buffalo, the Los Angeles County Museum of Art, the San Francisco Museum of Art, and the Corcoran Gallery of Art in Washington, DC, and spawning numerous adjunct presentations at smaller galleries.

Among Bill's circle were the designers Ray and Charles Eames, whom he first met in Ulm in 1955. In 1980 Bill visited Ray Eames—by then a widow—at her home in Los Angeles. The 1980s also saw a personal encounter with Andy Warhol, who produced two portraits of him, and finally with Donald Judd, several of whose works Bill purchased for his collection.

1 Cf. Thomas 2008, p. 170.

2 Cf. Donald Judd: "In the Galleries," in *Arts Magazine* (May/June 1963), reprinted in *Donald Judd: Complete Writings 1959–1975, Gallery Reviews, Book Reviews, Articles, Letters to the Editor, Reports, Statements, Complaints*, Halifax, New York 2005, p. 88.

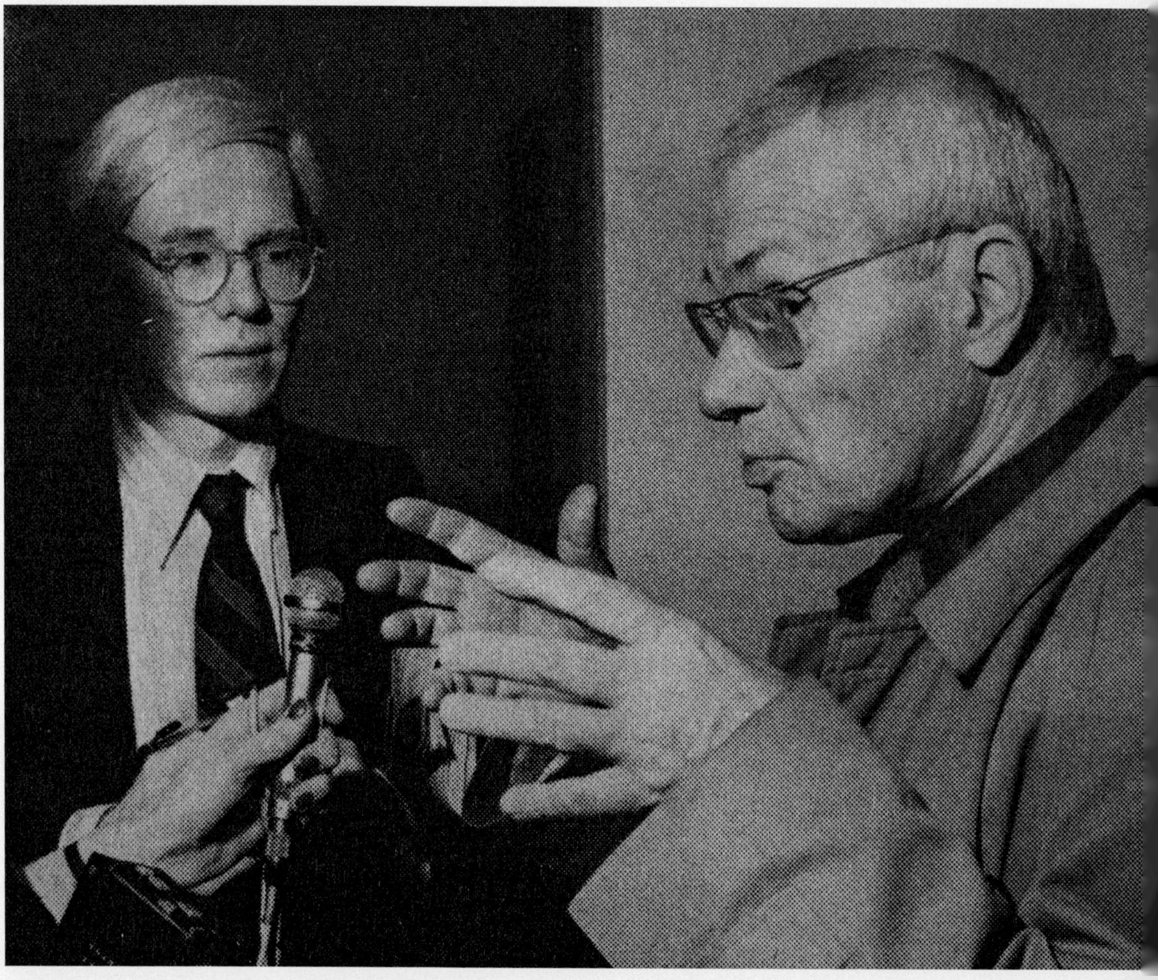

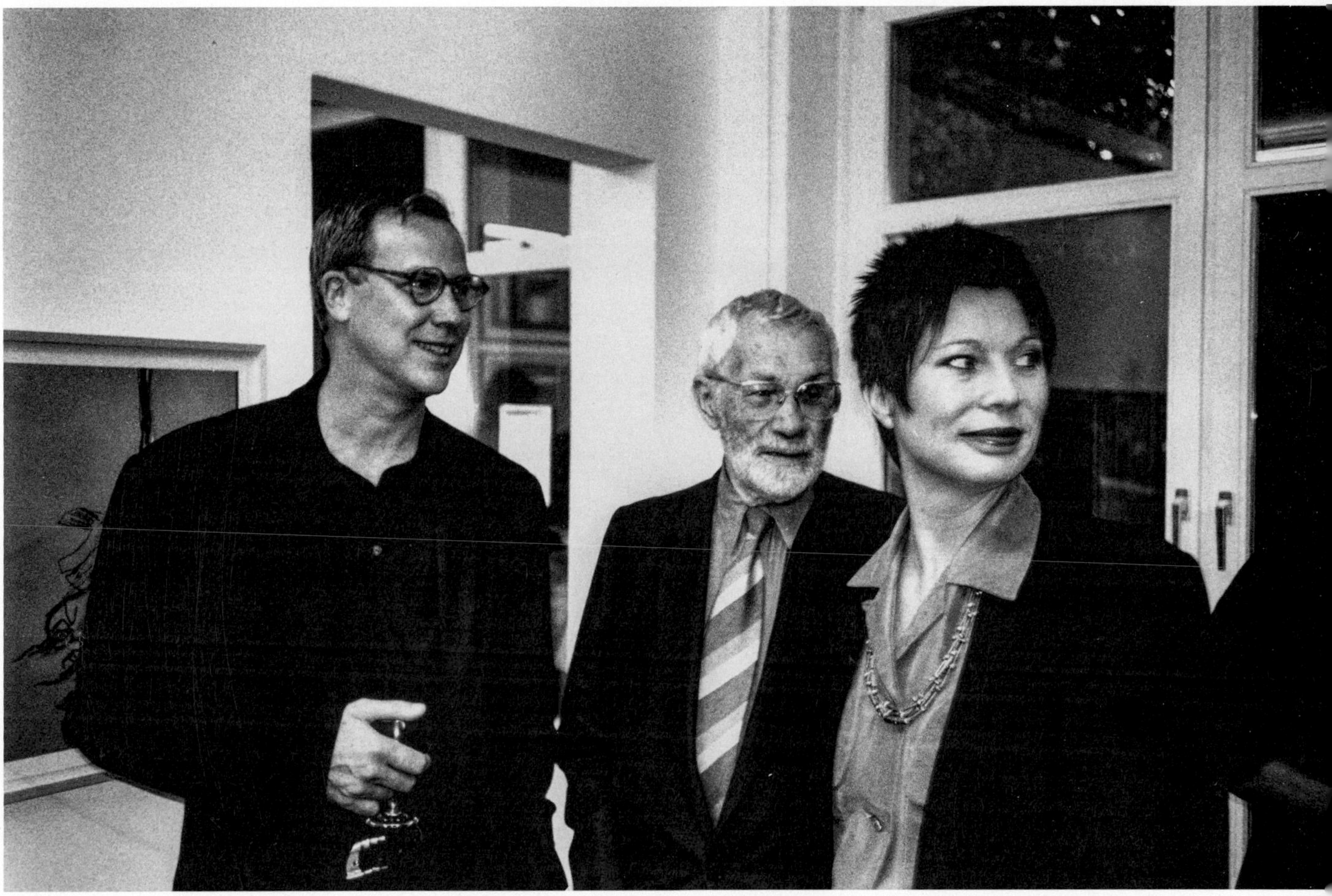

1991

Robert Wilson, Max Bill, and Angela Thomas Bill during the opening of the exhibition *Robert Wilson: Lohengrin Drawings and Other Works* at the Annemarie Verna Galerie, Zurich, September 1991. Despite their vastly different approaches, Robert Wilson and Max Bill held a deep respect for each other's work.

Angela Thomas Schmid,
photo: Niklaus Stauss

1978

Max Bill and Andy Warhol at the opening of Warhol's exhibition at the Kunsthaus Zürich in 1978.

Züri Leu, issue of June 2, 1978

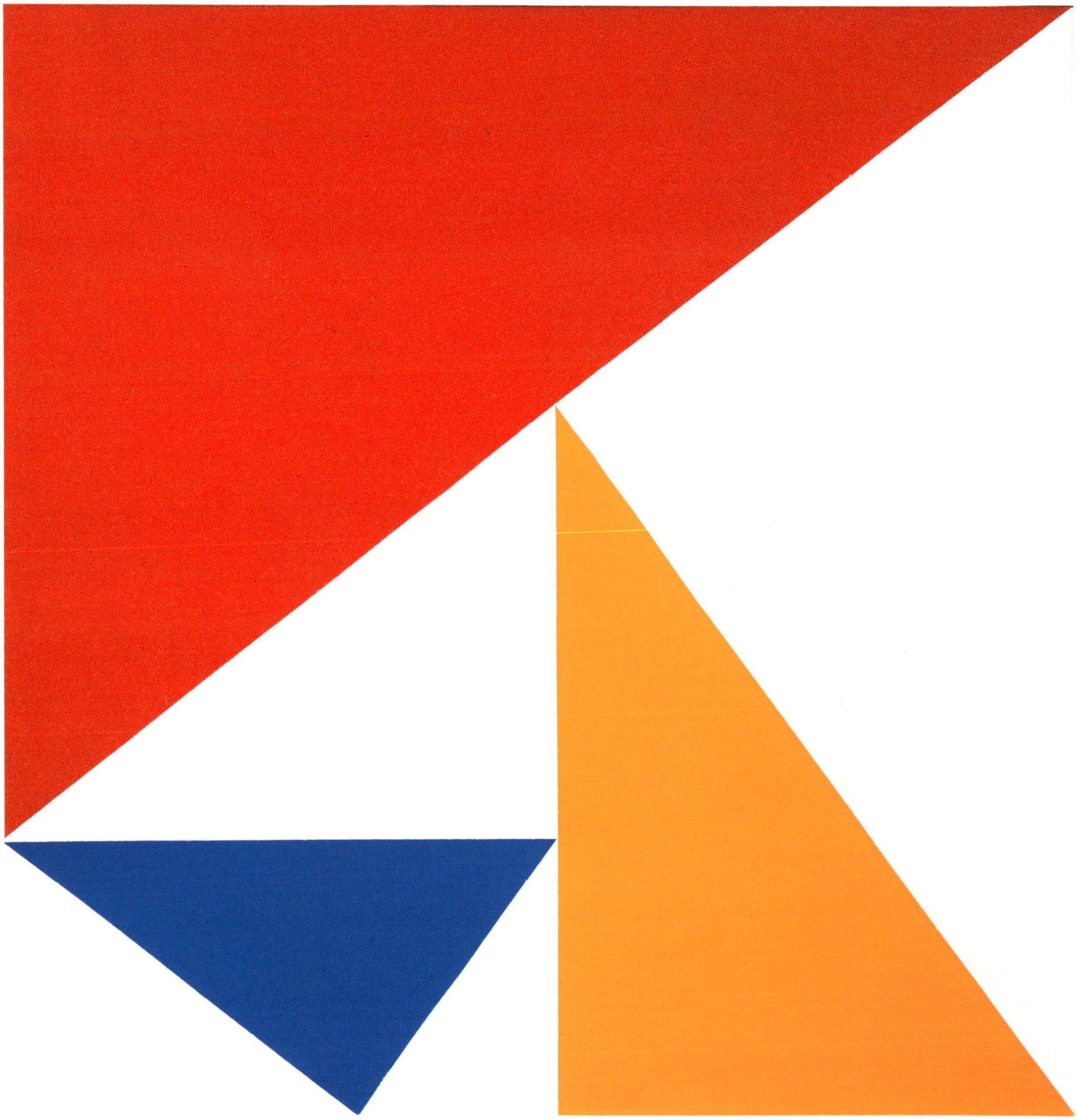

Max Bill
7 pythagoräische dreiecke als quadrat, 1978

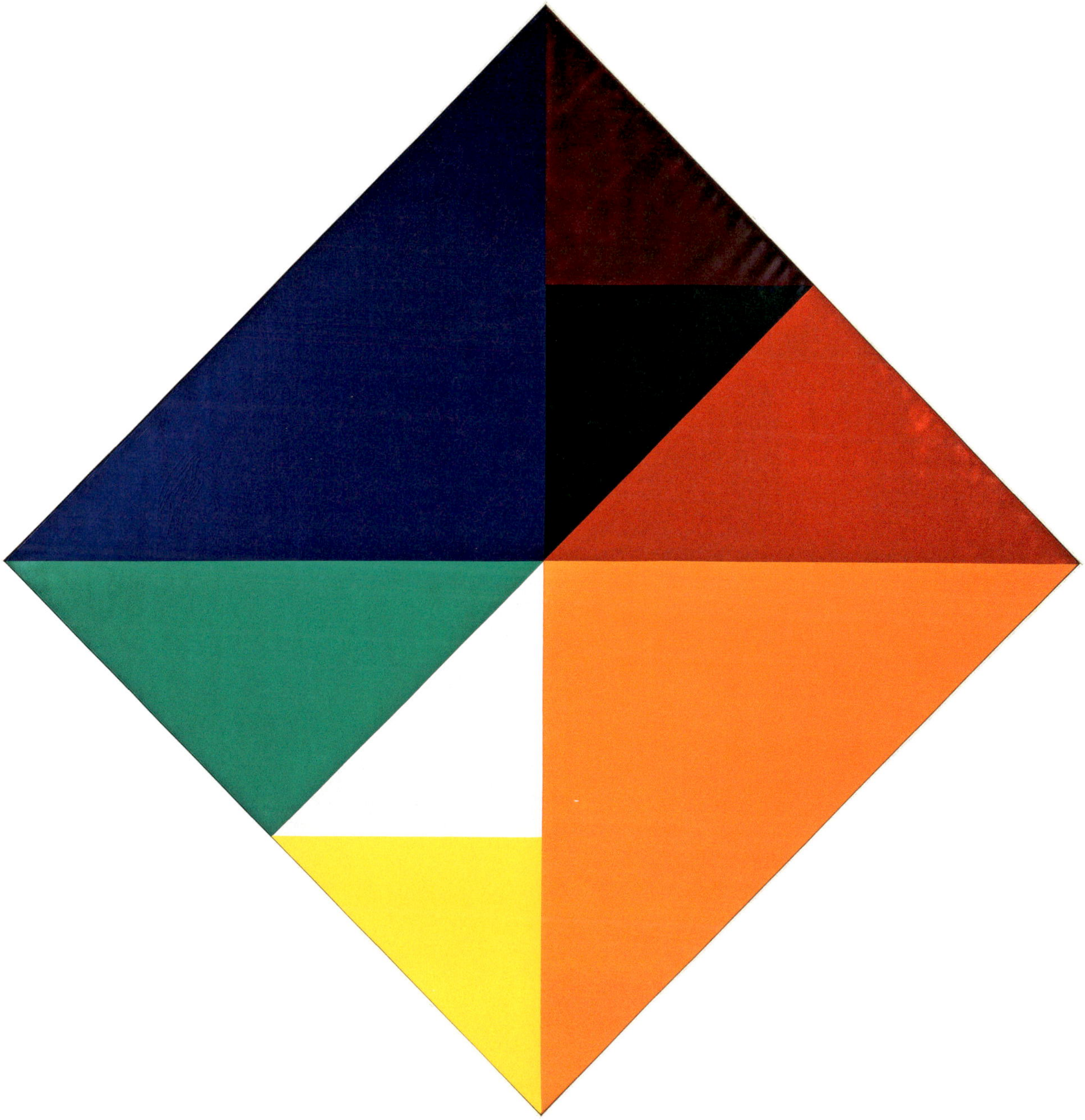

Max Bill
Untitled, 1970

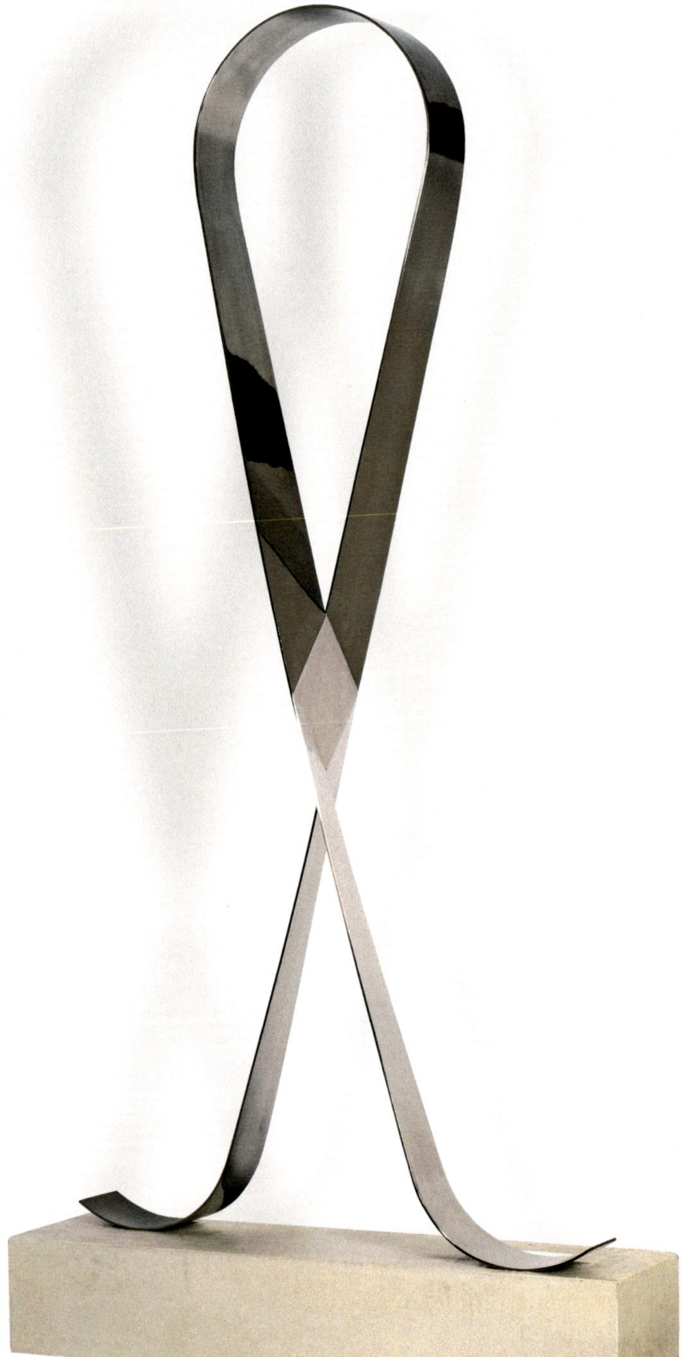

Max Bill
sechseckfläche um zwei quadrate, 1973

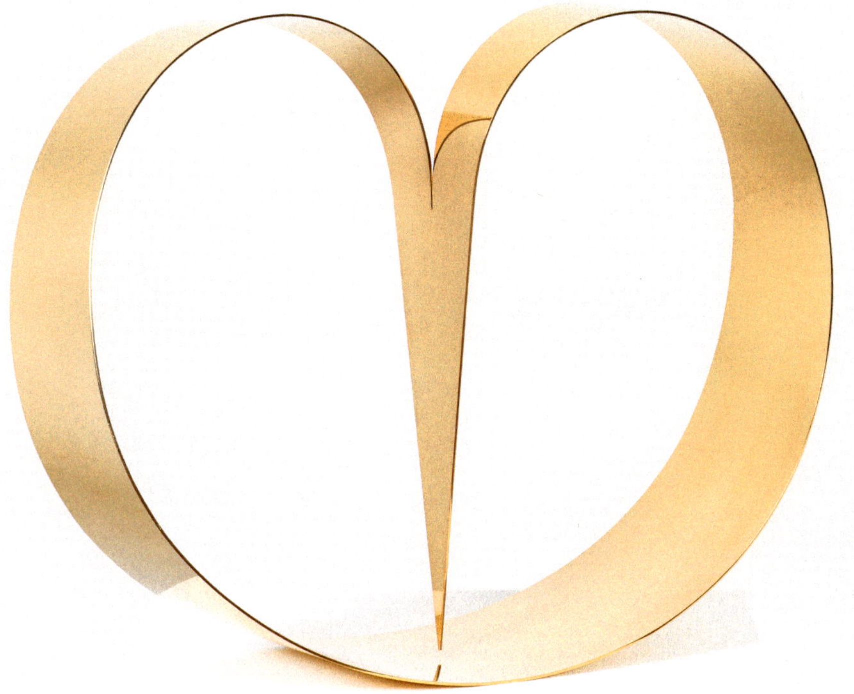

Max Bill
nach innen gekehrte fläche im raum mit zwei ecken, 1971

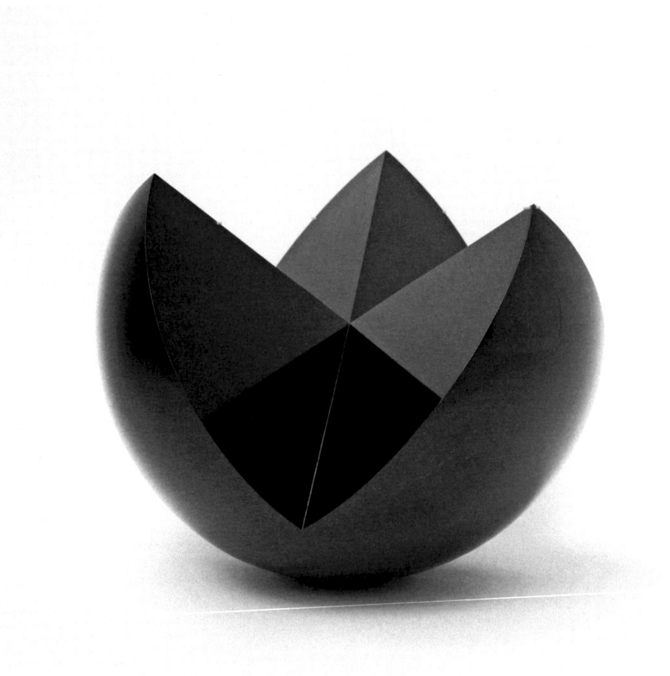

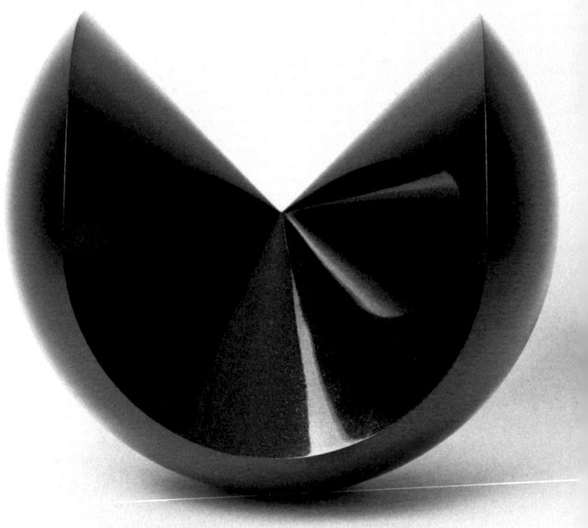

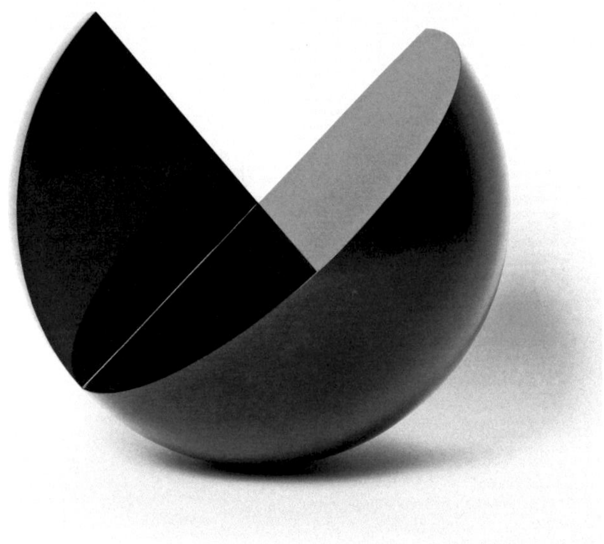

Max Bill
familie von fünf halben kugeln, 1965–1966

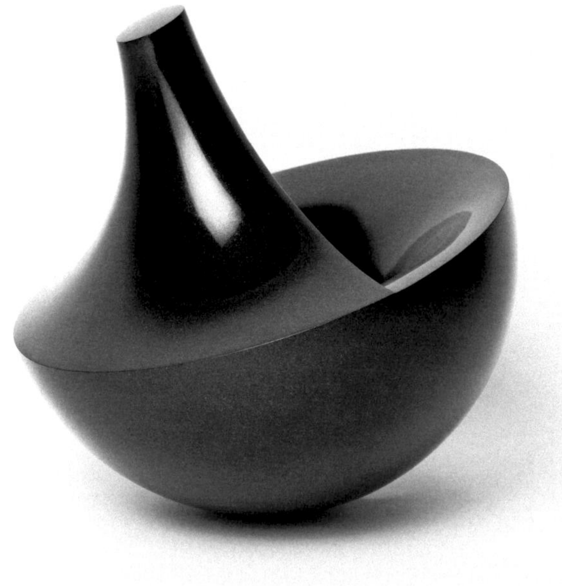

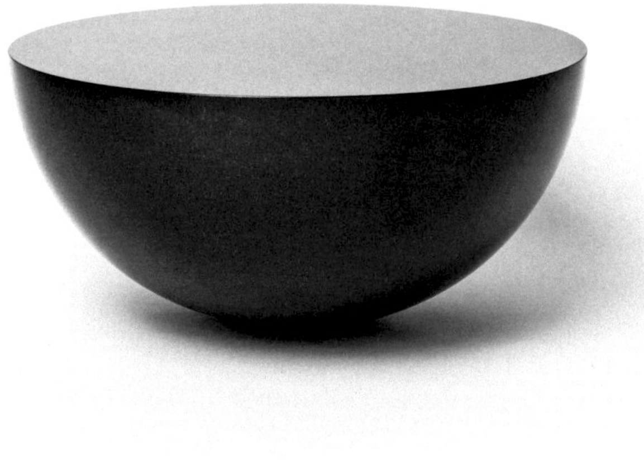

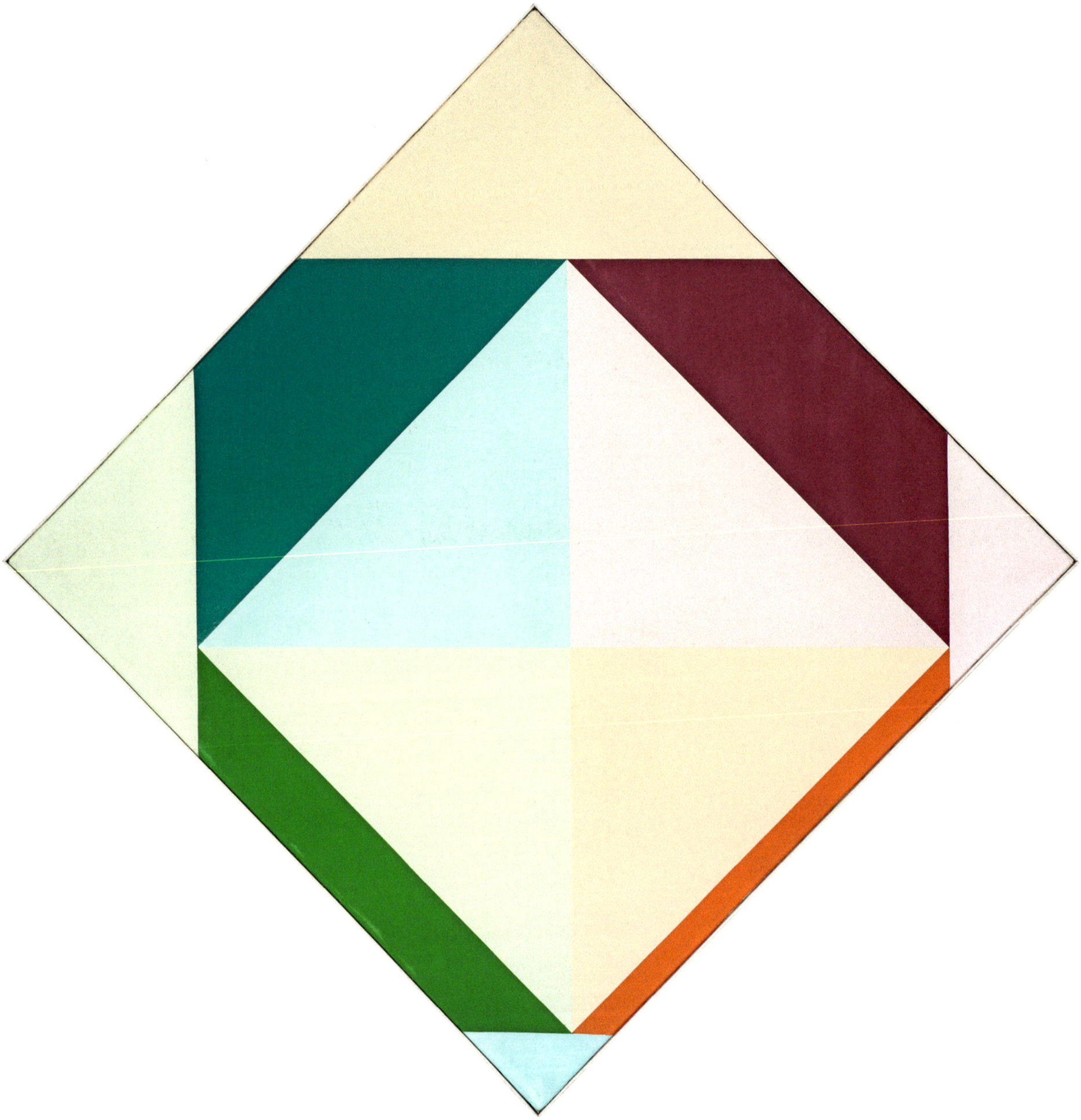

Max Bill
vier zonen im horizontal-diagonal-quadrat, 1963

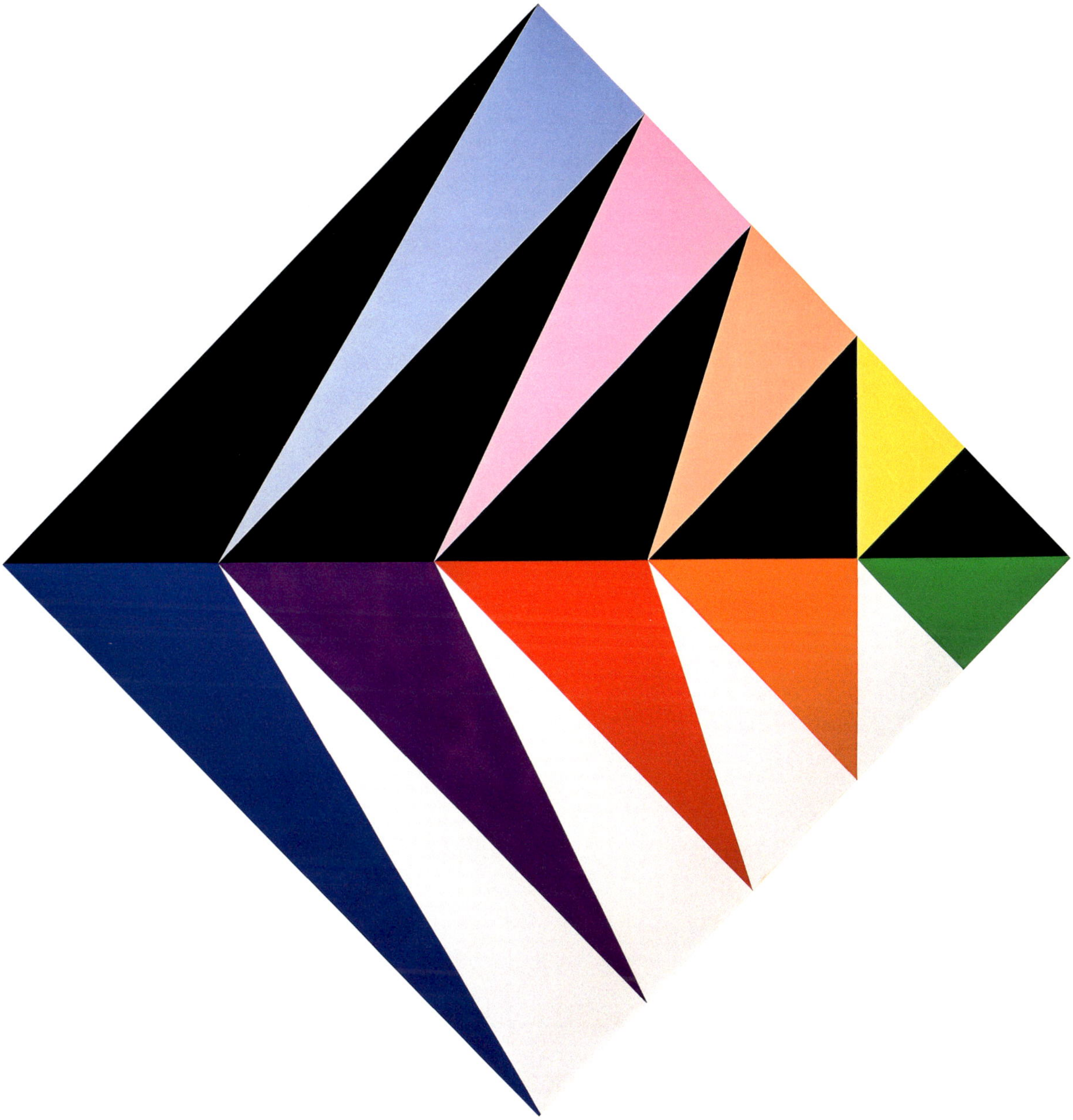

Max Bill
reflexe aus dunkel und hell, 1975

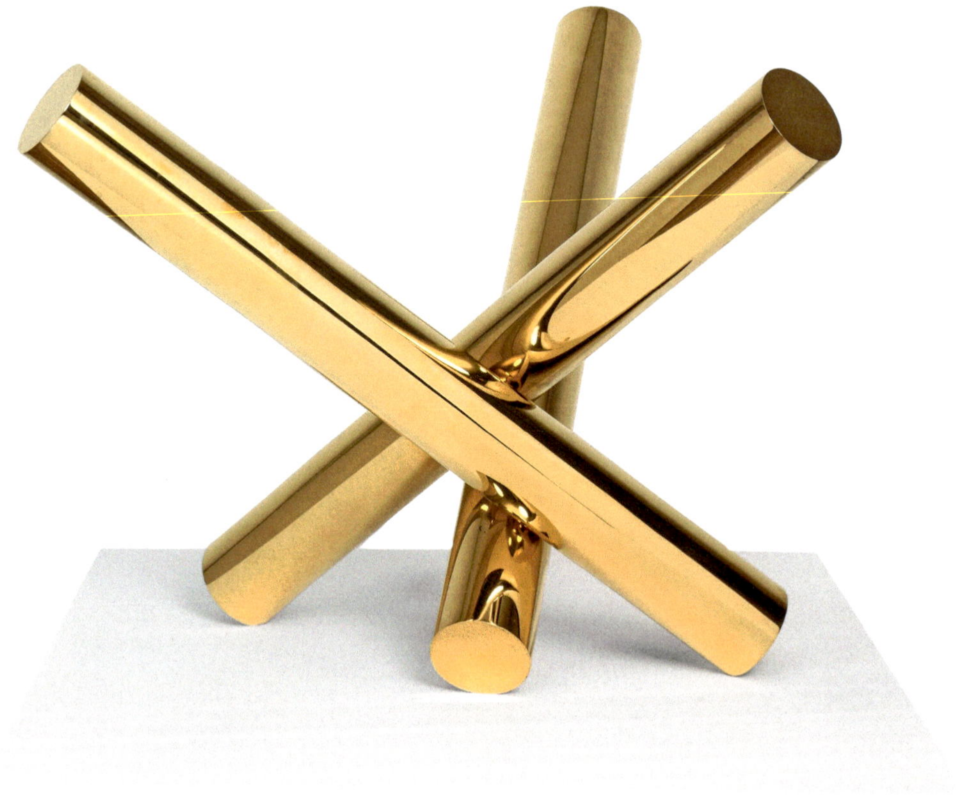

Max Bill
einheit aus drei gleichen zylindern, 1966

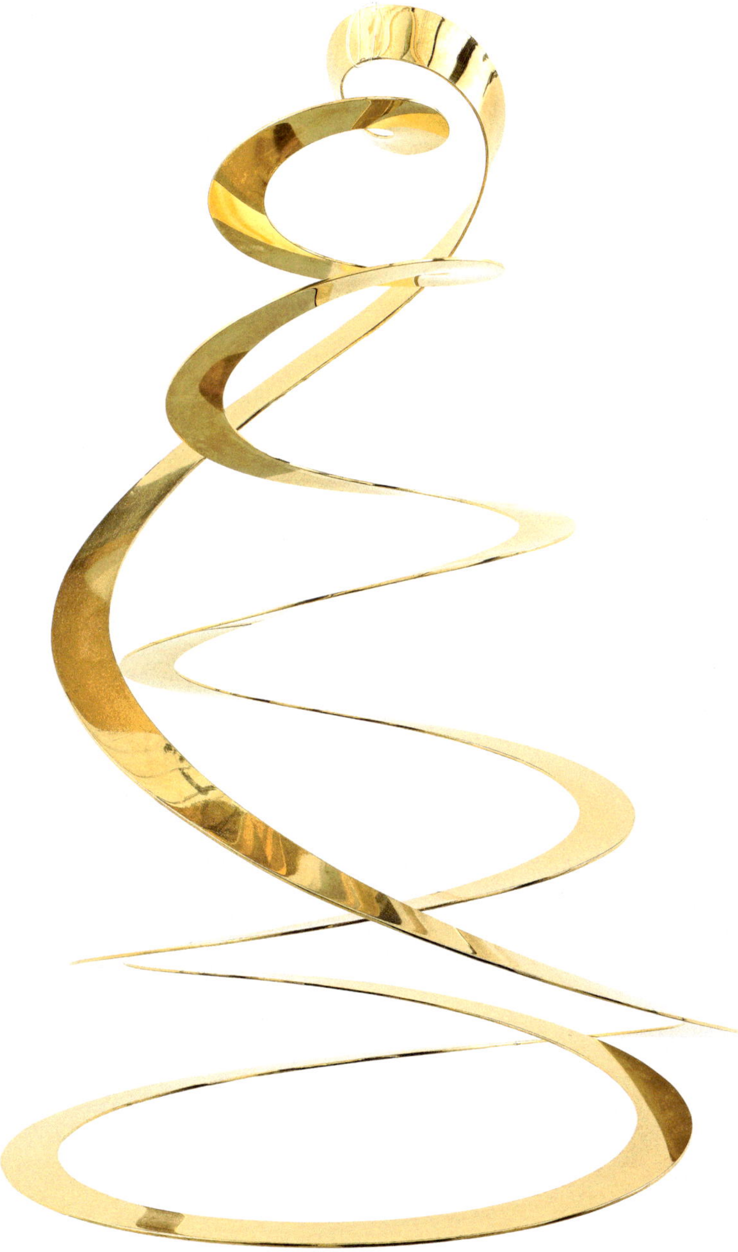

Max Bill
endlose spirale, 1973–1974

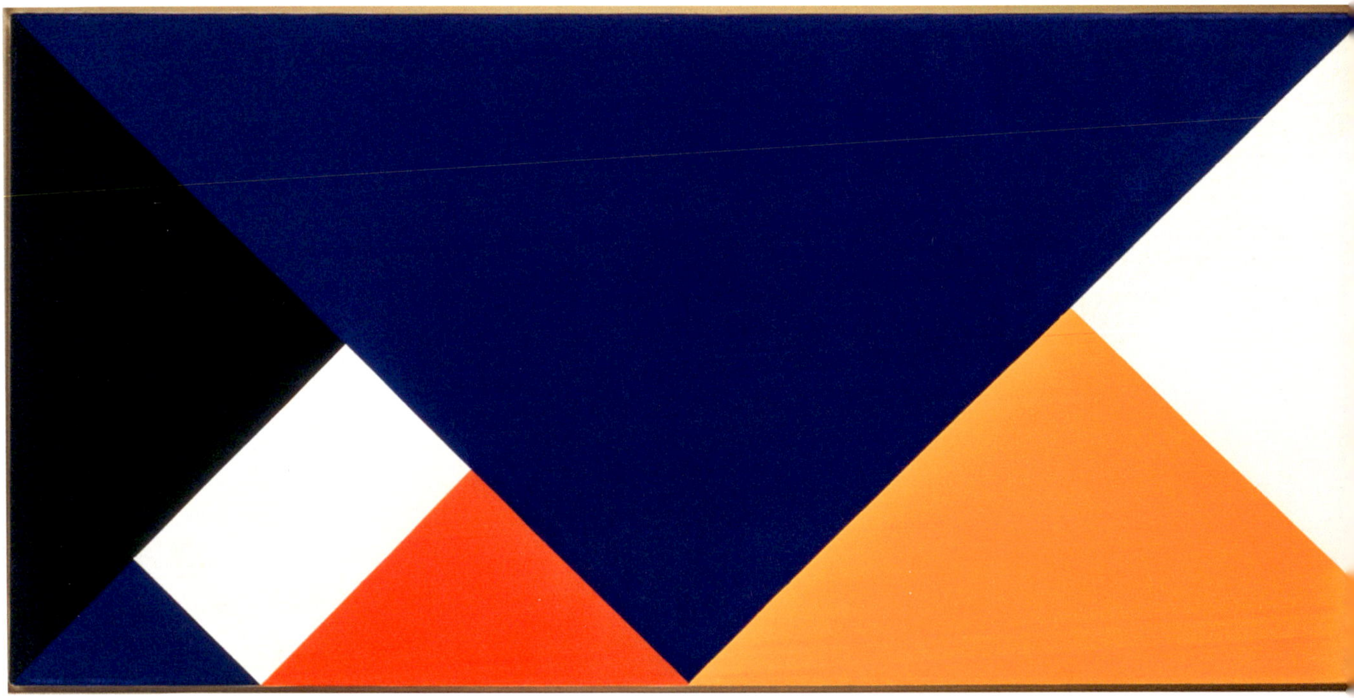

Max Bill
drei weisse akzente, 1970

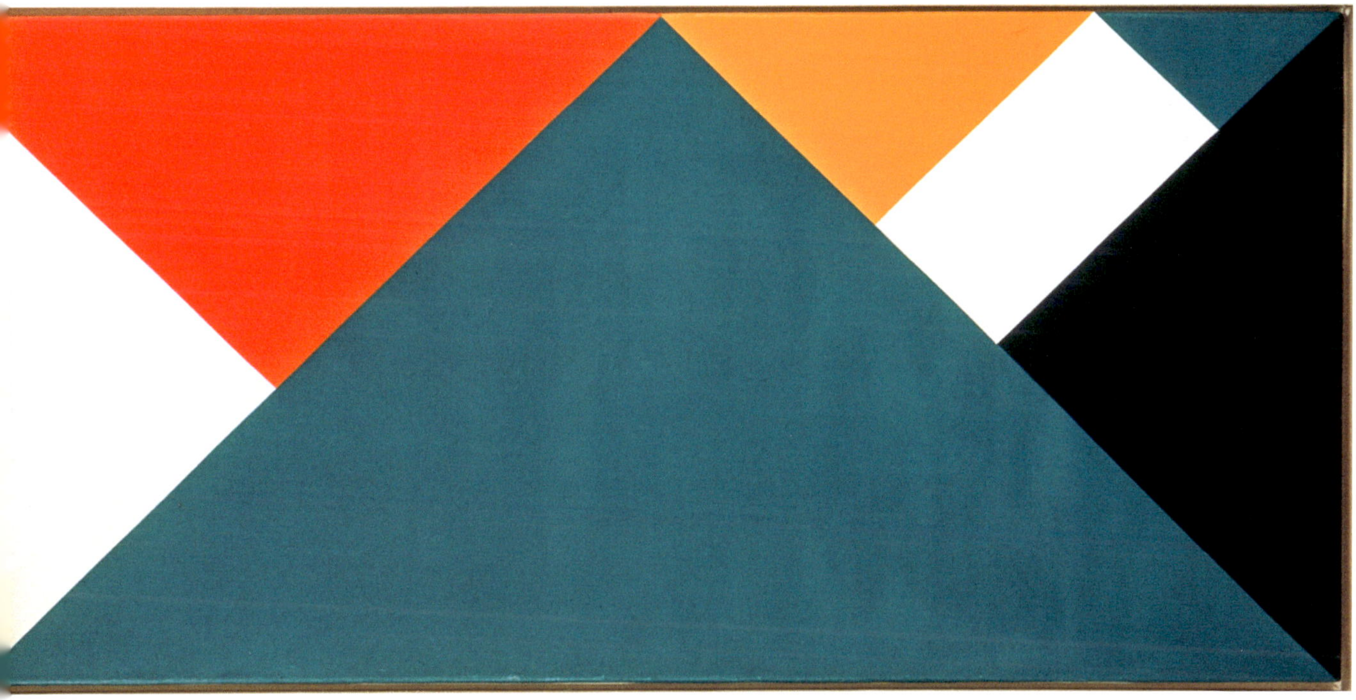

Max Bill
konstruktion aus zwei kugelförmigen ringen, 1965–1966

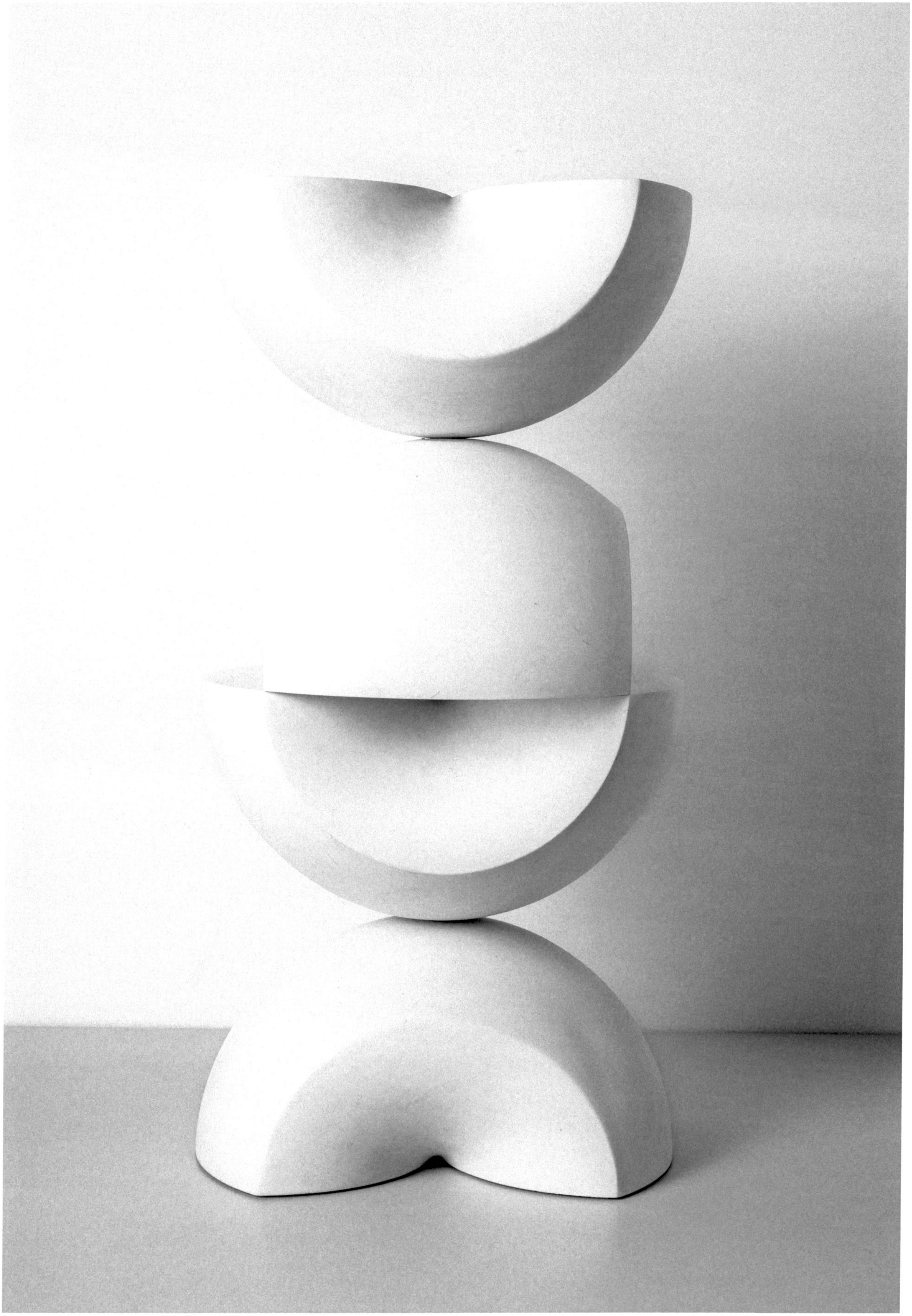

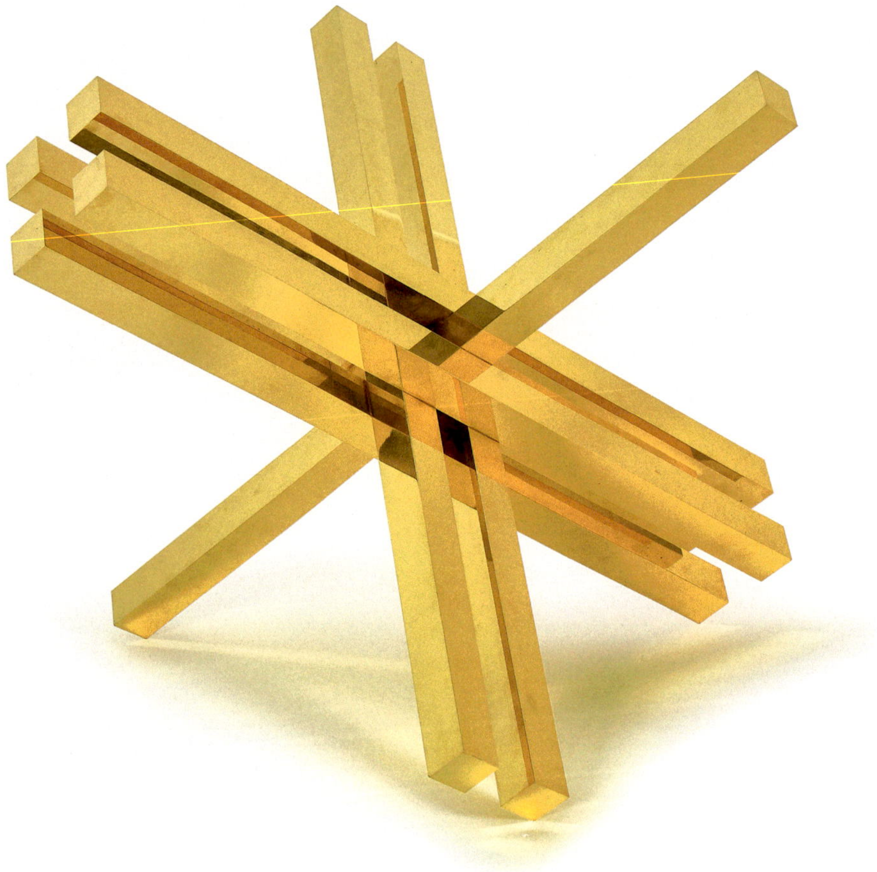

Max Bill
kern aus doppelungen, 1968

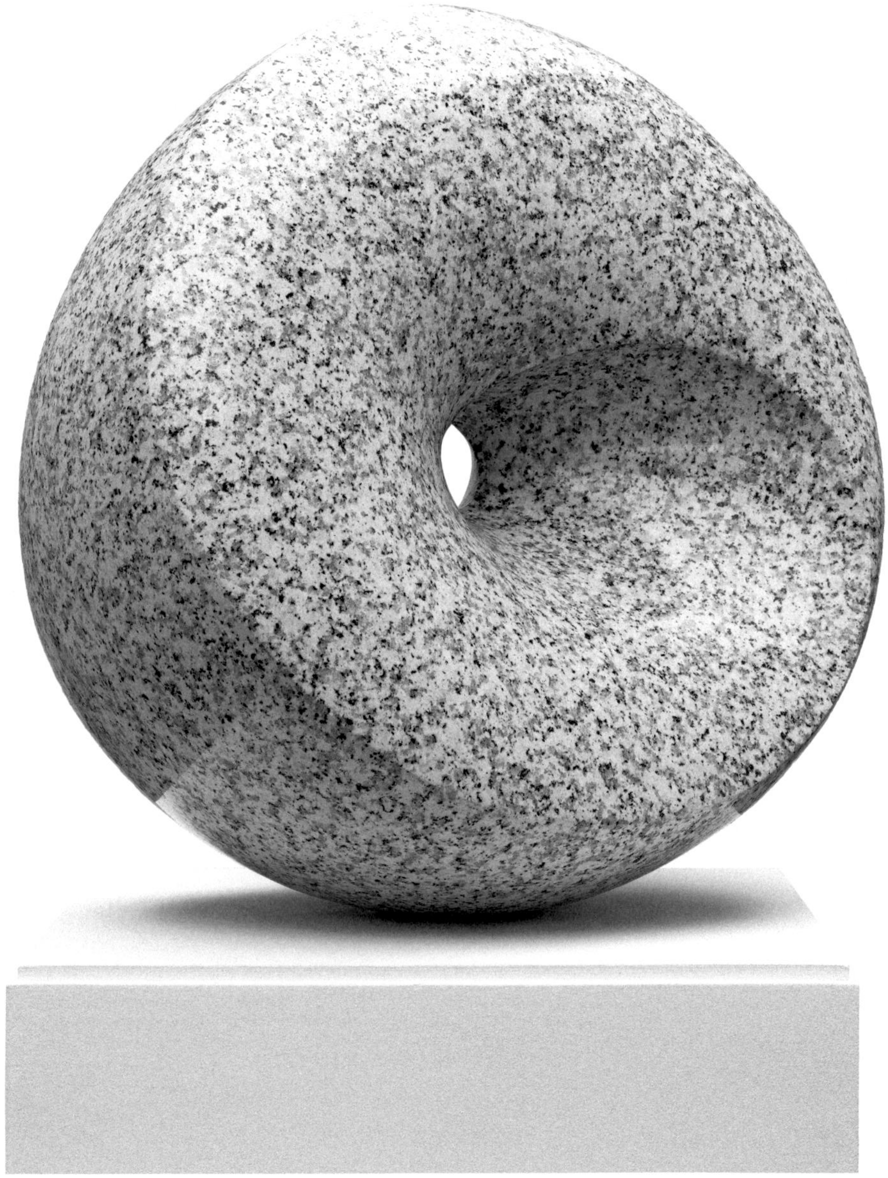

Max Bill
einheit aus kugel und endloser spirale, 1978/1983

Max Bill
drei schwarz und drei bunt zu weiss, 1983

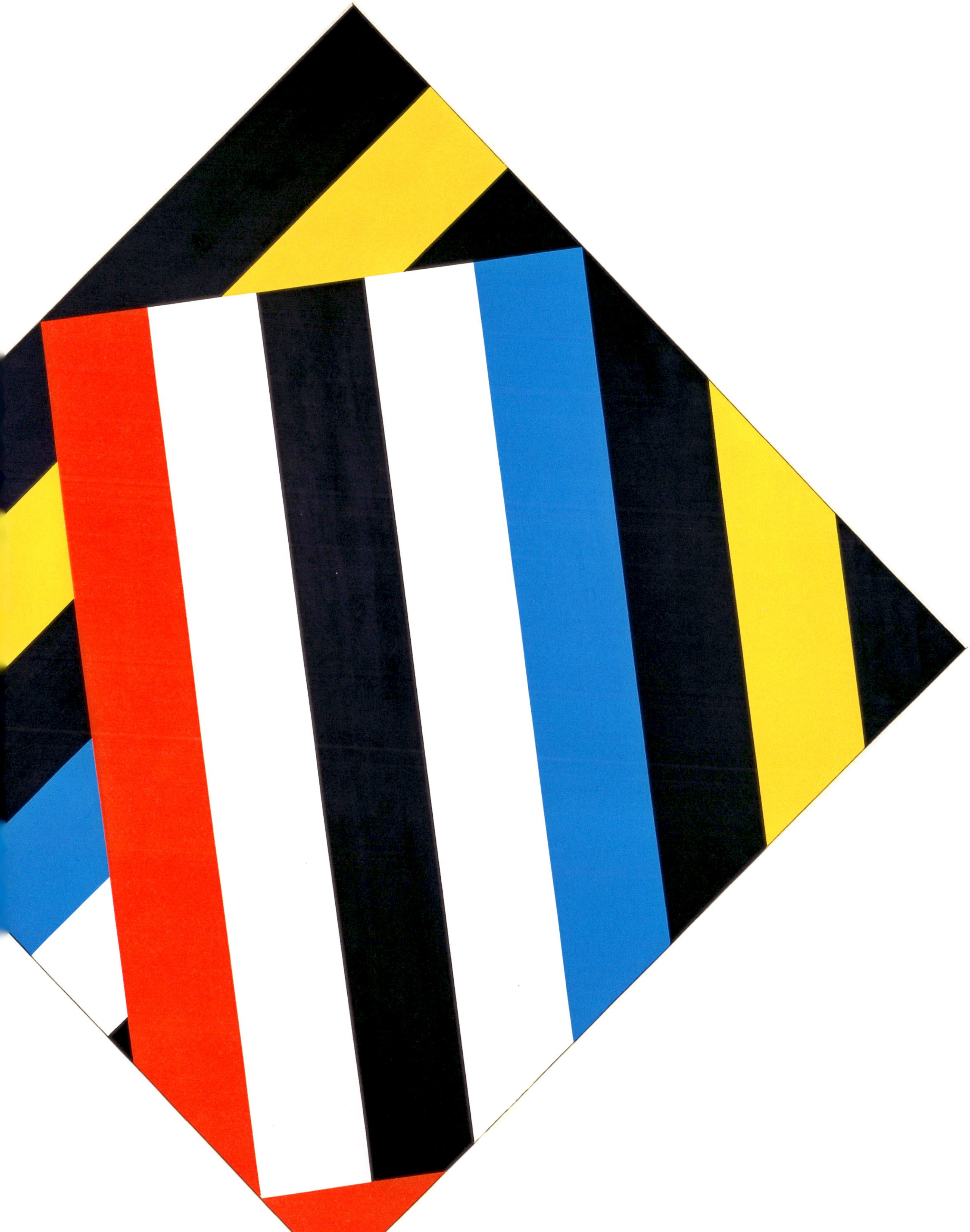

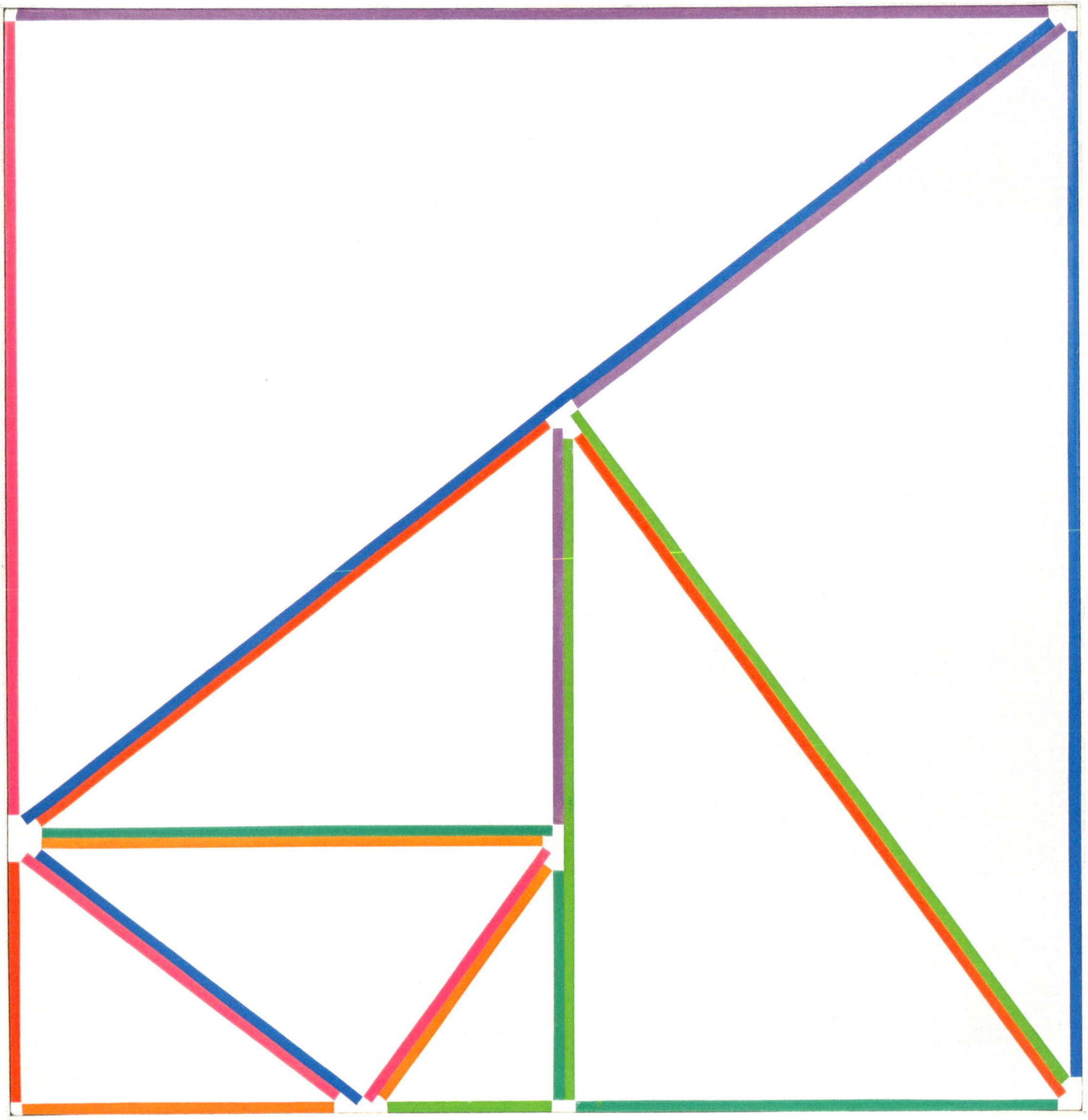

Max Bill
7 farben zu 7 pythagoräischen dreiecken im quadrat, 1980–1982

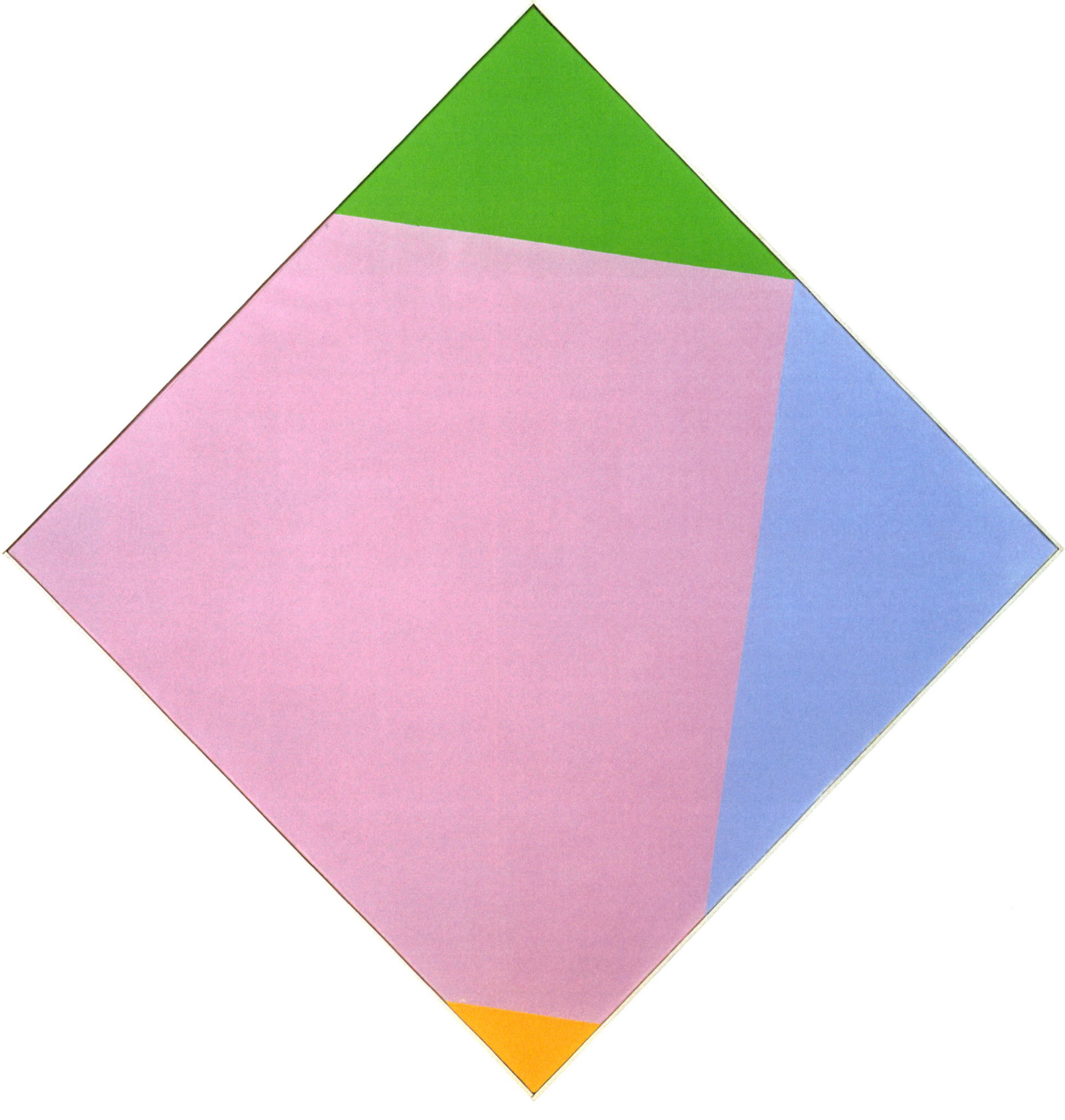

Max Bill
transcoloration aus lila, 1980–1986

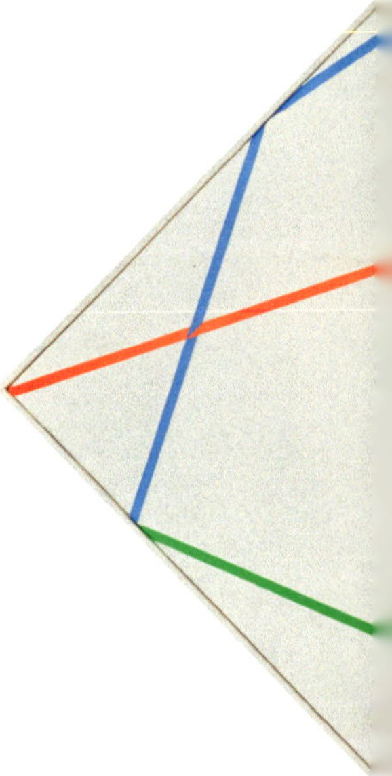

Max Bill
sechs dreiteilige linienzüge, 1983

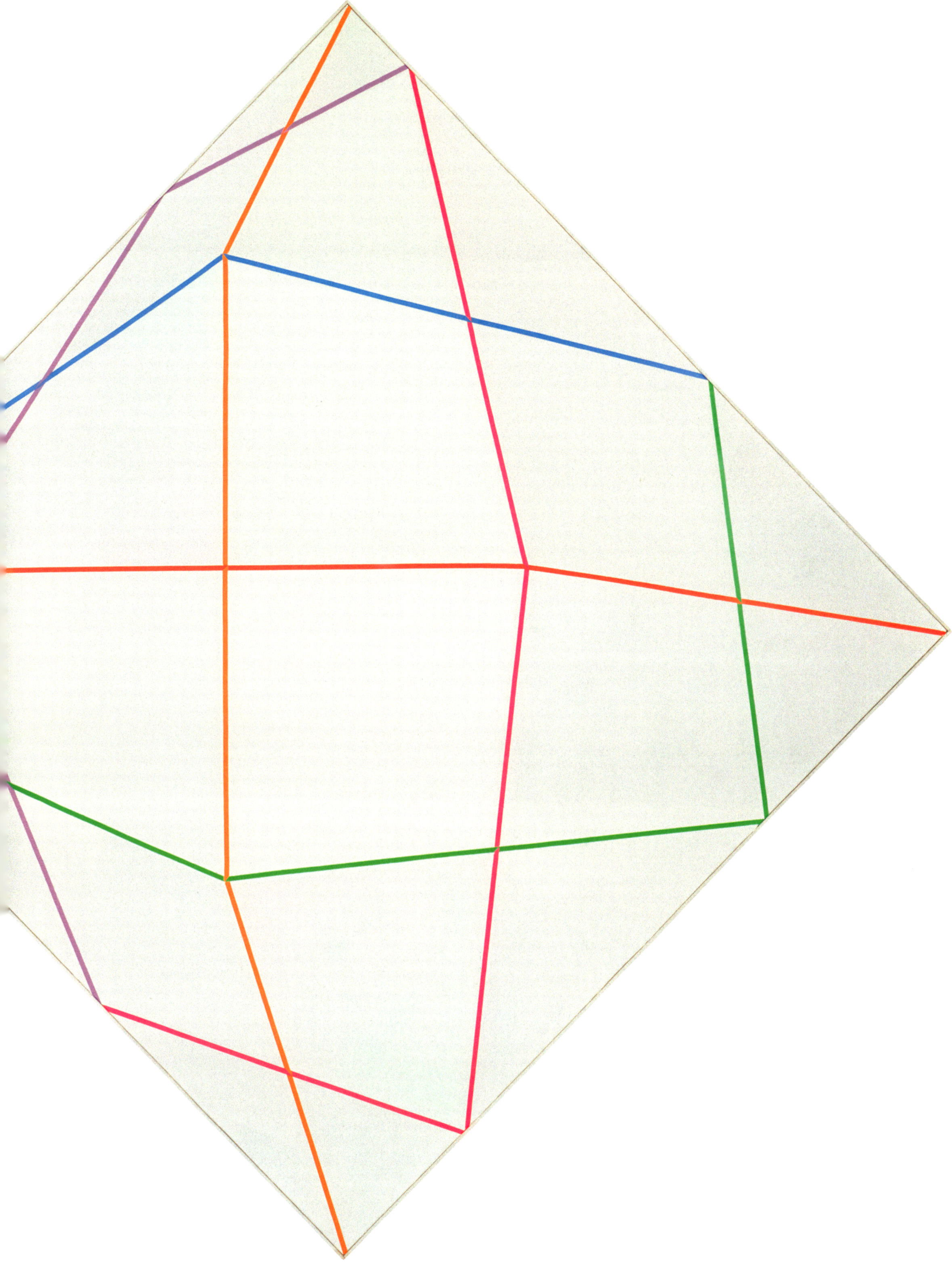

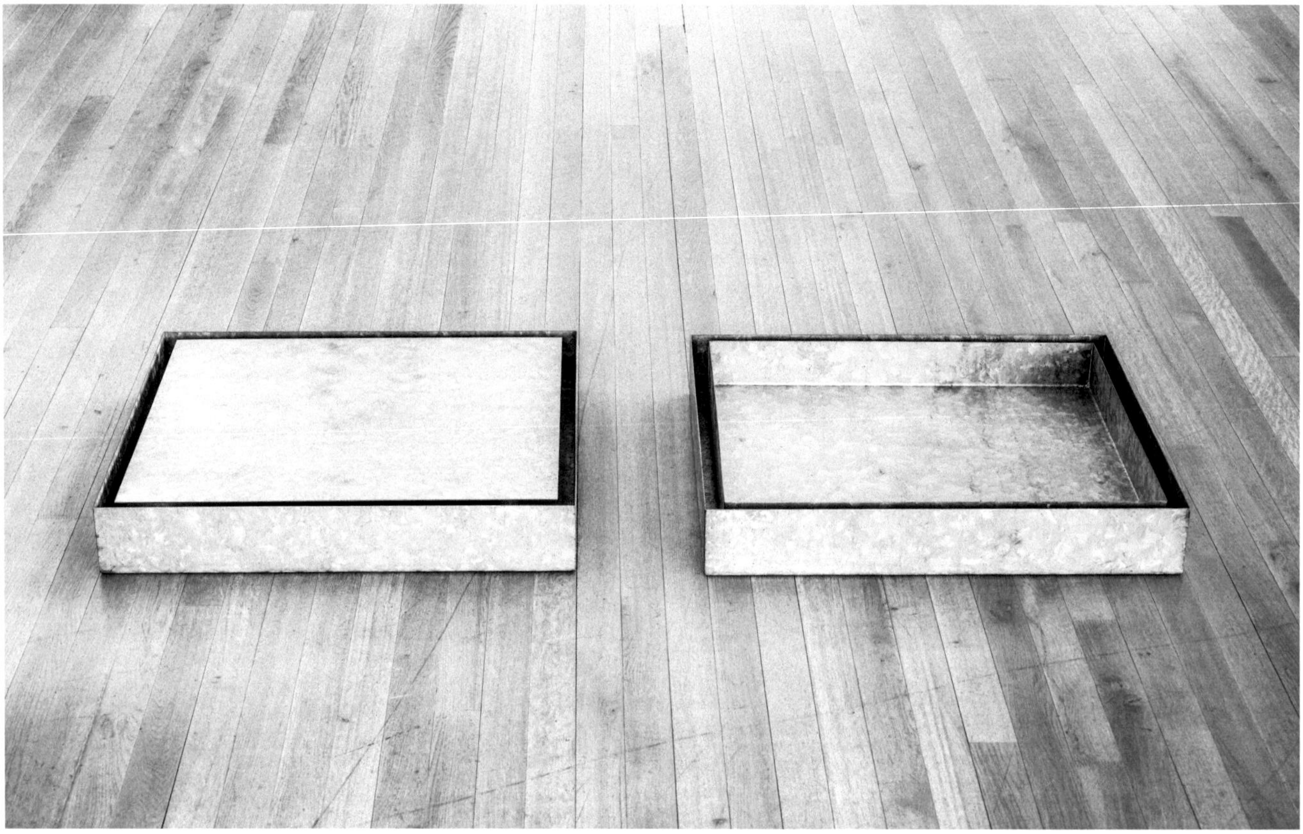

Donald Judd
Untitled (two floor sculptures
from a multi-part series), 1972–1973

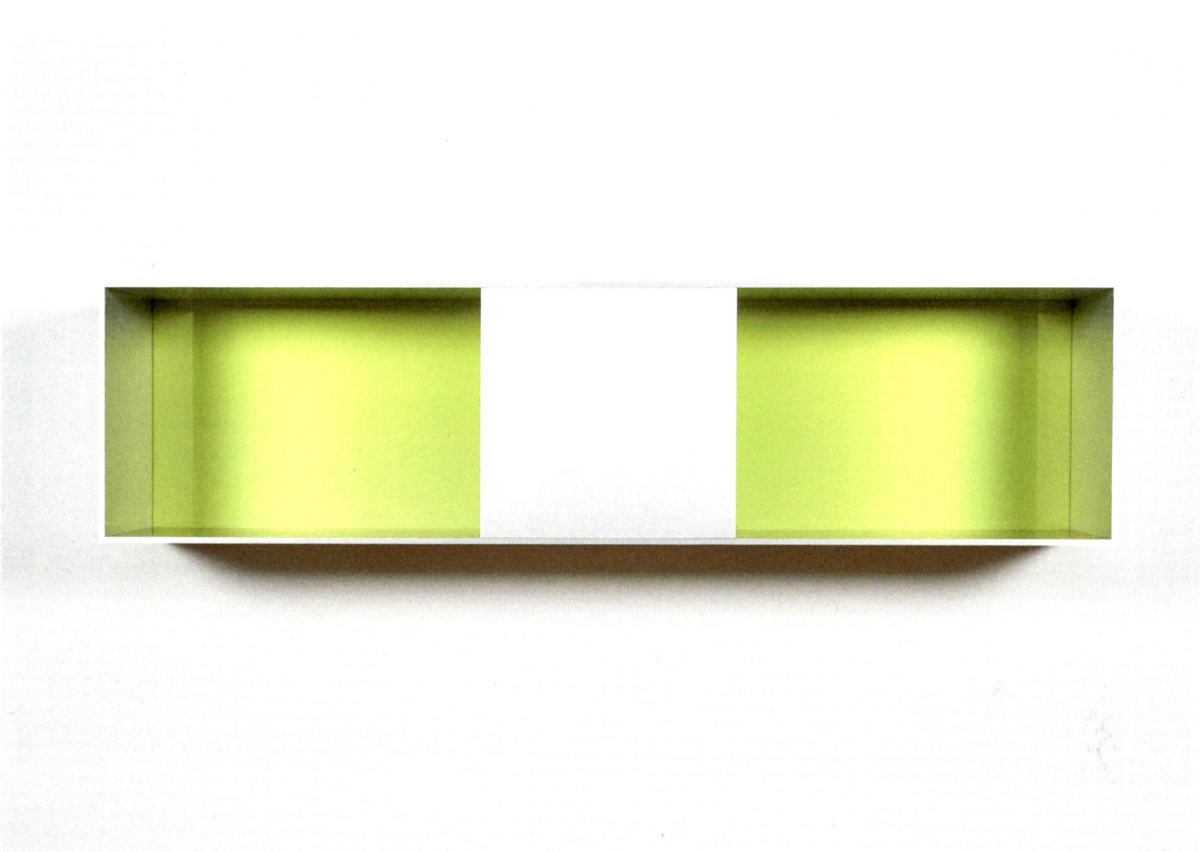

Donald Judd
Untitled (wall object from the
series: the moscow installation), 1991

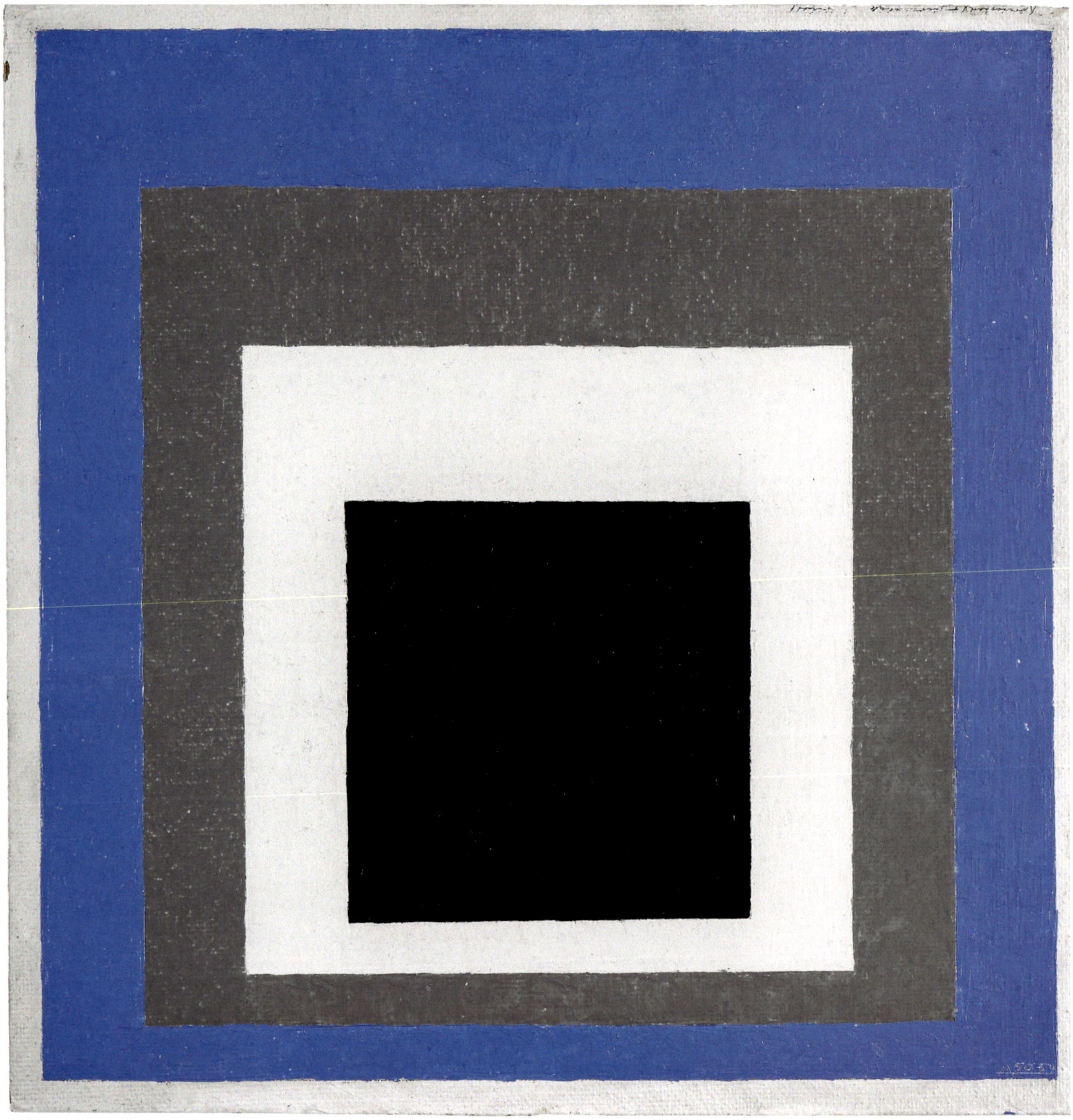

Josef Albers
Study for "Homage to the Square: Apodictic," 1950–1954

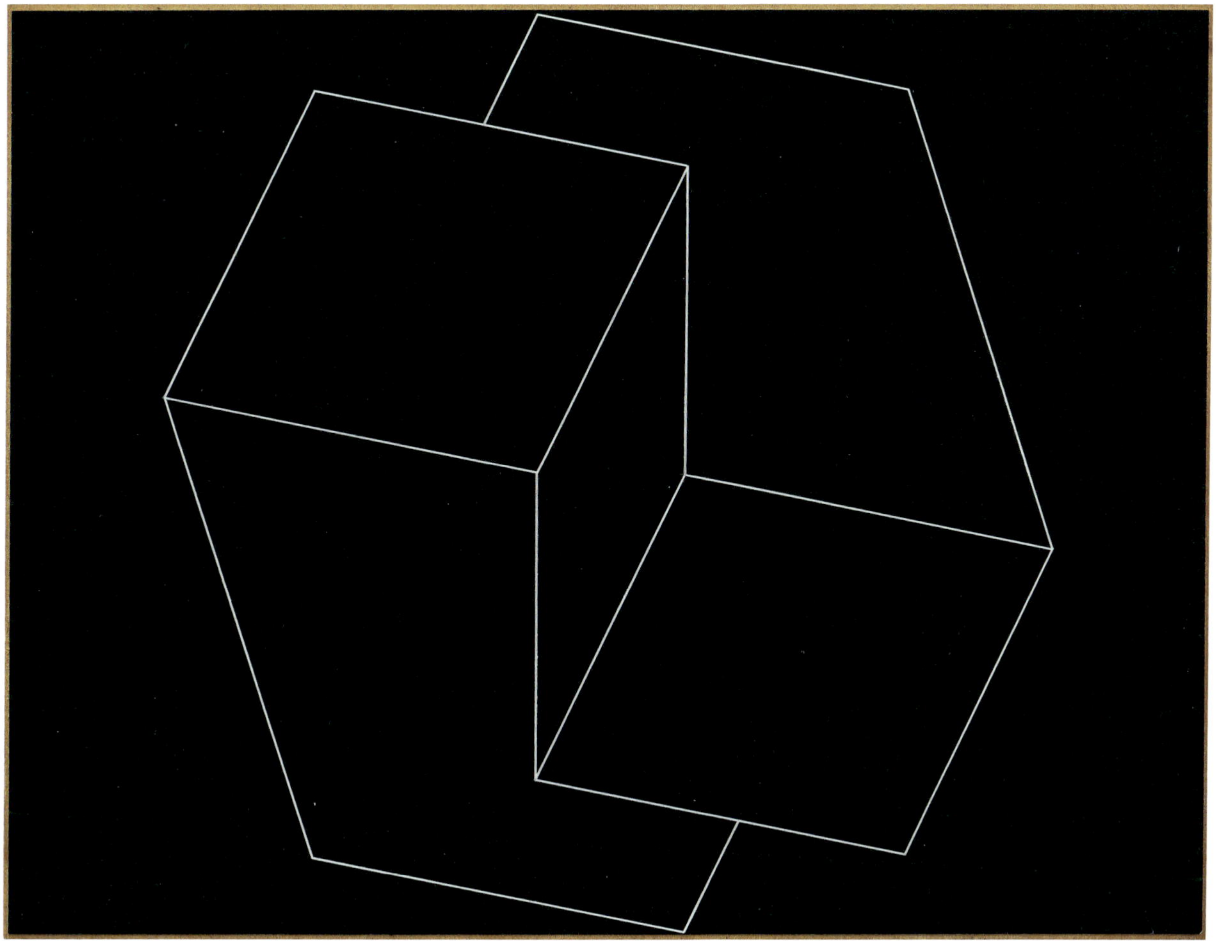

Josef Albers
u-12, strukturale Konstellation, 1955

Andy Warhol
Max Bill, 1980

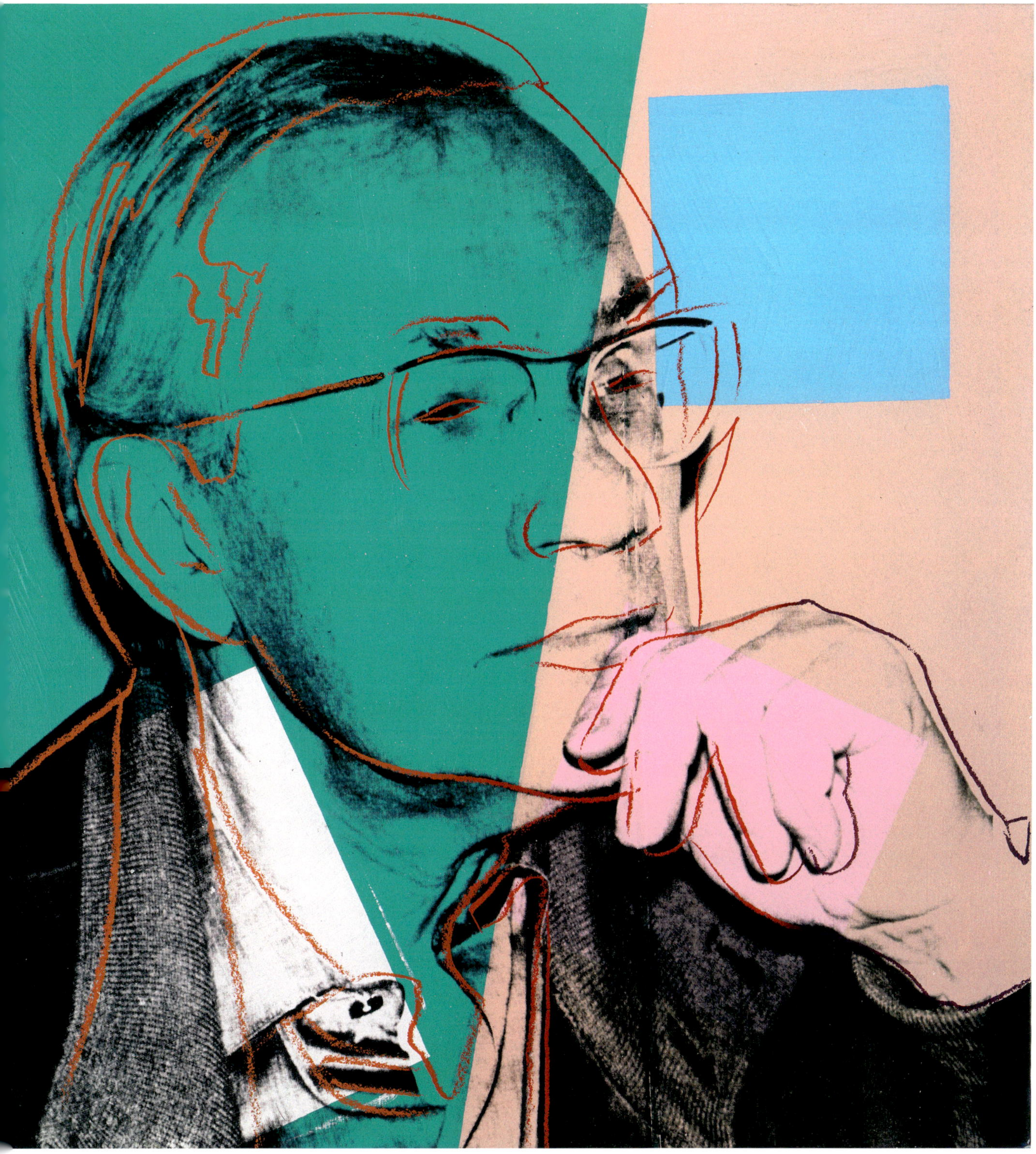

max bill

Angela Thomas Schmid

Bauhaus Constellations

The essay's title, *Max Bill Bauhaus Constellations*, which was first published in an extended form on the occasion of an exhibition of the same name at Galerie Hauser & Wirth in Zurich,[1] contains the root word *stella* (star) and the prefix *con-*, thus indicating a focus on work by Max Bill and the circle of artists to which he gravitated, among them many luminous figures.

The Back Story

If we were to look to images for insight on Max Bill's childhood and youth—which he partly spent in a reform school—we would come across an early self-portrait from 1925, showing a young man tormented by self-doubt and devastated by his parents' fighting; soon after the etching was made his mother would file for divorce (fig. 1). That same year, in a photograph taken in Paris, he brims with self-confidence. The reason was this: still at the tender age of sixteen, he had already had the opportunity to exhibit his early work (functional objects made at the Kunstgewerbeschule Zurich) at the *Exposition international des Arts décoratifs et industriels modernes* in Paris. Bill's work was chosen by Sophie Taeuber-Arp, who at the time earned a living—and supported her husband, Hans Arp—by teaching in the textile department at the same design school where Bill was training as a silversmith.

In May 1925 Bill traveled to Paris for the first time for the exhibition. Accompanied by Taeuber-Arp, who had taken him under her wing, he not only saw the Grand Palais, where his own work was on display; he also saw two contemporary buildings, presented as part of the exhibition, that fascinated him and aroused his interest in modern architecture: the *Pavillon de l'Esprit Nouveau* by Le Corbusier, and the Soviet pavilion, designed by the Russian architect Konstantin Melnikov. Back at school in Zurich, Bill took so many liberties that he was ultimately expelled. But during this time his artistic talents also led him to win a prestigious poster contest for the Suchard chocolate factory, which came with generous prize money. It opened up new horizons for him.

He strolled into a bookshop on Kirchgasse in Zurich, the Bücherstube Girsberger, where he bought the 1925 publication *Kunst-ismen*, edited by El Lissitzky and Hans Arp. In the book, various burgeoning avant-garde art movements (-isms) are defined by their protagonists. While in the bookshop, Bill also discovered a concrete reference to the Weimar-era Bauhaus, and learned that a new Bauhaus, designed by Walter Gropius, was to open in Dessau in December 1926. Bill purchased the first edition of the magazine *Bauhaus*, edited by Gropius and László Moholy-Nagy.

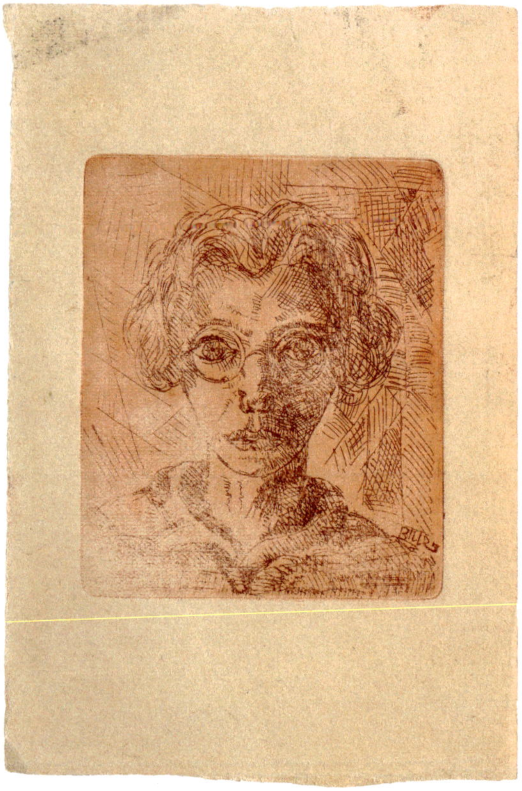

1 Max Bill, Untitled (early self-portrait), 1925, etching, 9.1 x 7.7 cm
max bill georges vantongerloo stiftung, haus bill zumikon
angela thomas and erich schmid
Courtesy Hauser & Wirth

Bill at the Bauhaus

Spurred by the buildings in Paris by Melnikov and Le Corbusier, Bill was inspired to become a modern architect himself. At eighteen years old, he took the Suchard prize money and traveled alone to Dessau—a considerable journey at the time. On April 20, 1927, he enrolled at the state Bauhaus with the matriculation number 151 (fig. 2).

That same month the Swiss, Basel-born architect Hannes Meyer was called to the Bauhaus. The new master was tasked with establishing the building and architecture department. Bill would have liked to study in Meyer's class, but he did not fulfill the admission requirements: according to the Bauhaus prospectus, to be eligible, prospective students had to either hold a *Mittlere Reife* certificate (equivalent to ten years of schooling) or have completed training in a relevant art or design field. Like every other new Bauhaus student, Bill had to begin with the preliminary course. Completing it would open the door to the individual workshops for metal, wood, mural painting, weaving, and the Bauhaus stage. The coursework in these workshops lasted two years, and only upon its completion would he qualify for Meyer's architecture department. Bill began his preliminary studies under Josef Albers, who had taught at the Bauhaus during its first incarnation in Weimar after being founded in the immediate aftermath of the military capitulation and the political chaos of the new republic. But when Bill arrived at the Bauhaus in Dessau, nearly a decade into the school's existence, unemployment, squalor, and shortages of everything and everyone still prevailed. Bauhaus master Albers was left with little choice but to send his students from the preliminary course to the garbage dumps, where they could purchase materials for their work at a reasonable price.

The Swiss architect Hans Fischli, who would later be named director of the Kunstgewerbeschule in Zurich, arrived at the Bauhaus a year after Bill and also completed Albers' preliminary course. On the subject Fischli said:

"[W]e were allowed to make anything from everything. we went to the scrapyard at the junkers plant [airplane and engine factory]—there was nothing that wasn't worth *something*; we went to the municipal landfill; behind our landlords' houses we searched for treasures that we would then transform into wondrous objects in the preliminary course. we were given themes for our work: dull and sharp, smooth and rough, explosive and static, heavy and light, round and angular. according to albers, anything else would have been a waste of valuable materials. he went so far as to require that the joints between the various parts be made without glue, cement, soldering, or welding. we even had to invent our own techniques for sticking, joining, weaving."[2]

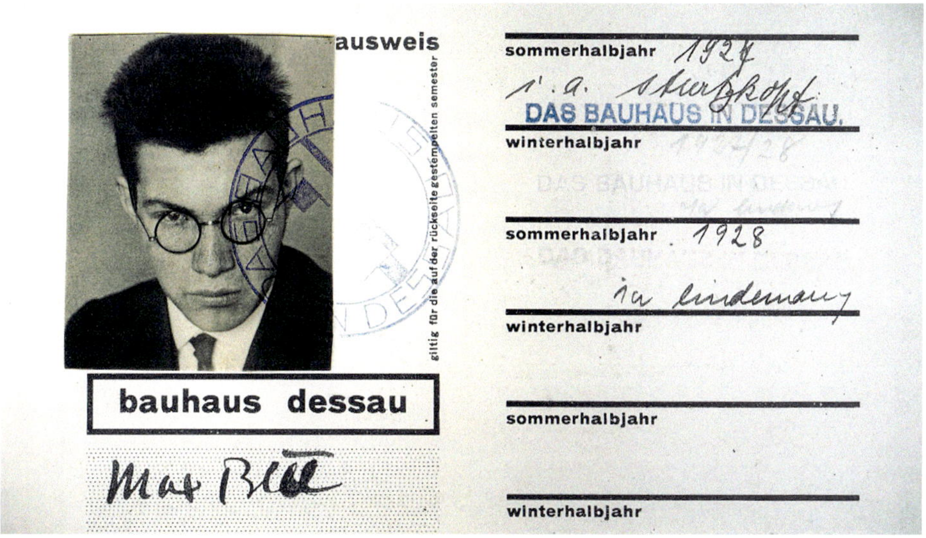

2 Max Bill's Bauhaus ID, 1927
max bill georges vantongerloo stiftung

In short, at the Bauhaus there was "a will to order." Appearing paradoxical at first, once we have understood Fischli's insight in all of its ambivalence we become privy to the nucleus of Bauhaus ideology and thus to Bill's basic principles. If we trace this ideology back to its historical extremes, it leads to the destructive attrition warfare of the World Wars, which both Bill and Fischli experienced and were deeply affected by. Hans Fischli and Max Bill both went on to teach and later serve as school directors: Fischli at the Kunstgewerbeschule in Zurich and Bill in Ulm. Guided by the premise "never again should materials be degraded to pomp and ostentation," in these roles they imparted to their students a sense of aesthetic moderation founded on the belief that all humans are equal.

Early Architectural Projects

Once at the Bauhaus, the young Max Bill—whose parents back in Switzerland eventually divorced on April 1, 1927—could finally breathe. The familial strife was behind him at last. Rebellious and anarchic, he now hungrily consumed an array of visual, spiritual, and erotic art. Bill subscribed to *Die Weltbühne*, an ambitious Berlin newspaper edited by writer Kurt Tucholsky and later by the pacifist Carl von Ossietzky. All the illustrious names of the day were published on its pages: Erich Mühsam, Lion Feuchtwanger, Else Lasker-Schüler, Robert Walser, Erich Kästner, Alfred Polgar, Carl Zuckmeyer, and Arnold Zweig. The pursuit of clarity became Bill's primary goal. In his own work it can be first observed in plans for three architectural projects that he completed for design contests while still in Dessau. On his own initiative he sent his design proposals to selection committees in Osaka and Zurich respectively.

In his preliminary course, Josef Albers stressed that designers must take responsibility for the products that they introduce to society. Bill became familiar with the fundamentals of design in Albers' interdisciplinary course. Outside of it, he (not yet twenty) independently developed two ambitious architectural projects for public competitions: the new Swiss state library at Hallwylstrasse 15 in Bern, which had to be submitted by October 1, 1927, and a five-story building in Osaka, for which the deadline was October 30, 1927 (fig. 3).[3] As Bill told me, he was compelled to rework the "first version" of his design for the Swiss state library (Dessau 1927) and consequently brought it to the post office a day too late. Since the postage date, not the date of delivery, was binding for the deadline, he begged the postwoman to set the stamp back a day, but she refused. The design thus remained in Dessau, where it was exhibited at the Bauhaus. Hannes Meyer, who had chosen not to submit his own design proposal for the competition, saw Bill's design in the exhibition.

Bill's design for a multistory house in Osaka arrived in Japan on time, earning him an honorable mention and modest runner-up prize money. Working together with Hans Fischli, Bill participated in another architectural design contest while in Dessau during the summer of 1928, for a kindergarten in a Zurich neighborhood center.[4] The duo was able to meet the deadline of June 25, 1928. The kindergarten, however, would be built by Hans Hofmann and Adolf Kellermüller. These three architectural projects demonstrate the strength of Max Bill's will to become a rational architect of modernist buildings. During the busy years that followed, he would try every avenue on his quest to realize this urgent ambition.

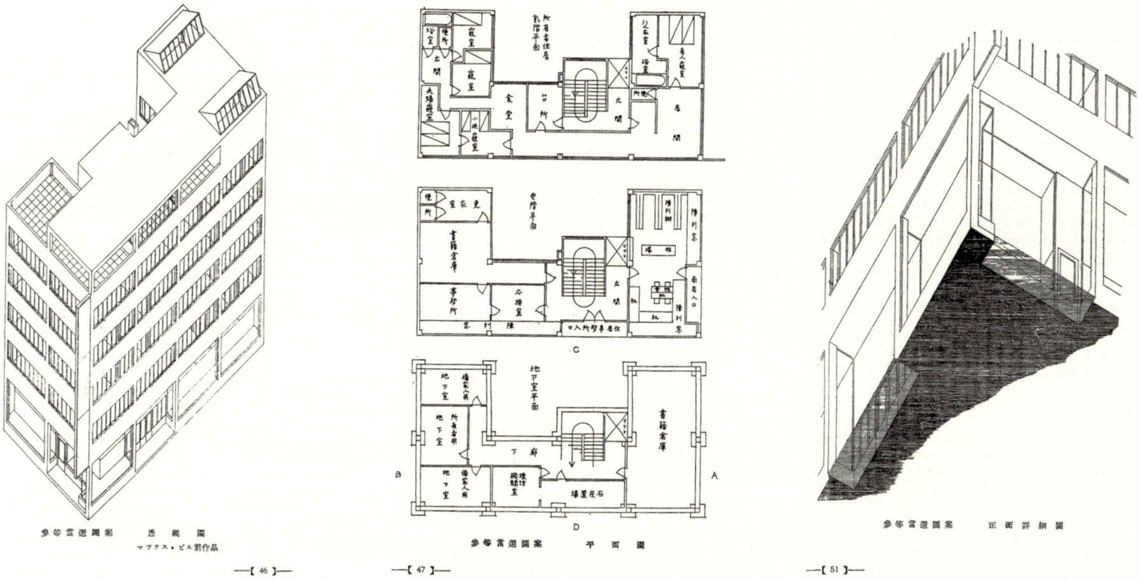

3 Max Bill, facsimile of the architectural plans for a five-story building with roof terrace in Osaka, 1927

max bill georges vantongerloo stiftung

Female Students at the Bauhaus

It can be assumed that Bill occasionally must have stumbled into the weaving workshop, where several of the female students that he happened to be attracted to were busy working. At any rate, as he later revealed to me, he fell in love at the Bauhaus four times. And so it was hardly a coincidence when, buoyed up by such visits, he suddenly started using yellow fabric to complete a geometric drawing in color (fig. 4).

Some of Bill's fellow female students smoked and wore their hair bobbed with bangs, as a symbol of their emancipation. They were refreshingly modern and lively, and they danced wildly at the Bauhaus parties. Through these encounters Bill discovered his own erotic appeal. Among the young women were Katt Both (née Anna Elisabeth Mathilde Both) and Hilde Rantzsch. They were already at the Bauhaus when Bill enrolled. The two friends took the young Swiss artist under their wing. At the time Bill lived two kilometers from the school in an attic apartment at Fichtenbreite 32. Hans Fischli would later become Bill's roommate. To earn a living, Rantzsch cleaned the Bauhaus weaving workshop. She made mostly figurative Surrealist art. Bill held on to two works that she made in 1927 (pl. p. 35). Together with Rantzsch and Fischli, Bill formed "gruppe z," an artist group "for new

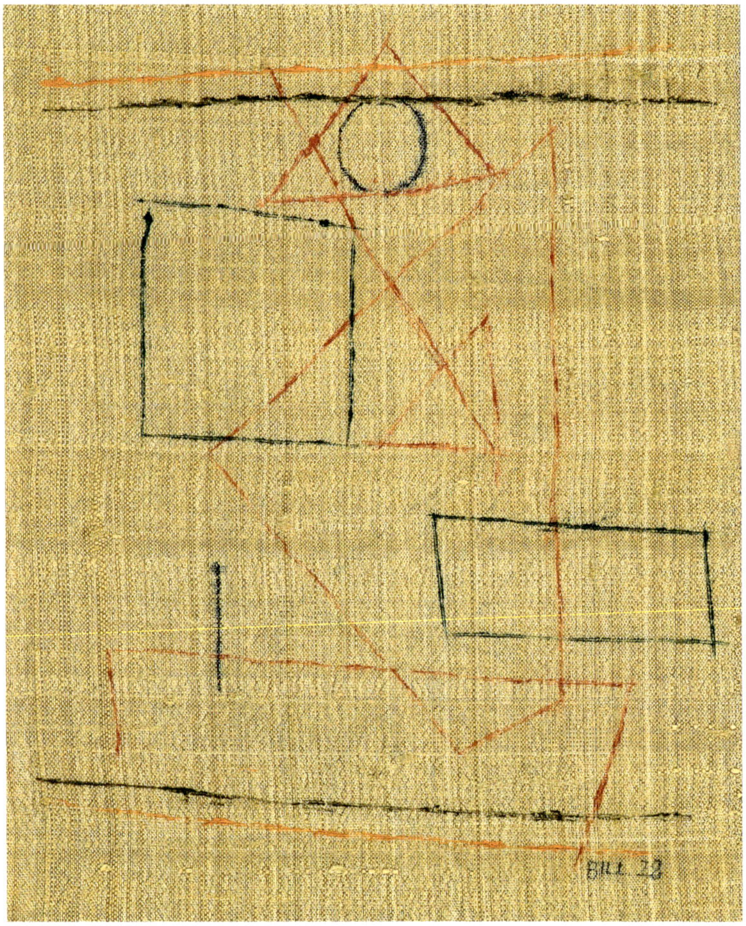

4 Max Bill, no. 3, 1928
Drawing on yellow fabric, 17 x 13.8 cm
max bill georges vantongerloo stiftung, haus bill zumikon
angela thomas and erich schmid
Courtesy Hauser & Wirth

painting, sculpture, etc." Shortly thereafter he designed their business card, writing in small print: "gruppe z, new painting, sculpture, etc., max bill painter, architect, secretary of gruppe z, dessau, fichtenbreite 32."

A few years later, after the Nazis had forced the Bauhaus to close, Bill and Rantzsch met again in Zurich. Rantzsch had emigrated to Switzerland, where for a period she worked in the studio of her fellow refugee and former teacher, Gunta Stölzl, who notably had been the only female Bauhaus master (of weaving). Bill designed her letterhead. Rantzsch nevertheless returned to Nazi Germany.[5] It is not known what became of her. Katt Both or "the girl with the beautiful eyes" (as the title of a portrait by Bill describes her), was three years his senior. She not only worked in the Bauhaus carpentry workshop, but, unlike Bill, also had the privilege of taking classes taught by Walter Gropius, Hannes Meyer, and Mart Stam in the Bauhaus architecture department. There is cause to believe that in mid-1928 she started taking Bill along to Stam's lectures on static equilibrium. Dutch architect Stam had recently arrived in Dessau as a visiting lecturer for "urban development and the fundamentals of architecture"; he remained there for approximately a year.

Bill and László Moholy-Nagy

While attending the preliminary course, Bill tried out the mural painting workshop, before being ultimately assigned to László Moholy-Nagy's metal workshop. We know this because a later design for *Untitled. Sketch for a mural with large O* (pl. p. 48), made in 1932, alludes to his taking up the subject of mural painting again.

Hannes Meyer, who in April 1928 had succeeded Walter Gropius as Bauhaus director, restructured the school's curriculum: from this point on, three days would be devoted to theoretical learning, and three to hands-on work. That meant fewer teaching hours and more time for discussions. It begs the question: was the new curriculum the reason why Bill was increasingly absent from Moholy-Nagy's class? Or was Bill—after having nearly completed training as a silversmith in Zurich—simply bored in the metal workshop? In any case, he was required to execute designs by Marianne Brandt—a task that he evidently thought to be beneath him. He could often be found on the banks of the Elbe, swimming and idling about, until one day Moholy-Nagy invited him to his studio in his master's house. Bill brought along his own watercolor paintings and spoke of his "maladie de la peinture" (painting sickness).

Looking back, Bill described his visit in the following terms: "László Moholy-Nagy invited me to his studio in 1927. He wanted to know why I no longer turned up at the Bauhaus metal workshop, which he ran. I told him that I would rather paint. I showed him pictures that I had brought along, and he showed me his." Here he added that Moholy-Nagy's "observations and advice remain with me to this day as criteria. A particularly characteristic picture demonstrated his artistic style, situated between Dutch and Russian constructivism."[6] Bill was referring to the painting *Q IV* (pl. p. 180),[7] which Moholy-Nagy made in 1923 during his tenure at the Weimar Bauhaus; it has its own style, with elements of both Dutch De Stijl and Russian Suprematism.

Thus, in the Bauhaus master's studio, Bill had the opportunity to see not only works that he had completed in Dessau, but also a number that dated back to the early days of the Bauhaus in Weimar.

Bill and Kandinsky

Kandinsky was born to well-to-do parents in Moscow and lived in Russia for thirty years, where he studied law and was ultimately appointed honorary professor at the University of Moscow. Kandinsky spoke and wrote fluent Russian and French, and from childhood he was able to read German, the language of his complex, seminal text *Über das Geistige in der Kunst*. After his time at the Bauhaus, Wassily Kandinsky emigrated to Paris. He and Bill remained in contact until the Russian artist's death on December 13, 1944. Bill republished several of his essays posthumously. Kandinsky taught at the Bauhaus between 1922 and 1933, both the obligatory foundational course on color theory as well as a free painting class that Bill attended as well.

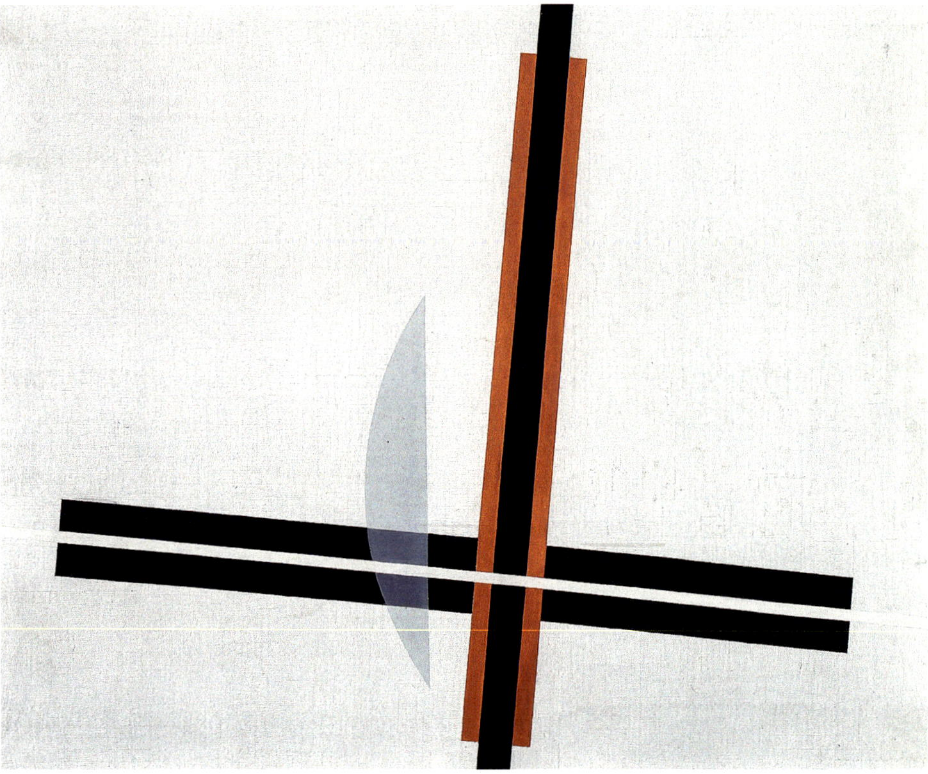

5 László Moholy-Nagy, Komposition Q IV, 1923
Oil on canvas, 102 x 123 cm
max bill georges vantongerloo stiftung, haus bill zumikon angela thomas and erich schmid
Courtesy Hauser & Wirth

Kandinsky thought that an artwork should become a "subject animated with a spiritual breath." Bill took up where the Russian artist left off, referring to his own oeuvre henceforth as "objects for spiritual use." His choice to replace the word *subject* with *object* is worth noting: Bill distanced himself from the spiritistic/subjective character of Kandinsky's work, favoring instead a mathematical/rational artistic style.[8]

Bill not only took an interest in Paul Klee's teaching notes (see the essay in this volume on pages 191–192), he also carefully went through the trunk of manuscripts that Kandinsky had left behind in the basement of his house—located in the exclusive Paris neighborhood of Neuilly-sur-Seine—and enjoyed an active written correspondence with his widow, Nina Kandinsky, whom Bill was acquainted with from the Bauhaus in Dessau. He visited her from time to time in France. She ultimately consented to a new edition of Kandinsky's publication *Punkt und Linie zu Fläche*, which Bill designed.

Bill on the Bauhaus stage

In late January of 1928, Bill, still attending the free painting classes, left the metal workshop and joined the Bauhaus stage and its workshop. It is possible that Clemens Röseler encouraged him to join. A fellow student and friend of Bill, Röseler (whose biographical data is unknown to me) had already been part of the stage workshop for some time and also painted. Bill's estate includes a composition by Röseler featuring a ship motif.[9] The Bauhaus stage was under the direction of Oskar Schlemmer, whom Bill already knew from "the human being," the master's obligatory, two-hour-long, weekly drawing class.

In addition to his own drawings, Bill kept a 1928 figurative drawing from Schlemmer's class made by his fellow student Alfredo ("Freddo") Bortoluzzi, who, together with Hans Fischli, Hilde Rantzsch, Annemarie Hennings, and Röseler, made up gruppe z.[10]

The stage workshop gave Bill free rein to his creativity. He appeared on the Bauhaus stage as an actor at least once, in a performance put on for the student body. He played the banjo in the Bauhaus band, having picked up the string instrument quickly thanks to the cello lessons he had taken as a child. Bill reminisced: "Oskar Schlemmer (1888–1943) was one of my teachers at the Bauhaus. For a time I worked on the Bauhaus stage, which he directed. To this day the theater remains a keen interest of mine [...]."[11]

Of all the Bauhaus masters, Schlemmer was reportedly the one who could be found with his students in the cafeteria most frequently. According to Bill's fellow student Fischli, members of the stage workshop had a special "aura" about them, "because everyone knew that they dwelled in the basement and had no funding, the schlemmer group had a peculiar virtue. when they walked around or sat at a table in the cafeteria, you always had to look twice: first came theatrics, and only then would they drink their milk from ordinary glasses."[12]

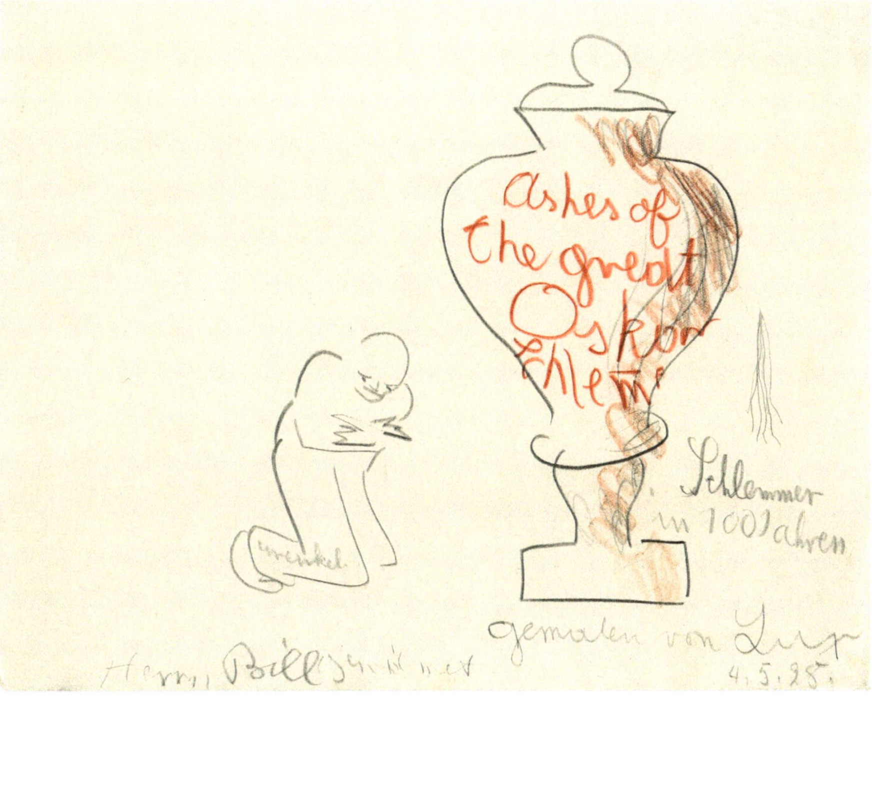

6 Theodore Lux Feininger, Ashes of the Great Oskar Schlemmer, Mai 4, 1928, Pencil and colored pencil on paper, 21.5 x 27.4 cm

max bill georges vantongerloo stiftung, haus bill zumikon
angela thomas and erich schmid
Courtesy Hauser & Wirth

Years later, Bill described what he had hoped for—and ultimately found—at the Bauhaus with the following words:

"It was as if you arrived at the Bauhaus acting on an irresistible urge, in hopes of finding something that would correspond perfectly with a modern attitude to life: a blend of education, science, experimentation, youthful exuberance, and cultural savvy. Once at the Bauhaus you no longer had to search for it consciously: you worked, you experimented, you discussed. The outside world became less and less interesting, because you were part of a community that brought together everything from the most important artists of our epoch to isolated, obnoxious overachievers who had washed up there by chance. From this group you searched out your friends and your even-more-endearing female friends; learning might have seemed superfluous at times, but you never forgot to work."[13]

Clemens Röseler was one of those friends that Bill had searched for and found at the Bauhaus. In a well-known photograph of student workers on the Bauhaus stage, Röseler can be found on the far left, next to Theodore Lux Feininger, holding a carpet beater aloft (pl. p. 21). Friends with Röseler himself, T. Lux Feininger may have been jealous of Bill, because in May 1928, T. Lux took a swipe at Bill by drawing a caricature mocking his apparent veneration of Schlemmer. It shows Bill bowing down in front of an urn holding the "Ashes of the great Oskar Schlemmer" (original in English). To the drawing he added the words "Herrn Bill gewidmet" (dedicated to Mr. Bill, fig. 5). Oskar Schlemmer was nevertheless still alive and kicking and Bill knew how to take a joke. For the rest of his life he would hold on to the caricature, to which he added his own—perhaps intentionally—orthographically incorrect note: "gemalen von Lux 4.5.28" (painted by Lux 5/4/28). As for the fact that T. Lux Feininger penned the caption in both German and English, according to his autobiography, so far only published in German, *Zwei Welten. Mein Künstlerleben zwischen Bauhaus und Amerika*, whenever he went to the cinema with his father—the German-American Bauhaus master Lyonel Feininger—they would subsequently discuss the film in English: something that he was particularly proud of.

In the fall of 1928, while Bill was practicing walking in circles on the stage, one of his classmates swung down from a trapeze and inadvertently crashed head first, into Bill's face. The collision knocked out several of Bill's upper teeth; he would have to wear a metal dental plate for the rest of his life.[14] The high cost of his dentist bills, largely paid for by taking out loans from his father, consequently forced Bill to terminate his studies at the Bauhaus. But the people he met and contacts he made while there would be of critical importance for his later career, and he kept in touch with many of them throughout the course of his whole life.

1 Angela Thomas Schmid: "max bill bauhaus constellations", in: Zurich 2019, pp. 5–55. The text has been abridged and lightly re-edited for the purpose of this publication.

2 Hans Fischli in *Hans Fischli. Malerei, Plastik, Architektur*, exh. cat. Zurich: Kunsthaus 1968, Zurich 1968, p. 28.

3 Thomas 2008, pl. p. 134.

4 Published under the English title "Max Bill and Hans Fischli: architectural competition project for a kindergarten and district center in Zurich, Dessau, 1928" in: Thomas 1993b, ill. p. 104.

5 The reason for Hilde Rantzsch's return to Germany is unclear. Perhaps she, like many other refugees in Switzerland, was sent back.

6 Bill 1976, p. 39.

7 There is reason to believe that Bill purchased the Bauhaus master's painting *Q IV* (1923) after it was exhibited at the Kunst Kabinett Klihm in Munich from June 2 until July 15, 1959, in the presentation *L. Moholy-Nagy 1895–1946, 20 Ölgemälde aus den Jahren 1920–1936*. Inserted into the pages of Bill's copy of the exhibition catalog was a letter from the gallery offering him the work *Q IV*, 1923, cat. no. 10. The catalog, which contains a black-and-white image of the work, also features a text by Moholy-Nagy's second wife (and widow), Sibyl Moholy-Nagy: "Moholy-Nagy und die Idee des Konstruktivismus." A black-and-white reproduction and an essay by Bill on *Q IV*, 1923, can be found in: Bill 1976, p. 39. The painting has been exhibited multiple times since Bill's death, on loan from Angela Thomas. It was, for example, presented in the exhibition *László Moholy-Nagy* at the gallery Annely Juda Fine Art in London in 2004. It was exhibited and reproduced in the catalog for *Albers and Moholy-Nagy: from the Bauhaus to the new world* at Tate Modern in London in 2006, and for the exhibition *László Moholy-Nagy* at Hauser & Wirth, London, 2019.

8 The German word *spiritistisch* (spiritistic) is not to be confused with the English term "spiritual." On the topic see also the passage in Schmid, 2008, in which Bill explains: "From my experiences at the Bauhaus and with my older colleagues in Paris I knew that I had to find a new path." He found it in music, with tones and harmonics that are "combined in mathematical intervals. And this made me realize that I also had to turn to mathematics in my painting and sculptures."

9 The estate is at the Haus Bill in Zumikon.

10 Annemarie Hennings was the daughter of the Dadaist Emmy Hennings from an earlier relationship prior to her marriage to Hugo Ball.

11 Bill 1976, p. 32.

12 Fischli 1968 (see note 2), p. 60.

13 Max Bill, 1947, quoted from: Thomas 2008, pp. 179–180.

14 For this reason, some individuals might have had the impression that Bill floundered when he spoke, or had a soft lisp. In actual fact it was the result of his having to wear the dental plate. A cameraman once took advantage of his misfortune, by filming Bill's lips at such an extreme close-up that they filled the entire screen thus presenting him in as unappealing a light as possible.

creative processes as logical method

Fabienne Eggelhöfer

Max Bill and Paul Klee

Max Bill began assiduously building up an international network of contacts during his time at the Bauhaus. After abandoning an apprenticeship as a silversmith at Zurich School of Arts and Crafts, he set off for Dessau in the spring of 1927 with the aim of studying architecture at the Bauhaus. As he had neither learned a trade nor was in possession of even an intermediate high school diploma, he first had to attend Josef Albers' preliminary course—as did most other students—before he could be admitted to one of the workshops. In addition to the preliminary course, Bauhaus freshmen were also required to attend Paul Klee's lessons on form and Wassily Kandinsky's on color. As Bill quit the Bauhaus before completing his course of study, his records do not tell us anything about his actual attendance of these classes. The former apprentice silversmith was assigned first to László Moholy-Nagy's metal workshop, which did not suit him at all. At the end of January 1928, therefore, he switched to the theater workshop taught by Oskar Schlemmer, whom he knew from the latter's "Human Being" drawing course. In parallel to his activities at the Bauhaus, Bill also worked independently on various architecture competitions and attended Klee and Kandinsky's free painting classes. Even the early days of his training were shaped by his interest in craftsmanship, architecture, and painting—the three disciplines that were to preoccupy him his whole life long.[1]

Reflecting on his experience at the Bauhaus in later years, Bill acknowledged that its fostering of interdisciplinary collaboration in pursuit of a better designed world had encouraged him in his own aspirations. Josef Albers' preliminary course in particular, he said, had taught him to question everything he knew and to fearlessly tackle new problems;[2] and it was again from Albers—with whom Bill stayed in touch right up to the former's death in 1976—that he had learned to develop objects out of the material.[3] For all his free experimentation, Albers had nevertheless insisted that every design act be discussed and explained in the group. In the world of early twentieth-century design this seemingly counterintuitive practice led to productive, dialectical, critical engagement. It also gave rise to new forms that were developed by venturing along hitherto unknown paths. Far from being some random product of the imagination, however, the design process itself was to be underpinned by logic at every stage—a balancing act that Paul Klee had come to master in his works, as in his teaching.

Klee's essay "exakte versuche im bereich der kunst" was published in the journal *bauhaus* in 1928. In it, Klee grappled with the dialectic of intuition and construction, of the spontaneous and the rational: "Where intuition is combined with exact research it speeds up the progress of research," he wrote. "Exactitude winged by intuition is at times best."[4] The essay was a commentary on the technical, rational approach that had come to prevail at the Bauhaus during those years. According such "exact research" an important role in design, Klee hailed it as a step in "our education towards the essential, towards the functional." By analyzing inner function, he argued, "we learn the prehistory of the visible." Yet this alone was not enough to create something, since creative processes demanded intuition, which could not be taught. Bill reprinted this text first in 1945, in the magazine *abstrakt/konkret* 7, and again in 1960, in the catalog of the exhibition *konkrete kunst. 50 jahre entwicklung* that he himself had curated.[5] Published alongside Klee's piece in that catalog were other groundbreaking texts on Concrete Art, including the De Stijl Manifesto, Theo van Doesburg's Concrete Art Manifesto (published in 1930 in the journal *art concret* under the title "Base de la peinture concret"), and texts by Georges Vantongerloo, Richard Paul Lohse, Georges Mathieu, Victor Vasarely, and Hans Arp. Although the exhibition featured the works of several artists from South America, not one of their numerous manifestos was published there.

The question of how much rational construction and how much intuition or playfulness is admissible in the artistic process was one on which most Concrete Art groups were divided. Even Bill, who had such a defining influence on Concrete Art discourse in Switzerland, was torn between these two poles. His first brief definition of Concretism was published in the catalog of *Zeitprobleme in der Schweizer Malerei und Plastik* of 1936, in which he opined that "although all creative design is stimulated by inspiration, it cannot be perfected without clear and precise forming."[6] Two years later he expanded on this, arguing that those works that might be perfected only through logical construction were "pure creations of the human spirit." The fundamentals, he continued, lay in "stereometric and planimetric regulation." Not that it was mathematics alone that led to works of art, since mathematics was effective only when coupled with the "inspiration of the mathematical approach."[7] Bill defined what he understood by the "mathematical approach" in another article which, like the aforementioned essay, was published first in the magazine *Das Werk* in 1949 and subsequently translated into various languages. The artist, he explains there, not only works with his or her own individual scales of value, but also has to rely on "empirical calculations." Whereas art always followed mathematical principles as a means of "imparting harmony to the whole," contemporary art was no longer a "naturalistic replica" achieved by means of perspective, but was rather a "primal image" based on mathematical models. "It must not be supposed that an art based on the principles of mathematics [. . .] is in any sense the same thing as a plastic or pictorial interpretation of the latter," wrote Bill. "The art in question can, perhaps, best be defined as the building up of significant patterns from the ever-changing relations, rhythms and proportions of abstract forms, each one of which, having its own causality, is tantamount to a law unto itself." The closer art approximated the mathematical way of thinking, he contended, the nearer it came "to the first cause or primal core of things."[8] In a letter to Georg Schmidt, Director of Kunstmuseum Basel, Bill made it clear that any imputation of "hard and fast calculations" to his sculptures was a "malevolent misunderstanding," since they were based only on "just as much mathematics as is necessary to make them 'crystalize out' and not simply stand there as fantasy products."[9] Whereas Klee did not use the term "mathematics" as such, his teaching at the Bauhaus rested on the same principles. Bill emphasized Klee's approach in a third amended version of his essay "Die mathematische Denkweise in der Kunst unserer Zeit": "also worth noting in this connection is the role of Paul Klee, whose 'pictorial thinking' is born of a pictorial logic that bears all the hallmarks of a theory in which geometric proportions are handled with imagination."[10] It was nature's own growth processes that initially served Klee as vivid examples of how forms come into being (fig. 1). Thus, when he asked his students to design leaf shapes, he instructed them not to copy an outline or to invent some fantasy form, but to follow nature's example by developing leaves from the inside out. "Inner necessity [is] the basis for form-creation," wrote Klee. "Underlying it is need. No vain toying with results, but rather an inner development, an active, necessary path to form."[11] Later, in Dessau, he dispensed almost entirely with concrete examples from nature to explain the emergence of geometric forms. His almost 3,900-page-long Bildnerische Gestaltungslehre (Theory of Pictorial Configuration) falls into three parts. Part one, the "General Part," explains the principles of figuration, in some cases citing examples from the world of nature and music. Part two, titled "Planimetric Configuration," is the longest of the three and is subdivided into nineteen chapters, beginning with "Paths to Form." There, Klee first explains the emergence, through movement, of the elementary geometric forms triangle, circle, and square and

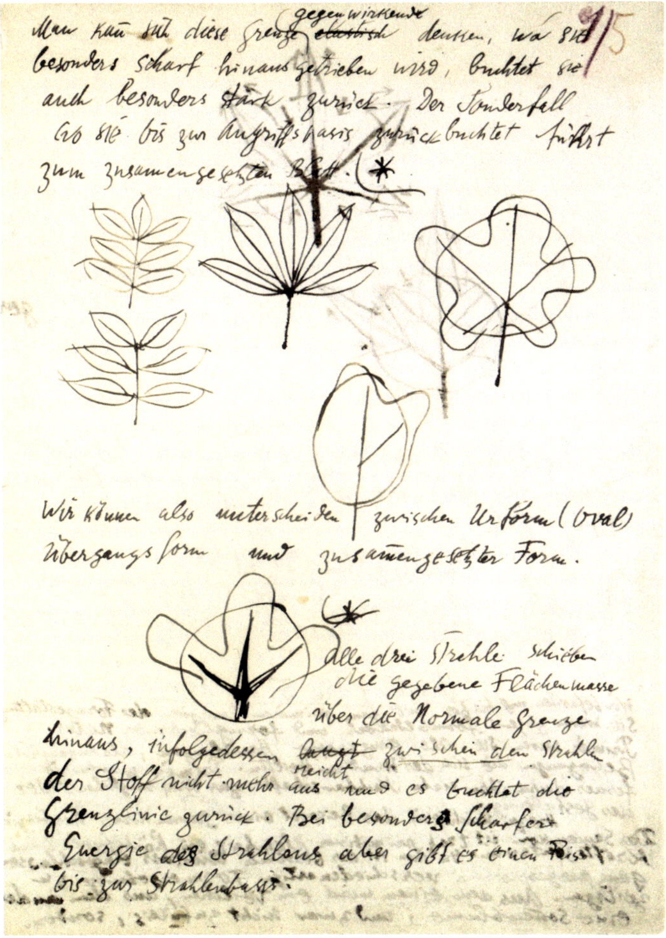

1 Paul Klee, Theory of Pictorial Configuration: I.2 Principal Order BG I.2/6, pen and colored pencil on paper, 22 x 14.4 cm
Zentrum Paul Klee, Bern

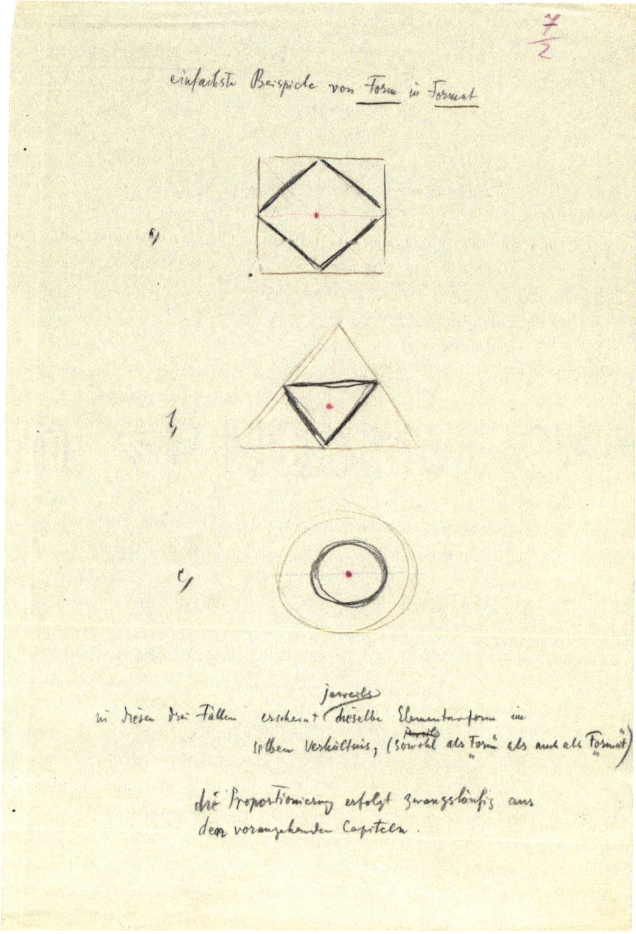

2 Paul Klee, Theory of Pictorial Configuration: II.7 Form in Format BG II.7/3, colored pencil on paper, 33 x 21 cm

Zentrum Paul Klee, Bern

then shows the many different ways in which they can be combined and modified (figs. 2 and 3). In part three this method is transferred to "Stereometric Configuration," by which Klee means configuration in space.[12] The focus here is always on the logical path to construction. His theory of creativity is summed up in the programmatic rallying cry: "Formation is good. Form is bad; form is the end, death. Formation is movement, act. Formation is life."[13] Klee, in other words, was concerned not with the end results, but with the process—with formation.

That Bill repeatedly appealed to his former Bauhaus master is hardly surprising, given Klee's emphasis on the logical derivation of form. It was Klee's "logic of process" that Bill regarded as a "direct continuation" of "what Klee understands by 'pictorial thinking.'"[14] Bill commented on his engagement with Klee in a conversation with Angela Thomas: "Back then, during my time at the 'bauhaus' (Dessau), I was interested in Klee's ideas and quite heavily influenced by them. Only much later did I fully grasp the theoretical background that Klee had elaborated; especially in connection with the systematic approach to picture-making that I myself would later undertake. I regard the theoretical work of Paul Klee to be of the utmost importance even today."[15] In Bill's view, Klee's teaching at the Bauhaus had been of ines-

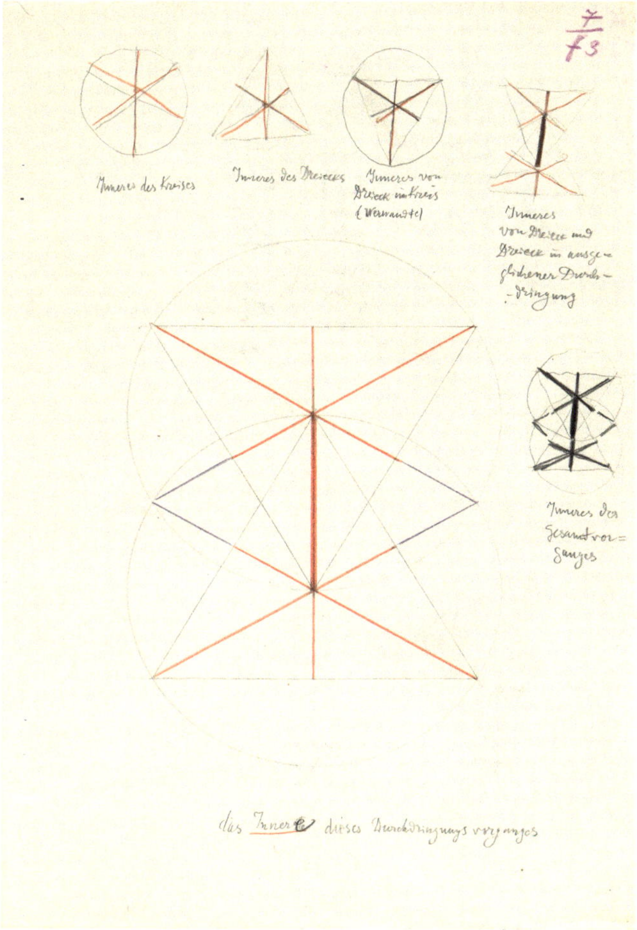

3 Paul Klee, Theory of Pictorial Configuration: II.9 Assembled Form BG II.9/45, pencil and colored pencil on paper, 33 x 21 cm
Zentrum Paul Klee, Bern

timable value to the emergence of Constructivist art.[16] Looking at the works of art that Bill himself produced while at the Bauhaus, it is not difficult to spot the similarities with some of Klee's works. Bill even suggested to his master that they swap paintings, a request that Klee diplomatically declined on the grounds that normally it was for the older artist to propose such a swap to the younger, and that was what he would do, if so inclined, when the time came.[17] On his teacher's fiftieth birthday in 1929, Bill gave him the work on paper *Hermaphrodith* (he appended the title himself), which is now at the Zentrum Paul Klee on permanent loan from a private owner (pl. p. 29). Klee, in return, sent Bill a card thanking him for his "softly powerful and consistently earnest" work.[18] But he did not return the sentiment—not even after Bill reconnected with him after he fled to escape the Nazis in late 1933. Bill visited Klee in Bern on several occasions. And in 1936 the works of both artists featured in the group show *Zeitprobleme in der Schweizer Malerei und Plastik* at Kunsthaus Zurich.[19] An article by Bill congratulating Klee on his sixtieth birthday was published in the *Neue Zürcher Zeitung*,[20] and of course Klee also received birthday greetings from Bill by post.[21] Only after Klee's death did Bill try yet again to swap works with him. Lily Klee, however, again rejected the idea, offering only to sell him one of her late husband's works at an especially low price—on condition that Bill neither disclose the amount nor resell it.[22] This is how Bill came to acquire Klee's painting *Rhythmie herbstlicher Bäume, 1920, 4*, the first of seven works by Klee that he would eventually buy which he gave to his wife Binia on the birth of their son Jakob on July 2, 1942.

Klee's death on June 29, 1940 and the Klee exhibitions at Kunsthaus Zurich, Kunsthalle Bern, and the Graphische Sammlung of ETH Zurich that followed shortly thereafter prompted Bill to write a number of newspaper articles.[23] He also offered a guided tour of the memorial exhibition at Kunsthalle Basel in the spring of 1941, which in his view was not properly understood.[24] Especially interesting is Bill's review of an exhibition at Kunsthaus Zurich that had been organized while Klee was still alive. In his write-up, Bill cast his erstwhile teacher as an "intermediate phenomenon" occupying the middle ground between Surrealism at one extreme and Constructivism at the other, and identified the essence of Klee's art as the dialectic between the conscious and unconscious, the intuitive and the rational. Klee, Bill concluded, had pointed out those paths "that might eventually lead to a natural, scientific and constructive order."[25] In a five-page article on Klee published in the magazine *Das Werk* he went even further, allocating several of Klee's works to the category of Concrete Art. Klee had thought about "exact constructions," he wrote, and had taught accordingly.[26] While it is certainly true that Klee, around 1930, began developing works consisting of geometric constructions and colored shapes (fig. 4) and that these had to do with his teaching, it is important to draw a distinction between what he taught and what he created.[27] His lesson notes did not serve him as studies, as has frequently been suggested—first and foremost by Jürg Spiller, who as editor of *Bildnerisches Denken* (1956) and *Unendliche*

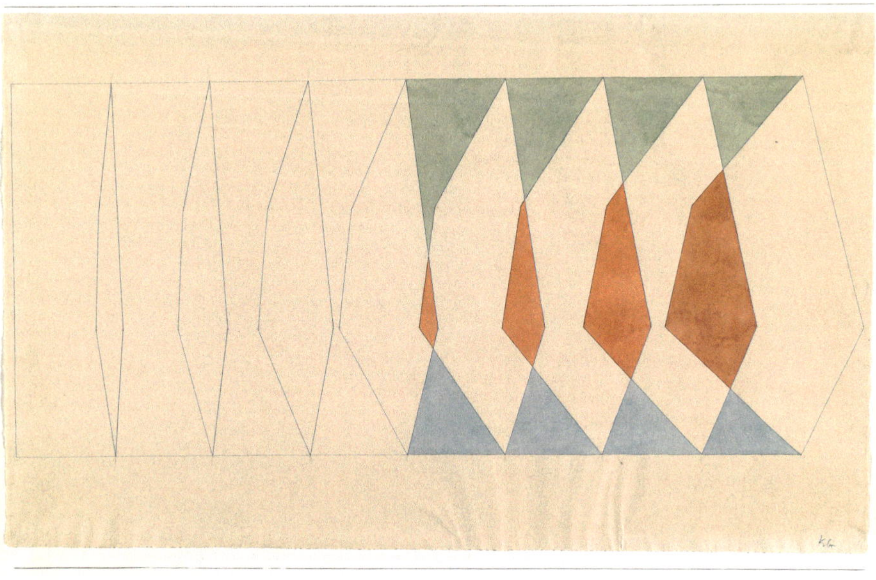

4 Paul Klee, Bewegung einer Figur (auf Grund von 1931 L 12), 1931, 53, pen, watercolor and pencil on paper on cardboard, 38.2 x 63.5 cm

Zentrum Paul Klee, Bern

Naturgeschichte (1970) juxtaposed the schematic sketches that Klee used for teaching with reproductions of his works.[28] His declaration of this as "proof" of Klee's translation of theory into practice[29] not surprisingly drew fierce criticism, even then. Bill, meanwhile, was apparently preparing a book that would present Klee's theory of pictorial configuration from a completely different angle. We know from two letters of his to Lily Klee dated the autumn of 1943 that he had met with her to talk about the possibility of publishing "klee's pedagogic work." In them he asks her for all Klee's teaching materials and stresses that apart from him, "no one would have the experience needed to compile the pedagogic work in its entirety, turning it into a usable whole that might provide those seeking avenues of artistic expression with clear guidance." That Bill had the audacity to take on such a project at all is actually quite astonishing, given how rarely he had attended Klee's classes on form.[30] But he saw "no alternative," he opined to Lily Klee, "to my devoting the coming winter to the bulk of the work on it."[31] In another letter to her he asked her for the notes that were still missing, since only when he had all the materials at his disposal could he form a proper picture of the task in hand.[32] Bill later complained that Lily Klee had given him only the "theoretical drawings," but not the texts belonging to them in the lecture transcripts.[33] Yet there never were any texts accompanying the geometric drawings, for although at the start of his career Klee wrote out his lectures word for word, he soon became confident enough not to need such detailed lecture notes.[34] The four lesson notes now in the estate of Max Bill were presumably acquired in connection with this project. It seems that Lily Klee was already in contact with Jürg Spiller by then and that he, too, was interested in Klee's teaching materials. But so eager was Spiller to reconstruct Klee's supposedly coherent "theory of art" that he changed the way the material was organized, removing single sheets from their original context and recombining them at his own discretion, even supplementing them with representations of his own. Bill confided his doubts about Spiller's work in a letter to Klee's son, Felix, even before the first volume, *Paul Klee: Das bildnerische Denken*, was published in 1956, prophesying that "it will certainly never be the book that passes on the legacy of Paul Klee's theory of pictorial configuration."[35] He therefore proposed that Helene Nonné-Schmidt, a former student of Klee who was still in possession of her own copious notes, should compile her own book of Klee's lessons. Felix had no objections to this undertaking in principle,[36] but when Schwabe Verlag, as the publisher of Spiller's work, inquired of him whether he had authorized the book that Bill and Nonné-Schmidt were planning, he reacted rather angrily to the premature publicity the project was attracting.[37] Ultimately, the book was never published. Nonné-Schmidt remained unconvinced by Spiller's compilation, and even considered it dangerous, arguing that it had degenerated into a mere "recipe book," as she wrote in a letter to Felix Klee of 1963. Thank goodness it was too expensive for most young people, she sighed, adding that "of course the book would not have stood a chance on the book market without all the many examples that Spiller had assembled almost entirely at random."[38] While from today's perspective, one can only concur with Bill and Nonné-Schmidt, Spiller's book sold well and is still all too often referenced, even today.

The time lag between Bill's time at the Bauhaus and his interest in Klee's theory of pictorial configuration was by no means unusual. Many students realized that they had not properly understood Klee's lessons at the Bauhaus only years or even decades after the event, and only then appreciated the significance of what he had taught them. Lena Bergner, for example, who was a student in the Bauhaus weaving workshop from 1925 to 1930, wrote how "his expositions were extremely important for us weavers as they helped us to advance beyond our all too playful designs and to produce more rigorous compositions. owing to his often all too short explanations, we often had trouble grasping the full meaning of his thoughts, which became apparent to us only much later when we were already practicing our profession."[39]

Max Bill, too, returned to Klee's Bauhaus teaching only when prompted to by his own lines of inquiry. Only then did he appreciate Klee's treatment of the "problems of constructivist art, which are structural and rhythmic, and related solely to the means of expression."[40] Klee's teaching notes in fact explain the very same creative processes that Bill, too, liked to apply: shifting, mirroring, rotating, warping, the rhythmic organization of area, the regular and irregular division of the picture plane—Klee calls this "dividual" versus "individual" organization—and progressive series. Then there are the color scales and contrasts, the primary and complementary colors, the notion of format and forms that interpenetrate or overlap. The titles of Bill's works really can be read as "recipes" telling us how he developed them. Any comparison of Bill's paintings and Klee's lesson notes would be bound to uncover numerous specific connections. To interpret Klee's lesson notes as the script for Bill's paintings, however, would not be helpful. The aim should rather be to show that Bill discovered in Klee's approach an attitude to form creation that accorded with his own. The pictorial processes that Klee taught at the Bauhaus and that Bill brought to bear in all his disciplines were to be applied in a series of logical steps. Both men were interested in the development of concrete forms using processes that rested on the fundamentals of configuration, and while they applied original, elementary, universal, and hence objective principles and conceptual models,[41] they selected their "operations" subjectively and intuitively. Both thus arrived at a successful synthesis of intuition and reason, even if with very different results.

1 For further details of Bill's training at the Bauhaus, see the essay by Angela Thomas Schmid in this catalog; pp. 173–183; Thomas Schmid: "max bill bauhaus konstellationen," in Zurich 2019; Bill 2008a; Ulrike Bestgen: "'... eine geistige, fortschrittliche Richtung' – Anmerkungen zu Max Bill," in Weimar 2007, pp. 11–21.

2 Bill 1979.

3 Hans Jörg Glattfelder: "Konstanz und Wandlung des Begriffs 'konkret' bei Max Bill," in Winterthur 2008, pp. 16–26, here p. 18.

4 Paul Klee: "exakte versuche im bereich der kunst," in *bauhaus. zeitschrift für gestaltung*, no. 2/3 (1928), p. 17, English translation "Exact Experiments in the Realm of Art," in *Paul Klee: Creative confession and other writings*, ed. by Matthew Gale, London 2013, pp. 18-19.

5 *abstrakt/konkret. bulletin der galerie des eaux vives zürich*, no. 7 (1945); cf. Zurich 1960, here pp. 20–21.

6 Cf. Zurich 1936, here p. 10.

7 Bill 1938, p. 251.

8 This text was published first in *Das Werk*, see Bill 1949a, and then, in an extended version, in Zurich 1949, n. p., Bill 1949. Translations to English, French and Spanish of the first version were published in Maldonado 1955.

9 Letter from Max Bill to Dr. Georg Schmidt, Conservator of the Public Art Collection Basel, June 10, 1949, Archiv Kunstmuseum Basel. I would like to thank Angela Thomas Schmid for alerting me to this.

10 Cf. Margit Weinberg-Staber 2001, p. 79.

11 Paul Klee: *Theory of Pictorial Configuration: I.2. Principal Order*, BG I.2/10, November 5, 1923, Zentrum Paul Klee, Bern.

12 All the teaching notes can be viewed online at www.kleegestaltungslehre.zpk.org (accessed: September 14, 2020). Introductions to each chapter in English see Fabienne Eggelhöfer, Marianne Keller Tschirren, "Bildnerische Gestaltungslehre: Teaching Pictorial Configuration," in *Paul Klee. Bauhaus Master*, exh. cat. Bern: Zentrum Paul Klee, Madrid: Fundación Juan March 2013, pp. 49–123.

13 Paul Klee: *Bildnerische Gestaltungslehre, I.2. Principielle Ordnung*, BG I.2/78, January 8, 1924, Zentrum Paul Klee, Bern.

14 Letter from Max Bill to Dr. Siegfried Salzmann, March 18, 1971, published in *Paul Klee und seine Malerfreunde. Die Sammlung Felix Klee*, exh. cat. Duisburg: Wilhelm-Lehmbruck-Museum 1971; Winterthur: Kunstmuseum 1971, Recklinghausen 1971, p. 124.

15 Max Bill in conversation with Angela Thomas, in Studen 1993, p. 24.

16 Max Bill: "bauhaus und 'abstraction-création' in Bezug auf die Entwicklung der konstruktiven Kunst in der Schweiz," in Winterthur 1981, p. 24.

17 Letter from Paul Klee to Max Bill, undated, probably November 1928, Bibliothek Max Bill, quoted after Thomas Schmid 2008, p. 269.

18 Postcard from Paul Klee to Max Bill, December 26, 1929, Bibliothek Max Bill, quoted after Thomas Schmid 2008, p. 267.

19 Sixteen works by Paul Klee and seven works by Max Bill, cf. Zurich 1936.

20 Max Bill: "Paul Klee. Zu seinem 60. Geburtstag," in *Neue Zürcher Zeitung*, 160, no. 2140, (December 17, 1939), Sunday Edition, p. 5.

21 Letter from Max Bill to Paul Klee, December 16, 1939, Zentrum Paul Klee, Klee family donation.

22 Letter from Lily Klee to Max Bill, July 1, 1942, Bibliothek Max Bill. I would like to thank Angela Thomas Schmid for alerting me to this.

23 Max Bill: "Paul Klee (1879–1940)," in *Neue Zürcher Zeitung*, 161, no. 977 (July 8, 1940), Morning Edition, p. 3; Max Bill: "Paul-Klee-Gedächtnisausstellungen," in *Die Weltwoche*, 8, no. 366 (November 15, 1940), p. 5.

24 I would like to thank Angela Thomas Schmid for alerting me to this.

25 Max Bill: "Zur Ausstellung Paul Klee im Kunsthaus Zürich. I, II," in *Neue Zürcher Zeitung*, 161, no. 326 (March 4, 1940), Evening Edition, p. 6; no. 332 (March 5, 1940), Evening Edition, p. 5. Bill also commented on the various publications in a letter to Lily Klee of October 26, 1940, now in the archives of the Zentrum Paul Klee.

26 Max Bill: "Paul Klee," in *Das Werk*, 27, no. 8 (1940), pp. 209–216, esp. pp. 214 and 215.

27 On the relationship between his teaching and work, see Fabienne Eggelhöfer: *Paul Klees Lehre vom Schöpferischen*, dissertation University of Bern, 2012, pp. 220–229; Michael Baumgartner: "Die 'Verwesentlichung des Zufälligen'. Paul Klees Zwiesprache mit der Natur," in *In Paul Klees Zaubergarten*, exh. cat. Bern: Zentrum Paul Klee; Oslo: Henie Onstad Art Centre; Bergen: Bergen Art Museum 2008/09, ed. by Zentrum Paul Klee, Ostfildern-Ruit 2008, pp. 23–45, esp. pp. 28–37; Jürgen Glaesemer: *Paul Klee. Handzeichnungen II. 1921–1936*, ed. by Kunstmuseum Bern and Paul-Klee-Stiftung, Bern 1984, pp. 234–239; Marcel Franciscono: *Paul Klee. His Work and Thought*, Chicago/London 1991, pp. 247–248.

28 Both books were published in English as *Paul Klee: The Thinking Eye. The Notebooks of Paul Klee*, ed. by Jürg Spiller, London/New York 1961, and *Paul Klee: The Nature of Nature. Notebooks, Volume 2*, London 1973.

29 *Paul Klee: The Thinking Eye* (see note 28), pp. 104–105.

30 Bill: "klee once told me how astonished he was that I should be one of the very few who had understood what his theory classes were all about, even though he (quite rightly) had no recollection of my having ever attended them," Letter from Max Bill to Dr. Siegfried Salzmann, March 18, 1971, reprinted in: Winterthur/Duisburg 1971 (see note 14), p. 124.

31 Letter from Max Bill to Lily Klee, September 27, 1943, Zentrum Paul Klee, Klee family donation.

32 Letter from Max Bill to Lily Klee, October 31, 1943, Zentrum Paul Klee, Klee family donation.

33 Letter from Max Bill to Felix Klee, September 14, 1952, Klee-Nachlassverwaltung, Hinterkappelen. I would like to thank the Klee family and Stefan Frey for allowing me to view this material.

34 For a more detailed account of Paul Klee's lessons at the Bauhaus, see Madrid 2013 (see note 12); *Paul Klee. Die Kunst des Sichtbarmachens. Materialien zu Klees Unterricht am Bauhaus*, exh. cat. Pfäffikon: Seedamm Kulturzentrum 2000, ed. by Kunstmuseum Bern, Paul-Klee-Stiftung, Seedamm Kulturzentrum Pfäffikon, Bern 2000 and www.kleegestaltungslehre.zpk.org (accessed September 14, 2020).

35 Letter from Max Bill to Felix Klee, September 14, 1952, Klee-Nachlassverwaltung, Hinterkappelen.

36 Letter from Felix Klee to Max Bill, September 29, 1952, Klee-Nachlassverwaltung, Hinterkappelen.

37 Letter from Felix Klee to Max Bill, January 8, 1953, Klee-Nachlassverwaltung, Hinterkappelen. Bill mentions the book in his letter to the publisher Paul Theobald and his wife: "this book will bee [sic]: grundlagen der gestaltung, die lehre von paul klee am bauhaus, geordnet und erweitert von helen schmidt-nonne [sic]." Letter from Max Bill to Paul Theobald, October 22, 1953, kindly provided by Geoffrey Goldberg, Chicago. I would like to thank Angela Thomas Schmid for alerting me to this.

38 Letter from Helene Nonné-Schmidt to Felix Klee, December 14, 1963, Klee-Nachlassverwaltung, Hinterkappelen.

39 Lena Bergner: "Unterricht bei Klee," in *form + zweck, fachzeitschrift für industrielle formgestaltung*, no. 3 (1979), pp. 60–62.

40 Letter from Max Bill to Dr. Siegfried Salzmann, March 18, 1971, reprinted in Duisburg/Winterthur 1971 (see note 14), p. 124.

41 Markus Zehentbauer's analysis of Bill's approach fits perfectly. See Markus Zehentbauer: "Der konkreteste Konkrete? Max Bill," in Ingolstadt 2012, pp. 45–52, esp. pp. 49–51.

max bill in paris

Crossovers and Overlaps or Concrete Art at the Frontiers

Guitemie Maldonado

The exhibition «*Art concret*» was held at the Galerie René Drouin on Place Vendôme in Paris from June 15 to July 13, 1945. Organized on the initiative of Nelly van Doesburg, it brought together thirteen artists who were either currently working or had worked in France, ranging from Jean Arp and Sophie Taeuber-Arp, Sonia and Robert Delaunay to Wassily Kandinsky and Piet Mondrian, and just under forty works that one assumes from the catalog to have been lent by the artists themselves, apart from those by Mondrian which belonged to the collections of Arp, Michel Seuphor, and Sonia Delaunay. The guillemets around the title, along with the gallery's past activities—that autumn it hosted Jean Fautrier's *Les Otages*—say a great deal about the situation of non-figurative art in Paris in the mid-1940s, the lack of knowledge and the scant recognition that it enjoyed. Apart from Theo van Doesburg, none of the Art Concret group founders[1] involved in publishing the only edition of the journal in Paris in April 1930 were included in the exhibition, not even Max Bill, despite being known in Parisian artistic circles, and having been the linchpin of the exhibition *konkrete kunst*, held the previous spring at the Kunsthalle in Basel,[2] as well as the driving force, along with Leo Leuppi and Richard Paul Lohse, behind the *abstrakt konkret* bulletin published by the Galerie des Eaux-Vives in Zurich.[3]

Organizing an exhibition such as *Art Concret* in Paris, a decimated city with its artistic milieu dispersed by the end of World War II, was certainly no mean feat, but it has to be said, contextual differences aside, that what made the Basel exhibition stand out, not with regard to scale but with regard to aesthetic ambition, was that the latter, as Serge Lemoine said, was a "testament to the privileged position enjoyed by Switzerland at that time, both closed in on itself, cut off from the rest of the world, yet preserving a certain number of research and ideals common to the West as a whole."[4] The catalog comprised no fewer than 179 entries, which just shows the expedients to which the organizers must have had to resort to bring more than fifty artists together, bang in the middle of the war, most of them living outside Switzerland (around half of them in Paris)—the graphic works, the Allianz group publications, and the photographs helped extend the perimeter beyond the frontiers, including works that could not be moved, while the Swiss public collections (the Kupferstichkabinett at the Öffentliche Kunstsammlung in Basel) and private collections (in Bern, Basel, Pratteln, and indeed Zurich) proved particularly well endowed with material. From all four corners of Europe as well as the United States, by way of the Soviet Union and Great Britain, the main proponents of what had been thought to be an autonomous artistic practice found themselves brought together under the umbrella of what aimed to be much more than simply an overview or an analysis of the movement. While Georg Schmidt, the Director of the Öffentliche Kunstsammlung Basel, gave a speech on the opening day, the catalog designed by Bill did the artists proud. It contains a dialogue on the modern art movements. "Ein

Zwiegespräch über moderne Kunstrichtungen," mentioning Mondrian's remarks about Neo-Plasticism,[5] an opinion piece by Bill, and an essay by Jean Arp.[6] The catalog for the Paris exhibition, a far more modest publication, opens with a quote from Arp introducing an unsigned essay[7] which traces the genealogy of Concrete Art from Cubism and Cézanne to its definition by Theo van Doesburg in "Comments on the basis of concrete painting" and the ambitious phrase "Creating a Universal Language,"[8] which one imagines must also have been chosen to echo the circumstances. Whereas if Bill retained anything from the 1930 manifesto, it was its sixth and last point: "striving towards absolute clarity,"[9] which, rather than a principle, concerned the means by which these were applied. This need for clarity was one of the leitmotifs of Bill's early writings. In 1944, he identified it in Constructive Art, which "aims to communicate the exact," and he designated it as one of the foundations of Concrete Art, which achieves autonomy because it is regarded as "an expression of the human spirit" and "is of that poignancy and clarity, of such perfection, as is to be expected of works derived from the human spirit." "In this sense, Concrete Art takes an active stance towards current events, it strives for law, ideal, order, and harmony, for absolute clarity, regularity, and thus, for reality itself."[10] Bill's concrete mindset adhered precisely to the conciliation that he operated between contradictory imperatives, or at least guidelines: "it is real and immaterial, unnaturalistic yet close to nature, it strives for the universal, but tends to the unique, it pushes back against the individualistic in favor of the individual."[11]

Between Paris and Basel, in 1944–45, between taking stock and looking ahead, but also between the 1930s and the 1940s—the aim of this lengthy preamble is to place Bill precisely at a time when, having finished his training, he identified and solidified his stances, in contact with the non-figurative artists gathered in Paris at the time, just when he fully grasped the idea of Concrete Art. Without him, it might have remained just one of many concepts, a simple response to the more or less general dissatisfaction with the term "abstract," and heralded a new chapter in history, following that of "a period of searching and of speculative experiments."[12] From the general to the specific, along with geography, chronology, and shared beliefs, there was also the international matter of abstract art and its universality, thrown into the spotlight at a key moment thanks to Bill and the inception of Concrete Art.

Max Bill and the Parisian melting pot (1925–1948)

Bill's first trip to Paris in 1925 was to visit the *Exposition internationale des arts décoratifs et industriels modernes*, a first encounter that set the tone for his later frequent visits from Zurich during the 1930s. Paris, toward which avant-garde exponents had gravitated for different reasons, abstract art in particular, gave him a chance to be part of this community. In 1932, he met Jean Arp there, whose wife Sophie Taeuber-Arp he knew from the Kunstgewerbeschule in Zurich; Jean Arp introduced him to Mondrian. He then met Georges Vantongerloo, who

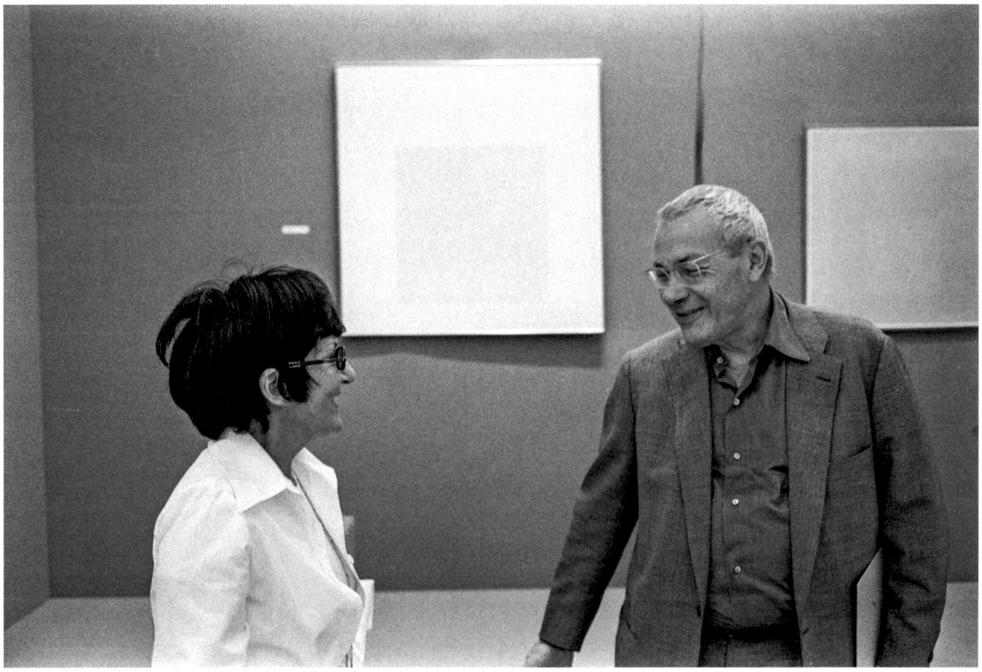

1 The gallerist Denise René with Max Bill at Art Basel, SIK-ISEA Zürich, Courtesy Fotostiftung Schweiz, photo: Maria Netter

became a friend of his; Max Ernst, with whom he went to Ticino; and he caught up again with Wassily Kandinsky, who had taught him at the Bauhaus. He also renewed his acquaintance with Antoine Pevsner, who introduced him to Marcel Duchamp and then František Kupka in 1945. As well as these individually formed relationships, some of which developed into real friendships, there was also the legitimacy conferred by what one might call the professional network that was becoming established around abstract art. Through Arp, Bill also became a member of the Abstraction Création association set up in 1931 and regularly took part in its activities (a journal and several exhibitions) until it disbanded in 1936. He took part in the *Réalités Nouvelles* exhibition in 1939, which briefly took up the baton for promoting an "art totally disconnected from a realistic view of nature"[13] and was a forerunner for the salon of the same name set up just after the end of World War II, in 1946. Bill's *dreiteilige einheit*[14] (pl. p. 111) featured in the catalog published on the occasion of the 1948 edition of the *Salon du Réalités Nouvelles*, followed by his *rhythmus im raum* in 1950, along with a translation of his opinion piece "ein standpunkt" of 1944.[15] However, Concrete Art was just one of the movement's many appellations, recorded in the Articles of Association lodged in 1946, which describe it as a direct descendant of Abstraction Création. A diagram, tracing the history of art from Impressionism to the Réalités Nouvelles, published in the 1948 journal, features Concrete Art in 1911 as a counterpoint to the abstract art practiced in France. Bill was among the artists who took part in the *Tendances de l'Art Abstrait*[16] exhibition at the Galerie Denise René (fig. 1) in 1948 and was awarded the Kandinsky Prize, set up by the artist's widow with the support of the gallery.

It was around this time, thanks to his interface with the Parisian milieux, that Bill was active in the Paris-based organization of international abstract artists which, informed by their joint endeavors, worked to promote their dissemination and their recognition. One of the rare photographs that remains of the exhibitions organized by Abstraction Création shows his *lange plastik* (pl. p. 47) in 1933 surrounded by paintings by Kurt Seligmann, Hans Erni, Serge Brignoni, Hans Fischli, Gérard Vuillamy, and even Enrico Prampolini, and alongside sculptures by Louis Conne, Vantongerloo, and Etienne Beothy. While Vantongerloo's piece was notable for its strictly orthogonal structure (similar work pl. p. 63), the other three shared a similar verticality, albeit harnessed in different ways—Conne's was irregular and punctuated with organic, even anthropomorphic excrescences, Beothy's was all undulations,[17] while Bill's was tapered and the only one to have an integral base, a fine white-painted iron tripod. Formal proximity did not stand in the way of specific approaches and, by choice and of necessity, Abstraction Création was a forum for broad non-figurative art, revealing and encouraging connections between artists of various persuasions. Aside from promoting artists through exhibitions, the association intended its journal to be a work of documentation and pedagogy, and it was also the trigger for the album *quinze variations sur un même thème* (pl. p. 61) which Bill began work on in 1935 and which he published through Mourlot in Paris in 1938. He claimed in the preface that he had published them not just to show the "infinite multiplicity of possibilities" inherent in Concrete Art, but especially to highlight the "methods," the "operations" that informed the compositions, to provide an "insight" into "their inner and outer workings" and the "contiguities" that they contained.[18] As a vehicle for these elucidations, the album of lithographs allowed for a relatively wide diffusion. While the association's plastic vocation is irrefutable, it was no less geared to transmitting that "artistic desire of the spirit that forms" that Georg Schmidt[19] derived from it, perhaps, or the interaction between the organic and the structure, which Ernst Kállai described as a result of "the vitality of form" and "construction ruled by laws"[20]—a particularly fruitful tension at that time.

Abstraction Création as a springboard (1931–1936)

Angela Thomas has described Bill coming across a copy of the Concrete Art manifesto in a bookshop in Paris one day in 1931—in other words, the same year as the foundation of Abstraction Création and the death of Van Doesburg in Davos, which were just a few months apart.[21] Reading the reflections on both Concrete Art and on the subject of mathematics[22] published by the artist as of the mid-1930s, it is fair to say that the manifesto can be discerned as a catalyst for the latter. In the years prior to his first written works, his developing artistic maturity played out through his plastic experiments, such as those he featured in the *Abstraction Création* journal. In the second 1923 edition, his 1931–32 *well-relief* (pl. p. 51) shares a page with his 1930–1931 *glasbild* (pl. p. 51, fig. 2)[23]; the photographs of the two works focus on their material dimension, highlighting the effects produced by the round cut-outs

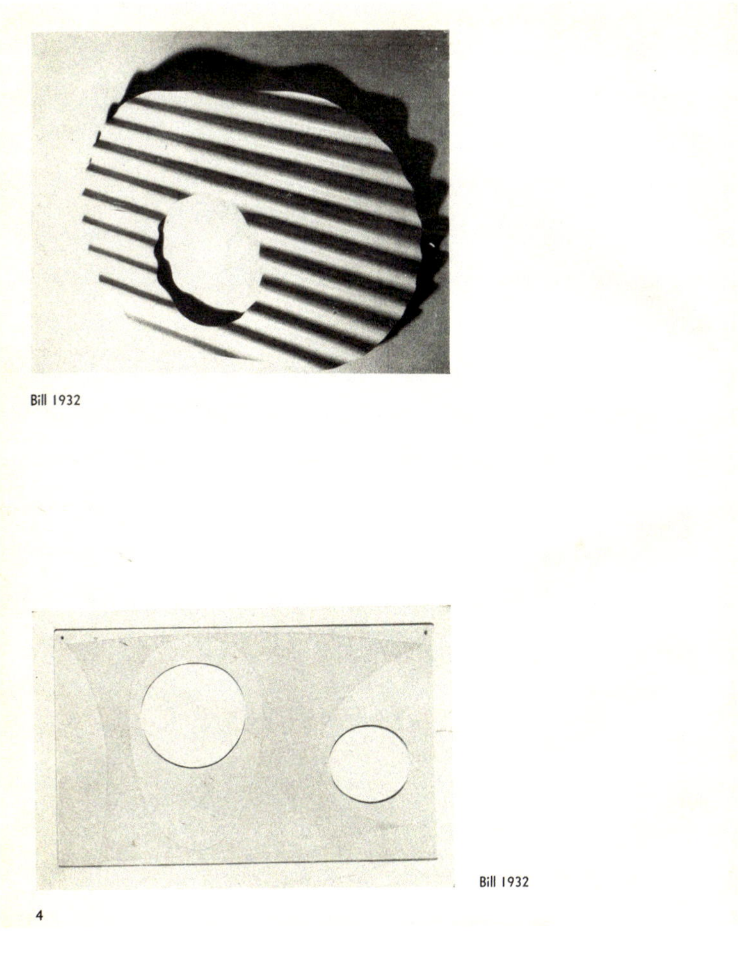

2 abstraction création
art non figuratif 1933, p. 4

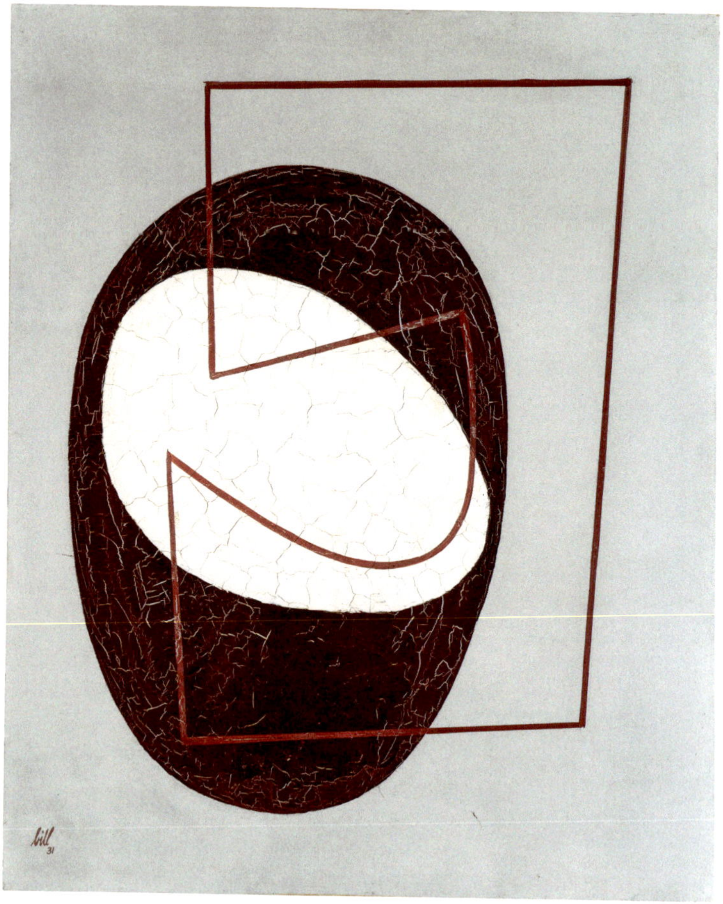

3 Max Bill, komposition 2, 1931,
Oil on plywood board, 43 x 53 cm
max bill georges vantongerloo stiftung, haus bill zumikon
angela thomas and erich schmid
Courtesy Hauser & Wirth

that they have in common—marked shadows and deformations in the former, and precise, fine outlines, sharp white discs in the latter. A perusal of the five editions of the journal suffices to note the frequency of artists' recourse to this sort of device (cut-outs, successions of images, plays of solids and voids, positive/negative shapes), from Arp to Ben Nicholson, by way of César Domela, Carl Buchheister, and Taeuber-Arp. In *well-relief*, composed simply of an O retrieved from a sign, its thickness making for what was then a recurrent form for Bill—whether it was a poster for the *n****kunst—prähistorische felsbilder südafrikas, kunstgewerbemuseum zürich* (pl. p. 50) exhibition at the Kunstgewerbemuseum in Zurich or *komposition 2* in 1931 or his 1932 *Untitled. Sketch for a mural with large O* (pl. p. 48), this closed and yet infinite form with an inside and an outside, which might be described as homothetic or at least concentric, seems to prefigure on the page the ribbons that he later subjected to different turns and twists, on their own or in multiples, and then deployed three-dimensionally in the space.

4 abstraction création
art non figuratif 1934, p. 5

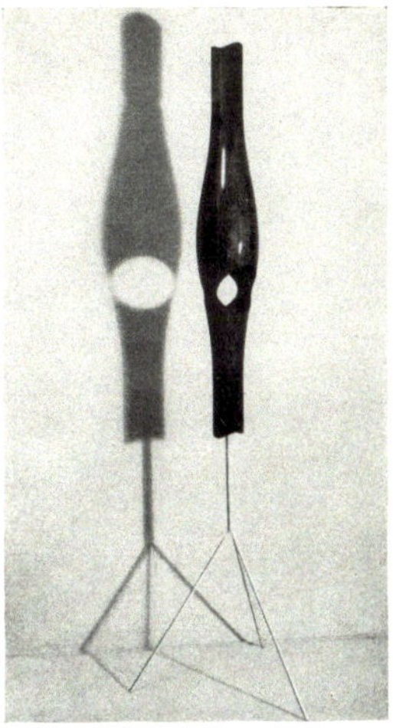

Bill

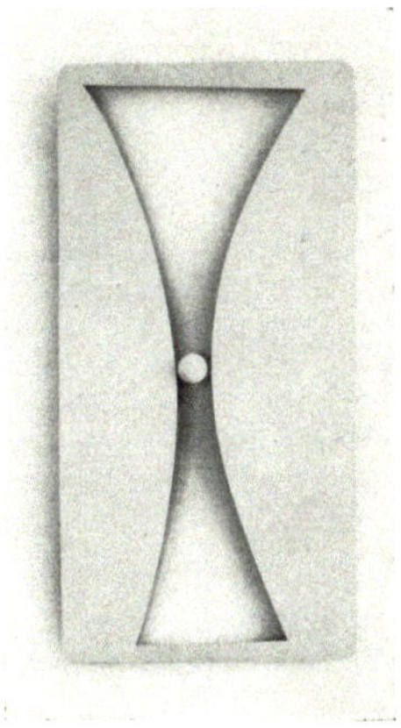

Bill

5

Bill's move to sculpture was also fueled by his exploration of the hollowed-out center—in a certain light, *lange plastik* projects its open silhouette on the wall, similar to the form that takes up the horizontal axis of his *glasbild* of the same year. Thus photographed, it was featured in the third edition of *Abstraction Création*, on the same page as his 1931 *relief mit weisser kugel* (fig. 4) which seemed to constitute its counterpoint image in negative—rather than flaring out, the shape, which is contained and not free like the sculpture, tightens around a marble at its centre, which forms the point of tension and balance of the work. Most of Bill's sculptural work involved similar exploration, *dreiteilige einheit* in particular, in which the two hollow discs, like lobes, fold in on each other to form a dynamic volume, both open and empty inside. Looking through the *Réalités Nouvelles* journal of 1950, it is clear just how widely these concepts of center, movement, interlocking, and winding were shared by Bill's contemporary sculptors.[24] Further confirmation is found in the singular evolution of a form by Etienne Beothy; a reproduction in the 1948 issue shows how it loops around the

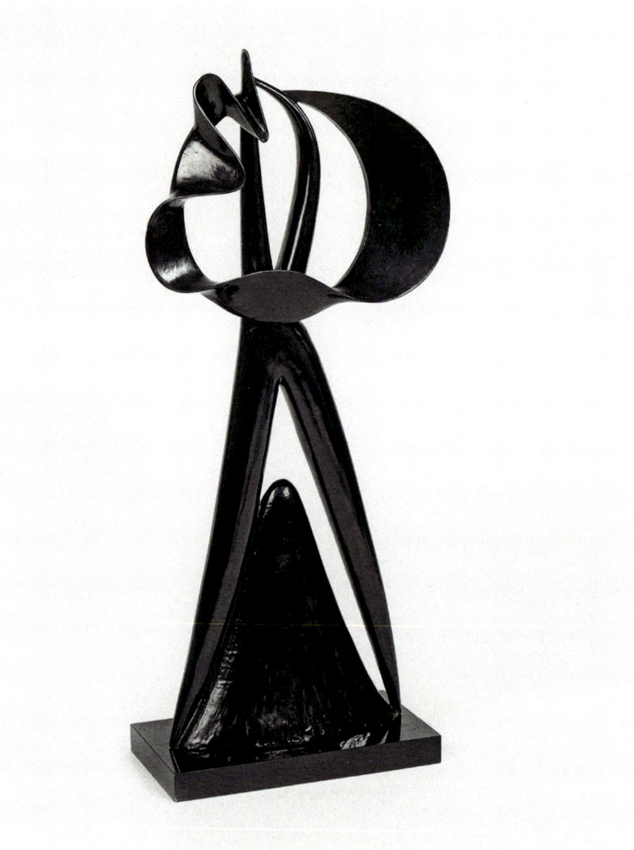

5 Etienne Beothy, Opus 099.
Don Quichotte (L'Homme d'esprit), 1947,
plaster, 73.6 cm

6 Etienne Beothy, Opus 111. Ionisation
(5 tours), Forme nucléaire I, 1949,
wood, 44 cm

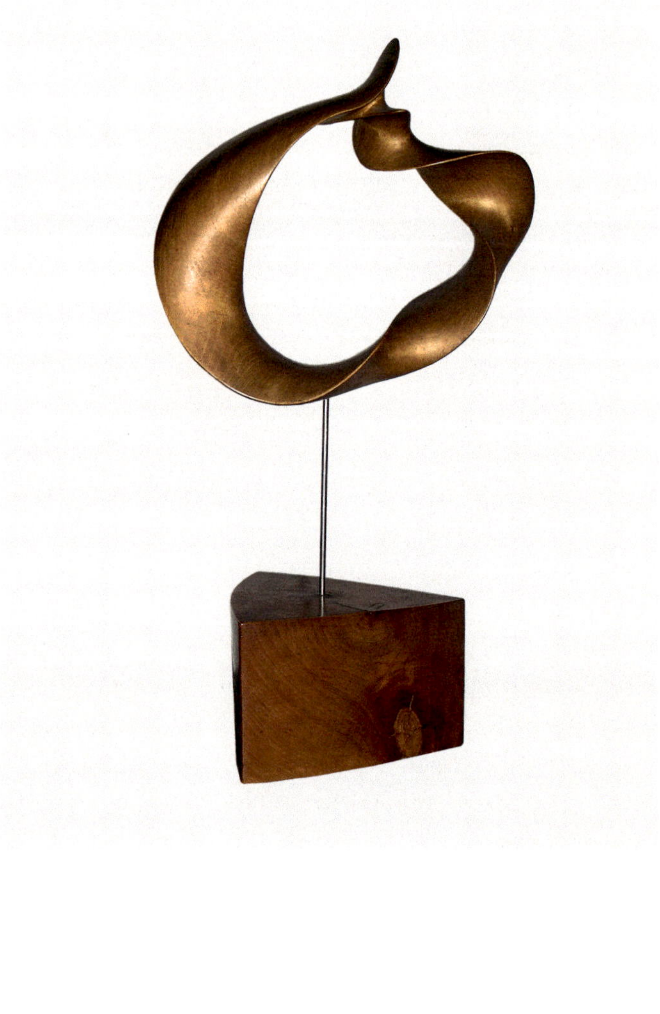

top part of a sculpture—*Opus 099. Don Quichotte (L'Homme d'Esprit)* of 1947 (fig. 5)—before descending and branching out, dividing upwards and downwards, conferring an anthropomorphic look to the work, whereas *Opus 111. Ionisation (5 tours), Forme Nucléaire I* from 1949 (fig. 6), published in the 1950 issue, consists of a similar ribbon that meets and closes around a floating void, twisting and entirely separate from the base. Were it connected to a body, the movement could be associated with dancing; here it simply imprints its rotation and its undulations on the space both inside and outside of it.[25] *unendliche schleife*, on which Bill embarked in 1935, was not unique, clearly, even though it achieved a remarkable simplicity and concentration. It is an outstanding example of his commitment to the themes of his time. Even more so if one considers that the trigger for the early research for this work was a commission from Marcel Breuer and an attempt to evoke the constant movement of flames.

Was Concrete Art Swiss? (1936 onwards)

We are not entirely done with this story of encirclings and overlaps. If the drivers of Abstraction Création such as *Réalités Nouvelles* congratulated themselves on recruiting their members from outside Paris,[26] it was an opportunity, at least for the former, to reaffirm the city's central role in the development of the Abstract Movement. For the latter it was a chance to float the idea of an association with fluid boundaries, as its name suggests. What marked the end of Abstraction Création for Bill coincided with the organization of the major exhibition *Zeitprobleme in der Schweizer Malerei und Plastik* at the Kunsthaus Zürich in June and July of 1936. It was in the catalog for the exhibition, devoted to Swiss artists, that the first of his texts on Concrete Art, "konkrete gestaltung," was published, in which he immediately asserted the founding principle of Concrete Art, which he frequently reiterated: "We call 'Concrete Art' works of art which are created according to a technique and laws which are entirely appropriate to then, without taking external support from experimental nature or from its transformation [. . .]."[27] From then on, the acculturation of Concrete Art in Switzerland seems to have truly taken off, to the extent that Serge Lemoine declared that Concrete Art was Swiss, just as "Fauvism, Cubism are French, Expressionism is German, Constructivism Russian and Dutch."[28] It has to be said that the commentators stuck to these geographical distinctions, despite the international, if not universal aspiration of this form of art. In his review of the 1948 *Salon des Réalités Nouvelles*, René Massat highlighted the "Alliance (*sic*) group, from Switzerland, [which] manifests itself with first class vitality and cohesion" [. . .] "in the vanguard of the fight for art that is both sensitive and in-

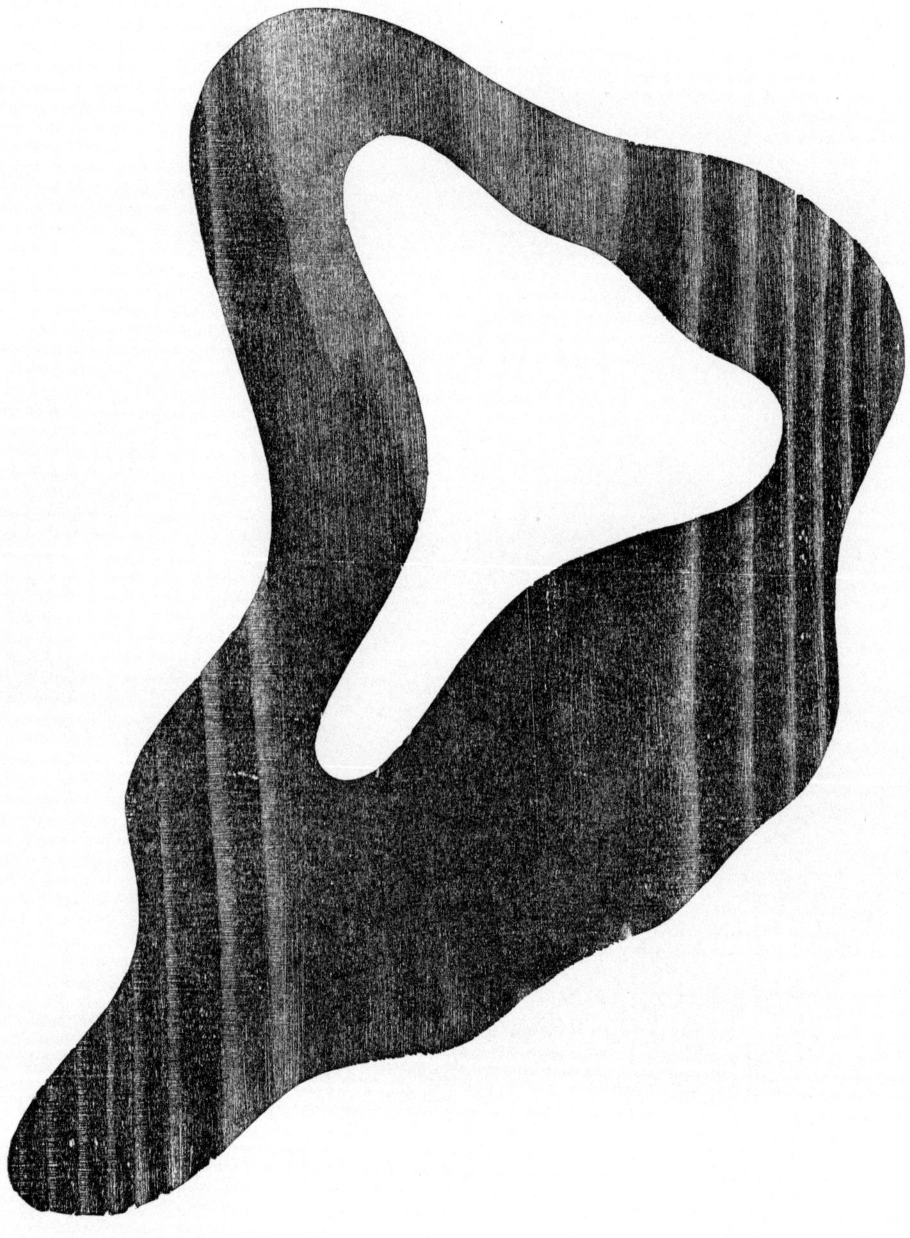

7 Hans Arp, Woodcut no. V from 11 configurations, 1930, 26.6 x 25.8 cm, edited by Max Bill and published by Allianz Verlag, 1945

tellectual";[29] the *Premier Bilan de l'Art Actuel 1937–1953* put together by Robert Lebel examines the general scene "from Abstract Art to Figurative Art," split into sections devoted to different practices (sculpture, engraving) and different countries, including an analysis of the situation in Switzerland by Isabelle Waldberg, which places Bill "at the head of Swiss Modernism."[30]

While taking stock of contextual specificities, these sorts of approaches run the risk of pigeonholing practices into forms of particularism, thus losing sight of their specific qualities, in other words, what allows them to come together with others, possibly geographically

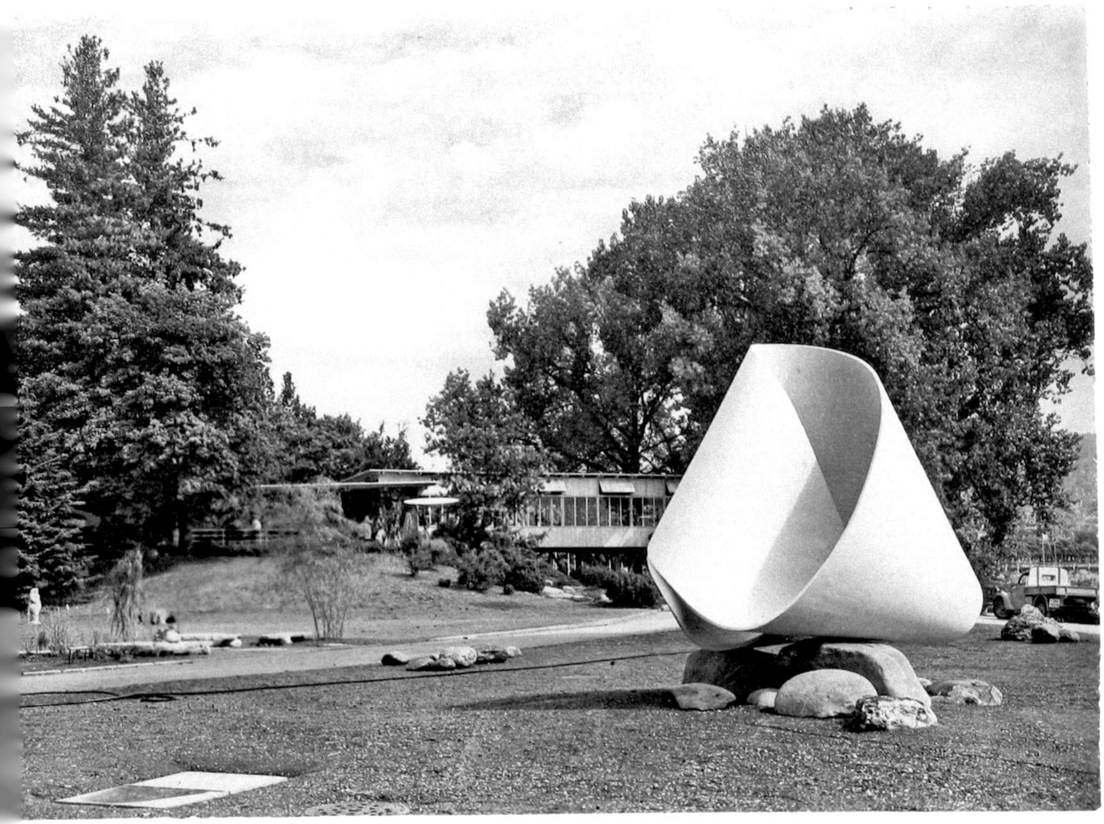

8 Postcard showing Max Bill's kontinuität, 1947
ETH Library Zurich, Image Archive

as well as chronologically distant. Bill's activities offer up two fertile avenues in this regard. In the 1944 exhibition *konkrete kunst*, a room, immortalized in a photograph, was given over to works by Arp, Mondrian, and Taeuber-Arp on the basis of their social, geographical, and creative proximity rather than their adhesion to an established group (pl. p. 76), showing the effect different sorts of intersections, such as that between the work of Arp and of Bill, could have on their thinking. The works published by Bill in the Allianz editions include Arp's *11 configurations*—woodcuts from different periods that he had sent Bill before he and Sophie Taeuber-Arp took refuge with him during World War II.

Plate V of the series, dated 1930, shows a similar configuration to Bill's O-shapes, executed in Arp's own irregular and undulating manner, along with Bill's description: "a black mark containing a white kernel, like a bowl."[31] In other woodcuts, these "kernel shapes" sometimes multiply in proximity to each other and sometimes they are embedded in each other. The kernel motif was a great help for thinking of Arp and Bill's sculptures together, those of the former full, thrusting their multiple protuberances and excrescences out from the center, while those of the latter turn, rotating around the same center, bypassing it or avoiding it, folding and refolding, in an endless movement of thrusts and tensions that seem to form the outlines as well as the internal structure. These similarities hold good for some open-air works, such as *kontuinität* (fig. 8), which was installed in 1947 on Lake Zurich, balanced on erratic boulders. Although they are in different registers, Bill's concept of endless continuity and movement, and Arp's growth or perhaps his concretion are similar, which allows us to think of Concrete Art as a logic of autonomous forms whatever their nature. Whether a sculpture is named *dreiteilige einheit*, like Bill's, or *Réalité Limitrophe*, like the one by Arp that was reproduced in the catalog for the 1945 exhibition *Art concret*, there is always the matter of tension, or contradiction as a founding principle for setting it in motion.

Thus, charting Max Bill's progress in Paris during the 1930s and 1940s, and his links to Abstraction Création, is not just a matter of observing his journey from maturation to maturity, noting connections between his individual trajectory and the collective approaches, between international aspiration and contextual specificity, and above all, between the different processes leading up to the execution of forms, but also of being able to trace the points of contact, the areas of friction, the overlaps, in order to think again about the formal input of Concrete Art seized at the frontiers.

1 Otto Carlsund, Theo van Doesburg, Jean Hélion, Léon Tutundjian, and Marcel Wantz signed the manifesto, "Base de la Peinture Concrète," published in the first edition of the journal.

2 Basel 1944. Organized and curated by Bill, held from March 18 to April 16, 1944.

3 Eleven editions between November 1944 and December 1945.

4 Serge Lemoine: "Konkrete Kunst, 1944," in *Art concret suisse: mémoire et progrès*, exh. cat., Dijon: Musée des Beaux-Arts, Dijon 1982, pp. 41–45, cf. p. 41.

5 Piet Mondrian: "Dialoog over de Nieuwe Beelding," in *De Stijl* (February/March 1919). English translation in Harry Holzman and Martin S. James (eds. and transl.): *The New Life: The Collected Writings of Piet Mondrian*, Boston 1986, pp. 75–81.

6 Jean Arp: "art concret," in Basel 1944, p. 11 f., a slightly adapted version of a text that first appeared in *Art of This Century*, ed. by Peggy Guggenheim, New York: Art of this Century Gallery, 1942; fragments were published in *Réalités Nouvelles*, no. 1 (1947).

7 According to Lemoine 1982 (see note 4), the author was held to be Jean Gorin, cf. p. 42.

8 Theo van Doesburg: "Commentaires sur la Base de la Peinture Concrète," in *Art Concret*, no. 1 (April 1930), p. 2; English translation "Comments on the basis of concrete painting," in *Theo van Doesburg*, ed. by Joost Baljeu, New York 1974, pp. 181 f.

9 "Base de la Peinture Concrète," in *Art Concret*, no. 1 (April 1930), p. 1; English translation "The basis of concrete painting," in Baljeu 1974 (see note 8), pp. 180 f.

10 Basel 1944, p. 9. Parts of it are reprised in French in *Réalités Nouvelles*, no. 4 (1950), p. 14.

11 Ibid., p. 10.

12 Doesburg 1930 (see note 8), p. 2.

13 *Réalités Nouvelles*, exh. cat., Paris: Galerie Charpentier, 1939.

14 *Réalités Nouvelles*, no. 2 (1948), p. 10.

15 *Réalités Nouvelles*, no. 4 (1950), p. 14.

16 *Tendances de l'Art Abstrait*, at the Galerie Denise René from October 22 to November 22, 1948.

17 *Femme Drapée. Forme et Rythme (Flamme Rythmoplastique). Opus 061*, 1933.

18 Max Bill: Preface to *quinze variations sur un même thème*, Paris 1938, n. p.

19 Georg Schmidt: "De la Variation d'un Thème dans les Beaux-Arts," in *XXe Siècle*, no. 4 (1938), p. 37.

20 Ernst Kállai: "Zu den Arbeiten von Max Bill," *Plastique*, no. 5 (1939), p. 13.

21 Angela Thomas, according to interviews with Max Bill, in the catalog *Max Bill*, Paris: Galerie Denise René, 1990.

22 In the journal, under the title "Les Problèmes de l'Art Concret," Jean Hélion devoted an essay to the relationship between art and mathematics, pp. 6–10.

23 *Abstraction Création*, no. 2 (1933), p. 4.

24 *Réalités Nouvelles*, no. 4 (1950), pp. 14 f.: *dreiteilige einheit* and *ein standpunkt* by Bill shared the double page with sculptures by Jonas, Reijers, Kallem, Descamps, and Uny.

25 In 1954, Beothy produced Forme *Nucléaire III. Opus 128*, a painted metal ring curved around a red sphere.

26 Edition 4 of *Abstraction Création* opened in 1935 with statistics pertaining to the origins of the "members and friends" belonging to the association: seventeen nationalities are represented (as many as at the *Salon des Réalités Nouvelles* in 1948), of which the Swiss formed the second largest contingent, after France (sixty-eight artists).

27 Bill 1936, p. 10; English translation Buffalo/Los Angeles/San Francisco 1974/75, p. 47.

28 Serge Lemoine; "Le Grand Passage," in Dijon 1982 (see note 4), cf. p. 3.

29 René Massat: "3ème Salon des Réalités Nouvelles," in *Le Courrier des Arts et des Lettres* (July 23, 1948), p. 1.

30 Isabelle Waldberg: "En Suisse, in *Premier Bilan de l'Art Actuel. 1937–1953*, Paris 1953, p. 255.

31 Max Bill: "Commentary on Plate V." in *arp: 11 configurations*, Zurich 1945, n. p.

imprecise precision

Max Bill and Concrete Art in Brazil

Heloísa Espada

The enduring impact of Max Bill's work in Brazil continues to provide fertile ground for debate. The importance of his work for the evolution of Concrete Art and design in the country is beyond doubt. Yet the words of the "Manifesto Neoconcreto" warning of the risk of a "dangerous rationalist exacerbation"[1] in Concrete Art still resonate in contemporary interpretations of Bill's oeuvre. His visit to São Paulo, Rio de Janeiro, and Belo Horizonte in 1953[2] elicited both admiration and opposition. The criticism of modern Brazilian architecture that he voiced on that occasion met with great displeasure at the local level. Referring to Oscar Niemeyer's works, Bill spoke of "anarchy," "antisocial waste," "disorder," "barbarism," a "decorative spirit," and "irresponsibility."[3] In response, the architect Lúcio Costa[4] called Bill "prejudiced" and disqualified him by writing that "the well-known artist is, strictly speaking, neither an architect nor a painter, nor a sculptor, but rather, fundamentally, a shape-maker ('designer')" who does not limit himself to designing products.[5] The controversy occurred two years after the major Bill retrospective at the Museu de Arte de São Paulo (MASP) and after his piece *dreiteilige einheit* (1947/48) had been awarded the Grand Prix for Sculpture at the first São Paulo Art Biennial hold at the Museu de Arte Moderna (MAM-SP). Bill's work, in other words, was already known and revered in the country, which provides a scale for the degree of Lúcio Costa's irritation.

This text focuses on the less objective aspects of Bill's relationship with Brazil.[6] Without passing over the controversial character of his opinions about the country, a subject that I will return to later, I want to explore how some of the more underlying aspects of the Swiss artist's output resonated in the Concrete and Neo-Concrete Art coming out of Rio de Janeiro and São Paulo. Bill's investigations into concepts such as precision and imprecision, continuity and discontinuity, multiplicity and unity, finitude and infinitude, permanence and change, show that his interest in mathematics, especially in topology and non-Euclidean geometry, involved not only the ideals of clarity and order, but, above all, the paths sought by science to deal with the irregular, the unpredictable, and the ineffable. Often, his works based on a strict formal logic call attention to a random detail. In his paintings, for example, color is used primarily as an expressive means to define the rhythm of a surface, oftentimes without following any pattern. What influence could these personal, and, in the case of Bill, always subtle, choices have on Concrete Art in Brazil?

The starting point for my deliberations is the Swiss artist's solo exhibition at the MASP in 1951. As the biggest retrospective of his work up to that point, it featured thirty-eight of his paintings, nine sculptures, fourteen graphic-design works (books and posters, among others), and twenty-seven photographs showing architectural projects, industrial design work, urban planning proposals, exhibition layouts, as well as sculptures in the public space (fig. p. 108 bottom).[7] All of the pieces

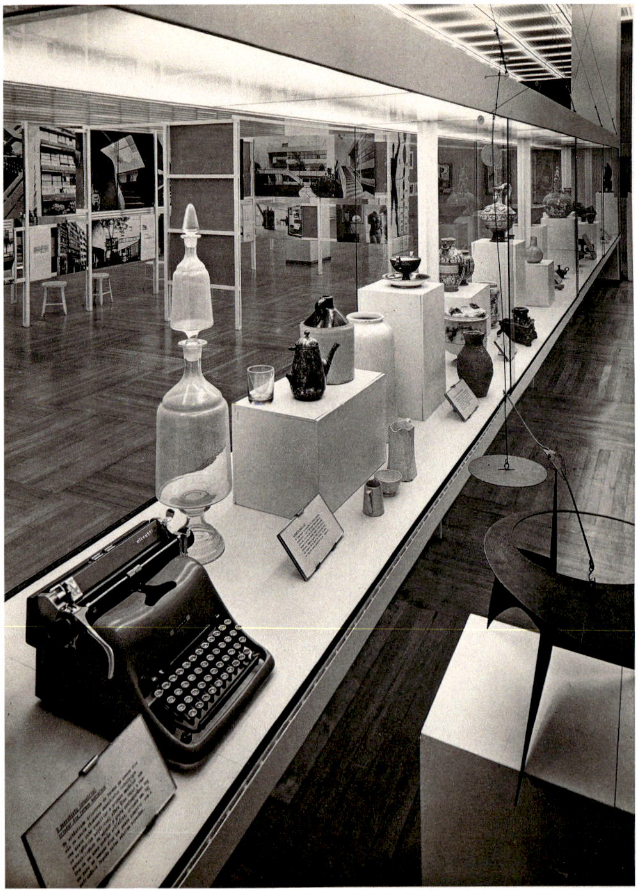

1 Showcase of forms at the old MASP on Rua Sete de Abril, São Paulo, c. 1958
Instituto Moreira Salles Collection, photo: Peter Scheier

and projects had been realized between 1936 and 1949 and thus painted a fairly representative picture of Bill's ideas about Concrete Art.[8] Exemplary works such as *quinze variations sur un même thême* (1935–1938), *konstruktion mit schwebendem kubus* (1935/36) (pl. p. 61), *unbegrenzt und begrenzt* (1947), and *dreiteilige einheit* (1947/48) (pl. p. 111) were also included, and the latter would be transferred to the first São Paulo Art Biennial months later. The exhibition did not receive much press coverage, but it did make a profound impact on the art scene. Especially artists based in the southeast of the country, such as Waldemar Cordeiro, Geraldo de Barros, Willys de Castro, Hércules Barsotti, Abraham Palatinik, Ivan Serpa, and the critic Mário Pedrosa went to see it. Mary Vieira and Almir Mavignier emigrated to Europe that same year after visiting the exhibition. They both became close to Bill and, in 1954, enrolled as students at the Hochschule für Gestaltung (HfG) in Ulm. Alexandre Wollner, who had helped set up the exhibition at the museum, was the third Brazilian to join the first class of the German school.

Bill's ideas, however, had already permeated Brazil's art scene even before his exhibition opened. Pietro Maria Bardi, director of the MASP, had started negotiations to bring the exhibition to the museum as early as 1948, but scheduling conflicts and discussions about having it travel to other cities in Latin America had caused several delays. The retrospective finally opened on March 1, 1951, following a solo exhibition by Le Corbusier and coinciding with the inauguration of the Instituto de Arte Contemporânea, Brazil's first design school, which for three years was housed at the MASP. All of this clearly points to an objective of approaching modern art from a broad perspective — one that also included architecture, urbanism, and design.

In its early years the museum was housed in one floor of the Diários Associados building[9], in São Paulo downtown. After being closed for renovations the museum reopened in June 1950 with the Le Corbusier's retrospective. On that occasion, Lina Bo Bardi, who was in charge of this remaking, expanded the area and redesigned the presentation of the museum Pinacoteca housing works from the Renaissance and European Modernism. To separate the gallery reserved for works from the collection from the space used for temporary exhibitions, the

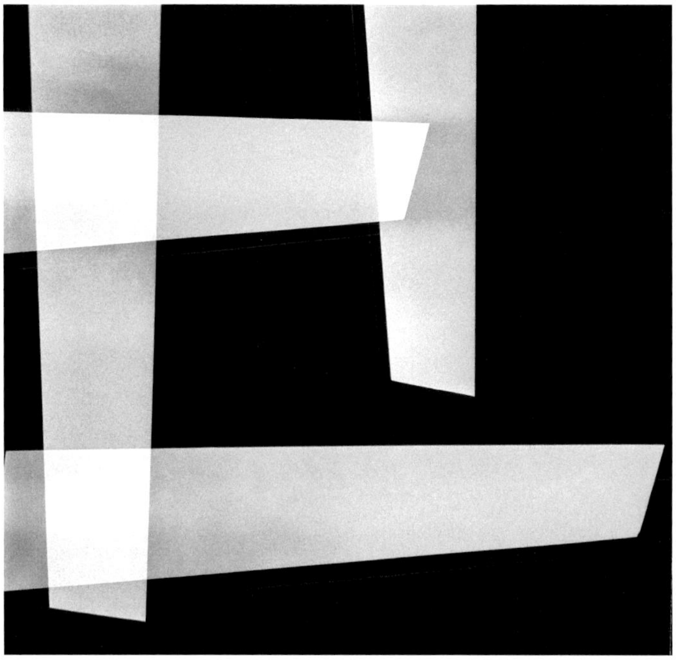

2 Geraldo de Barros, Fotoforma, 1950. Silver gelatine print, 28 x 27 cm
Coleção Fernanda Feitosa e Heitor Martins, São Paulo, Instituto Moreira Salles Collection

architect designed a glass cabinet called a "showcase of forms," whose contents showed a close affinity with the concept of the exhibition *Die gute Form*, which Bill had organized in Basel in 1949. The MASP showcase contained objects from different eras, artisanal as well as industrial, alongside organic forms as examples of "good design"— meaning instances where form and function closely and elegantly corresponded. An Olivetti typewriter, a Vigorelli sewing machine, a piece of a tree trunk, ethnographic objects, and household items were displayed alongside a painting by Ingres and an architectural design by Le Corbusier, for example (fig. 1).

Another sign that Bill's ideas were already circulating in Brazil even before the opening of his solo show was the small photographic exhibition *Fotoforma* by Geraldo de Barros, which took place in January of 1951. In a text written for the occasion, Pietro Maria Bardi discussed Barros's encounters with the works of Wassily Kandinsky, Piet Mondrian, and Bill.[10] The exhibition is considered a landmark of abstractionism and, more specifically, of modern photography in Brazil. Most of the images were obtained using experimental photographic techniques ranging from overlays to scratches, cuts, and assemblages of negatives and papers. The most abstract series, called *Fotoformas*, consists of multiple exposures of an object or a scene in the same frame. For example, the artist photographed the same open backlit doorway four

3 Hércules Barsotti, Branco/Preto, 1961. Oil on canvas, 100 x 50 cm

Acervo do Museu de Arte Contemporânea da Universidade de São Paulo

times on the same piece of film, while rotating his Rolleiflex, producing an overlapping geometric form (fig. 2). The doorway thus works as a modular shape. The technique was planned, but not completely controlled—the execution of an imagined concept that would reveal itself only after the film was developed. Sometimes the artist even extended the creative process into the laboratory, experimenting with new cuts and creating new compositions from the same frame. As such, the *Fotoformas* are different compositions of the same formal idea, which is almost always a synthetic and geometric image. As in Bill's work, Barros's formal variations on a theme have a musical quality and induce a recurring visual movement that could be likened to the oil painting *kühle teilung* (1943) (pl. p. 84), which would be shown at the MASP a few months later.

Some of Bill's individual works reveal his interest in the space between the regular and irregular. The painting *sechs gleichlange linien* (1947) (pl. p. 89), for example, is based on six elements of the same size. The painting seems to be the result of chance, as if it had originated in a *cadavre exquis* composed entirely of lines. Very thin, light, and sinuous, these lines are reminiscent of organic and flaccid shapes. They suggest the attraction between bodies that are very close, but do not touch. Listless in their appearance, the lines here mainly serve a decorative and seductive purpose, which transcends the effects that can be explained by *Gestalt*.

Creating a geometry that went beyond the rational dimension of perception was the goal of several artists in Brazil. São Paulo native Hércules Barsotti, who can be considered a Concretist or Neo-Concretist, worked with the concept of creating corpuses through flexibly composed geometries. In *Branco/Preto* (1961) (fig. 3) he compromises the stability of the white rectangle of the canvas by subtly altering it. Black lines on the side of the frame suggest a slight inclination of the plane out into the surrounding space. The white screen is like an empty but susceptible area, subject to minimal pressure. The form seems to result from the tension between the notion of resistance and the possibility of adaptation. Barsotti was interested in small imperfections and movements capable of creating ambiguous concepts of space, plane, and depth. Although they were made using different methods, *Branco/Preto* and *sechs gleichlange linien* both transcend the sphere of the rational and both suggest some kind of relationship between the viewer's imagination and his or her body.

Bill presented at least four sculptures based on continuous metal loops at the MASP: *unendliche schleife aus einem kreisring I* (1947–1949), *unendliche schleife aus einem kreisring II* (1947–1949), *fläche durch eine linie begrenzt* (1948/49), and *dreiteilige einheit* (1947/48). The congruence between the notions of interior and exterior and between the finite and infinite, in addition to the open and uninterrupted structure of the latter work, captivated several Brazilian artists. The effect it had on the work of Lygia Clark is perhaps the most emblematic example. The Moebius strip made its first appearance in the artist's work in 1963, in her performance *Caminhando*. Armed with scissors and a paper Moebius strip, the artist continuously cut along the length of the paper strip until there was nothing left to cut. In addition to breaking with the concept of interior and exterior, *Caminhando* introduced an element of chance into Clark's process and brought the artist closer to organic, protean forms. Soon after this performance, she created a series of sculptures, *O dentro é o fora*, made from continuous bands of stainless steel that showed a strong affinity to Bill's investigations. She then stepped beyond the interests of the Swiss artist and developed the *Trepantes* series, which consisted of flexible bodies suspended from the ceiling or mounted on tree trunks. In 1964, in a series known as "soft works" *(obres moles)*, the artist started to produce rubber objects that were even more unstable and dynamic than her previous pieces (fig. 4). According to Mário Pedrosa, who had followed Clark's work since the early 1950s, with the "soft works" the artist achieved "a perfect expression of her dilacerated thinking between art and non-art, between creation and non-existence."[11] From that point on she would move away from the production of art objects and become increasingly involved with studies of the body.

A combination of immobile and dynamic elements, predictability and chance—through audience participation—also marked the work

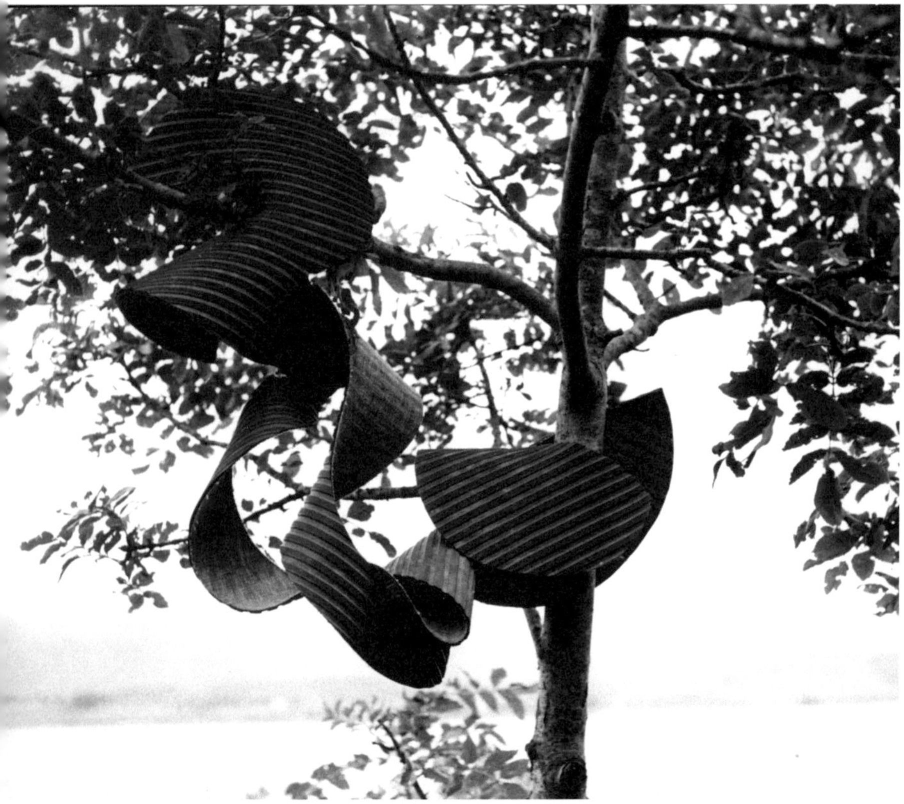

4 Lygia Clark, Obra mole, 1964, synthetic rubber, variable dimensions, diameter 50 cm

Courtesy Associação Cultural Lygia Clark, photo: Guy Brett

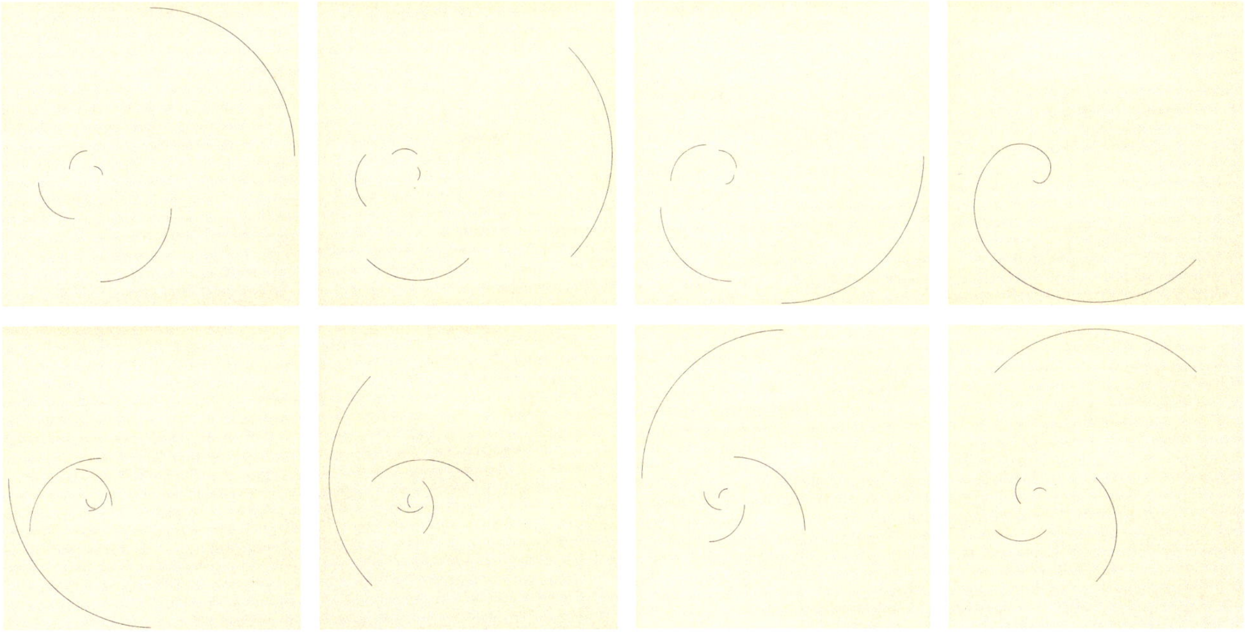

5 Mary Vieira, zeiten einer zeichnung 2. max bill zum geburtstag, 1952/53, 8 serigraphs in a folder, 24 x 24 cm

Spiral Press, Bern

of Mary Vieira. For her, Bill's exhibition at the MASP was a confirmation of her own experiments with geometric sculptures that, starting in 1948, she had conducted in relative isolation in Minas Gerais. In 1949 she developed her first *Polivolumes*—pieces that combine a fixed structure with plates or circles that revolve around an axis whenever they are touched by the audience. These works offer infinite possibilities of configuration based on pre-fixed elements. With her *Polivolumes*, the artist devoted herself to investigating the configuration of shapes as a consequence of movement, which in turn was a result of sometimes unpredictable impulses.

Vieira regarded Max Bill as a master: "in max bill and his works I found the parameters I sought. His attitude toward artistic work was a model for me in every way."[12] Shortly after moving to Switzerland in 1951, the artist produced two series of eight lithographs, *zeiten einer zeichnung. max bill zum geburtstag* (1952/53) (fig. 5), in which she explored different possibilities of populating a plane with a fixed set of curved and straight lines. In both cases, the length of the lines increases incrementally in a mathematically controlled way. In each series, the engravings are organized in pairs, according to which arrangements of the lines are most closely related to each other. Each pair tells the "story" of a virtual turning motion that accompanies the contraction and expansion of the lines. This process of directing the gaze over time with progressive and smooth changes modifies our spatial perception of the plane.

Lawrence Alloway discusses the philosophical differences between geometric works made by avant-garde artists in the early twentieth century and the geometric art that emerged after 1945 in a text written for the catalog of a monographic Max Bill exhibition that toured from Buffalo to Los Angeles and San Francisco in 1974/75. While Mondrian and his peers possessed a Platonic optimism that made them believe in the exceptional powers of geometry, wrote Alloway, "the geometrics of post-war art acquired a kind of existential base: geometry is no longer regarded as a mysterious symbolizing agent; it is, on the contrary, humanized. Order is taken as an arbitrary proposal of the artist's, a personal project against the void."[13] The reasons for this void, to which Alloway refers, however, were very different between Europe and Latin America. While Europe was having to cope with a land devastated by war, in Brazil the challenge was to survive political structures rooted in slavery that had never so much as contemplated the idea of a collective social project.

In 1953, Max Bill compared Rio de Janeiro to "a bombarded city."[14] After praising an upper-class housing project designed by Lúcio Costa, he said that he thought "it was a mistake to build only luxurious buildings when there existed such a problem with public housing."[15] The artist was quick to recognize the urbanistic problems caused by inequality, as well as the limits of modern architecture in such a scenario. The Concrete Art that emerged in Brazil in the 1950s was a phenomenon mainly middle- and upper-class artists from the southeast, the wealthiest and most-industrialized region in the country, partook in. While the artistic output of that era can be viewed as the personal and arbitrary undertakings of the artists who engaged in it, it can also be understood more broadly as the utopia of a specific social class which, for a period of just over a decade, believed it was possible to reconstruct the country on new foundations.

[1] "Manifesto Neoconcreto," in *Jornal do Brasil*, Sunday supplement, Rio de Janeiro, March 22, 1959. The manifesto is generally attributed to the poet and critic Ferreira Gullar, although the text was signed by Amilcar de Castro, Franz Weissmann, Lygia Clark, Lygia Pape, Reinaldo Jardim, and Theon Spanudis alongside Gullar.

[2] Max Bill was in Brazil in June of 1953 at the invitation of the Ministry of Foreign Affairs to give a series of lectures. He returned to the country only a few months later as a member of the jury for the second Art Biennial at the Museu de Arte Moderna, São Paulo (MAM-SP).

[3] Max Bill: "O arquiteto, a arquitetura, a sociedade," lecture held on June 9, 1953 at the Faculty of Architecture and Urbanism, University of São Paulo, printed in *Depoimento de uma geração*, edited by Alberto Xavier, São Paulo 2003, pp. 158–163. See also Max Bill's interview with Flávio Aquino: Flávio Aquino: "Max Bill critica a nossa moderna arquitetura," *Manchete* (June 1953), reprinted in *Arte concreta paulista: documentos*, edited by João Bandeira, São Paulo 2002, pp. 32–33.

[4] The Brazilian architect and urbanist Lúcio Costa (1902–1998) was a pioneer and chief theorist of modern Brazilian architecture from the 1930s to the 1960s. He was also the author of the Pilot Plan for Brasília.

[5] Lúcio Costa: "A nossa arquitetura moderna. Oportunidade Perdida," *Manchete* (July 1953), reprinted in Bandeira 2002 (see note 3), p. 34.

[6] The main reference work on the subject is the book by García, first published in English as María Amalia García: *Abstract Crossings: Cultural Exchange between Argentina and Brazil*, Berkeley 2019. See also Rodrigo Otávio da Silva Paiva: *Max Bill no Brasil*, Berlin 2011.

[7] Paiva 2011 (see note 6), p. 41.

[8] Both Bill and the MASP wanted the exhibition to travel to Buenos Aires and other Latin American cities, which ultimately did not happen owing to scheduling problems and, above all, difficulties with the Brazilian customs office.

[9] Diários Associados was a set of communications companies (journals, newspapers, and radio stations) belonged to Assis Chateaubriand, the businessman who created the MASP in 1947. In the 1940s, the first museum's base occupied one floor of the Diários Associados headquarters in São Paulo downtown. The renovation headed by Lina Bo Bardi in 1950 expanded the MASP area to a second floor on this building.

[10] Pietro Maria Bardi: *Fotoforma*, exh. booklet, São Paulo 1951.

[11] Mário Pedrosa: "A obra de Lygia Clark," in *O Estado de São Paulo* (December 28, 1963), reprinted in Otília Arantes (ed.): *Acadêmicos e modernos: Textos escolhidos III*, São Paulo 2004, p. 351.

[12] Mary Vieira, cited from *Mary Vieira: o tempo do movimento*, exh. cat., São Paulo and Rio de Janeiro: Centro Cultural Banco do Brasil 2005, p. 23.

[13] Lawrence Alloway in Buffalo/Los Angeles/San Francisco 1974/75, p. 12.

[14] Aquino 1953 (see note 3), p. 32.

[15] Ibid., p. 33.

max bill (1955)

tomás maldonado

Excerpts with Commentary by María Amalia García

Tomás Maldonado's book *Max Bill* synthesizes the Swiss artist's strong connections to the South American postwar scene. This artful edition—nearly square in format (21 x 22 x 1.5 cm.), with letterpress type, red cloth binding and a paper dust jacket (fig. 1)—is exemplary of the modern approach to layout given its use of the grid system, the sans serif typography (in the manner of the Futura font), and the uniformity and synthesis of its graphic design. In addition to the standard print run, the edition was completed with sixteen special copies containing an original two-color lithograph by Bill and signed by the artist. The book included an introduction by Maldonado on Bill's multifaceted production, four key texts by the Swiss artist ("The mathematical approach in contemporary art", "A monument", "Differential living quarters as a city element," and "Form, function, beauty"), and black-and-white photographs of his visual art, design work, and architecture. The quadrilingual edition (Spanish, English, German, and French) indicated the desire for a broad international reach, of clear benefit to both Bill and Maldonado as well as to the fledgling publishing house. Without a doubt this book was the tremendous bet on which the publishing house directed by Jorge Grisetti was launched, Nueva Visión, which emerged from the magazine of the same name founded by Maldonado in 1951. In 1955, alongside *Max Bill*, works by Wilhelm Worringer ("Problematik der Gegenwartskunst") and Juan Carlos Paz ("Introducción a la música de nuestro tiempo") also appeared. These editions, geared toward a burgeoning professional and university audience, made available in Spanish key materials on modernism's development which had previously been inaccessible in the language.

Maldonado, in his introduction to the book, presents Bill as an artist who has reached the pinnacle of modernism's ambition, with his integrated, all-encompassing practice of the visual arts and sense of continuity among them. Faced with the centrality that individual expression in contemporary art acquired in the mid-1950s (abstract expressionism, informalism, tachisme), Maldonado saw in Bill's working methods a rational and coherent approach to the creation of visual moments. Maldonado argued that, unlike other avant-garde trends (such as De Stijl, which sought, by employing a limited vocabulary, to make the modern world visible), Bill's work implied a new approach to understanding stylistic coherence. Form was for Bill "the sum of all functions in harmonious unison," so that the material structure became a mediating element between the function of the object and its beauty. As such, Maldonado pointed out that the versatility of this method was that it was "equally applicable to the creation of a sculpture or of a pavilion, or a brush or a table." Proceeding from the same rational and intelligible impulse, concrete art and good form (*Gute Form*) were complementary approaches to the creation of both artistic and utilitarian forms.

Publishing a book on Max Bill had been a longstanding project: Maldonado had been eager to publish a monograph on the Swiss artist ever since he met him at his home in Zurich in 1948. In 1950 Maldonado

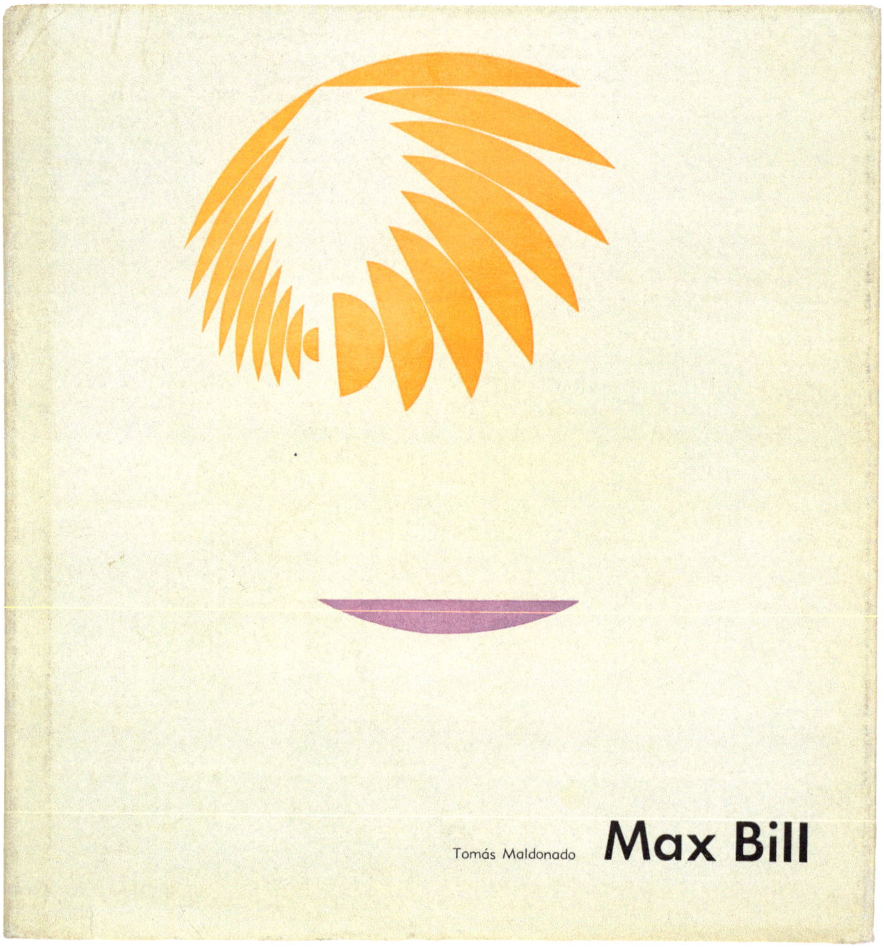

1 Dust jacket for Tomás Maldonado, *Max Bill*, 1955, with a print by Bill

already had a version very similar to the monograph published in the Nueva Visión book, which he sent to Pietro Maria Bardi, director of the Museu de Arte de São Paulo, hoping it might be included in a catalog for an exhibition of the artist held at the São Paulo museum in March 1951. Although the catalog of that exhibition was never produced, it makes sense to situate the Nueva Visión book in connection to the São Paulo exhibition. Another important point of reference for *Max Bill* is the 1952 publication of Bill's book *Form*, which gave life to the idea of Good Form through a highly varied visual repertory of natural elements and artifacts. In terms of its graphic characteristics (the square format, sans serif typeface, and grid-system layout), *Form* also seems to have been a key reference for *Max Bill*, given the close proximity between their respective dates of publication (figs. 2, 3).

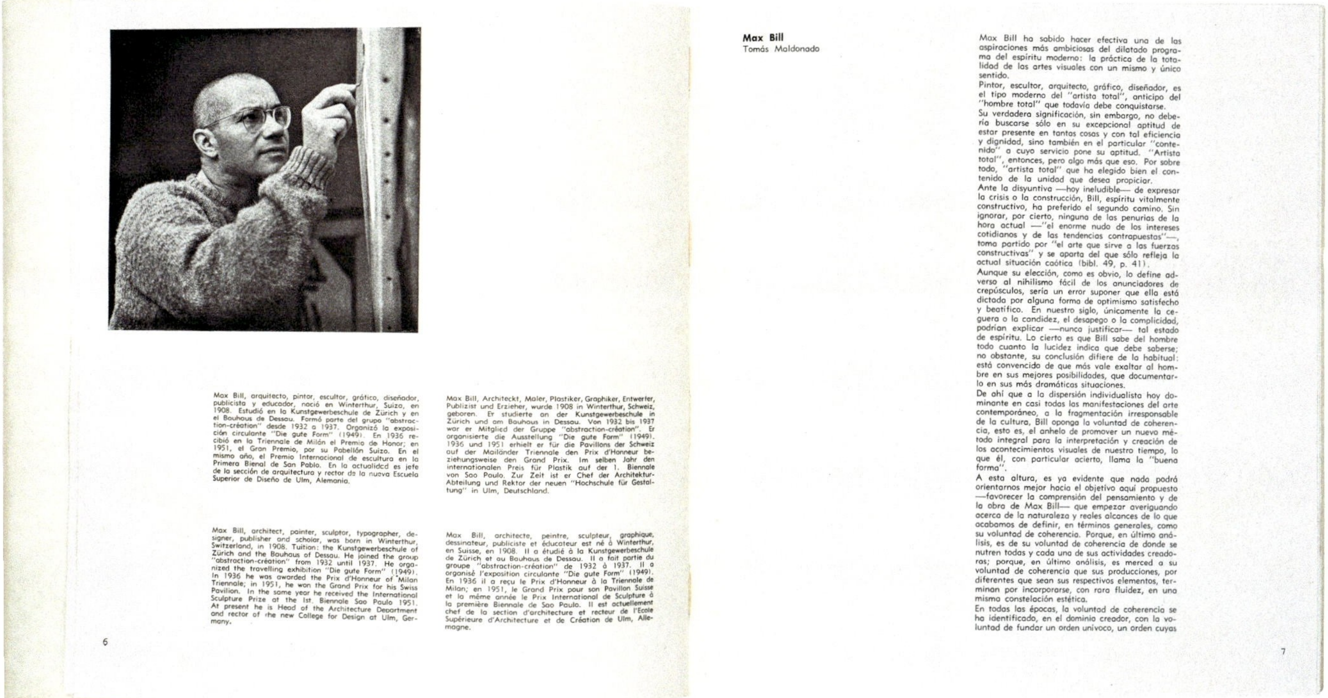

2 Pages 6 and 7 from the layout of Tomás Maldonado, *Max Bill*, produced in a square format, with a sans-serif font and grid system

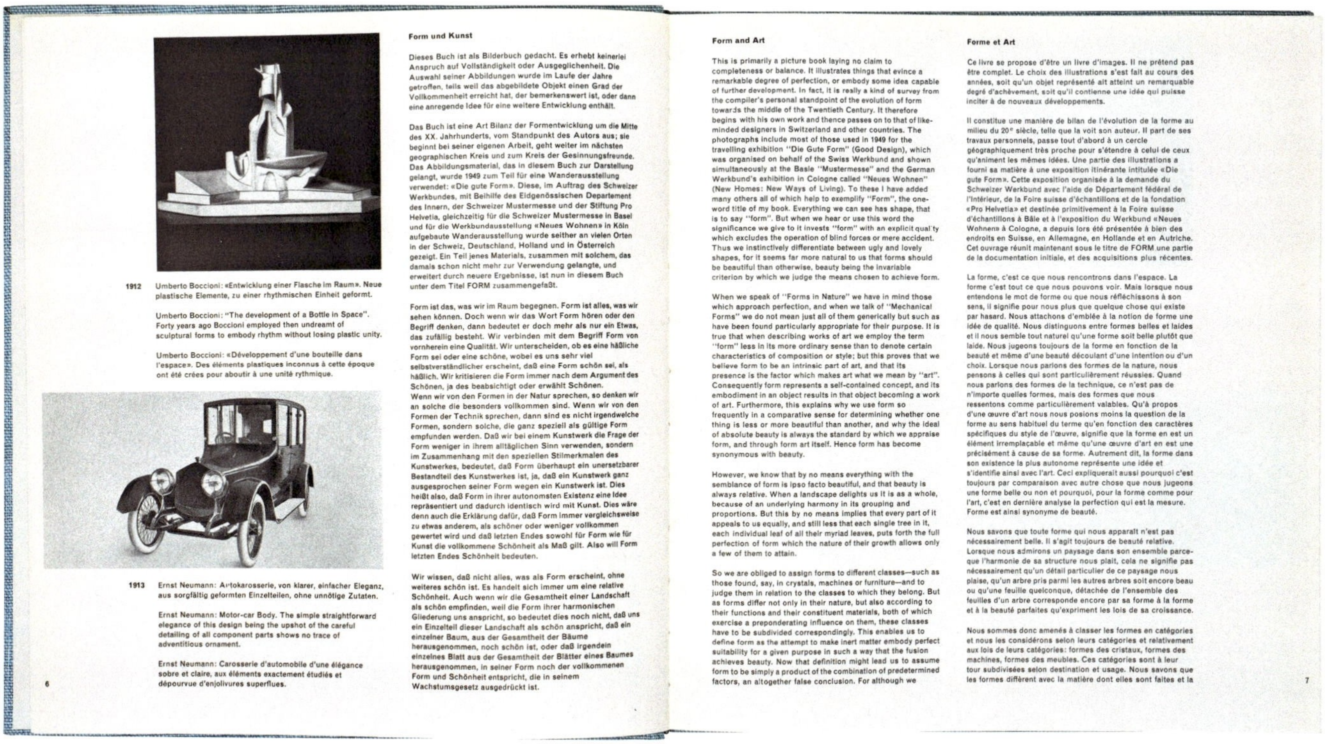

3 Pages 6 and 7 of Max Bill's design for his monograph *Form*, 1952, which was a crucial source of inspiration for Maldonado's book

This book was unequivocally the result of the fruitful artistic and intellectual bond between Maldonado and Bill; it illustrated the array of intense dialogue between the Swiss artist and his Argentine and Brazilian artists, critics, and institutions. At Bill's invitation, Maldonado joined the faculty at the HfG Ulm in 1954: and although the relationship at first continued to be one of mutual accord, disagreements over how to conceive of industrial production emerged as the decade wore on. However, notwithstanding these misunderstandings between the two, Maldonado's *Max Bill* was, for a long time, the only extant publication to explore the work and thought of this Swiss artist.

tomás maldonado *max bill*, 1955 (excerpts)

Max Bill has achieved one of the most ambitious aspirations of the wide program of the modern spirit: the practice of all visual arts with one same and only sense.

Painter, sculptor, architect, typographer, industrial designer, he is the modern type of the "total artist," a forerunner of the "total man," still to be conquered.

His real significance, however, should not be sought only in his exceptional ability to be present in so many things with such efficiency and dignity, but also in the particular "content" which his aptitude serves. A "total artist" therefore, but even something more; above everything else, a "total artist" who has well chosen the content of the unit he wishes to favor.

Before the dilemma—today unavoidable—of expressing crisis or construction, Bill, a vitally constructive spirit, has chosen the second road. Perfectly aware, certainly, of all the predicaments of the present times—"the enormous knot of daily interests and of opposing trends"—he follows "the art which serves constructive forces" and stands aloof from that which only reflects the present chaotic situation.[1]

Although his selection, as is obvious, defines Bill as contrary to the easy nihilism of the announcers of twilights, it would be a mistake to suppose that it is dictated by any form of satisfied and beatific optimism. In our century, only blindness or candor, indifference or complicity, might explain—but never justify—this state of mind. What is true is that Bill knows about Man all that lucidity points out should be known; nevertheless, the conclusion he arrives at differs from the customary; he is convinced that it is far more valuable to exalt Man within his better possibilities than to record his most dramatic situations.

Thus, against the individualistic dispersion today prevailing over practically all the expressions of contemporary art, against the irresponsible fragmentation of culture, Bill opposes the will of coherence, that is, the desire to promote a new and integral method for the interpretation and creation of the visual events of our time, what Bill calls, so very aptly, the "good form."

At this stage it is already evident that nothing can lead us better towards the objective herein set forth—to make easier the comprehension of the thought and the work of Max Bill—than to start a survey of the nature and real scope of what we have just defined, in general terms, as his will of coherence. Because, in the last analysis, it is from that will of coherence that each and every one of his creative activities are nourished; because, in the last analysis, thanks to his will of coherence, his production, however different the respective elements may be, ends by incorporating itself, with uncommon fluidity, into one only aesthetic constellation.

In any age the will of coherence has identified itself, in the field of creation, with the will of establishing one univocal order, of which the component parts respond to one sense and illustrate one same spirit. Generally speaking, the ultimate aspiration was, in most cases, that of imposing compulsive poetics to which, willingly or unwillingly, all forms created by the community should necessarily be subjected and pay tribute. Or, in short, a stylistic preceptive. A style.

[...]

In our time, new ways of defining and achieving coherence have begun to make themselves known. Furthermore, the notion itself of style, back from the ostracism to which the modern movement had condemned it, reappears today radically transformed.

On studying it, one may see that the notion of style has had an extraordinary and ambiguous fate in our century.

Theo van Doesburg asserted in his time that "the idea of style, as the annulment of all styles" constituted the foundation of neoplasticist poetics; Walter Gropius, on his part, recalled, not so long ago, that "the purpose of the Bauhaus had never been to disseminate a style." The fact is that in the period of the "De Stijl" and the Bauhaus, what we conclusively know today was only suspected at the time, that is, that the so-called "nonstylistic style," advocated by those trends, ended up, in the long run, as another victim of a process of solidification; that the forms and figures discovered with such daring and fervor, forms and figures born of rebellion, ended up by losing their original spontaneity and vitality, calcifying·themselves finally into a style, perhaps more attractive, but no less limited for that reason.

[...]

In the midst of this tangled fabric of problems—of "non-stylistic styles" that promise "final solutions" but end by being manners; of styles which the modern world acknowledges it needs but nevertheless rejects,—some few creators, profiting from experience accumulated from 1910 up to the present, seem to be on the road to success insofar as articulating a new position is concerned. This new position, as we have already stated, fundamentally favors a new understanding of coherence and style.

The work of Bill is one of the best illustrations of this new position. His paintings, his sculptures, his architectural work, his industrial designs, all express a firm will of coherence and point out, therefore, towards a style. But, to tell the truth, the coherence and the style that derive from his work are of a very particular nature. Bill asserts, in fact, that we should orient ourselves towards the ideal condition wherein all forms, from the smallest object to a city, should also be conceived as "the sum total of the functions in harmonious unison" ("Form, function, beauty"). This must not be construed, however, in the sense that Bill, like the Abbé Batteux in the XVIII century, pretends to submit all creative activities to the tyranny of "one same principle". No. The task of Bill is another. The results obtained by him are different too. His work shows a new type of coherence, open, dialectical, a real plural unity; for that reason, then, the style is neither dogmatic nor closed. On the contrary, it is a coherent, constructive style, but at the some time essentially creative, always assisted by phantasy or surprise. To put it in other words, in Bill the will to uniform does not prevail over the will to form. That is why his style is at the same time responsible and free. The style of the years to come. Because against all predictions, the years to come shall not create a hermetic culture, suspended in time.

Bill, commenting on Adolf Loos, asserts: "A unity of style (Stileinheit) begins to insinuate itself, a unity which cannot be achieved by the mere adding of superficialities of style."[2] At first sight, this formulation would not differ from those set forth at the end of the last century by the pioneers of functionalism. Something, however, makes it stand by itself. For Bill, "superficial styling" is not always ornamental. There also is a modernistic "superficial styling," not ornamental, which goes over the form without being able to show an intimate relationship with it. Such is the case of forms which, according to Bill, "look very attractive and modern in a superficial sort of way"; forms whose "pretty façade often hides technical drawbacks". Thus we get to the central theme, that is, the one which will point out the manner and the reason of the forms conceived by Bill—whether artistic or industrial. We refer to the fundamentals of his doctrine on form. "For us it has become self-evident—says Bill—that beauty cannot be developed from function alone. But we can demand beauty that is equal in quality to function, i. e. that it should, so to speak, be part of function."[3] From this, undoubtedly, may be inferred a more dynamic formulation of the relationships between function and form, less mechanized than that stated by [Louis] Sullivan: "form follows function." In Bill, form and function are not related in a lineal, successive and continuous manner, but in a parallel, simultaneous and discontinuous manner. "We define form—he writes—as the attempt to make inert matter embody perfect suitability for a given purpose in such a way that the fusion achieves beauty." But he hastens to tell us: "Now that definition may lead us to assume form to be simply a product of the combination of predetermined factors, an altogether false conclusion."[4]

[...]

Let us observe, to this respect, how his severe methods of structuration never turn against his creative autonomy. We might even dare to say that his strictness lies in his freedom.

In a certain sense, it is identified with it. This synthesis—unusual for some—of terms as opposed as these, is, in our opinion, one of the most promising facts of contemporary visual culture. The peculiar nature of the structuration methods confirms that the constructive spirit, notwithstanding the unfavorable situations already pointed out, is re-establishing, step by step, its revolutionary continuity.

All right. But what do these structuration methods consist of? What are their characteristics? For Bill, a form organizes itself according to its own "law of development" and taking as a starting point its own inner data. It is from the dialectics of form, from its peculiar manner of being born, and never from pre-established proportional or harmonic outlines, that methods of structuration must be inferred.

In his "Fifteen variations on one theme"[5] Bill, between 1935 and 1938, tried to give practical examples of these ideas. The productiveness of the method was surprising. These fifteen images more than proved that a structural theme, if born in compliance with a "law of development" and not arbitrarily, admits "an infinite multiplicity of possibilities." This means that the new type of structural theme contributes, in fact, to enlarge illimitedly the resources of art, but shows, at the same time, its astonishing adaptability to any other field of creation. The method is equally applicable to the creation of a sculpture or of a pavilion, of a brush or a table.

In the strictly artistic field, the fifteen images of Bill have, moreover, other implications. Georg Schmidt, with particular insight, has stated[6] that they change the traditional idea of variation—formal variation, in time, of an "external" theme to art—to another idea of wider scope—formal variation, in time and in space, of an "internal" theme to art. In other words, in the past, what displaced itself, what was in relative freedom, was a theme foreign to art, while the artistic structure of the work, with slight modifications, remained constant. With Bill, what displaces itself is a theme intrinsic to art; what is in perfect freedom is artistic structure itself.

The trend of Bill in painting-sculpture is concrete art. The term "concrete art," coined by van Doesburg in 1930, used by Bill in his writings of 1936, by Arp and Kandinsky in 1938, is the one which can best help us in the appreciation of the true nature of this new artistic trend. Let us make clear, incidentally, that by "new artistic trend" no new "ism" must be understood. Concretism is not concrete art. "An 'ism'—says Bill—is never the real thing, it is always something that substitutes what is real."

Actually, it is only a short time ago that concrete art began to make itself known as an independent aesthetic conduct. At first, it did not pretend to be at all a new artistic trend; it only sought to be a new way—the best and the most appropriate—of designating the old artistic trend known as abstract, or abstract art. In Italy, for instance, the term "concrete art," particularly during the last postwar period, is commonly used in this sense, that is, instead of the expression "abstract art." And nothing more.

However, this division between abstract art and concrete art, which began by being a difference in name, tends at present to assume another meaning. In our opinion, it becomes increasingly evident that abstract art differs from concrete art; that both expressions are the labels of essentially different artistic facts. This change, undoubtedly, has been favored, above all, by the creative contribution of the outstanding group of Swiss concrete artists—Max Bill, Camille Graeser, Richard P. Lohse, Verena Loewensberg—who have opened new perspectives to a definition of concrete art on new bases.

But what are, after all, the differences between concrete art and abstract art? Bill said recently that abstract art was an art of transition. Let us add that, like all processes of transition, this one is achieved by degrees.

[...]

The first abstract art pretends to be a sublimated chronicle of reality, hence its frank difference with concrete art, the aim of which, as has been so often said, is not to record reality but rather to create it. In the second, on the other hand, the difference is more qualitative than quantitative. It takes place on a subtler plane; without grandiloquence.

Bill has recently added new shades that help to clear up a large part of these problems. The distinctive elements of concrete art, elements "which are only very partially seen in the majority of the paintings and sculptures at present considered abstract," would be—for Bill—"the production of fields of energy, with the help of color" and "the creation of certain rhythms, which could not be originated otherwise."[7]

In this manner, the boundaries between abstract art and concrete art are far more precise. We know that the new realities of concrete art are not either born of the abstract or the fictitious, that they do not resort to mirages nor do they manufacture them, but we also know now that in these new realities, however objective they pretend to be, it is always possible to detect the utilization on the part of their creator, of such notions as "field" and "rhythm," which, in themselves, lead us to more complex and subjective worlds.

The fact is that, in substance, the works of concrete art, in contradiction to what has so often been stated, are not only objects. They are also facts. Facts which happen, which flow. And what is important, facts that happen and flow among us. That is, facts we can perceive, we can see coming or going, to which we get near or from which we draw away. Perception and communication.

The opinions of Bill regarding two-dimensionalism in the work of art—the old problem of the "plane within the plane" mentioned by Mondrian—radically uproot a great number of viewpoints of the primitive concrete art. "Any painting—writes Bill—formerly considered as a two-dimensional surface, is now transformed into space and part of a pluridimensional phenomenon, in which the perpetually changing real space and the psychic space superimpose themselves. For this reason, a painting is not something two-dimensional, since we conceive it in relation to its effect—its sense—and not as an object enclosed within itself."[8]

Certainly, many are amazed at these so frequent displacements in concept of concrete art. They would prefer a more stable doctrine; a dogma, if possible. But concrete art is no more and no less than a method. A method, on the other hand, in constant renewal and confirmation.

The creative process of concrete art starts with the "image-idea" ("Bild-Idee") and is achieved with the "image-object". It is "an ideological concept which, made visible and translated into a painting, has given birth to a concrete object."[9] For further clarity let us recall, moreover, that Bill defines "concrete" as "what exists in fact, what is not only thought of, what is not concept only."[10] In other words, concrete art stresses the objective, the verifiable, practically verifiable character of the final image: "a reality which can be controlled and observed."[11] This should not be understood in terms of adhering to a narrow and short-sighted pragmatism; a type of objectivity where any form of projection or subjective creation is excluded. Certainly, concrete art sets itself one object, but we should at all times keep it in mind, a "rich" object. An object whose confirmation requires, in fact, all the available data, and also, especially, perceptive data.

It is evident that the "image-idea" is transformed into an "image-object" through toil, that is, through the handling of artistic elements and technical media. However, if this is successfully achieved, it is undoubtedly because the handling has been assisted at all times by a congruent, constructive method: on one hand, with the "image-idea"; on the other hand, with the "image-object." Aesthetic experience teaches which is the peculiar development of each "image-idea" and its possible objectification, in other words, what is its "law of development" and its applicability. It is, finally, from this "law of development" from which the methodological constants of concrete art are deduced. For this reason, concrete art is, Bill states, "the pure expression between form and law."[12]

[...]

The new unity of painting-sculpture-architecture will not be achieved, as in the Renaissance, by the mechanical and artificial superimposing of different artistic "genres." The unit will have to be set forth in terms of fusion. Of fusion in space. "It is in space—Bill states—that sculptural, pictorial and spatial creation may rise to unity."[13] This fusion shall be achieved on the basis of speculative contributions of painting and sculpture, but neither painting nor sculpture shall lose their independence or waive their specific functions. As regards the case of painting in particulor, it is well to recall that the problem of its survival or disappearance is, above all, a practical problem, closely linked to the objective conditions (social and technical) of creation.

Strictly speaking, as long as artistic work depends on craftsmanship's resources, as long as nuclear energy and electronic machines, for instance, are not placed at the service of spiritual creation, but, to a certain extent, go against it, painting shall continue to be the more logical solution and that which offers the best guarantees to the artist. No one can deny that nowadays, painting "covers" a whole field of creative requirements which no other media can satisfy with equal success.

Bill's position regarding the problem of the relationship of Art and Science has two aspects: Science (mathematics) as a regulating method and Science as a source of inspiration of concrete art themes. We have already referred to the former, incidentally, when mentioning the "Fifteen variations on one theme." Let us now consider the second aspect.

In his article: "The Mathematical Approach in Contemporary Art,"[14] Bill suggests the need of formulating what could be called the new themes of concrete art. Instead of proposing—as has been done from Luca Pacioli down to our days—the use of Science exclusively as a regulating method of Art, Bill points out that it is necessary to start considering Science under a new light, that is, as the main source of new themes. This should not be interpreted as Bill advising to leave aside all regulating mathematical-geometrical method and paint, like the Douanier Rousseau, "under the dictates of his dead wife" (Kandinsky); what he really upholds is that Science ought to be present in the form as also in the content of a work of art. And this should not be understood, either, in a literal sense, as a mechanical reproduction of new realities discovered by modern Science, because this would be, after all, a new form of naturalism, naturalism on another scale, but as senseless as traditional naturalism. His purpose is different: what he really advocates is that the "aesthetic" conscience of "space-time"—constituting the raw material of concrete art—accompany and express the modifications and enrichments noticeable in the "scientific" conscience of the space-time. Concrete art should direct its themes in this sense, even when the efforts required from the creators to achieve this be increased day by day.

It is precisely in the artistic production of Bill—as also in that of Georges Vantongerloo—where this new trend of themes begins to appear with exemplifying clarity. Bill's sculptures, subtly referred to "curved and not oriented spaces" of topology, speak to sensibility in a language never heard heretofore. His "Continuity" [pl. p. 80 top] and his "Tripartite Unity" [illus. p. 111] are among the works of higher lyrical content of contemporary sculpture. Before them a complex feeling made of giddiness and bewilderment, of curiosity and enchantment gets hold of the spectator. It is a glimpse of other dimensions not yet intuited, but which, thanks to these works, man has begun to conceive with increasing anxiousness, as if changing a flat world for another one of infinite dimensions. Actually, this is a new triumph of artistic knowledge.

The new theme trend is also manifest in the pictorial production of Bill. Certain notions as continuous-discontinuous, precise-imprecise, limited-unlimited, which constitute his favorite thematic repertoire, are, undoubtedly, filtrations coming from the most up-to-date scientific expression.

Let us briefly consider the results: let us analyze, briefly too, the manner in which these notions are artistically objectified.

In these last few years, Bill has advanced in the sense of giving great importance to the pictorial "field," to what is not a figure. The result has been the "ineffable image." A type of image where all the scientific notions to which we have alluded above are included. It is evident that the need of devitalizing plastically the figures in favor of a greater expressive emphasis of empty surrounding space, can only be achieved in two ways: through the "virtualization" of the figures by means of lines and dots, or by the sfumato of lines and dots. But the lines, dots and sfumatos help to invalidate the traditional concept of precision—as was understood until Mondrian—to give way to a new concept—the imprecise-precision. Imprecise-precision because in works of art of this type the purpose is constructive, even when certain external resources be diffuse and not very strict. The lines (straight, curved, undulated, or spiral), the dots and the sfumatos are not used for ornamental or naturalistic purposes, but as to express a secret organizing will of the image itself. In the painting "Unlimited-limited," for instance, the sfumato retains its frank structural strength: the spectator realizes that, after all, the sfumato can be looked at—even when a certain preparation is necessary—with the "naked eye," that is, as a new pure element of concrete art, without volumetric reminiscences of any kind.

As may be seen, the present theme trend of concrete art is imbued with scientific notions. Nevertheless, these are not the only elements that make it up. Undoubtedly, there is also an aesthetics, a manner of defining beauty. There is also an ethics, a way of trusting in man. Because artistic doing, as any doing, is tantamount to taking sides, not only in relation with given values, but with all values and all possible realities. The artist models the matter of his art not only with his humors and vapors—as Baudelaire wished him to—but also with his ideas. And these ideas are of a very different origin and complexion. The reality of concrete art is extremely complex because it is a reality designed for communication. It deals with the most difficult material: meanings—with visual meanings.

The art of Max Bill conveys its content to the spectator. Through the work of this extraordinary artist, men can slowly become aware of their own power of invention, order, clarity, and beauty. Perhaps they cannot yet understand them completely—very often, many of the cobwebs that nowadays weaken their artistic sensibility must be brushed off from the eyes—but the truth is that all men have here the possibility of taking a glimpse into the wonderful.

This text was first published in an unabridged version in Maldonado 1955. It was written by Tomás Maldonado as an introduction to his publication on Max Bill—the first-ever monograph on the latter. Apart from this introduction, it contained texts by Max Bill himself, numerous illustrations relating to his work, a comprehensive bibliography, and a list of exhibitions. All texts were featured in Spanish, English, German, and French. Translation by María Luisa Uriburu.

[1] Max Bill: "La pittura concreta", in: *Domus*, no. 206, February 1946, pp. 37–43, here p. 41. Article with illustrations by Bill, Klee, Lohse, Mondrian, Albers, Malewitsch, Hinterreiter, Taeuber-Arp, Vantongerloo, and Kandinsky.

[2] Bill 1949b, reprint in: Gerd Hatje (Ed.): *Idea 53, International Design Annual – Internationales Jahrbuch für Formgebung – Annuaire International des Formes Utiles*, Stuttgart 1952, pp. 10–12, here p. 12.

[3] Ibid., p. 10.

[4] Bill 1952, p. 8.

[5] Max Bill: *quinze variations sur un même thème*, Paris 1938.

[6] Georg Schmidt: "La variation d'un même thème dans les beaux arts" in: *XXe siècle*, no. 4, 1938, pp. 37 f., here p. 37.

[7] Max Bill: "De la surface à l'espace", in: *XXe siècle*, no. 2, 1951, pp. 59–65, here p. 62.

[8] Ibid., pp. 60.

[9] Max Bill: "Max Bill spiega la pittura concreta", in: *sele arte*, first year. September/October 1952, pp. 11–16, here p. 12.

[10] Max Bill in: *Zürcher konkrete Kunst*, exhibition catalog Stuttgart: Galerie Lutz & Meyer; München: Galerie Otto Stangl, 1949.

[11] See Bill 1952, p. 12.

[12] Max Bill in: *Zürcher konkrete Kunst*, exhibition catalog Stuttgart: Galerie Lutz & Meyer; Munich: Galerie Otto Stangl, 1949.

[13] See Bill 1951, p. 65.

[14] Bill 1949a.

max bill and american art

Lynn Zelevansky

My first trip to Brazil was in 1989 as a very junior curator at the Museum of Modern Art (MoMA) in New York. I was sent by Kynaston McShine—then senior curator in the museum's department of painting and sculpture—with the assignment of finding an artist who would be appropriate for MoMA's *Projects* program, which focused on emerging artists or those who were less known to the museum's audiences. I was to view that year's São Paulo Bienal, and learn what I could in a week that was jam-packed with studio and museum visits. Kynaston, who was supremely well connected, arranged for me to be guided through São Paulo and Rio de Janeiro by two experts in contemporary Brazilian art: Ivo Mesquita and Paulo Herkenhoff.

Tired of the overblown aspects of the New York art world at the end of the 1980s, it was a pleasure for me to experience the unique sensibilities, intelligence, and creative energy of the Brazilians, most of whom were all but unknown in New York at the time. For a budding curator, this was paradise, but for Ivo and Paulo it was not enough. They wanted me to understand that Brazilian art had its own trajectory, apart from Europe and the United States. In 1989, few books and articles on Brazilian art had been translated, so they took it upon themselves to begin my education into that history, in front of the art when possible, through pictures in books and films, and by introducing me to the artists themselves. The biggest shock for me in that intense week was the importance of Max Bill to the development of Brazilian art in the decades after World War II. I was floored. It seemed impossible that the unique, sophisticated, and enormously inventive work of artists such as Lygia Clark, Lygia Pape, Hélio Oiticica, and, from a younger generation, Cildo Meireles, whose work I ultimately showed at MoMA, would have been related in any way to Bill's. In truth, I hardly knew Bill's work. I had a vague notion of a form of geometric abstraction, but no one I knew—at MoMA or elsewhere—discussed this artist.

I certainly did not know that Bill saw himself primarily as an architect, and that, in addition to architecture and his career as a painter and sculptor, he was a renowned industrial and graphic designer and typographer, and an educator who, in concert with others, designed both the building and the curriculum for the Hochschule für Gestaltung (HfG) in Ulm, Germany, following World War II.[1] His sense of social responsibility, which infused everything he did, resulted in both underground actions (joining the Resistance during the Spanish Civil War and World War II) and formal politics (serving on the Council of Zurich (1961–1968) and the National Council of Switzerland (1967–1971), advocating for controversial environmental and anti-apartheid issues).[2] My understanding of how wide-ranging Bill's achievements were, and how significant he was as a model, began on that first trip to Brazil. Bill did not single-handedly chart the direction of art in Brazil, but his notion of Concrete art (konkrete Kunst)—a systematic approach to abstraction that originates in mathematics and logic but also allows for the role of intuition—reverberated in Brazil, supporting the development of many of the country's most forward-looking artists.[3]

Nothing like this happened in the United States. When Bill made his first trip there in June 1953, it was as a designer. He attended Aspen, Colorado's International Design Conference, where he was a major speaker. The conference was oriented towards the business side of design, and Bill was a dissenting voice. Reflecting his formative experiences as a student at the Bauhaus, he believed that designers needed to take responsibility for everything they sent into the world; their focus should be on making people's lives better, not making money. The Los Angeles designer Gere Kavanaugh, who was at that conference and heard Bill speak, remembers that his lecture generated a good deal of debate.[4]

Bill visited New York on the way back to Europe and briefly engaged with that art world when Rose Fried threw a party in his honor at her gallery. Apparently he was already known in some quarters of the city, as his work had appeared there for the first time three years earlier in a group exhibition at Galerie Chalette in Manhattan. That 1950 exhibition, titled *Construction and Geometry in Painting: From Malevich to "Tomorrow,"* confirmed his situation as an intermediary between two generations: that of his Bauhaus teachers, some of whom were also included in the show, and his own.

Bill was a consistent presence in the United States between 1963 and 1975. During that period, he showed every few years at the Staempfli Gallery in New York and garnered significant American collectors, among them Nelson Rockefeller, who acquired one of Bill's works for his sculpture garden.[5] In 1965, he was included in MoMA's landmark exhibition, *The Responsive Eye* (often remembered as a celebration of "Op art," the show presented its share of jarring optical illusions, but was actually a broad survey of abstract visual experiences, some extremely subtle). Bill also had important collectors in Chicago:[6] the Art Institute of Chicago included him in *Sculpture of the Twentieth Century* (1952) and *Sculpture: A Generation of Innovation* (1971); and he had a solo show at the Arts Club of Chicago (1969). His most significant exhibition in the United States, simply titled *Max Bill*, was a retrospective organized by the Albright Knox Art Gallery in Buffalo, New York, which toured to the Los Angeles County Museum of Art, the San Francisco Museum of Art, and the Corcoran Gallery in Washington, DC (1974/75) (fig. 1). In addition, between 1958 and 1982 he was included in five Carnegie Internationals—the closest thing that the United States has to Documenta or the Venice Biennale—and Galerie Denise René, Paris, and Hans Mayer, Dusseldorf showed him at Art Chicago in 1984.

Other activities also brought Bill to the United States. He was made an honorary member of the American Institute of Architects in 1964, and in 1980 he curated a retrospective exhibition of the work of his good friend Georges Vantongerloo, which toured to the Los Angeles

County Museum of Art. This occasioned a visit with Ray Eames. She, together with her husband Charles Eames, was among America's most famous designers, and Charles had taught at Bill's Ulm School of Design in 1955. Photographs taken in 1958, when Charles returned to Ulm for a lecture, confirm the warm friendship that had developed between Bill and the Eameses. Unfortunately, Charles had died two years before Bill's 1980 visit, but Bill renewed the connection with Ray Eames (fig. 2).

Despite all this attention, Bill's inclusion in the 1982 Carnegie International and the 1984 edition of Art Chicago were essentially outliers.

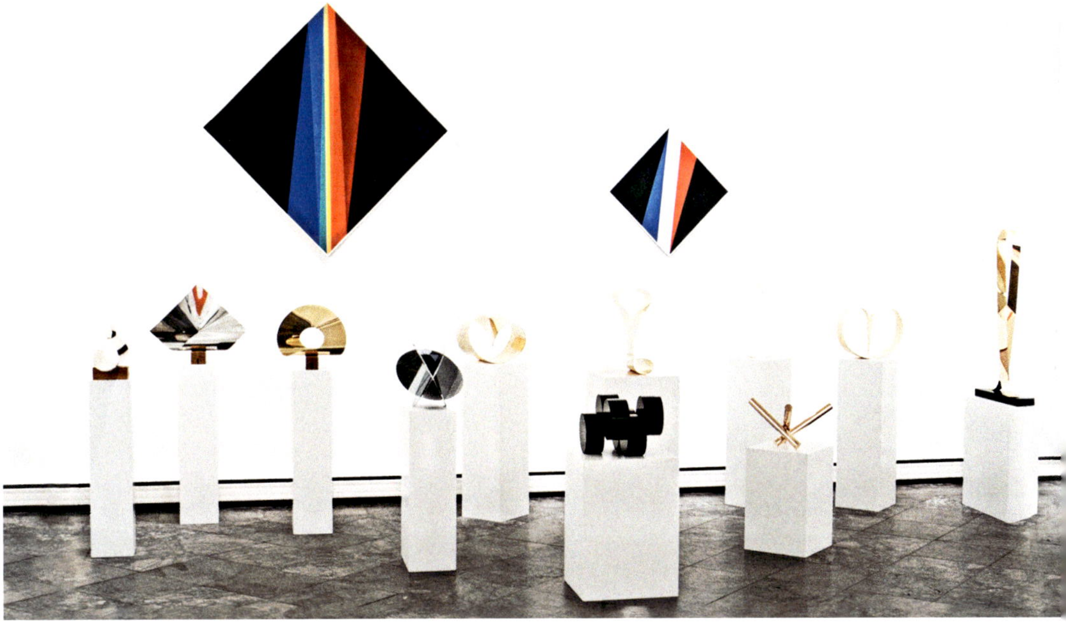

1 View of the Max Bill retrospective at Albright Knox Art Gallery, 1974/75
Albright Knox Art Gallery

While he continued to show extensively in Europe, after 1975 he seems to have all but disappeared from the consciousness of the American art world. Bill knew many well-known American artists—Jasper Johns and James Lee Byars are just two examples—but it seems that, for him, the most important friendships were with an older generation, many of whom taught him at the Bauhaus. These were people who influenced his art and life. It is not surprising, then, that Josef and Anni Albers were his closest friends in the United States. When Albers was at Black Mountain College, he invited Bill to teach there, just as László Moholy-Nagy had invited him to teach at the New Bauhaus in Chicago. Bill declined both offers, but Albers, already a US citizen, taught twice at the Ulm School (fig. 3).[7]

While Bill's associations with younger American artists may have lacked the intensity of his ongoing relationships with the older Europeans who had helped to form him, influence did flow from Bill to some of this new generation. Among those who were in Europe in the late 1940s

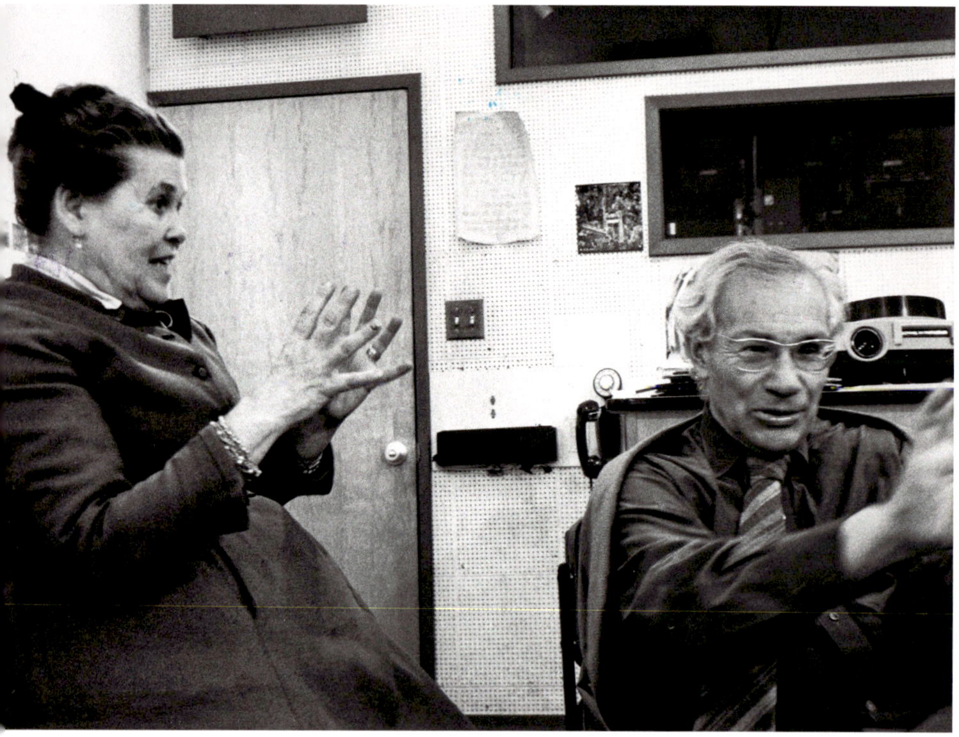

2 Max Bill visited Ray Eames in Pacific Palisades in 1980
Photo: Angela Thomas Schmid

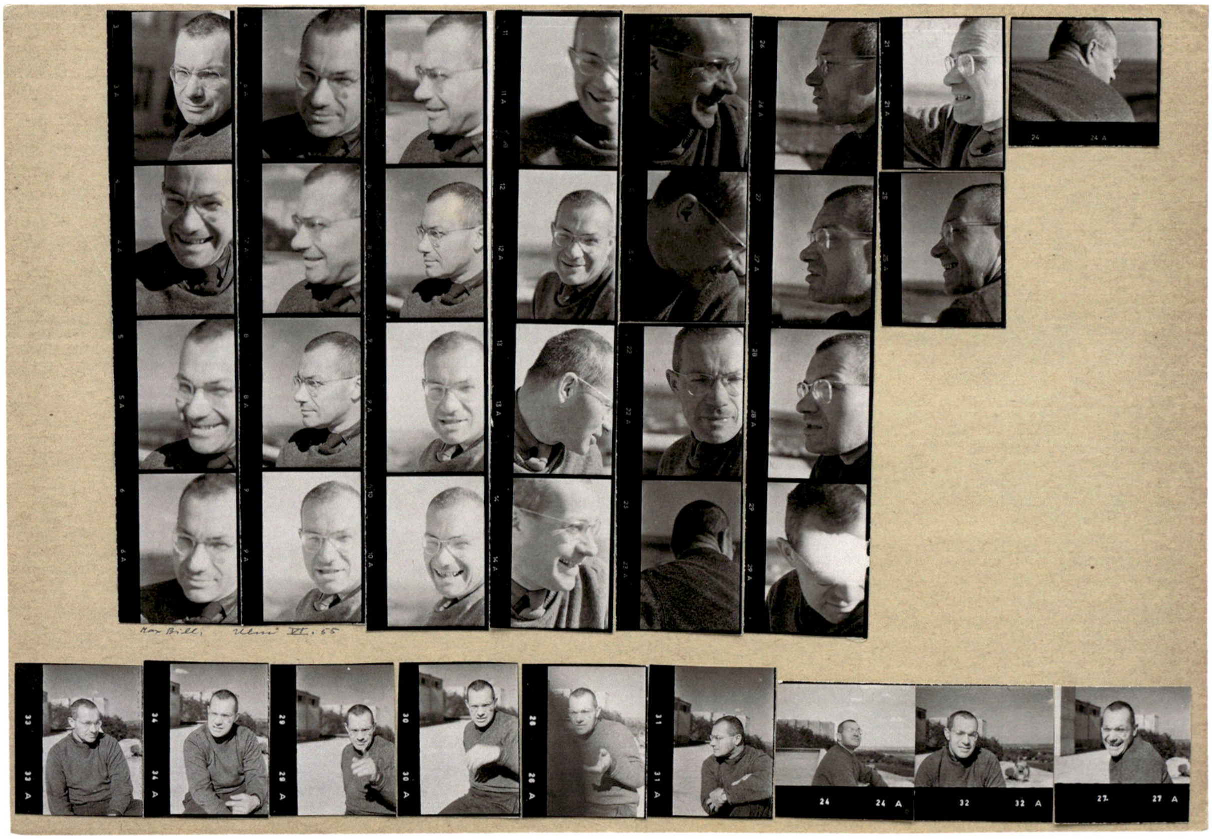

3 Series of portraits of Max Bill, taken by Josef Albers 1955 in Ulm
Guggenheim Collection

and early 1950s, and encountered Bill's work there and were swayed by it, was the photographer William Klein, who was making paintings at the time. Ellsworth Kelly, who was in Paris on the GI bill,[8] was intrigued by Bill's work when he saw it at Galerie Denise René in Paris in 1950, and when he heard about the school Bill was forming in Ulm thought that he might teach there, though that did not come to pass.[9]

Bill had a strong relationship with George Rickey, who was of his generation (fig. 4). Rickey included him in his book, *Constructivism: Origins and Evolution*, noting that Bill was "the dominant figure" for Constructivism in Switzerland, and that he had expanded upon and given intellectual muscle to Theo van Doesburg's notion of Concrete art.[10] It should be said that Bill defined Concrete art humanistically, adding the possibility of beauty and the role of intuition to works that originated in logic and mathematics.[11]

Robert Wilson, the experimental theater director, playwright, and visual artist, recounted his friendship with Bill.[12] In October 1989 he inscribed a catalog for him, writing: "For my great artist friend a million flower petals for you. Lots and Lots of Love."[13] Wilson and Bill met in 1981 in Munich, when Bill attended a performance of Wilson's play, *The Golden Windows*, and had a drink with him afterwards. Bill greatly admired Wilson's work (the feeling was mutual) and, soon after, acquired a drawing by Wilson, made in relation to the play that he had seen. Some years later, they found themselves together in Moscow on a speakers' program, and they spent time perusing that city. Wilson writes that they shared "a number of things in common: a love of architecture, which I had studied, and interest in city and landscape architecture, and furniture." He owns one of Bill's library stools and says that it has always been one of his favorite pieces of furniture. On April 7, 2005, he wrote the following poem in memory of Bill:

Max was Bill
Bill was just Bill
Simple semiply Bill
A philosopher simple.

When asked whether he thought that Bill was influential for artists in the United States, Wilson wrote, "I think Max had an influence on many artists in the United States, especially those with a love and passion for architecture." He remembered having a conversation with Donald Judd years ago, in which Judd told him how much he admired Bill.[14] The gallerist, Paula Cooper, who knew Judd well, agrees that Judd admired the Swiss polymath.[15]

In 1973, Judd had an exhibition in Zurich at Galerie Annemarie Verna, which specialized in the work of American and Italian artists of the 1960s. Judd did not come to Switzerland for that show, but Bill, a passionate collector who loved living with beautiful objects, bought

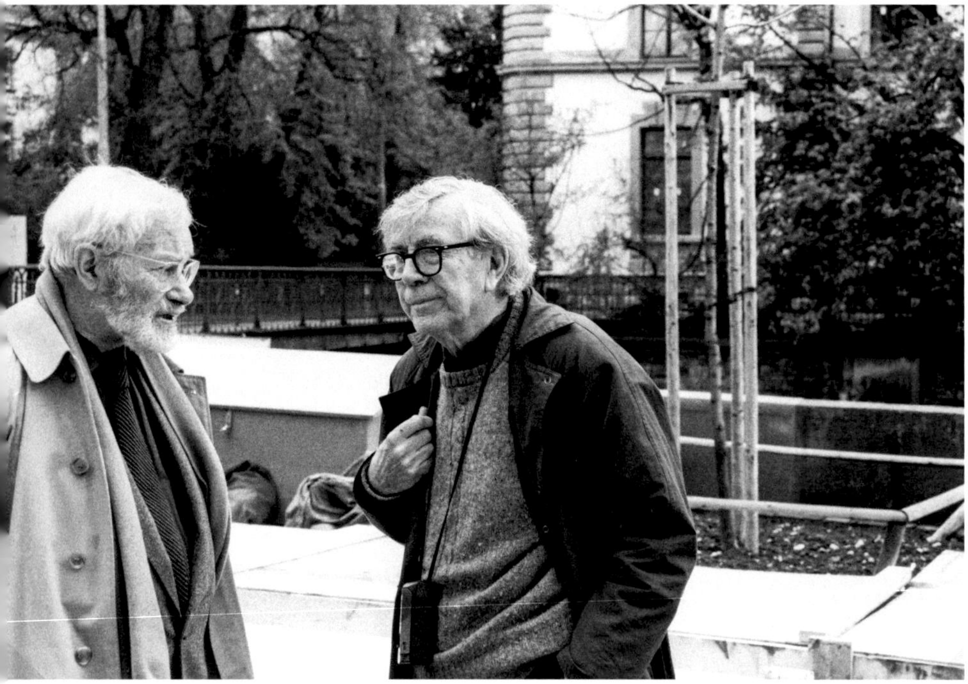

4 Max Bill and George Rickey in 1990 in Zurich
Photo: Angela Thomas Schmid

two works by Judd from that first exhibition (pl. p. 166).[16] Gianfranco Verna remembers that Bill, a very curious person, always attracted to new things that might inspire his own work, came often to the gallery to see the art of younger people. Verna feels that one of Bill's great achievements was as a collector.[17] His holdings consisted predominantly of important work by that older generation of modernists to which he felt so close, including his Bauhaus teachers, Albers, Wassily Kandinsky, Paul Klee, Moholy-Nagy, Oskar Schlemmer, and Kurt Schwitters, as well as his good friends, Sophie Taeuber-Arp and Georges Vantongerloo, along with pieces by other renowned modernists. Among the younger artists, in addition to Judd and Wilson, Bill owned pieces by Piero Manzoni, Andy Warhol, and Keith Haring.[18]

Judd was also a collector, but in his earlier years he was not as open-minded as Bill. When he first came to Switzerland, with little knowledge of Swiss art, Judd pronounced the work there "respectable" but "not good enough."[19] This echoes his *Arts Magazine* review of Bill's 1963 solo exhibition in New York. When he calls Bill's paintings "able," he was, in effect, damning with faint praise. In assessing the quality of the sculpture, however, he deemed it "first rate."[20]

As a critic, Judd was conscientiously evenhanded in assessing artwork. In the decades after World War II, though, there was a strong bias against European contemporary art in some quarters of the New York art world, one that Judd apparently shared. American artists and their supporters had lived under the hegemony of Europe since the birth of the republic. For the first time, they occupied the international spotlight, and were not eager to share it. In a 1964 interview, Judd announced, "I'm totally uninterested in European art, and I think it's over with."[21] It was fine with him if "the structures, values, feelings of the whole European tradition [...] all [went] down the drain."[22] It took him a while to shed this attitude, which was emblematic of two generations of the most prominent American artists, but he did.[23] In 1980, he told the critic Rudi Fuchs, "We took it for granted that we in America would invent everything anew. We were so eager. But then there was [Richard Paul] Lohse here, and we should have been aware of that but we did not know."[24] In 1988, Judd organized exhibitions of the work of Lohse in his Marfa, Texas, and New York City spaces.

When he opened up to the possibility of showing a Swiss artist of the older generation, Judd chose Lohse over Bill, whom we know he admired. Bill and Lohse had much in common, personally as well as professionally. Both were political and active in the Resistance during World War II. They were both well-respected designers as well as artists. They were both leaders in the community of Concrete artists in Zurich. In his *Arts Magazine* review of Bill's work, Judd had praised the sculpture, so he might have chosen to show it; but although Bill sought to exclude associations to nature from his art, his sculpture, reinforced by the frequent use of pedestals, recalls earlier European modernism, making the works decidedly different from those with which Judd surrounded himself in Marfa and New York City. Judd clearly appreciated Bill's sculpture for what it was, but Lohse's paintings, systematic and modular in approach, were more reflective of Judd's concerns and those of his US cohort.

Aside from what must have been a brief encounter at Bill's 1963 Staempfli Gallery opening, Bill and Judd seem to have had only one meeting. In the late 1980s, Judd was living in Switzerland, close to a workshop that was fabricating his sculpture. He invited Bill, along with a few other people, to his home there for drinks.[25] By all reports, the conversation did not involve art or even go that deep, yet the two artists shared many deeply felt interests.[26] That said, they also had very different temperaments and, born twenty years apart, they reflected values associated with their distinct generations. As a result, they approached their common concerns in dissimilar ways. Both were passionate about architecture. Neither was a trained architect, but both lived in homes that they designed or renovated. Bill, gregarious by nature, chose architecture as his primary profession and his personal identity. His widow Angela Thomas remembers that, when they checked into a hotel and Bill had to state his profession, he would write "architect." He had an architecture office in Zurich, separate from his house, where his art and design studios were located. According to his son, Jakob Bill, about a dozen of his father's buildings are still standing out of approximately eighty projects, which he says is not a lot for an architect.[27] Verna reports that he was always unhappy that he did not have more commissions.

Judd—not gregarious—decided against architecture as a profession early in his life because "in architecture it was necessary to deal with clients and the public. That seemed impossible to me, as did the business of a firm."[28] His attitude toward architecture changed when he discovered that he could be his own client and control the spaces in which his art was seen. He did not know how to make an architectural plan, and never created a building from scratch. Rather, he used preexisting structures, and got out of those prosaic buildings beautiful spaces that were previously hidden and unseen. Verna believes that this was Judd's great achievement in architecture, and that, above all, space was his medium. Judd was working for himself, while Bill retained those Bauhaus values that dictated a focus on societal responsibilities.

This held true for their design work, as well. Both artists designed furniture (fig. 5). For Bill, in addition to his humanistic values, this involved concepts of function and mass production. Judd, in contrast, told Verna that he created tables, chairs, beds, etc. for himself, because in Marfa he couldn't find anything that was "aesthetically respectable." Verna believes that Judd's furniture design entailed the working through of a formal alphabet, and that he couldn't have cared less about comfort. Perhaps Judd's admiration for Bill was based less on individual art works and more on his ability to function in so many fields at such a high level. Bill's accomplishments as an architect, artist, designer, typographer, educator, curator, and politician are remarkable. It is hard to imagine how he achieved so much in a single lifetime.

In 1993, Bill received the Praemium Imperiale prize, which has been called the Nobel Prize for culture. In the documentary film, *Max Bill—the master's vision* by Erich Schmid (2008), viewers can feel the excitement around the ceremony in Japan.[29] The jurors were heads of state, Helmut Schmidt, Jacques Chirac, and Edward Heath, among others. Bill was very famous in Japan. Angela Thomas reports that once, when they were at a Los Angeles hotel with Ray Eames, and Eames and Bill were on the dance floor thoroughly enjoying themselves, Thomas was approached by some Japanese men who were almost overwhelmed at seeing Bill in the flesh. They told her, "In Japan he is like a god."[30] This is thanks to several successful Japanese designers who had studied at the Ulm school and carried Bill's philosophy and strategies home with them in the 1950s.

Unlike the contemporary art worlds of Brazil and Japan, which were in formation when they encountered Bill's ideas and could apply them, artists in the United States did not see Bill's work with any consistency until the 1960s, at which point the generation that might have been influenced by him was already artistically mature and could look back on an internationally renowned cohort of artists that had emerged from their own soil. Most significantly, Americans never got to see all of Bill. They only saw his painting and sculpture. Compare

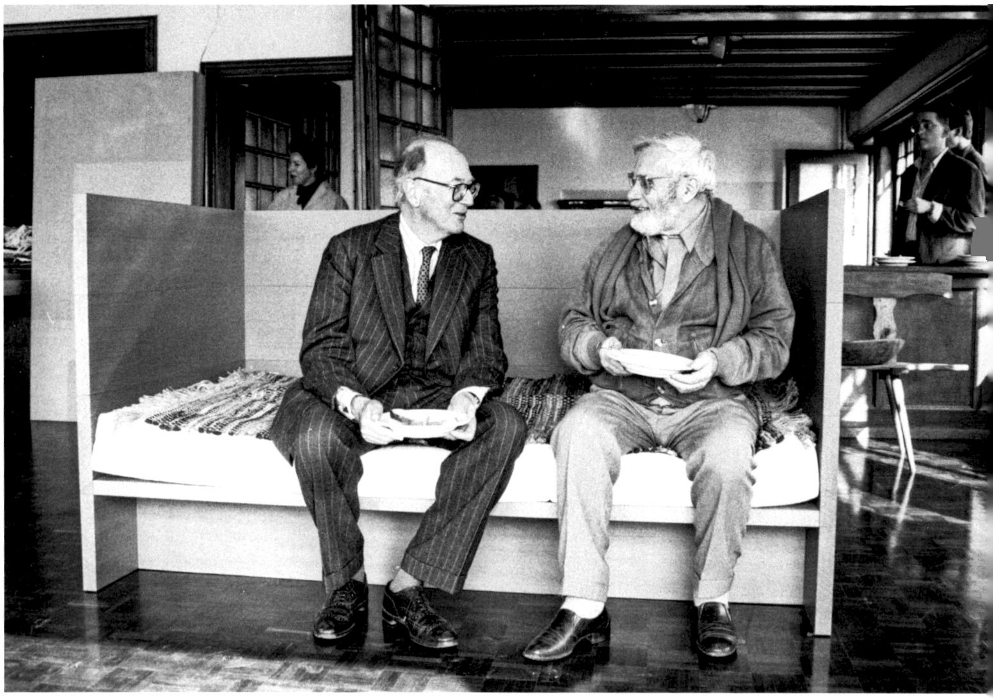

5 Max Bill and Paul Jolles sitting on the bed that Donald Judd built himself, Küssnacht am Rigi, 1990
Photo: Angela Thomas Schmid

Bill's 1951 exhibition at the São Paulo Museum of Art (MASP) with his one major museum exhibition in the United States, the retrospective that was organized by the Albright Knox Art Gallery in 1974/75. The Brazilian show, reflecting the ideology of a very young and adventurous institution, included not just painting and sculpture, but also Bill's architecture and design, without ranking one form above another. Pietro Maria Bardi and Lina Bo Bardi, who conceived the museum, had "an expanded view of art that was based on the supposition that art is the result of its environment, and therefore encompasses all the countless artistic manifestations of a culture."[31] Including several disciplines together, seeing how Bill's philosophy carried through from one to another allowed visitors to get a sense of the broad applications of his approach, and the prodigiousness of his output.

The Albright Knox retrospective took the traditional approach, including only Bill's "fine art," painting, sculpture, and prints. The exhibition was a success, so much so that an additional venue, the Corcoran Gallery, was added to the tour after the show opened. Robert Hughes wrote a glowing review of the exhibition in *Time* magazine, calling it "a revelation," and deeming Bill "one of the great colorists of modern art."[32] In Los Angeles the reviews were universally positive. The *LA Times* printed a photograph of Bill with his works and captioned it: "Without Compromise—artist—environmentalist Max Bill". During this period, the first global oil crisis elevated public consciousness concerning the environment and Bill, always concerned with environmental issues, was especially vocal on the subject. Art critic Henry J. Seldis, clearly impressed with Bill's many and diverse achievements, wrote:

"Bill—a professorial-looking bespectacled man of ideas—certainly knows how not to waste his efforts as he pursues his multitudinous activities as artist, architect, parliamentarian and environmentalist with methodological calm and deep conviction."[33]

Clearly, Bill was greatly appreciated in some prestigious circles in the United States. He had a strong impact on some there who had the opportunity to understand his far-ranging achievements, but he was not influential in the manner that he was in Brazil or Japan. Seldis calls him "a man of ideas."[34] He was also a man of action, and so much of the vitality of his endeavors comes from the diversity of his activities, painting, sculpture, architecture, ecology, yes, and also design and pedagogy, and politics. In the United States, we have yet to experience, in exhibition form, the thing that made him extraordinary.

[1] "The school was built to house the activities described in the program that Max Bill, Inge Scholl, and Otl Aicher had drawn up between 1950 and 1951." Guillermo Zuaznabar and Neus Moyano: "Max Bill and the HfG Ulm: Lines of Division," in Madrid 2015, p. 50.

[2] Angela Thomas Schmid in: Schmid, 2008.

[3] Ronaldo Brito: *Neoconcretism: Vértice e ruptura do projeto construtivo brasileiro*, ed. by Funarte/Instituto Nacional de Artes Plásticos, Rio de Janeiro 1985, p. 105.

[4] Author's telephone conversation with Gere Kavanaugh, August 18, 2020.

[5] Note from Angela Thomas Schmid, October 1, 2020.

[6] For example, Geoff Goldberg reports that Bill first wrote to his father, an architect, in 1948 about his father's design of a gas station, which Bill wanted to include in a book, and they became friends. Bill had a big influence on Goldberg's grandmother, who was an artist. The family collected Bill's work. Email from Geoff Goldberg to the author, July 28, 2020.

[7] Angela Thomas Schmid in conversation with the author, August 22, 2020.

[8] The G. I. Bill of Rights was a law passed in the United States in 1944 to help veterans re-enter the workforce. Among other things, it provided aid for education.

[9] Information from Yve-Alain Bois, author of the Ellsworth Kelly catalog raisonné, via an email from Mary Anne Lee, the Ellsworth Kelly Foundation. Bois believes that ultimately Kelly's and Bill's ideas about art turned out to be very different.

[10] George Rickey: *Constructivism: Origins and Evolution*, revised edition, New York 1995, p. 62 and pp. 149–151.

[11] See Karin Gimmi: "On Max Bill," in Madrid 2015, p. 14.

[12] Email from Robert Wilson via his assistant, Max Koltai, August 3, 2020.

[13] Photograph of the page, which is dated October 1989, from Angela Thomas Schmid.

[14] Email from Robert Wilson via his assistant, Max Koltai, August 3, 2020.

[15] Email from Anthony Allen at Paula Cooper Gallery to the author, August 25, 2020.

[16] Clément Dirié: "Meet the Vernas, the pioneering gallerist couple who brought Minimalism and Arte Povera to Zurich," in *Art Basel/Year 49*. The works by Judd that Bill purchased are each: *Untitled*, 1972/73, 58.5 x 68.5 x 10.5 cm, galvanized iron; today located in the max bill georges vantongerloo foundation.

[17] Author's taped interview with Gianfranco Verna, August 26, 2020. Verna was extremely helpful with valuable insights into the relationship between Bill's concerns and Judd's. Unless otherwise stated, all insights and opinions credited to Gianfranco Verna come from this interview.

[18] Bill bought the Haring for a museum he was designing, which never came to fruition. It was to be in a park with a number of schools around it. He believed that the Haring would attract young people. Interview with Angela Thomas Schmid (see note 7).

[19] Verna interview (see note 17).

[20] Donald Judd: "Max Bill," in *Donald Judd: Complete Writings, 1959–1975*, Halifax/New York 2005, p. 88.

[21] Bruce Glaser: "Questions to Stella and Judd," in *Minimal Art: A Critical Anthology*, ed. by Gregory Battcock, Berkeley/Los Angeles/London 1995, p. 154.

[22] Ibid., p. 150.

[23] For example, the influential New York School painter, Barnett Newman, claimed that he and his US contemporaries were freeing themselves of "the impediments of memory, association, nostalgia, legend [and] myth [...] that have been the devices of European painting." Quoted in Donald Judd: "Barnett Newman," in *Studio International* (February 1979), pp. 66–69.

[24] Quoted in Rudi Fuchs: "Donald Judd (Artist at Work)," in *Donald Judd*, ed. by Nicholas Serota, New York 2004, p. 1.

[25] The Vernas found these fabricators for Judd. Gianfranco Verna interview (see note 17).

[26] Both Gianfranco Verna and Angela Thomas Schmid were present at this meeting, and they both reported this to the author.

[27] Manuel Fontán del Junco: "Everything Goes Hand in Hand: A Conversation with Jakob Bill," in Madrid 2015, p. 28. The average output of renowned architects is difficult to gauge, but Frank Lloyd Wright, for example, built 511 buildings of which 432 are still standing. Mies Van der Rohe built approximately seventy-eight buildings. Louis Kahn built about thirty-two.

[28] Donald Judd: "Kunst und Architektur," in *Donald Judd. Architektur*, exh. cat. Münster: Westfälischer Kunstverein, Münster 1989, p. 195. Cf. Renate Petzinger: "Specific Elements in Donald Judd's Architecture," in *Kunst and Design: Donald Judd, Preisträger der Stankowski-Stiftung 1993*, Berlin 1993, p. 131.

[29] Angela Thomas Schmid in the film, *Max Bill—the master's vision* (see note 2).

[30] Ibid.

[31] Milene Soares Cara: "MASP, the Bardis and Design in Brazil," cf. http://www.mac.usp.br/mac/conteudo/academico/publicacoes/anais/modernidade/pdfs/MILENE_ING.pdf (accessed October 15, 2020).

[32] Robert Hughes: "Superb Puritan," in *Time* (November 18, 1974), p. 58. In his 2012 obituary for Hughes, critic Randy Kennedy noted that Hughes was often "a traditionalist scourge." https://www.nytimes.com/2012/08/07/arts/robert-hughes-art-critic-whose-writing-was-elegant-and-contentious-dies-at-74.html (accessed October 15, 2020). A print version of this obituary appeared in *The New York Times*, Section A (August 7, 2012), p. 16.

[33] Henry Seldis: "Max Bill sees Art as a Model for Life," in *Los Angeles Times* (December 19, 1974).

[34] Ibid.

Works in the Exhibition

If not mentioned otherwise, all works are the property of the main lenders of the exhibition:
max bill georges vantongerloo stiftung,
haus bill zumikon, angela thomas and erich schmid,
Courtesy Hauser & Wirth

Josef Albers (1888–1976)

Tectonische Gruppe, 1925
Sandblasted flashed, painted cameo glass
29.6 x 45.6 cm
pl. p. 38/39

Study for "Homage to the Square: Apodictic", 1950–1954
Oil on hardboard
40.4 x 40.4 cm
pl. p. 168

u-12, strukturale Konstellation, 1955
Engraving on Formica on wood
49.1 x 65.1 x 2.5 cm
pl. p. 169

Hans Arp (1886–1966)

Formes préadamites, 1945
Cherry wood relief
27.2 x 25.5 x 2 cm
pl. p. 66

Max Bill (1908–1994)

Table, undated
Wood, metal
74 x 56 x 56 cm

Selbstporträt, 1926
Oil on canvas
50 x 65 cm

Ich, ein Katzenmensch, 1927
Indian ink and watercolor on paper 17.2 x 13 cm
pl. p. 28

Zwei Freundinnen, Katt und Hilde, 1927
Drawing and frottage on paper
18 x 21 cm
pl. p. 28

Das Sternenpaar und der kleine Luftgeist, 1928
Colored sheet
30.2 x 20.2 cm
Private collection, Switzerland; on loan to Zentrum Paul Klee, Bern
pl. p. 31

Düstere Bewegungen (Stilleben), 1928
Gouache and watercolor on paper
27.4 x 23.2 cm
pl. p. 25

Mondansingender Hund, 1928
Ink and watercolor on paper
22.5 x 29.5 cm
Private collection, Switzerland; on loan to Zentrum Paul Klee, Bern
pl. p. 26

Was man nur auf dem Bilde sieht, 1928
Ink and colored pencil on cloth
19 x 13 cm
pl. p. 24

Der kleine Jammer König, 1929
Indian ink and watercolor on Japanese paper
33 x 34.5 cm
pl. p. 27

Ein Schiff unter der Sonne, 1929
Watercolor and ink on paper
44 x 32 cm
pl. p. 30

Hermaphrodith, 1929
Oil on paper on cardboard
63.5 x 40.5 cm
Private collection, Switzerland; on loan
to Zentrum Paul Klee, Bern
pl. p. 29

glasbild, 1930–1931
Crystal glass, sandblasted on one side
60 x 100 cm
pl. p. 51

Poster: n****kunst—prähistorische felsbilder
südafrikas, kunstgewerbemuseum zürich, 1931
Letterpress, linoprint
127 x 90 cm
Zürcher Hochschule der Künste / Museum
für Gestaltung Zürich / Plakatsammlung
pl. p. 50

Poster: wohnausstellung neubühl, Zürich, 1931
Letterpress, linoprint
128 x 90.5 cm

well-relief, 1931–1932
Iron, synthetic resin paint
80 x 120 cm
pl. p. 51

Untitled, 1932
Watercolor on cardboard
16.9 x 21 cm
pl. p. 48

Untitled. Sketch for a mural with large O, 1932
Gouache
21.6 x 30.9 cm
pl. p. 48

Poster: wohnbedarf—paul matzinger, basel, 1932
Linoprint
127.5 x 91 cm
Zürcher Hochschule der Künste / Museum
für Gestaltung Zürich / Plakatsammlung
pl. p. 49

lange plastik, 1933
Wood, white painted iron
200 cm
pl. p. 47

Draft for facade Pestalozzi & Co, 1934
Pencil and gouache on tracing paper
29.7 x 53.8 cm
pl. p. 54/55

konstruktion, 1934
Oil on wood
50 x 60 cm
pl. p. 52

schwarze plastik, 1934
Wood
28.5 x 20 x 10 cm
pl. p. 53

3 variations, 1935
Oil on plywood
60 x 50 cm
pl. p. 52

quinze variations sur un même thème, 1935–1938
16 prints, lithograph on paper
each 32 x 30 cm
pl. p. 61

Poster: zeitprobleme in der schweizer malerei
und plastik, kunsthaus zürich, 1936
Letterpress, linoprint
99.5 x 69 cm
Zürcher Hochschule der Künste / Museum
für Gestaltung Zürich / Plakatsammlung

Draft drawing for the Swiss pavilion,
IX. Milan Triennale, 1936
Pencil, colored pencil, and watercolor on paper
21 x 29.8 cm
pl. p. 57

Draft drawing for the Swiss pavilion,
IX. Milan Triennale, 1936
Pencil and colored pencil on paper
22.6 x 41.2 cm
pl. p. 56

konstruktion aus 30 gleichen
elementen, 1938–1939
Metal, gold plated
30 x 90 x 16 cm
pl. p. 58/59

konstruktion in messing, 1939
Brass
144 cm
Kunsthaus Zürich, donation
of the artist, 1986
pl. p. 46

konstruktion aus drei quadratgrössen
(denkmal für pythagoras), 1939–1941
Brass, gold plated
90 x 90 x 80 cm
pl. p. 60

konstruktion mit 10 vierecken, 1940–1943
Oil on canvas
90 x 75.6 cm
Kunstmuseum Bern
pl. p. 83

acht-teiliger rhythmus, 1942
Oil on canvas
90 x 60 cm
pl. p. 78

horizontal-vertikal-diagonal-rhythmus, 1942
Oil on canvas
160 x 80 cm
pl. p. 97

konstruktion mit 3 quadraten, 1942
Oil on canvas
66.5 x 33 cm
pl. p. 96

kühle teilung, 1943
Oil on canvas
72.5 x 72.5 cm
pl. p. 84

rhythmus in vier quadraten, 1943
Oil on canvas
30 x 120 cm
Kunsthaus Zürich, 1968
pl. p. 94

Poster: die farbe—kunstgewerbemuseum zürich, 1944
Lithograph, pasted image
128 x 90.5 cm
Zürcher Hochschule der Künste / Museum
für Gestaltung Zürich / Plakatsammlung
pl. p. 92

Poster: konkrete Kunst, Kunsthalle Basel, 1944
Linoprint
128 x 90.5 cm
Zürcher Hochschule der Künste / Museum
für Gestaltung Zürich / Plakatsammlung
pl. p. 87

Typewriter Patria, Redesign: 1944
(design: Otto Haas 1936)
Metal casing, shrink-coated, synthetic keyboard,
wooden carrying case
12 x 40 x 34 cm
Zürcher Hochschule der Künste / Museum für
Gestaltung Zürich / Designsammlung

umgekehrt laufende spirale, 1944
Steel wire, wooden base
23.5 x 18 x 4 cm
pl. p. 88

magische chromographie, 1944–1946
Oil on canvas
72 x 108 cm
Kunstmuseum Winterthur, gift of the Frawa AG, 1969
pl. p. 90

Poster: USA baut, kunstgewerbemuseum zürich, 1945
Offset print
127 x 90 cm
Zürcher Hochschule der Künste / Museum
für Gestaltung Zürich / Plakatsammlung
pl. p. 99

konstruktion aus drei kreisscheiben, 1945–1946
Brass, chrome plated
ø 50 cm
pl. p. 81

kühles gleichgewicht, 1946
Oil on canvas
72 x 72 cm
pl. p. 98

kontinuität, 1946/1982
Copper, gold plated
41 x 36 x 48 cm
pl. p. 80

sechs gleichlange linien, 1947
Oil on canvas
98 x 70 cm
pl. p. 89

sechseck im raum mit gleichen seitenlängen,
1947/1965
Brass
72 x 104 x 51.5 cm
pl. p. 91

46656 horizontale und vertikale relationen, 1948
Oil on canvas
50 x 50 cm
Private collection, Switzerland

sechseckfläche im raum, 1948
Metal, chrome plated
38 x 40 x 23 cm
pl. p. 79

fläche im raum, 1948–1971
Brass, gold plated
65 x 60 x 38 cm
pl. p. 80

Dreibeinstuhl, design: 1949
Shaped birch plywood, solid frame
75 x 43.5 x 52 cm
Zürcher Hochschule der Künste / Museum
für Gestaltung Zürich / Designsammlung
pl. p.93

Dreirundtisch with angular legs, design: 1949
Linoleum, maple wood
Zürcher Hochschule der Künste / Museum
für Gestaltung Zürich / Designsammlung

Poster: pevsner—vantongerloo—bill, kunsthaus
zürich, 1949
Letterpress, linoprint
100 x 70 cm
pl. p. 86

Quadratrundtisch, design: 1949
Linoleum, maple wood
69 x 90 x 90 cm
Zürcher Hochschule der Künste / Museum
für Gestaltung Zürich / Designsammlung
pl. p. 93

Höhensonne, design: 1951
Enameled metal, nickel plated
60 x 14.5 x 14.5 cm
Zürcher Hochschule der Künste / Museum
für Gestaltung Zürich / Designsammlung
pl. p. 116

Kreuzzargenstuhl, design: 1951,
Shaped maple plywood, solid beech wood frame
78 x 48 x 52 cm
Zürcher Hochschule der Künste / Museum
für Gestaltung Zürich / Designsammlung
pl. p. 120

Chair for the Swiss pavilion,
IX. Milan Triennale, 1951
Wood
Zürcher Hochschule der Künste / Museum für
Gestaltung Zürich / Designsammlung
pl. p. 121

fläche im raum durch eine linie begrenzt,
c. 1952/1994
chrome-nickel steel
138.5 x 280 x 70 cm
pl. p. 123

22, 1953
Marble, base: granite
78,8 x 58,5 x 57 cm
pl. p. 119

unendliche fläche in form einer säule, 1953/1993
Brass, chrome plated
130 x 6 x 6 cm
pl. p. 85

(together with Mary Vieira)
Wire model for "unendliche schleife"
(hfg Ulm), 1953/54
Wire, cardboard
14 x 20 x 18 cm
pl. p. 126

(together with Hans Gugelot)
Ulmer Hocker, 1954
Varnished wood
45 x 39.5 x 28.5 cm
pl. p. 117

zwei zentren (grün + orange), 1956
Oil on canvas
101 x 200 cm
pl. p. 115

blau gefasst, 1956
Oil on canvas
59 x 113 cm
pl. p. 118

quadrat im quadrat, 1960
Oil on canvas
80 x 80 cm
pl. p. 125

Poster: konkrete kunst—50 jahre entwicklung,
helmhaus zürich, 1960
Letterpress, linoprint
128 x 90.5 cm
Zürcher Hochschule der Künste / Museum
für Gestaltung Zürich / Plakatsammlung

verteilung 4 : 3 : 2 : 1, 1960
Oil on canvas
100 x 100 cm
pl. p. 124

Stacking chair, 1961
Plywood and steel
80 x 40 x 40 cm

vier zonen im horizontal-diagonal-quadrat, 1963
Oil on canvas
121 x 121 cm
pl. p. 150

konstruktion aus zwei kugelförmigen ringen,
Carborundum
51 x 26.5 x 26.5 cm
pl. p. 157

familie von fünf halben kugeln, 1965—1966
Black granite
Diameter each 32 cm
pl. p. 148

einheit aus drei gleichen zylindern, 1966
Brass, gold plated
Each element 54 cm
pl. p. 152

kern aus doppelungen, 1968
Brass, gold plated
50 x 60 x 50 cm
Kunstmuseum Bern,
Anne-Marie und Victor Loeb-Stiftung, Bern
pl. p. 158

pavillon skulptur II, 1969/1975
Wood
315 x 315 x 315 cm

drei weisse akzente, 1970
Oil on canvas
70 x 300 cm
pl. p. 154

Untitled, 1970
Oil on canvas
200 x 200 cm
pl. p. 145

nach innen gekehrte fläche im raum mit zwei ecken,
1971
Brass, gold plated
45.5 x 56 x 19 cm
pl. p. 147

vier verschränkte farbgruppen, 1971
Oil on canvas
120 x 120 cm

sechseckfläche um zwei quadrate, 1973
Chrome steel
306.5 x 154 x 38 cm
pl. p. 146

endlose spirale, 1973—1974
Brass, gold plated
41 x 25.5 x 26.5 cm
pl. p. 153

reflexe aus dunkel und hell, 1975
Oil on canvas
120 x 120 cm
pl. p. 151

rhythme de couleurs du pays de brancusi, 1976—1977
Oil on canvas
50 x 300 cm

7 pythagoräische dreiecke als quadrat, 1978
Oil on canvas
100 x 100 cm
pl. p. 144

einheit aus kugel und endloser spirale, 1978/1983
Montorfano granite
56 x 56 x 39 cm
Collection Museum Haus Konstruktiv, Zürich,
donation by the Silva-Casa Stiftung
pl. p. 159

7 farben zu 7 pythagoräischen dreiecken im quadrat,
1980—1982
Oil on canvas
150 x 150 cm
pl. p. 162

transcoloration aus lila, 1980—1986
Oil on canvas
100 x 100 cm
pl. p. 163

drei schwarz und drei bunt zu weiss, 1983
Oil on canvas
200 x 200 cm
pl. p. 161

sechs dreiteilige linienzüge, 1983
Oil on canvas
200 x 200 cm
pl. p. 164/165

Lygia Clark (1920–1988)

Bicho Monumento a todas as situações, 1960–1964
Aluminum
25.3 x 25.3 x 0.6 cm (flat folded)
Private collection, Switzerland

Bicho—Projecto para um Planeta, c. 1960
Aluminum
Diameter 30.8 cm
Grażyna Kulczyk Collection
pl. p. 130

Theo van Doesburg (1883–1931)

Composition in half tones, 1928
Oil on canvas
50 x 50 cm
Kunstmuseum Basel, Hans Arp Donation, 1966
pl. p. 72

Nélida Fedullo (1920s–2011)

Untitled, c. 1949
Indian ink and tempera on paper
69.5 x 50.5 cm
ISLAA Institute for Studies on
Latin American Art, New York
pl. p. 136

Ohne Titel, 1950
Tempera on paper
71.1 x 50.2 cm
ISLAA Institute for Studies on
Latin American Art, New York
pl. p. 136

Lyonel Feininger (1871–1956)

Marine, 1923
Ink and watercolor on paper
28 x 37.9 cm
Zentrum Paul Klee, Bern; donation Livia Klee
pl. p. 34

Fritz Glarner (1899–1972)

Relational Painting No. 101, 1959
Oil on canvas
72 x 67 cm
pl. p. 107

Camille Louis Graeser (1892–1980)

Konstruktion, 1949
Colored ink drawing on paper
35.9 x 50.9 cm

Konstruktion mit sechs Farbakzenten, 1949
Oil on canvas
40 x 60 cm
Aargauer Kunsthaus Aarau;
gift of the Camille Graeser-Stiftung, Zürich
pl. p. 101

Hans Hinterreiter (1902–1989)

Studie 419A, 1949
Tempera on paper
16.5 x 21.9 cm
pl. p. 104

Alfredo Hlito (1923–1993)

Formas y líneas en el plano, 1953
Oil on canvas
103 x 103 cm
ISLAA Institute for Studies on
Latin American Art, New York
pl. p. 138

Enio Iommi (1926–2013)

Construcción, 1945
Painted iron, marble
54 x 49 x 33.5 cm
Galerie von Bartha
pl. p. 135

Ritmos espaciales, 1945
Metal wire, wood
c. 64 x 50 x 40 cm
Daros Latinamerica Collection, Zürich
pl. p. 134

Donald Judd (1928–1994)

Untitled (two floor sculptures; from
multipart series), 1972–1973
Galvanized steel plate
10 x 58.3 x 68.5 cm
pl. p. S. 166

Untitled (wall object from the series:
the moscow installation), 1991
Aluminum, plexiglass
25 x 100 x 25 cm
pl. p. 167

Wassily Kandinsky (1866–1944)

Untitled (circle and stairs), 1928
Ink and watercolor on paper on cardboard
49 x 19.3 cm
Private collection, Switzerland; on loan
to Zentrum Paul Klee, Bern
pl. p. 32

Dessin no. 26, 1931
Indian ink and ink on paper
22 x 18 cm

Paul Klee (1879–1940)

Kinder vor der Stadt, 1928, 59
Oil transfer drawing and watercolor
on paper on cardboard
29.6 x 30/30.5 cm
Zentrum Paul Klee, Bern
pl. p. 33

modell 7a dreidimensional, mit Achsen= und Punktbindung, 1931, 7
Pen, colored pencil, and pencil on paper on cardboard
44.5/44.8 x 57.6/58.1 cm
Zentrum Paul Klee, Bern
pl. p. 36

Constructiv-impressiv, 1927, 32
Oil on cardboard
58 x 44 cm
Zentrum Paul Klee, Bern
pl. p. 37

František Kupka (1871–1957)

composition néo-plastique, c. 1930
Gouache on paper
28 x 27 cm
pl. p. 71

Leo Leuppi (1893–1972)

Variation VI, 1947
Oil on canvas
61 x 53 cm
Aargauer Kunsthaus Aarau; permanent loan from Kultur- und Sozialstiftung Möbel Pfister
pl. p. 100

Verena Loewensberg (1912–1986)

Untitled, 1947
Oil on canvas
48 x 48 cm
Aargauer Kunsthaus Aarau
pl. p. 106

Richard Paul Lohse (1902–1988)

Dynamische Konstruktion, 1942
Oil on cardboard on Pavatex
90 x 90 cm
Private collection
pl. p. 102

Poster: Unsere Wohnung—Wanderausstellung des Schweizerischen Werkbunds, Kunstgewerbemuseum Zürich, 1943
Lithograph
65 x 90 cm
Zürcher Hochschule der Künste / Museum für Gestaltung Zürich / Plakatsammlung
pl. p. 103

Tomás Maldonado (1922–2018)

Construcción de 2 elementos, 1953
Oil on canvas
100 x 70 cm
ISLAA Institute for Studies on Latin American Art, New York
pl. p. 139

Almir Mavignier (1925–2018)

Poster: Südamerika, c. 1953
Offset print
83 x 40.5 cm
Zürcher Hochschule der Künste / Museum für Gestaltung Zürich / Plakatsammlung
pl. p. 132

flimmerndes quadrat, 1956
Oil on canvas
55 x 55 cm
pl. p. 133

László Moholy-Nagy (1895–1946)

Fotogramm (positiv), 1924
Negative photogram, mounted
39.7 x 29.7 cm
pl. p. 40

Komposition TP 5, 1930
Oil on Formica
28.5 x 20.5 cm
pl. p.41

Piet Mondrian (1872–1944)

Tableau no II (with grey and black), 1925
Oil on canvas, 50 x 50 cm
Kunstmuseum Bern, Sammlung Professor Dr. Max Huggler, donation 1966
pl. p. 73

Antoine Pevsner (1884–1962)

Colonne développable de la victoire, 1946
Brass, first version
104 x 79 x 67 cm
Kunsthaus Zürich
pl. p. 69

Lidy Prati (1921–2008)

Concreta N° 2-B, 1948
Oil on canvas
60 x 60 cm
ISLAA Institute for Studies on Latin American Art, New York
pl. p. 137

Hilde Rantzsch (1908– ?)

Untitled, 1927
Watercolor and ink on paper
28.5 x 20.5 cm
pl. p. 35

Oskar Schlemmer (1888–1943)

Untitled, 1922
Ink on paper
47 x 33.5 cm
pl. p. 35

Performance sequence with figurines for "Das triadische Ballett" and requisites from the "Bauhaus-Tänze", Bauhaus-Bühne Dessau, c. 1928
Drawing on paper
28.2 x 22.3 cm

Sophie Taeuber-Arp (1889–1943)

Composition à rectangles, et carrés pavés de cercles, 1939
Oil on canvas
20.1 x 28 cm
Kunstmuseum Bern, Anne-Marie und Victor Loeb-Stiftung, Bern
pl. p. 67

Untitled (from the portfolio "fünf konstruktionen"), 1941
Serigraph
31.8 x 30.5 cm
pl. p. 68

Joaquín Torres-García (1874–1949)

Formas animicas en rojo y negro, 1938
Tempera on cardboard
80.7 x 50.8 cm
Daros Latinamerica Collection, Zürich
pl. p. 65

Georges Vantongerloo (1886–1965)

Groupe y = -ax2 + bx + c y'= -2ax + b y'=-ax2 + bx + c / -2ax + b, 1931
Wood, paint
67 x 53.5 x 51 cm
pl. p. 63

Courbes, 1939
Oil on masonite
60 x 42 cm
pl. p. 62

Mary Vieira (1927–2001)

zeiten einer bewegung: a + b, 1952–1955
Perforated black anodized aluminum
each 216 x 24 x 24 cm
Galerie von Bartha
pl. p. 128

ritmo no espaço: 2: tensão-expansão (model), c. 1952
Metal wire and granite
31 x 50 x 45 cm
Private collection, Switzerland
pl. p. 127

(together with Max Bill)
Wire model for "unendliche schleife" (hfg Ulm), 1953/54
Wire, cardboard
14 x 20 x 18 cm
pl. p. 126

Poster: brasilien baut, kunstgewerbemuseum zürich, 1954
Offset print
127 x 90 cm
Zürcher Hochschule der Künste / Museum für Gestaltung Zürich / Plakatsammlung
pl. p. 129

Friedrich Vordemberge-Gildewart (1899–1962)

Untitled (composition no. 155), 1946
Oil on canvas
120 x 80 cm
pl. p. 70

Andy Warhol (1928–1987)

Max Bill, 1980
Acrylic and silkscreen ink on canvas
101.6 x 101.6 cm
Bischofberger Collection, Männedorf-Zurich, Switzerland
pl. p. 171

Hanns Robert Welti (1891–1934)

Untitled (surrealistic composition with seven-branched chandelier), undated
Oil on canvas
66 x 72 cm
pl. p. 105

Alexandre Wollner (1928–2018)

Poster: IV Bienal, Museu de Arte Moderna São Paulo, 1957
Offset lithograph
96 x 66 cm
Museum für Konkrete Kunst, Ingolstadt
pl. p. 131

Bibliography

Ades 1989
Dawn Ades: *Art in Latin America: The Modern Era, 1820–1920*, London 1989.

Alberro 2017
Alexander Alberro: *Abstraction in Reverse: The Reconfigured Spectator in Mid-Twentieth-Century Latin American Art*, Chicago/London 2017.

Bachmann 2019
Pauline Bachmann: *Pure Leiblichkeit. Neokonkretismus in Brasilien (1957–1967)*, Bern et al. 2019.

Basel 1944
konkrete kunst, exh.cat. Basel: Kunsthalle Basel 1944, Basel 1944.

Berlin 2010
Das Verlangen nach Form—O desejo da forma. Neoconcretismo und zeitgenössische Kunst aus Brasilien, exh. cat. Berlin: Akademie der Künste 2010, ed. by Robert Kudielka et al., Berlin 2010.

Bern 2017
The Revolution Is Dead. Long Live the Revolution! From Malevich to Judd, From Deineka to Bartana, exh.cat. Bern: Kunstmuseum Bern and Zentrum Paul Klee 2017, ed. by Michael Baumgartner, Kathleen Bühler and Nina Zimmer, Munich/London/New York 2017.

Bill 1936
Max Bill: "konkrete gestaltung", in *Zeitprobleme in der Schweizer Malerei und Plastik*, exh.cat. Zurich: Kunsthaus Zurich 1936, Zurich 1936, p. 10.

Bill 1938
Max Bill: "Ueber konkrete Kunst", in *Das Werk: Architektur und Kunst*, vol. 25, 8 (1938), pp. 250–256.

Bill 1942
Contribution by Max Bill, in *allianz. vereinigung moderner schweizer künstler*, exh.cat. Zurich: Kunsthaus Zurich 1942, Zurich 1942, n. p.

Bill 1944
Max Bill: "ein standpunkt", in *konkrete kunst*, exh.cat. Basel: Kunsthalle Basel 1944, Basel 1944, pp. 9–10.

Bill 1952
Max Bill: *Form. A Balance Sheet of Mid-Twentieth-Century Trends in Design*, Basel 1952.

Bill 1954
Max Bill: "The Mathematical Approach in Contemporary Art," in *Arts and Architecture*, 8 (1954), trans. by P. Morton Shand, pp. 20–21.

Bill 1957
Max Bill: "Ein Denkmal," in *Das Werk: Architektur und Kunst*, vol. 44, 7 (1957), pp. 250–254.

Bill 1976
Max Bill in *Du. Die Zeitschrift der Kultur*, 424 (June 1976), pp. 12–69.

Bill 1979
Max Bill: "lehren am und aus dem bauhaus," in *form + zweck, fachzeitung für industrielle formgestaltung*, 3 (1979), p. 66.

Bill 2008a
Jakob Bill: *max bill am bauhaus*, Bern 2008.

Bill 2008b
max bill—funktion und funktionalismus. Schriften 1945–1988, with essays by Jakob Bill, Max Bill, Dietmar Guderian, Michael Hilti, ed. by Jakob Bill, Bern 2008.

Bill 2010
Max Bill: "Beauty from Function and as Function," in: *Form, Function, Beauty = Gestalt* (Architecture Words 5), London 2010, pp. 32–41.

Buffalo/Los Angeles/San Francisco 1974/75
Max Bill, exh.cat. Buffalo: Albright-Knox Art Gallery; Los Angeles: County Museum of Art; San Francisco: Museum of Art 1974/75, ed. by James N. Wood and Max Bill, Buffalo, NY 1974.

Cohn 2010
max bill, mavignier, wollner. 60 years of constructive art in brazil, ed. by Peter Cohn, São Paulo 2010.

Davalle 2016
Verónica Davalle: "América Latina, la otra sede de la HfG de Ulm," in *Revista Chilena de Diseño: creación y pensamiento*, vol.1, 1 (2016), pp. 53–63.

Fleischmann/Bosshard/Bignens 1999
Gerd Fleischmann, Hans Rudolf Bosshard, and Christoph Bignens: *Max Bill. Typography, Advertising, Book Design*, Sulgen 1999.

Frankfurt 2013
alex wollner brasil. design visual, exh.cat. Frankfurt: Museum Angewandte Kunst 2013/14, ed. by Klaus Klemp, Julia Koch, and Matthias Wagner K, Tübingen 2013.

García 2019
María Amalia García: *Abstract Crossings. Cultural Exchange between Argentina and Brazil*, trans by Jane Brodie, Oakland, CA 2019.

Geneva 1972
Max Bill, exh.cat. Geneva: Musée d'art et d'histoire 1972, Geneva 1972.

Hartsuyker 1968
Enrico Hartsuyker: "Urbane Plastiken: zum Schaffen von Mary Vieira," in *Das Werk: Architektur und Kunst*, vol. 55, 10 (1968), pp. 669–673.

Herford 2008
Max Bill. No Beginning, No End, exh.cat. Herford: Marta Herford. Museum für Kunst, Architektur, Design 2008, Zurich 2008.

Hüttinger 1977
Eduard Hüttinger: *Max Bill*, Zurich 1977.

Ingolstadt 2012
Die Idee Konkret: konkrete Kunst als ideengeschichtliche Entwicklung, exh.cat. Ingolstadt: Museum für konkrete Kunst Ingolstadt 2012, ed. by Tobias Hoffmann, Cologne 2012.

Judd 1963
Donald Judd: "In the Galleries," in *Arts Magazine* (1963); reprinted in *Donald Judd: Complete Writings 1959-1975: Gallery Reviews, Book Reviews, Articles, Letters to the Editor, Reports, Statements, Complaints*, Halifax, NS 1975, p. 88.

Lindinger 1987
Herbert Lindinger: *HfG Ulm. Die Moral der Gegenstände*, Berlin 1987.

Los Angeles/Miami 2004/05
Beyond Geometry. Experiments in Form, 1940s–70s, exh.cat. Los Angeles: County Museum of Art; Miami: Miami Art Museum 2004/05, ed. by Lynn Zelevansky, Cambridge, MA/London 2004.

Madrid 2011
Cold America. Geometric Abstraction in Latin America (1934–1973), exh.cat. Madrid: Fundación Juan March 2011, Madrid 2011.

Madrid 2015
Max Bill, exh.cat. Madrid: Fundación Juan March 2015, ed. by Manuel Fontán del Junco and María Toledo, Madrid 2015.

Maldonado 1955
Tomás Maldonado: *Max Bill*, Buenos Aires 1955.

Mavignier 2002
Interview mit Almir Mavignier, by Tobias Hoffmann and Frank Schmidt, Hamburg 2002, www.mavignier.com/hfg.html (accessed April 13, 2021).

Meister/Meister-Klaiber 2018
Daniel P. Meister and Dagmar Meister-Klaiber, *Einfach komplex—Max Bill und die Architektur der HfG Ulm*, Zurich 2018.

Merklinger 2013
Martina Merklinger: *Die Biennale São Paulo. Kulturaustausch zwischen Brasilien und der jungen Bundesrepublik Deutschland (1949–1954)* (Image, vol. 41), Bielefeld 2013.

Münster/Paris 1978
abstraction—création 1931–1936, exh.cat. Münster: Westfälisches Landesmuseum für Kunst und Kulturgeschichte; Paris: Musée d'art moderne de la Ville de Paris 1978, Paris 1978.

New York 2001
Abstract Art from the Rio de la Plata. Buenos Aires and Montevideo 1933-1953, exh.cat. New York: The Americas Society 2001, New York 2001.

Paris 1997
Années 30 en Europe. Le temps menacant, exh.cat. Paris: Musée d'art moderne de la Ville de Paris 1997, Paris 1997.

Roth 1951
Alfred Roth: "Der Schweizer Pavillon an der 9. Triennale in Mailand 1951: Ausstellungsarchitekt Max Bill SWB, Zürich," in *Das Werk: Architektur und Kunst*, vol. 38, 9 (1951), pp. 266–268.

Rotzler 1977
Willy Rotzler: *Constructive Concepts: A History of Constructive Art from Cubism to the Present*, Milan 1989.

São Paulo 2000
mavignier 75, exh.cat. São Paulo: Museu de Arte Moderna 2000, ed. by Delmar Maviginer, São Paulo 2000.

São Paulo 2005
Mary Vieira. O tempo do movimento, exh.cat. Rio de Janeiro: Centro Cultural Banco do Brasil, Rio de Janeiro; São Paulo: Centro Cultural Banco do Brasil, São Paulo 2005.

Schmid 2008
Max Bill—the master's vision, documentary produced by Erich Schmid, Ariadnefilme GmbH, Zumikon 2008.

Spitz 2002
René Spitz: *hfg ulm. The View behind the Foreground. The Political History of the Ulm School of Design 1953–1968*, Stuttgart 2002.

Spitz 2014
René Spitz: *HfG Ulm. Concise History of the Ulm School of Design. Notes on the Relationship between Design and Politics* (A5/06), ed. by Jens Müller, Zurich 2014.

Studen 1993
max bill, exh.cat. Studen: Fondation Saner 1993, ed. by Angela Thomas, Studen 1993.

Stuttgart 2005/06
max bill. maler, bildhauer, architekt, designer, exh.cat. Stuttgart: Kunstmuseum 2005/06, ed. by Thomas Buchsteiner and Otto Letze, Ostfildern-Ruit 2005.

Thomas 1983
Angela Thomas Jankowski: "sophie taeuber-arp 1889–1943," in *Sophie Taeuber-Arp*, exh.cat. Ascona: Museo Comunale; Bottrop: Moderne Galerie Quadrat 1983, Ascona 1983, pp. 35–58.

Thomas 1990a
Angela Thomas: "gespräch mit max bill," in *Max Bill*, exh.cat. Ludwigshafen a. R.: Wilhelm-Hack-Museum 1990, Stuttgart 1990, pp. 11–30.

Thomas 1990b
Angela Thomas: "D'apres des entretiens avec Max Bill," in *Max Bill*, exh.cat. Paris: Galerie René 1990, Paris 1990, n. p.

Thomas 1991
Angela Thomas: "max bill and Italy," in *max bill*, exh.cat. Milan: Lorenzelli Arte 1991, ed. by Luciano Caramel and Angela Thomas, Milan 1991, pp. 18–23.

Thomas 1993a
Angela Thomas: "gespräch mit max bill," in *max bill*, exh.cat. Studen: Fondation Saner 1993, ed. by Angela Thomas, Studen 1993, pp. 7–38.

Thomas 1993b
Angela Thomas: "Max Bill: The Early Years. An Interview," in *DAPA: Journal of Decorative and Propaganda Arts 1875–1945*, no. 19 (1993), pp. 98–119.

Thomas 2005
Angela Thomas Schmid: "max bill und georges vantongerloo," in *max bill, maler, bildhauer, architekt, designer*, exh.cat. Stuttgart: Kunstmuseum Stuttgart 2005, ed. by Thomas Buchsteiner and Otto Letze, Ostfildern-Ruit 2005, S. 32–34.

Thomas 2008
Angela Thomas: *mit subversivem glanz*, vol. 1: 1908–1939, Zurich 2008.

Thomas 2011
Angela Thomas: "Shared viewpoints and cultural appreciation," in *max bill. five decades*, exh.cat. London: Annely Juda Fine Art 2011, London 2011, n p.

Ullmann 2016
Larissa Ullmann: *Max Bill. Kurator und Vermittler konkreter Kunst*, master thesis, University of Zurich, Zurich 2016.

Valencia 1990
Arte abstracto. Arte concreto. Cercle et Carré, exh.cat. Valencia: IVAM Centre Julio Gonzáles, ed. by Gladys C. Fabre, Valencia 1990.

Varela 2012
Elisabeth Catoia Varela: *Critica e Narrativa: A visita de Max Bill em 1953*, www.anpap.org.br/anais/2012/html/simposio4.html, 07/09/2013 (accessed November 25, 2020).

Weimar 2007
Max Bill. Die Schönheit der Ratio. Das Bauhaus und die Folgen 2, exh.cat. Weimar: Klassik Stiftung, Neues Museum 2007, Weimar 2007.

Weinberg Staber 2001
Sind auf einer Leinwand eine Frau, ein Baum oder eine Kuh etwa konkrete Elemente? Konkrete Kunst: Manifeste und Künstlertexte (Studienbuch 1, Stiftung für konstruktive und konkrete Kunst), ed. by Margit Weinberg Staber, Zurich 2001.

Winterthur 1981
Konstruktive Kunst 1915–45. Dreissiger Jahre Schweiz, exh.cat. Winterthur: Kunstmuseum Winterthur 1981, ed. by Kunstmuseum Winterthur, Rudolf Koella, Ludmila Vachtová, Winterthur 1981.

Winterthur 2008
Max Bill: Aspekte seines Werks, exh.cat. Winterthur: Kunstmuseum Winterthur and Gewerbemuseum Winterthur 2008, Sulgen 2008.

Zurich 1936
Zeitprobleme in der Schweizer Malerei und Plastik, exh. cat. Zurich: Kunsthaus Zurich 1936, Zurich 1936.

Zurich 1949
Antoine Pevsner, Georges Vantongerloo, Max Bill, exh.cat. Zurich: Kunsthaus Zurich 1949, Zurich 1949.

Zurich 1954
Brasilien baut: Moderne brasilianische Architektur—Neue brasilianische Graphik—Plastiken von Mary Vieira, exh. cat. Zurich: Kunstgewerbemuseum der Stadt Zurich 1954, Zurich 1954.

Zurich 1960
konkrete kunst. 50 jahre entwicklung, exh.cat. Zurich: Helmhaus Zurich 1960, Zurich 1960.

Zurich 2019
max bill bauhaus konstellationen, exh.cat. Zurich: Hauser & Wirth 2019, Zurich 2019.

Zurfluh 2014
Lukas Zurfluh: *"construire une exposition . . .," Die architektonische Konzeption der Schweizerischen Landesausstellung Expo 64 als Praxis der politischen Kultur*, doctoral thesis, ETH Zurich, 2014.

Image Credits

Aargauer Kunsthaus Aarau, photograph: Jörg Müller, pl. pp. 101, 106, photograph: Alexandra Roth, pl. p. 100

Associaçao Cultural Lygia Clark, photograph: Guy Brett, fig. 4, p. 214

Galerie von Bartha, Basel, photograph: Jonas Hänggi, Basel, pl. p. 135, photograph: Ben Koechlin, pl. p. 128

Fotoarchiv Kunsthalle Basel, photograph: Atelier Eidenbenz, fig. p. 76

Kunstmuseum Basel, photograph: Martin P. Bühler, pl. p. 72

Bauhaus-Archiv, Berlin, fig. p. 20, 21

bpk-Bildagentur, Berlin/Guggenheim Collection, fig. 3, p. 236

Kunstmuseum Bern, pl. p. 67, 73, 83, 158

Schweizerische Nationalbibliothek, Bern, pl. p. 204, fig. 5, p. 215

Zentrum Paul Klee, Bern, Bildarchiv, pl. p. 26, 29, 31, 32, 33, 34, 36, 37, 47, 52 (bottom), 70, 79, 85, 104, 105, 107, 119, 122–123, 126, 127, fig. p. 142, pl. p. 148–149, 150, 157, 166, 167, fig. 1, p. 187, fig. 2, p. 188, fig. 3, p. 189, fig. 4, p. 190, fig. 1, p. 220, fig. 2 and 3, p. 221

Albright-Knox Art Gallery, Buffalo NY, fig. 1, p. 235

Christine Dufour-Beothy, fig. 5 and 6, p. 202

Privatsammlung, photograph: Conradin Frei, pl. p. 102

Stadt Ingolstadt, Museum für Konkrete Kunst, Ingolstadt, photograph: Wilfried Petzi, pl. p. 131

Instituto Moreira Salles Collection, fig. p. 108, fig. 2, p. 211, photograph: Günter Flieg, fig. p. 111, photograph: Peter Scheier, fig. 1, p. 210

Lidy Prati archive. Courtesy of the Polastri Prati family, fig. p. 113

MASP Research Center, fig. p. 109

Bischofberger Collection, Männedorf-Zürich, Switzerland, pl. p. 171

Triennale Milano—Archivio Fotografico, photograph: Crimella, fig. p. 75

ISLAA Institute for Studies on Latin American Art, New York, pl. p. 136 (both), 137, 138, 139,

Acervo do Museu de Arte Contemporânea da Universidade de São Paulo, fig. 3, p. 212

© René Spitz, photograph: Hans G. Conrad, fig. p. 9, 108 (top), 110, 112 (both)

Muzeum Susch, pl. p. 130

HfG-Archiv Museum Ulm, fig. p. 140, photograph: Sigrid von Schweinitz, fig. p. 22, 23

Museum Wiesbaden, Archiv Vordemberge-Gildewart, photograph: Ed Restle, fig. p. 42, 44

Kunst Museum Winterthur, photograph: Hans Humm, Zürich, pl. p. 90

max bill georges vantongerloo stiftung, haus bill zumikon, angela thomas and erich schmid, Courtesy Hauser & Wirth, pl. p. 24, 25, 27, 28 (both), 30, 35 (both), 38-39, 40, 41, fig. p. 43, pl. p. 48 (both), 51 (both), 52 (top), 53, 54—55, 56, 57, 58—59, 60, 61, 62, 63, 66, 68, 71, 78, 80 (both), 81, 84, 86, 88, 89, 91, 96, 97, 98, 114—115, 117, 118, 124, 125, 133, 144, 145, 146, 147, 151, 152, 153, 154—155, 160—161, 162, 163, 164—165, 168, 169, fig. 1, p. 174, fig. 2, p. 175, fig. 3, p. 177, fig. 4, p. 178, fig. 5, p. 180, fig. 6, p. 181, fig. 3, p. 200, photograph: Thomas Cugini, pl. p. 141, photograph: Hans Finsler, pl. p. 77 (top), photograph: Margit Weinberg-Staber, fig. p. 23

Angela Thomas Schmid, Zumikon, fig. 2, p. 236, fig. 4, p. 238, fig. 5, p. 241, photograph: Carmen Martinez, fig. p. 45, photograph: Niklaus Stauss, fig. p. 143

Daros Latinamerica Collection, Zürich, photograph: Peter Schälchli, Zürich, pl. p. 65, 134

ETH-Bibliothek Zürich, Bildarchiv, pl. p. 205

gta Archiv / ETH Zürich, Alfred Roth, fig. p. 74 (top)

Kunsthaus Zürich, pl. p. 46, 69, 94—95

Museum für Gestaltung Zürich, Plakatsammlung, ZHdK, pl. p. 49, 50, 87, 92, 99, 103, 129, 132

Museum für Gestaltung Zürich, Designsammlung, ZHdK, pl. p. 93 (both), 116, 120, 121

Sammlung Museum Haus Konstruktiv, Zürich, photograph: Stefan Altenburger, pl. p. 159

SIK-ISEA Zürich, Courtesy Fotostiftung Schweiz, photograph: Maria Netter, fig. 1, p. 197

© 2021 Stiftung Ernst Scheidegger Archiv, Zürich, Foto: Ernst Scheidegger: fig. p. 42, 74, 77

Zürcher Hochschule der Künste, Medien- und Informationszentrum, fig. 2, p. 199, fig. 4, p. 201

Imprint

This catalog is published on the occasion of the exhibition
max bill global
Zentrum Paul Klee, Bern
September 15, 2021 to January 9, 2022

The exhibition has been supported by

Kanton Bern
Canton de Berne

Burgergemeinde
Bern

ERNST GÖHNER STIFTUNG

haus bill

isla
INSTITUTE FOR STUDIES ON LATIN AMERICAN ART

wb form

JUNGHANS
GERMANY. SINCE 1861

prohelvetia

Concept: Fabienne Eggelhöfer
Editors: Fabienne Eggelhöfer, Nina Zimmer
Editorial team: Myriam Dössegger, Kai-Inga Dost
Translations: Kathleen Heil, Bridget Mason, Bronwen Saunders, Lisa Schons
Copy editing: Colette Forder, Lisa Schons
Proofreading: Colette Forder
Design: Sabine Hahn
Image editing, printing, and binding: DZA Druckerei zu Altenburg GmbH, Thuringia

Verlag Scheidegger & Spiess
Niederdorfstrasse 54
8001 Zurich
Switzerland
www.scheidegger-spiess.ch

Scheidegger & Spiess is being supported by the Federal Office of Culture with a general subsidy for the years 2021–2024.

ISBN 978-3-85881-877-5
German edition ISBN 978-3-85881-697-9